FROM LENIN
TO MALENKOV

The History of World Communism

by

Hugh Seton-Watson

FREDERICK A. PRAEGER
New York

BOOKS THAT MATTER

Published in the United States of America in 1953
by Frederick A. Praeger, Inc., Publishers, 105 West
40th Street, New York 18, N. Y.

Sixth Printing, 1955

Library of Congress Catalog Number 53-9522

Lithographed in the United States of America

14939

Contents

v

Introduction

BOTH the subject and the literature of communism are vast. Communism is a theory, which professes to explain philosophy, religion, history, economics and society. Communism is a vocation, whose devotees accept its discipline in every part of their private and professional lives. Communism is a science of conspiracy, a technique of wrecking and subversion. Communism is a revolutionary movement, a political force which operates in a social environment, which recruits its members from various classes of society, and marshals its armies against various political opponents.

Each of these aspects of communism has its literature. In the field of theory there are the works of the masters—Marx, Engels, Kautsky, Plehanov, Luxemburg, Lenin, Trotski, Stalin—and many works of commentary. On the vocation we have the testimony of ex-communists, including imaginative writers of the stature of Silone, Serge, Plisnier and Koestler. On the conspiracy there are both official documents and a rich assortment of memoirs by ex-communists and others, of varying degrees of reliability. On the revolutionary movement there is a wealth of raw material in the reports of congresses of the Comintern and of the individual parties, and in the miscellaneous periodicals published by them. On the Russian Revolution and the Soviet regime there are a few analytical works of great merit, and some outstanding studies of the French and Chinese parties have recently appeared.[1] The most important survey of the communist movement as a whole— with special emphasis on the Comintern—is Franz Borkenau's *The Communist International*, which appeared in 1938 and dealt mainly with the events of 1918–1919 and of the 1920's. The same author's recent work,[2] which appeared when the present work was in the press, has carried the story forward, for Europe only, to 1950, with fuller chronological detail but less acute analysis than his first book. But in the field of comparative analysis of communist movements, on the world scale, much more remains to be done.

[1] A. Rossi, *La physiologie du parti communiste*, Paris, 1948; B. Schwarz, *Chinese Communism and the rise of Mao*, Harvard, 1951.
[2] *European Communism*, 1953.

It is to this last aspect that the present work is intended to be a contribution. It thus deals with only a part—though an important and rather neglected part—of the phenomenon of communism. Readers who seek to understand the whole phenomenon can hope to find only partial enlightenment in these pages—even if this book achieves its limited objective. They will certainly need also to acquaint themselves with Marxist-Leninist theory, preferably from the original sources, as well as from one of the better commentaries.[1] Their understanding would also be increased by the study of some of the works of imaginative literature which have a bearing on the mentality of communist man and woman.[2]

The philosophical and psychological sides of communism are barely mentioned in the present work, not because they do not interest me, or because I have not studied them, still less because I do not consider them important, but because there is a limit to what one work can contain, and because in my opinion they have been treated in other works far more authoritatively, and with far more literary distinction, than I could aspire to.

The present work is intended to be both less and more than a survey of communism in the world to-day or a history of communist movements. The method is neither chronological history nor contemporary political geography, but comparative historical analysis. Whenever possible, comparisons are made between different social and political situations, and different successful or unsuccessful attempts by communists to seize power.

The distinction between communist movements before and after seizure of power cannot be pushed too far. The development of the state machine and the social structure of the Soviet Union had so important an effect on the actions of communist movements outside the Soviet Union that I have found it impossible to omit from these pages a summary of the main features of Soviet social and political evolution. In fact about one-quarter of the book is devoted to Soviet internal affairs. The Russian Revolution, the internal struggle in the Bolshevik party, the Five Year Plans and the *Yezhovshchina* all profoundly affected world communism. The Stalinist regime has become the ideal for all communists, and the phrase 'world revolution' to-day means the extension of the Stalinist regime to all countries of the world. It is thus obvious that the world communist movement is unintelligible without some

[1] For example, R. N. Carew Hunt, *The theory and practice of communism*, 1949; F. Wetter, *Il materialismo dialettico sovietico*, Rome, 1950.
[2] C. Plisnier, *Faux passeports*, Paris, 1938; A. Koestler, *Darkness at noon*, 1942; V. Serge, *L'affaire Toulaev*, Paris, 1950.

knowledge of the Stalinist system. The Stalinisation of Eastern
Europe has made necessary a comparison between the 'popular
democratic' regimes and that of the Soviet Union. This is still
more necessary in the case of communist China, whose claim to be
considered as a distinct form of government is supported not only
by the great differences that separate China from both Russia and
Europe, but also by the specific statements of the Chinese communist leaders themselves. These are problems which cannot be
ignored in the present work. Therefore, though it is principally
concerned with communist bids for power, about one-quarter of it
is devoted to communists in power, in Russia, Eastern Europe and
China.

An important aspect of the Stalinist regime, which does not
usually receive attention in books on communism, is its treatment
of national and colonial problems. The countries in which the
communists have achieved their greatest successes are countries
of mixed or uncertain nationality or colonial subjection. Russia,
China, the Balkans and South-East Asia are the obvious examples.
Lenin carefully studied and systematically exploited national and
colonial tensions. In this field Stalin was his diligent and ingenious,
if not always successful, pupil. Communist propaganda directed
to Asian peoples has made much of the Soviet claim to have
'solved' national and colonial problems. The true position of
non-Russian nationalities in the Soviet Union however bears
little relation to the propagandists' picture. This contrast between
reality and propaganda in the national and colonial problems is
an important part of the history of the communist movement.
I have therefore devoted to it more space than the reader will
have expected.

If I can make any claim to an original approach to the subject,
it is in my emphasis on the relationship of communist movements
to social classes and to the internal balance of political power in
their respective countries. Both in the last chapter, and in the discussions of the main attempts by communists to seize power,[1]
I have tried to indicate the principal social and political conditions
that have helped or hindered communists in their recruitment of
supporters and in their onslaught on the state machine. In the
sections that describe or discuss the Soviet and the 'popular demo-

[1] The German and Hungarian revolutions; the Chinese revolutions of 1927 and
1946-8; the Popular Front in Spain; the resistance movements; the Stalinisation of
Eastern Europe. Problems of power are especially discussed on pp. 53-8, 59-63,
142-9, 153-4, 206-8, 271-7, 210-27, 248-60, 330-47.

cratic' regimes, I have stressed the distribution of power and the trends of social development. I have tried throughout the book to keep to these two central themes. But in order to explain social and political situations it has frequently been necessary to mention other factors, such as the economic development of the Soviet Union or the effects of international diplomacy. Distinctions between politics and economics, and between internal and foreign politics, are in reality no more than convenient fictions, which have to be abandoned when they cease to be convenient.

The comparative study of social and political systems is less developed in the 'free world', and is confined within narrower limits, than it should be. West European and American sociologists do not appear to have fashioned all the intellectual tools that the job needs. Modern Marxist writings on social classes do not help. Marx was a great pioneer of social science. Anyone who wishes to understand the modern world, whether he love or hate communism, must be a 'post-Marxist'. Pre-Marxist social thinking is as useful as pre-Newtonian scientific thinking. But things have happened in the world since Marx died, especially in the socially and economically backward countries to which Marx, quite understandably, paid little attention. The cant phrases of contemporary Stalinist hacks on proletariats and Lumpenproletariats and labour aristocracies; on rich and medium and poor peasants; on petty bourgeois and national bourgeois and bureaucratic bourgeois and compradore bourgeois; on good landowners and bad landowners and patriotic landowners and reactionary landowners—all serve rather to confuse than to enlighten those who seek the truth. Marxist writing on social problems, in the era of Stalinist imperialism, has become overlaid first with a political, then with a moral, and finally with a zoological varnish. To distinguish accurately between hyenas, jackals, running dogs, paper tigers, reptiles, misanthropes, cannibals and other disagreeable animal types requires a mental subtlety to which the non-Stalinist infidel can hardly attain.

But the social problems remain, and whoever wishes to understand the communist movement must grapple with them. If my efforts, unaided by special skill or special intellectual equipment, can stimulate the sociologists to reveal the truth, they will have served a purpose.

The essence of my theme is the effort of communists to win recruits, to seize and to wield power in their respective lands. My emphasis is therefore on those national communist movements whose efforts seem to me at different times to have been the most significant. I have thus paid little attention to the international agencies of communism, even to the Comintern itself. I have referred to Comintern congresses which dealt with a problem of interest to one or more important communist parties, but have made no attempt to recount the history of the Comintern or of such subsidiary organisations as Profintern, Krestintern or Red Aid. Nor have I attempted to penetrate the mystery which surrounds the dissolution of the Comintern in 1943, and the operation of post-war communist internationl organisations. Not only are these subjects veiled in mystery: I am not sure that they are important. The essential fact is that, at least since the 5th Comintern congress in 1924, the international communist movement has been subject to the orders of Moscow. Whether this control is exercised by foreign communists, established in a central office in Moscow or some other Soviet-controlled city, who transmit the orders of the Soviet leaders to their respective parties; or whether the orders come to the national parties directly from Soviet officials, without passing through a central office of Comintern or Cominform—is an interesting question for a specialist in institutions, and an important question for a counter-intelligence officer. But for the analysis of the social basis of communist movements, and of communist bids for power, it is of small significance.

The internal organisation of communist parties is a more important subject. But this has already been well described and analysed by many competent writers. I have devoted some space to the organisation of the Soviet party. I have broken no ground: the facts are generally known. My interpretation of the trends in the Soviet party, for whatever it is worth, is my own. I have also briefly discussed some special features of the organisation of the Chinese party, and the growing divergence of the Yugoslav party from the Soviet model. The internal organisation of the other communist parties has not been discussed. It is in fact in all cases a close imitation of the Stalinist adaptation of the Bolshevik original.

Throughout the book I have been trying to look at communist movements from the outside, not from the inside. This approach has its defects: so has its opposite, the method adopted by ex-communists. Not only, as explained above, is the present work not an attempt to cover the whole phenomenon of communism: it is not intended even to cover the whole field of the communist revolutionary movement. No work yet published has covered this, and I do not believe that the job can be done for many years yet. But bits of the job can be done. Various works by ex-communists have explained the technique of communist conspiracy, the way a communist lives, and the peculiar *mystique* of which the 'steel-hard Bolshevik' elite of party members are possessed. These points are hardly mentioned in this work, not because I do not realise how important they are, not perhaps even because I am mentally incapable of understanding them, but because they have been well described and analysed by others better qualified. What I have tried to do has not been done by the ex-communists. It is in a more or less systematic manner to relate communist activity to the real social forces, and the real balance of political power, within which it operated. My subject is in short the impact of the communist movement on the outside world, and of the outside world on it.

It may be convenient here to summarise for the prospective reader the contents of this work. It is best to precede this by a summary of the seven main phases in the history of the international communist movement. Each phase is closely linked with a phase in the development of Soviet Russia.

The first phase, the years 1918 to 1920, corresponds with the civil war in Russia. It is a period in which revolutionary feeling was widespread. Its most important events were the revolutions in Finland, Germany and Hungary, the establishment of national states in Eastern Europe, and labour unrest in Italy. During these years the revolutionary movements in Europe were not directed from Moscow. The Comintern was founded in March 1919, but it was not until after the second congress, held in the late summer of 1920, that it was in a position to attempt to direct international communist activity.

The second phase, from 1921 to 1928, corresponds to the N.E.P. and the struggle between Stalin and the Left Opposition in Russia. In Europe revolutionary feeling declined, and communists suffered defeats in Germany, Bulgaria, Poland and Britain. In Asia there were small communist gains in Java and Japan in the early 1920's and sensational victories followed by sensational defeat in China in 1927. The international movement was effectively subjected to the central leadership of the Comintern by 1921, to the Soviet party by 1924, and to Stalin by 1927.

The third phase lasts roughly from 1928 to 1933, and corresponds to the First Five Year Plan in Russia. The new 'left' economic policy introduced by Stalin required the disgrace of the 'right' elements both in the Russian party and the world movement. A new 'extreme left' policy of the Comintern doomed the European parties to impotence. The world slump weakened the economic and political power of the working class everywhere. In Germany increasing misery led to the victory not of communism but of Hitler. In Asia there were no striking communist successes, but in remote provinces of China Mao Tse-tung was building his power machine.

The fourth phase, from 1934 to 1939, corresponds to the period of the Popular Front tactic. But it is not a homogeneous period. At first the Soviet government's fear of German and Japanese aggression coincided with similar fears by masses and intellectuals in many lands. Anti-fascist slogans won communism wider popularity than it had ever known. In Russia too the new policy was popular, for it extolled the glories of Russia's past, appealed to Russian patriotism, and for a time even brought a milder internal regime. The turning point came towards the end of 1936. Within Russia the greater freedom was withdrawn, a purge began in the party, and this led during 1937 to the mass cataclysm known to history as the *Yezhovshchina*. In Europe the failures of Blum's government and the 'appeasement' policy of the British government were discouraging factors, and the progress of the Japanese in China was strategically more important to Russia than was the course of events in Spain. The Popular Front slogans were still proclaimed by the communist parties right up to August 1939, but the *Yezhovshchina* and the declining interest of Moscow in France or Spain deprived the Popular Front policy of its substance already by mid-1937.

The fifth phase is the period of the Nazi-Stalinist honeymoon, from 1939 to 1941. It is marked by gains in territory to the Soviet Union, loss of influence by European communist parties, and some—though not very efficient—help by the Comintern to the Nazi war effort.

The sixth phase is the period of the Grand Alliance and the Resistance Movements, from 1941 to 1945. During these years the communists recovered more than they had lost. In China ever since 1928 Mao Tse-tung had been building his army and his civil power in the 'liberated areas': the Popular Front policy brought him further support, the Nazi-Stalinist pact had little effect on his fortunes, and the Grand Alliance was on the whole beneficial to him. In the Balkan Peninsula, France, Italy and

South-East Asia the communists were able to increase their
strength by their role in the resistance. The end of the war was
followed by a period of transition, not unlike that of 1937–39.
The slogans of the Popular Front and the Grand Alliance were
still official doctrine during 1945 and 1946. But in Eastern Europe
'co-operation' between communists and non-communist democrats was interpreted in a manner that suited only the communists;
in Western Europe relations between the communists and their
partners grew more and more tense, until in the spring of 1947
the communists were excluded from the governments of France
and Italy; while in Asia communists and nationalists were at war
in China from the summer of 1946, and hostilities began between
the French and the communist-led Vietminh at the end of that year.

The seventh phase formally opened with the foundation of the
Cominform in the autumn of 1947. It was a period of extremism,
accompanied in many cases by violence. Strikes in France and
Italy were defeated, risings in Indonesia and India were suppressed,
risings in Malaya and Burma achieved a measure of success. A
year later came the sensational breach between the Yugoslav and
Soviet communist leaders. Since 1948 Stalinist regimes have been
consolidated in the East European satellite states, Mao Tse-tung's
form of communist totalitarianism has entrenched itself in China,
the Yugoslav regime has evolved further from the Stalinist model,
war has continued in Indochina and broken out in Korea, but in the
lands beyond the border zone between the Stalinist and the free
worlds communist movements have made no significant gains.
The death of Stalin in February 1953 will probably prove to have
inaugurated a new phase.

The main facts about each of these phases are well enough
known. I have not tried to tell them again in detail. Some facts
of course I have had to mention, for without them my attempts at
analysis and comparison would be meaningless. Inevitably most
space has been given to the most important communist parties—
the Russian, Chinese, French and German.

The arrangement is partly chronological, partly regional and
partly analytical. The first two chapters, on European society
before 1914 and on the Russian Revolution, are almost entirely
analytical. The third chapter concerns European communism in
1918 to 1920. Its emphasis is on a comparison of the German and
Hungarian revolutions with the Russian, and on events in the
borderlands between Germany and Russia. There is also some
discussion of events in Italy and of the first two congresses of the

Comintern. The fourth and fifth chapters are more chronological, and deal with communist policy in Russia and in Europe during the 1920's. The sixth chapter discusses—with a superficiality of which I am only too aware—the impact of the West on Asian societies, as the background to the rise of revolutionary nationalism and communism in Asia. The seventh chapter deals with communism in Asia in the 1920's. Its main emphasis is of course on the Chinese events of 1927, but there is also some discussion of communism in Java and Japan. The eighth chapter describes Stalin's Revolution, the years 1928 to 1939. Here relatively small space is given to the collectivisation of agriculture and five year plans, on which there is a large literature available in English (though I hope that I have noted the essential features), and relatively large space is devoted to the position of the non-Russian nationalities and to the *Yezhovshchina*, subjects much less known to European and American readers, but no less important for the development of international communism. The ninth, tenth and eleventh chapters are chronological, dealing respectively with the periods of Popular Front, Nazi-Stalinist pact, and Resistance Movements, and covering and discussing events in Europe, Asia and Latin America. The twelfth, thirteenth, fourteenth and fifteenth chapters are again regional: they concern respectively post-war Russia, Eastern Europe, China, and communism in the non-Stalinist world. The last chapter is purely analytical. It discusses the political and social conditions that favour or hinder the communist cause, and raises some of the problems of resistance to communism. That it does not provide ready-made 'solutions' to the problems should not, I feel, be made a reproach. To push back, even by a few inches, the boundaries of ignorance and illusion is more useful than to pontificate about miraculous short cuts to salvation that do not exist. Utopian optimism and defeatism are, to use a Stalinist phrase, 'equally harmful deviations'.

In conclusion I must thank Mr. D. J. Footman, who read the whole typescript, and Mr. G. F. Hudson, who read the sections on Asia, for their advice and encouragement. Many others have helped me, especially those who took part in the Seminar on Twentieth-century Revolutions at St. Antony's College, Oxford, in 1951-2. A special word of gratitude to the staff of the Library of Chatham House, for their courteous and efficient help. And finally to my wife, for help and encouragement at all stages.

CHAPTER ONE

Europe before 1914

C OMMUNISM derives from the European socialist movement,
and this has a double origin, in the industrial revolution and
in the development of radical political ideas.

The industrial revolution created the industrial working class,
which replaced the peasantry at the base of the social pyramid. The
peasants, scattered among countless villages, were less accessible
to political influences than the workers, concentrated in towns.[1]

Precursors of socialism, champions of equalitarian ideas of a
rather crude kind, can be found not only in the eighteenth century but in the Middle Ages, and even in the ancient world. In
the nineteenth century Saint-Simon, Fourier, Cabet and others
propounded doctrines which contained some of the elements of
modern socialism. Karl Marx called them 'utopian socialists',
and claimed for himself the title of 'scientific socialist'. The first
crude attempts to put socialist doctrines into practice were made
in France in 1848 and in the *Commune* of 1871.

All this is well known. So are Marx's doctrines. But it is not
enough, in order to explain the background to European socialism
and communism, to point to these well-known facts. There were
great social and political differences between European countries,
which were reflected in the different development of their labour
movements.

Most western writers on socialism assume that the history of
socialism is simply the history of western labour, and that anything outside north-western Europe, France, Germany and north
Italy is a quaint subject for erudite experts. More recently a school
of western experts on Leninism has appeared: among them is a
tendency to ignore western development. But an understanding of
modern communism requires at least some knowledge of labour
movements throughout Europe, and this requires at least some

[1] In Britain more than half the population was urban already before 1850. In
Germany the percentage of urban to total population rose from 36 in 1871 to 60 in
1910; in France from 34 in 1876 to 44 in 1911.

1

knowledge of the main social, political and cultural features of Europe in 1914. Moreover these need to be regarded without blinkers, whether of orthodox Marxism, of western liberalism or of conservative nostalgia.

The following brief survey of European society in 1914 suffers inevitably from oversimplification. I hope however that it may provide some guidance for the student of communism.

The economic, social and cultural borderlines of 1914 did not always coincide with state frontiers. But as it was within the framework of states that labour movements had to operate, the survey has to be made within that framework.

ECONOMIC AND SOCIAL DIVISIONS

The extreme economic categories are the predominantly industrial states and the almost purely agrarian. Of the first Britain is the most complete example. Germany too was predominantly industrialised in 1914, though certain large regions—especially the provinces east of the Elbe—remained agricultural. The opposite extreme are the Balkan countries. Of these Serbia and Bulgaria may with little exaggeration be termed purely agrarian, while in Roumania and Greece the first beginnings of industry (oil and shipping) could be observed.

Between these two extremes it is possible to distinguish three types. The first may be described as countries of mixed society. Here industry was already important, was becoming more important, and was to be found in most parts of the country, but did not yet absorb a predominant portion of the nations' labour or wealth. Urban influences were spreading to the countryside, and the differences in outlook and way of life between peasant and townsman were rapidly diminishing. To this type belonged France, the Low Countries and Scandinavia. The second type were countries where this mixed type of economy coexisted with the purely agrarian. The best examples were Italy, Spain and Austria. Here Piedmont and Lombardy, Catalonia, German-Austria and Bohemia had mixed economies; south Italy and the islands, central and southern Spain, Galicia and Dalmatia were agrarian; while Tuscany, parts of Castile and Mediterranean Spain, and Moravia fell somewhere between. The third type were agrarian societies with important industrial islands. Hungary, Poland and Russia were the best examples. The Budapest area, Polish Silesia, Warsaw, Łódź, the Moscow area, the Donets Basin, and St. Petersburg were great industrial centres, with large and modernly equipped factories, but a few miles outside the industrial towns was an agrarian society at least as primitive as that of southern Italy or southern Spain, and little less primitive than that of the Balkans.

These five types contained different admixtures of industrial and agrarian economy. It is now necessary to say a few words about the classes of industrial and agrarian society.

In industrial society the dominant element was the business class of great industrialists and bankers. It had been formed partly from the landowning class and partly from the merchants of the pre-industrial age. At the base of the social pyramid the factory working class replaced the peasantry. In Britain this process had made decisive progress by the middle of the nineteenth century, in Germany early in the twentieth. Between the industrialists and the workers was the ill-defined 'middle class', with its three main sub-divisions of small business men and managers, professional men and civil servants. The three sub-divisions were closely interconnected, rather than three separate castes. Under a system of liberal economy the small business man had a high social prestige, the professional man was recognised as a useful citizen but was not elevated into a prophet, and the civil servant was encouraged to regard himself as servant rather than master. But though this was generally true of all industrial societies, there were considerable variations due not to economic but to political or cultural factors. Thus, the professional man enjoyed higher prestige and influence in France and Italy than in Britain, the bureaucrat in Germany than in France, the business man in Britain than in Germany.

In agrarian societies the traditionally dominant class were the great landowners, of more or less ancient aristocratic origin. During the nineteenth century however this landowning class lost much of its power, not only in countries that became predominantly or largely industrialised, but also in countries still mainly agrarian. A living had to be found for younger children of the landowning nobility. Towards the end of the century a general crisis of European agriculture ruined many landed estates, and caused even eldest sons to look for an occupation off the land. They became army officers, bureaucrats, professional men or business men. Their distribution between these occupations varied according to political and cultural factors. In Britain and Scandinavia sons of the nobility were less unwilling to enter business than in Germany or Eastern Europe. In Prussia, Hungary and Russia the bureaucracy was swollen with impecunious nobles. These, rather than their

more prosperous fellows who retained their landed estates, became the ruling class in the political sense. But on the land the
noble landowners remained dominant up till the First World War.

There were countries however where there were no landowners,
or where they played a minor part. In France the peasants had
acquired ownership of the land in the greater part of the country
as a result of the Great Revolution. In Scandinavia and the Low
Countries peasant ownership was widespread during the nineteenth century. In the Balkans, the Turkish conquerors had destroyed the old landowning class in the fifteenth century; when
Turkish rule was overthrown in the nineteenth, the land became
the property of the peasants. In Serbia, Bulgaria and Greece in 1914
large landowners were not a significant political or economic
force. It was from the peasantry that the new ruling class of these
countries—bureaucrats, army officers, merchants and professional
men—was formed.

In the industrial or mixed societies of the countries of Western
Europe, the peasantry was increasingly affected by urban influences.
Urban bourgeois and medium farmer, urban worker and farm
labourer, were growing more and more like each other. In the
agrarian societies of Eastern Europe, townsmen and peasants
lived in different centuries. Here the peasantry formed the base
of the social pyramid. Illiteracy, primitive methods of production
and the habits of mind of serfs but recently emancipated, partly
accounted for the peasants' poverty. From the end of the nineteenth century a still more important cause was overpopulation.
The number of persons engaged in agriculture per unit of agricultural land was higher than in Western Europe, and this discrepancy was growing. The rural surplus of population grew faster
than either the output per acre or the supply of jobs outside
agriculture. Already before 1914 large parts of Russia, Poland,
Italy and the Balkans suffered from overpopulation on the land,
and this was threatening to become a serious danger in most of
eastern and southern Europe. Marx's prophecy of the concentration of wealth and poverty was at least partly justified in the
peasant lands. A rural semi-proletariat constituted an increasing
proportion of the peasantry, and the process seemed likely to
continue. At the other extremity a class of rich peasants was
appearing. This latter process has however been greatly exaggerated by Marxist writers, both in Russia and elsewhere. In Russia
itself, it was official policy, during the Premiership of P. A.
Stolypin (1906–11), to encourage the formation of this class,

known in Russia as *kulaks*. In some parts of Russia and of other East European countries *kulaks* were without doubt an important factor: in other parts they hardly existed. Moreover the economic process must be distinguished from its social consequences. Even where *kulaks* were powerful, it is doubtful whether any consciousness of class conflict existed within the peasantry. The peasants as a whole were aware of their class interests against the great landowners, and against the towns: the class struggle of poor peasants against rich was little more than a theory of Marxist intellectuals. The theory was, in certain cases and at certain periods, based on economic realities, but it had not become a real factor in the life of the peasants.

In Russia and Eastern Europe an industrial working class was growing rapidly in the first decade of the twentieth century. The great majority of these new workers were unskilled, and their standard of living was as low as that of the poorer peasants. Not only were they materially poor, and exposed to exploitation by their employers, but they suffered from the mental and emotional bewilderment that resulted from the loss of one social environment—village life—which was not yet compensated by absorption in a new society. This twofold misery of the East European worker in 1910 has its parallel in the situation of the British worker early in the nineteenth century.

The middle class in agrarian societies was small both in numbers and in influence. Of the three sub-divisions, the business element was the weakest. In many cases it consisted of persons of a nationality different from that of the surrounding countryside and even of the towns—Jewish or German in Poland, Hungary, Roumania and Russia; Greek or Armenian in the Balkans. The professional element was relatively more important. It was essentially a product of western cultural influence. It arose partly in response to economic demands—for the skills of the modern world, and for jobs for children of noble families—and partly as a result of the deliberate policy of the enlightened despots—Joseph II of Austria, Alexander I of Russia. At the turn of the nineteenth and twentieth centuries intellectuals enjoyed in the countries of agrarian economy a prestige and influence out of proportion to their numbers, and relatively much greater than those of their more numerous and more cultured counterparts in northern and western Europe. The third sub-division, the bureaucracy, was the most important of the three. The growth in its numbers during the nineteenth century was due partly to the demand for jobs for children of the nobility and partly to the expanding field of action of the state. It was especially marked in countries in which the development of industry came late, and was brought about not so much by private initiative as by government policy. Of this Russia is the most striking example. The numbers of the bureaucrats increased more rapidly than the national wealth, and their real income remained low. When thousands of individuals possess power over the lives of citizens but are themselves poor, the incentive to corruption is very strong. This is still more the case when the legal system is cumbrous, obsolete and unjust, and the evasion of its more irksome features can command a market price. Russia and the Balkan states provide good examples. More pernicious than this mass petty corruption was the large-scale corruption sometimes practised by individuals highly placed in the government machine, who, uncontrolled by representative institutions, were able to sell valuable privileges to wealthy buyers, domestic or foreign, for really high prices.

POLITICAL SYSTEMS

The political systems of Europe before 1914 varied from the completely parliamentary to the almost completely despotic. The most democratic parliamentary system, in the double sense that suffrage was universal and that the government was responsible to the elected assembly, was in France. In Britain government had been responsible at least since the reign of Victoria, but there were still gaps in the franchise. In Scandinavia and the Low Countries too parliamentary government was well established. The stronghold of autocracy was Russia. In 1905 Tsar Nicholas II had been obliged to grant the beginnings of a constitution, but he was able two years later to take back most of his concessions. Police, army and bureaucracy were at his command, and he could appoint and dismiss ministers as he chose. The parliament (*Duma*) was elected on an unrepresentative franchise and was seldom able to make itself felt. Between these two forms of government were various transitional types. Germany and Austria had parliaments elected by universal suffrage, but ministers were chosen by the monarchs and responsible only to them. The parliament of Prussia, from which was formed the Prussian state government, which in most matters affecting the daily life of the people was 'the government' of two-thirds of the population of Germany, was elected by an unrepresentative franchise. Italy appeared to have a genuine parliamentary system, with universal suffrage since 1912 and ministries responsible to parliament. This was however modified by the fact that in the south elections were managed by the local landowners or bureaucrats, who were thus in a position to offer blocks of unrepresentative deputies to party leaders seeking to form governments. In Spain these conditions prevailed in most of the country, the local *caciques* managing elections which were not even nominally based on universal suffrage.[1] In Hungary the franchise was extremely restricted, and though in Budapest at least the urban bourgeoisie could vote freely, in the countryside everything depended on the landlord. In Roumania the situation was similar. In Serbia, Bulgaria and Greece there was universal suffrage and the ministries were nominally responsible to the parliaments. The working of parliamentary government was however hindered by the ignorance and apathy of many of the peasant voters, intimidation at the polls (to some extent equalised by the fact that several parties had their own bands of toughs), and the interference of the monarchs. In general the trend of the last decade before the war was towards parliamentary government. Freedom of speech and conscience was fairly generally recognised, at least in the towns, and the press reflected most political opinions present in each country. Even in Russia there was immensely more freedom in 1914 than in 1900.

EDUCATION

Education was essentially a western phenomenon. The educational systems of Eastern Europe, which made great progress from the middle of the nineteenth century, were copied from those of the West. France was the usual model, but by the end of the century Germany was also being widely imitated. The British and Scandinavian systems were less well known. In north-western lands education largely derives from Protestantism, from the habits of Bible-reading and of forming individual opinion first on religious and then on other matters. The connections between Protestantism and individualism, and between individualism and economic enterprise, are obvious, and have often been discussed by historians and sociologists. If education stimulated enterprise, economic development also created a demand for educated people. In France the ideas of the Great Revolution, themselves the product of the educated *élite* of the eighteenth century, enormously stimulated the growth of schools and universities. The right to education became

[1] *Cacique* is an American Indian word. In Spanish political parlance it came to mean a local boss.

one of the principal rights of the French citizen. In Prussia the growth of schools was a result of the enlightened despotism of the monarchs, and the demand for skilled and efficient soldiers. This factor was also important in Piedmont. In Hungary, southern Italy and Spain the process was much slower, but influences from France, Piedmont and Germany were felt and considerable progress was made. In the Balkan states, as soon as liberation from the Turks was secured, democratic ideas and the demand for skilled people combined to push education at a rapid pace. If the progress was both qualitatively and quantitatively less than was hoped, this was due rather to the poverty of the young nations rather than to ill will by their rulers. In Russia the progress of education was irregular yet impressive. Periods of enlightenment alternated with periods of obscurantism. An attempt was made to prevent the education of persons of humble social origin. But the needs of the modern world could not be ignored, and the methods of the obscurantists were not efficient. By 1914 Russian education had enormously advanced.

There is a difference between the educational systems of the western (industrial or mixed) and eastern (wholly or predominantly agrarian) countries which has had great political consequences. In the West education has been developed at all levels, in response to a demand for all levels of education and because the different levels have been dependent on each other. In the East education has been developed disproportionately at the top—in the higher strata of society and in the more advanced forms. In Russia and in the Balkan countries excellent universities grew up at a time when village schools were miserably poor and badly staffed, many villages had no school at all, and many children did not go to the schools that were within their reach.

This disproportion in the educational systems of eastern and southern Europe accounts in part for the phenomenon of the frustrated intelligentsia, the central problem in revolutionary movements of the twentieth century. East European university graduates were little if at all inferior to their western counterparts. They belonged to the nineteenth or twentieth centuries. But their less fortunate compatriots in the villages were living in the eighteenth or sixteenth centuries. This contrast between themselves and their own peoples horrified the more generous spirits. They felt themselves obliged to serve their peoples, to raise them to their own level, and to fight against all those who had, or appeared to have, an interest in keeping them in their backward state. To these idealist motives for discontent were added personal material

motives. As the numbers of the educated increased, it became more
difficult to find jobs for them in the free professions, the distended
bureaucracy or the still small business class. It was these young
intellectuals, appalled at their peoples' plight and dissatisfied with
their own positions, who learned, whether during visits abroad or
within their own countries' universities, the political ideas of nineteenth-century Europe. It was they who introduced liberalism,
nationalism and socialism to eastern and southern Europe. It was
from their ranks that the leadership of revolutionary movements
was formed.

RELIGIONS

Religious influences were an important factor in the political and
social differences within Europe. Protestantism was dominant in
northern and north-western Europe, but there were also important
Protestant minorities in central Europe among Slovaks and Hungarians and among some of the German minorities in the east.
Catholicism was dominant in the greater part of Mediterranean
Europe and the middle Danube, and had two northern outposts,
Poland and Lithuania in the east and Ireland in the west. Orthodoxy was dominant on the lower Danube, in the Balkan peninsula
and the whole of European Russia. Islam was still strong in parts
of the south-east, especially in the valleys of Bosnia and Macedonia
and along the Black Sea coast from Thrace to Crimea.

In countries where the rulers were Catholic or Orthodox, the
Catholic and Orthodox churches were more or less thoroughly
associated with the political regime, and were beneficiaries of the
economic and social system. Political and social reformers thus
found themselves fighting the churches. The identification of
political freedom and progress with anti-clericalism, or even with
atheism, was first made by the eighteenth-century French *philo-
sophes*, the first historical example of the modern phenomenon of
the disaffected intelligentsia. The identification spread through
most of Europe, partly as a result of the political role of the
churches in other countries, partly as a ready-made importation
from France. In countries where Catholicism or Othodoxy was
the religion of the people, oppressed by rulers of different faith, the
democratic movements were not to the same extent in conflict with
the church. Examples are Catholic Poland and Ireland, Orthodox
Serbia and Bulgaria.

In Protestant countries the churches were not so closely associated with the political system, and that system was in any case

less despotic. The connection between Protestantism and liberalism has already been mentioned. Thus in Britain and in Scandinavia democratic movements were not anti-clerical, even if individual democrats were anti-clericals or even atheists. The exception to this statement is Germany. Ever since Luther the German Evangelical Church was closely associated with the power of the princes, and later shared in the odium which attached to them. German democrats were therefore more often anti-clerical than British or Scandinavian, though less than French or Spanish.

It is important to distinguish between the decline of religion in Western Europe and the attack by reformers and revolutionaries on religion in the East. The decline was the result of scepticism, connected with the development of natural science. The scepticism may or may not be justified, and its consequences for society may or may not be harmful. But the process was not accompanied, at least in the twentieth century, by outbursts of fanaticism and violence, nor did the sceptics need to replace their lost faith by another to serve with equal passion. In Britain and Scandinavia, especially, democrats who still believed would go for their religion to church or chapel and for politics to their party meetings: politics and religion were kept in separate compartments. In Eastern Europe the political party had to take the place of religion. The old religion had been abandoned not from a sceptical attitude but from a passionate belief that it was wrong and unjust. The new ideology had to satisfy spiritual needs as well as provide a course of political action. This was especially the case in Russia from the 1860's onwards. Something of this attitude to revolutionary politics can also be found in Spain and the Balkans. In France and Germany it was to be found earlier in the nineteenth century, but by 1914 scepticism rather than anti-religious fervour was the prevalent attitude to religion among those who were not still believers.

THE PROBLEM OF NATIONALITIES

Another important factor in the background to European socialism is the problem of nationalities. In Western Europe states usually coincide with the limits of nations. In Britain the demands for Scottish and Welsh home rule have not hitherto caused great trouble. In Switzerland a single nationality has been formed from people among whom three languages are spoken. More serious problems are the conflict between Walloons and Flemings in Belgium and the claims of Catalan and Basque nationalism in Spain. But even these are small in comparison with the multitude of national conflicts that were to be found in Eastern Europe before the First World War. The Austro-Hungarian and Russian empires were multi-national states: in the former the German-Austrians and Hungarians enjoyed a privileged position, in the latter the Russians claimed complete supremacy.

The problems were complicated by differences in cultural level between nationalities within one state. In most cases the level of the subject nations was inferior to that of the dominant. Examples are the Poles in Prussia, the Slovaks in Hungary and the Tatars in Russia. In others the level was the same—Germans and Czechs in Bohemia; Russians, Ukrainians and Georgians in Russia. In others the subject nation was culturally more advanced than the dominant nation. The obvious examples of this in Eastern Europe were the Poles, Balts and Finns in Russia: in the West the Catalans in Spain were similarly placed. There were special cases where a minority belonging to one subject nation was socially and culturally dominant over a majority of another subject nation with which it lived. Examples are the Poles in the Russian Ukraine, the Swedes in Finland and the Italians at the north-east corner of the Adriatic.

THE LABOUR MOVEMENTS

The combination of these economic, social, political, cultural, religious and national factors determined the nature of the labour movements which grew up throughout Europe at the turn of the nineteenth and twentieth centuries. The conditions most favourable to a peaceful and democratic labour movement were a numerous working class with a high proportion of skilled workers within it; strong and generally accepted parliamentary institutions; a high general level of education; the habit of religious tolerance; and ethnical homogeneity. The conditions most likely to produce a violent and fanatical revolutionary movement were a social structure based on a primitive and poor peasantry and a small unskilled working class little if at all less primitive or poor; a political system based on bureaucratic despotism; an educational system producing an intelligentsia ideally rebellious and personally dissatisfied; the habit of religious persecution and support by the church to political tyranny; and diversity of nationalities within one state. The countries in which the first set of conditions were most nearly realised were Britain and Scandinavia, to a lesser extent France. The countries in which the second set of conditions most nearly prevailed were Russia, Hungary and Spain, to a lesser extent the Balkan countries. Germany, Austria and Italy, geographically located between the two groups of countries, held also in respect to these conditions an intermediate position.

The labour movements of all European countries had in common the same body of doctrine, socialism, more or less derived from Marx. But in practice the differences in the conditions outlined above, between northern and western Europe and southern and eastern Europe, produced very different movements. In the north and west the labour leaders were themselves usually workers; their own forces were the organised workers; the enemy forces were the capitalists and their various supporters; and the field in which the struggle was fought was one of parliamentary liberty and trade union rights. In the south and east the leaders were usually in-tellectuals; their own forces were an indeterminate mass which at times included peasants, craftsmen, small shopkeepers, unskilled labourers and a few skilled factory workers, but whose solid core consisted largely of intellectuals or semi-intellectuals; the enemy forces were bureaucrats, to a lesser extent landowners and only in the third place capitalists; and the field of struggle was one in which at best parliamentary liberties and trade union rights were insecure, and at worst persecution drove the movement into a conspiratorial underground.

The clearest example of a workers' movement led by workers was the British. The British workers had to fight hard for their trade unions in the middle of the nineteenth century, but they suc-ceeded, partly because their growing importance in the economy brought them influence and power, partly because a liberal form of government could not for long refuse them without denying its own principles. In Britain too the intellectual had little cause for frustration, ideal or personal. There was a demand for his abilities in political and economic affairs. Though there will of course, in every place and age, always be some intellectuals who have a grudge against society, this was not in nineteenth-century Britain a characteristic of intellectuals as a group. The opposite extreme was Russia. The nature of the political and social system drove almost all educated Russians into opposition. The very word 'intelligentsia', first invented in Russia, included the notion of opposition. The few educated men and women who supported the regime did not count as members of the intelligentsia. From its ranks was formed a minority of professional revolutionaries, who created socialist parties at a time when an industrial working class hardly existed in Russia. In Russia moreover workers were forbidden to form trade unions.at all until 1906, and even after

this the unions' powers were extremely small. Strikes continued
to be illegal up to the 1917 Revolution. Thus not only the relative
unimportance of the working class, but the political system itself,
hindered the development of a workers' movement led by workers,
while the same political system favoured the production from
the intelligentsia of revolutionary theorists and organisers.

France and Germany lie between these extremes. In France
the working class was relatively small in numbers, but enjoyed
considerable freedom and was politically turbulent. The insurrection of the Lyon silk workers in 1834, the role of the workers in the
Revolution of 1848, and the Paris *Commune* of 1871, are the obvious examples. The French intelligentsia had little cause to be
frustrated. Its social prestige was extremely high, and there was
as much demand for the services of the educated man in French
society as in British. There were of course causes for indignation
in France as elsewhere, but there was nothing to compare with the
contrast between the centuries (nineteenth-century intellectual and
sixteenth-century peasant) that prevailed in Russia and the Balkans.
But the motive for disaffection of the intelligentsia in France was
provided, not by objective conditions, but by tradition. Since the
eighteenth century a large part of the intelligentsia had been in
revolt against all established institutions. In particular the struggle
against the church and the army was vigorously pursued. This
struggle had of course a solid foundation in facts, but what is important here is not the essence of this or any other political controversy, but the predisposition of a large part of the French
intelligentsia in favour of any doctrine that sounded 'progressive'.
One may speak of a certain conservatism of revolution in nine-
teenth- and twentieth-century France. The slogan *pas d'ennemis à
gauche* has remained strong until our own time. Intellectuals therefore played, side by side with working-class organisers, a large
part in the French labour movement.

In Germany the role of workers in the labour movement was
relatively greater than in France. In the first years of the German
labour movement the workers had fewer legal rights than in France,
but their role in the national economy was larger and grew more
rapidly. But at the turn of the century the German labour movement was on the whole a workers' movement led by workers.
Yet at least in the early years intellectuals played an important
part. In Germany as in France, intellectuals enjoyed great social
prestige and could find useful and well-paid occupations. But the
political absolutism which continued until the 60's, and was by no

means eliminated even after the foundation of the German Empire, provided an irritation that was lacking in France or Britain. This was especially true for intellectuals of Jewish extraction, who suffered first from legal discrimination and later from less concrete social barriers. The most striking example of a disaffected German-Jewish intellectual of the mid-nineteenth century is of course Karl Marx himself. Another was Ferdinand Lassalle. Among intellectuals who were influential in the German labour movement on the eve of the First World War may be mentioned Eduard Bernstein, Karl Kautsky, and Roza Luxemburg, all incidentally Jews.

The Balkan labour movements conformed to the Russian pattern. The first socialist groups were created by intellectuals, and in 1914 the working class was barely an important social force. It is worth noting that the three most prominent pioneers of Balkan socialism —Svetozar Marković in Serbia, Dimiter Blagoev in Bulgaria, and Dobrogeanu-Gherea in Roumania—had learned their ideas in Russia.[1] In Hungary and Poland, where by 1914 the working class was already considerable, workers' leaders were more important than in the Balkans or Russia, but the role of intellectuals was rather greater than in Germany. From this point of view the German-Austrian and Czech movements may be roughly compared with the German, the north Italian and Spanish with the French. In southern Italy there was something comparable to the intelligentsia of the East: its most eminent example was the Neapolitan Marxist Antonio Labriola. In Scandinavia the development was much as in Britain. The Finnish movement was essentially of the Scandinavian type, but was complicated by the cultural differences between the Swedish minority and the Finnish majority, and by Finland's association with Russia.[2]

The role of Jews in the socialist movements, mentioned already in connection with Germany, deserves a few words. In Austria, Hungary, Poland and Roumania the Jews formed a far higher proportion of the population, and were relatively far more influential in professional and business circles, than in Germany. The same was true in the western borderlands of Russia. In the interior of Russia residential and educational discriminations reduced the

[1] Marković was a pre-Marxist, essentially a disciple of the Russian theorist Chernyshevski. Blagoev founded the earliest Marxist study group in Russia, in 1885. In 1891 he founded the Bulgarian Socialist Party. In 1918 he founded the Communist Party. Dobrogeanu-Gherea, whose original name was Katz, was a member of the Land and Liberty organisation in Russia in the 1870's.
[2] Finland was connected with Russia from 1809 onwards by a personal union, the Russian Emperor being also Grand-Duke of Finland. In the 1890's the Russian government began a policy of russification of Finland.

number of Jews, but there were still many among the most
eminent intellectuals and business men of the two capitals St.
Petersburg and Moscow. In all the lands mentioned, Jews were in
effect excluded from agriculture and from the bureaucracy. The
most successful Jews became prosperous capitalists and eminent
lawyers or doctors. But the great majority of Jews, especially in
Poland, Roumania and Russia, were extremely poor shopkeepers,
craftsmen or workers. As the Jewish population multiplied, each
generation faced increasing competition for diminishing means
of livelihood. The presence of the more prosperous Jews, firmly
entrenched in business and the professions, was resented by the
growing number of young educated Poles, Roumanians and Russians who were looking for jobs in these directions. This provided
a solid economic motive for anti-semitism, which of course also
had much older religious and cultural origins. Anti-semitic violence
was however directed as much against the Jewish semi-proletariat
as against the Jewish capitalists. The bleak economic prospects,
and the growing political insecurity, drove the younger Jews
either to Sionism, which promised a solution away from their
present homelands, in the ancient fatherland of Palestine, or to
revolutionary movements which promised equal rights for all
citizens within a socialist republic. It is thus not surprising that
there were many Jews in the socialist movements of Russia,
Poland and Roumania. In Austria and Hungary the position of
the Jews was much better. Many had become assimilated, felt
themselves, and were accepted by others as, Austrian and Hungarian patriots. Yet here too the Jewish background was favourable for sympathy with revolutionary ideas, and many leading
Austrian and Hungarian socialists were Jews.

THE SECOND INTERNATIONAL

Marx's attempt to create an international socialist organisation,
the First International of 1863–76, had been a failure. Six years
after his death, in 1889, a Second International was formed. In
the years up till 1914 it enjoyed considerable prestige among both
friends and foes of socialism. Its most important member parties
were the German and the French, but the parties of most other
European states also belonged. The International was a loose
organisation, which paid too much importance to formal unity to
insist on rigid doctrines that might bring a split. The same was
also the tendency of most member parties, which while paying lip

service to Marxist orthodoxy allowed divergences to exist within their ranks. A split was considered the greatest evil, at all cost to be avoided. But though the unity of the Second International was thus always more apparent than real, yet the parties belonging to it did share certain common problems. Of these the two most important were the relations between the socialist party and the trade unions in each country, and the party's attitude to political power.

In Britain the trade union movement was already old and strong before a political party of labour was formed at all. It was when the Taff Vale case showed the trade unions that their rights depended on the goodwill of the legislature that they decided to support a separate political movement of labour. The Labour Party appeared in the Parliament of 1906 as an important minority group, but by 1914 the majority of British workers had not yet been convinced that at election time they should vote for Labour rather than for Liberals or Conservatives. In Russia the opposite was the case. A socialist party had been formed already in 1877, a Marxist party in 1898, but there were no trade unions until 1906. Such workers' organisations as existed were regarded by the party as instruments for seizure of power, not as bodies with an independent task to perform. In France socialist parties and trade unions grew up side by side. Their memberships overlapped, but their leaderships and their functions were quite distinct. They were equals in the eyes of the workers, and respected each other's independence. In Italy the socialist party was older than the trade unions, but the latter were able to assert their independent status. In Germany the most powerful trade unions were closely connected with the Social Democratic Party. There were however also separate Catholic and Liberal trade unions.

In the years before 1914 appeared a movement known as syndicalism. Its followers maintained that the working class should seize power by 'direct action' in the industrial not the political field. Parliamentary action, they believed, was a waste of time. The only effective method was the revolutionary general strike. This trend was quite strong in the French and Italian trade union movements on the eve of war, and there were some echoes of it in Britain. Its main stronghold was Spain. Syndicalism, associated with anarchist ideas on the abolition of the state, was strong among the factory workers of Barcelona and the agricultural labourers of Andalusia. It is interesting that, though the prophet of anarchism was a Russian, Michael Bakunin, it should have gained ground among the Latin nations and not in Russia. There did exist in Russia a trend among the workers opposed to political action and urging that all efforts be devoted to the daily struggle for economic interests. But this trend ('Economism' or 'Liquidatorism', as it was variously named by Lenin) was a moderate not a revolutionary trend. It had nothing in common with revolutionary syndicalism. Rather it resembled the policy of the most moderate elements in the British labour movement.

Marx had prophesied the concentration of wealth in the hands of a few capitalists, accompanied by progressive impoverishment of the masses. We have seen that in agricultural Eastern Europe the second part of this prophecy had been to a large extent justified, but that the first part had not. In industrial Western Europe the opposite was the case: there had indeed been an impressive growth of capitalist monopolies or quasi-monopolies, but the standard of living of the working class had not fallen but improved. The West European workers of 1910 were very different from the miserable British proletariat of 1840. Moreover the middle class in the towns and the peasants in the countryside of Western Europe remained numerous, influential and prosperous. There was no prospect that in the near future the workers would form an overwhelming majority of the population except in Britain, and neither in Britain nor elsewhere in the north-west were the workers a desperate proletariat. In these circumstances there were two possible courses of action for the socialist parties. One was to abandon the ideas of class struggle and revolution as romantic anachronisms, and to collaborate with social classes other than the workers and with democrats who were not socialists. The other was to prepare armed insurrection by a minority, in the belief that if the workers through their party took the lead, a large part of the peasantry and a section of the middle class could be persuaded to follow.

The first course could take the form either of a coalition between a socialist party and 'bourgeois' parties, or of an extension of a socialist party's membership and programme so as to recruit many who were not workers and were at least lukewarm about socialism. In the 1920's and 1930's this second variation was adopted by the British and Scandinavian labour parties, the first by the German, French and other socialists. But before 1914 no socialist party could bring itself to adopt either course. It was urged in the German party by Eduard Bernstein, who proposed to 'revise Marx', and thus created the word 'Revisionism', later a term of abuse in left socialist and communist circles. But Bernstein, though not expelled from the party, was rebuked by it. Similar trends within the French and Italian parties were also defeated.[1]

The opposite policy, revolutionary action, was also rejected by the party leaders. In Germany it was advocated by Roza Luxemburg, in Italy by Benito Mussolini. In the French and Italian movements, as we have seen, the left wing was on the whole syndicalist. The special case of Russia will be examined in greater detail in the next chapter.

The leaders of the great socialist parties in practice pursued a policy of uneasy compromise, seeking not so to antagonise either the right or the left wing as to drive it out of the party. They talked like revolutionaries and acted like moderate reformers. This policy had different effects in different countries. In France, where the battle for political democracy had been won after the victory of the *Dreyfusards*, a policy of opposition to all bourgeois parties was for the time perfectly sound. In Italy, where the absence of political democracy in the south was a weapon which could be used by the Right against the socialists in Italy as a whole, the wisdom of such a course was more doubtful: co-operation with middle-class radicals might well have benefited the socialists. In Germany, where government was not responsible to the Reichstag, and the restricted Prussian franchise was still in force, refusal to co-operate with the progressive sections of liberalism and political Catholicism to attain the limited objective of political democracy was probably harmful to the socialists. While thus abstaining from parliamentary action, the socialist leaders avoided any concrete preparations for revolutionary action, which after all might in the future become a practical possibility. They thus had the worst of both policies.

SOCIALISM AND NATIONALITIES

In East European socialist movements the national problem played an important part.

Socialist parties of subject nations had to consider the problem of national independence if they were to win a mass following: at the same time, being in constant conflict with the nationalist bourgeoisie of their own nations, they felt a certain aversion for nationalist demagogy. They had to steer between two dangers. One was that in their desire to recruit the masses they would

---

[1] Millerand was expelled from the French Socialist Party after he had accepted office in Waldeck-Rousseau's government in 1899. Bissolati was expelled from the Italian party for supporting the Italian invasion of Libya in 1911.

forget their socialism and become mere radical nationalist parties, the other was that in their emphasis on the internationalism inherent in socialist doctrine they would antagonise the bulk of the workers. The Polish socialist movement is the best example of these difficulties. The Polish Socialist Party (P.P.S.), founded in 1892, was divided between nationalist and internationalist wings. The extreme internationalists broke off in 1900 to form a separate party, Social Democracy of Poland and Lithuania (S.D.K.P.L.). Their leader Roza Luxemburg—who later became prominent in the German socialist movement—argued that the partitions of Poland should be maintained, and that the future of the Polish workers lay within the great economic units of the Russian, Austrian and German empires rather than within an independent Polish state. The left wing of P.P.S. did not definitely renounce the aim of independent Poland but stressed autonomy for the present, and laid the main emphasis on the usual points of a socialist programme. The nationalist wing, or 'Revolutionary Fraction', led by Jozef Piłsudski, was so preoccupied with national independence, regarded as an aim attainable in the near future, that it neglected all else.

The strength of the Russian revolutionary movement in 1905 made the left wing of P.P.S. for a time more powerful than the right, and brought it close to the S.D.K.P.L. The defeat of the Russian movement after 1907 had the opposite effect. On the eve of the First World War the nationalist trend was uppermost in the Polish socialist movement.

Socialist parties of dominant nations were confronted with the same problem. The socialist emphasis on economic factors naturally gave support to the argument that the great economic units of Russia and Austria should be preserved. A certain more or less conscious pride in membership in a nation that had created a great state reinforced the economic argument. Some socialists however deliberately reacted against this tendency towards 'Great Power chauvinism'. The Austrian and Russian Marxists in fact produced different solutions for the national problem.

The Austrians Otto Bauer and Karl Renner devised a system of cultural autonomy and personal nationality, by which the citizens of Austria would owe political loyalty to the central government while for all matters affecting their language and culture they would be governed by autonomous institutions elected by members of each nationality regardless of place of residence.

This solution was rejected by the Russian Bolshevik leader Lenin on the ground that it gave both too little and too much. It would not satisfy those who wished for complete independence, and it would perpetuate a problem which a more radical treatment could solve. Lenin believed that the future socialist republic must be a centralised state, but was willing that any subject nationality of a larger state, which wished for its own independent state, should secede. Having seceded, it should set up its own centralised socialist republic. There was no place for federalism in his plans. The same principle held for the party as for the state. Each socialist party must be centralised. No section of the party could claim special autonomy on grounds of nationality. This brought Lenin into conflict with the Jewish Marxist party, the Bund, which wished, while remaining within the Russian Social Democrat Party, to be recognised as the sole representative of the Jewish workers of Russia. Lenin's views were also incompatible with those of Roza Luxemburg, who insisted that under no circumstances must Poland become an independent state. Lenin also disapproved of the reorganisation of the Austrian socialist party, on federal lines, at the end of the 1890's.

Lenin's attitude to the national problem was thus essentially opportunist. He regarded nationalism as a nuisance, which diverted the people's anger from its true enemy, the capitalists, against neighbour nations, which were not really its enemies. The hatred of Poles against Ukrainians, Russians against Jews, or Armenians against Tatars, was exploited by the Tsar's bureaucrats to keep the oppressed disunited. In order finally to remove this nuisance, the right to full self-determination 'up to the point of separation' must be recognised. It could be hoped that when the subject nations saw that they were being given this right, they might prefer not to make use of it, and to remain united in one state with brother nations. But if they insisted on separation, they must not be prevented.[1]

Neither Bauer's nor Lenin's policy was more than an attempt at a theoretical solution of an extremely complicated and important problem. Events were to show that no clearly defined principle could·deal with it.

[1] The clearest account available in English of Russian Marxist discussions of the nationality problem is in E. H. Carr, *The Bolshevik Revolution*, Vol. I, pp. 253–75 and 410–28. The classical texts are O. Bauer, *Die Nationalitätenfrage und die Sozialdemokratie*, Vienna, 1907; Karl Renner ('Rudolf Springer'), *Grundlagen und Entwicklungsziele der österreichisch-ungarischen Monarchie*, Vienna, 1906; and J. V. Stalin, *Marxism and the national and colonial problem*, 2nd English edition 1936.

One of the main concerns of the Second International, in the last years before 1914, was the prevention of war. It was widely believed that a general strike by the workers of the great industrial countries, and particularly of Germany and France, could frustrate the schemes of those whom socialists regarded as imperialistic warmongers. But when the crisis of 1914 came, the general strike was not even attempted. The great French socialist orator and denouncer of war, Jean Jaurès, was struck down by an assassin, and the French and German socialist parties voted for their countries' war efforts.

CHAPTER TWO

Lenin's Revolution

RUSSIAN SOCIALISM

SOCIALIST ideas became known to Russian intellectuals in the 1850's. The problem was how to fit them to the social reality of Russia. The pioneer of Russian socialism, N. G. Chernyshevski, took a special interest in the village commune, a self-governing peasant institution which dated at least from the seventeenth century and whose powers were strengthened under the settlement by which serfdom was abolished in 1861.[1] The first Russian socialists believed that if the peasants could be educated to socialist ideas, the commune could be transformed into the basic organ of a socialist society. In this way Russia could escape the miseries of capitalism, experienced by Western Europe in its industrial revolution, and could pass straight from its existing quasi-feudal social order to socialism. This view, which is generally known as Populism, with certain modifications, enjoyed strong support in Russia right up to 1917. The Populists for the first twenty years were not clearly separated from the Marxists. Marx's views were known in Russia from the beginning of the 1870's and he was greatly admired by the Populists, who regarded themselves as his pupils. They believed that his doctrines should be adapted to Russian conditions. Marx himself was open-minded on the question whether Russia could by-pass capitalism. As late as 1883, the year of his death, he wrote that Russia still had 'the rarest and most suitable opportunity, ever offered to a country, to avoid the phase of capitalistic development', but that if the Russian revolution were delayed and the opportunity so missed, Russia would 'fall under the sway of the ineluctable laws' of capitalism.[2]

That the introduction of socialism would require a revolution was generally believed. But the first Russian socialists were

[1] The best brief account available in English of the commune is in G. T. Robinson, *Rural Russia under the old Regime* (1929).

[2] Marx's words are printed in full in Y. Gardenin, *K pamyati N. K. Mihailovskovo*, Paris, 1904.

strangely indifferent to the political struggle in the narrower sense. They believed that their task was to propagate socialist ideas to the peasants, who when once converted would make a great social revolution, without bothering about such bourgeois shibboleths as constitutions and parliamentary liberties. But the peasants were not much impressed by the propaganda, and the police arrested the propagandists and the courts sentenced them to long terms of imprisonment. It became clear that the bourgeois liberties, which would have permitted them to preach their views without fear of police persecution, were worth having. The first socialist organisation, Land and Liberty, founded in 1877, split two years later on the issue of political action. One section, which took the name People's Will, decided to devote itself to the attainment of a constitution, and to use the weapon of assassination. It was a highly disciplined conspiratorial group. Its members were few, and consisted of intellectuals and a few urban workers but not of peasants. Despite its small numbers, it defeated the vast machine of the Imperial Russian police and on 14th March 1881 killed Tsar Alexander II. But it did not secure a constitution or civil liberties: the autocratic regime continued, more rather than less severe, for another twenty-four years. The conspirators were rounded up by the police and the organisation effectively ceased to exist.[1]

For the next years Russian socialism grew up in exile in Western Europe. In Switzerland in the mid-1880's was formed the most important Marxist group under G. V. Plehanov, who had begun his revolutionary career in Land and Liberty. For twenty years Plehanov urged two important arguments. The first was that all hopes of the transformation of the commune into an institution of socialism were utopian, and that Russia must in fact pass through capitalism. The second was that the working class must take part in the struggle for political liberties, that mere concern with economic interests was not enough. These arguments were supported at the end of the 90's by younger men from inside Russia, of whom the most important were V. I. Ulyanov—better known as Lenin—and Y. O. Martov. In 1898 was founded the Russian Social Democratic Party, in 1902 the Socialist Revolutionary Party, a modern form of the old Populist movement. Both joined the Second International. In 1903 was held the 2nd Congress of the Social Democrats, at which took place the split into two factions, known as

[1] An excellent account of the conspiracy is D. J. Footman, *Red Prelude*, 1944. On Populism there is a vast literature in Russian. Far the best and most thorough survey in a western language is Franco Venturi, *Il Popolismo russo*, Milan, 1952, 2 vols.

Bolsheviks and Mensheviks. Various attempts were later made to bring the factions together, and for a time formal unity was restored. In fact however the differences were never overcome, and in 1912 the breach became final. Thereafter there were two Russian Marxist parties. There is no doubt that personal issues, and the confidence of Lenin in his own Marxist infallibility, played a large part in the split. But there were also serious political differences, which grew more serious as the years passed, and the split remained.

BOLSHEVIKS AND MENSHEVIKS

The main difference concerned the organisation of the party. In Lenin's view the party must be the 'vanguard of the proletariat'. It must lead the working class, as the working class must lead other classes into revolution. Left to itself, the working class would think only of day-to-day economic problems, of what Lenin, with the British example in mind, contemptuously called 'trade unionist tactics'. The party must not follow the 'elemental' movement of the workers, must not become a 'tail' to the working class, but must lead the workers forward, understanding their true interests better than they themselves. The party must be a band of 'professional revolutionaries', bound by an iron discipline. Quality must come before quantity. No one must be admitted to the party who would not completely subject himself to its leaders and put the claims of the party on his time and efforts before all others.[1] Several of Lenin's opponents at the 1903 Congress, especially Martov, agreed with most of this. But they did not wish to make the conditions of membership quite so arduous. It was on a disagreement as to the phrasing of the first article of the party statute, defining the qualifications of membership, that the split took place.

During the following years the difference widened. It concerned the role of the party in political life. Up to 1905 conspiratorial methods were clearly necessary, as the Imperial Russian regime allowed no freedom of speech, meeting or association. On the necessity of 'illegal' activity there was thus no difference. But the regime which emerged from the troubled period 1905–7 was no longer the same. Considerable liberties were available. Economic progress was extremely rapid. The working class was growing in numbers, skill and influence. The intelligentsia had much more

[1] Lenin first laid down this doctrine in his pamphlet, *What is to be Done?* published in Switzerland in 1902.

scope for its abilities, much less cause for frustration. Russia was beginning to resemble western bourgeois countries. In these conditions a legal mass movement of the workers, on western lines, could hope to achieve results. To many of the workers' leaders inside Russia, the old type of conspiratorial party appeared a reactionary anachronism. Those who held this view wished to 'liquidate' the old party and build a new movement. They received increasing sympathy from the leaders of the Mensheviks in exile. Lenin however furiously stuck to his old policy. He violently attacked 'Liquidatorism' inside and outside Russia. He accused those Mensheviks who supported the 'Liquidators' of the sin of 'Revisionism' already introduced into the German Social Democratic Party by Bernstein.[1] To the Mensheviks Lenin appeared a cantankerous utopian, who in any case could not be trusted as a colleague. Every year of peaceful development in Russia seemed to confirm their views.

Another difference between Bolsheviks and Mensheviks concerned the role of the peasantry. Lenin believed that the working class must make the peasantry its ally, and could only do this by giving it what it most desired, the land. About one-sixth of the arable land of Russia, including some of the best quality, was still held by noble landowners. The peasants, suffering from the growing pressure of population and using backward methods of cultivation, passionately desired this land. The Socialist Revolutionary Party proposed to socialise all land, including that held by peasants as well as by landlords, and then to grant to individual peasant households the use of such land as they needed for their families on the principle of 'labour ownership'. Once this had been done, they believed, socialism could be built in the Russian village. Lenin had no use for the principle of 'labour ownership', which he regarded as 'petty bourgeois utopianism'. But in practice he supported the Socialist Revolutionary policy, for two reasons. Firstly, it was clear to him that this was what the peasants wanted: 'labour ownership' would take the land away from the noble landowners and give it to the peasants. If the workers were to have the peasants as allies, they must give them what they wanted. Secondly, Lenin believed that the destruction of large estates would remove the remnants of feudalism from Russian rural society and make possible a rapid development of capitalism. The peasantry would be rapidly differentiated between a rural bourgeoisie and a rural proletariat. The latter would be the ally of the working class

[1] See above, p. 17.

in its final struggle with the bourgeoisie in town and country. The Mensheviks were less interested in the peasants than were the Socialist Revolutionaries or Bolsheviks. To them the important problem was the relationship between the workers and the urban bourgeoisie, which they saw increasingly in terms of a West European social and political system. They favoured the expropriation of the noble landowners, but they held that the expropriated land should not be divided among the peasants but be administered by popularly elected authorities on the peasants' behalf. This policy was known as 'municipalisation'.

BOURGEOIS AND SOCIALIST REVOLUTIONS

The peasant question was linked with the general theory of the coming revolution. In the Socialist Revolutionaries' view, the establishment of 'labour ownership' would essentially complete the revolution. Thereafter Russia would be a socialist country, though no doubt many years of effort would be necessary to build real socialism. But Mensheviks and Bolsheviks were agreed that the coming revolution would be a 'bourgeois revolution', which would do for Russia essentially what 1789 did for France. It would replace the Tsar's autocracy by a parliamentary republic. But Lenin believed that 1905 had shown that the bourgeoisie of Russia was not capable of carrying through a bourgeois revolution. In 1905, he argued, the bourgeoisie had compromised with the autocracy and supported it against the masses. This would happen next time too. Betrayal of the revolution by the bourgeoisie could only be prevented if the revolution were led by the proletariat. The proletariat must do the job of the bourgeoisie for it. It must bring under its leadership all the revolutionary forces in the country, including the overwhelming majority of the peasantry and a large part of the urban lower middle class. The proletariat would be led by 'its' party—here Lenin of course had in mind his own Bolshevik group. Thus under the leadership of the Bolshevik party would be formed a 'revolutionary democratic dictatorship of the proletariat and peasantry'. With the autocracy overthrown, the Bolsheviks would hold the key positions. Having led to its triumphant conclusion the bourgeois revolution, they would be well placed to carry on the next stage, the socialist revolution that was to replace government in the interests of the bourgeoisie by government in the interests of the proletariat.[1] How soon this second

---

[1] These views were first clearly expressed by Lenin in his pamphlet, *Two Tactics of Social Democracy*, published in Switzerland in 1905.

stage would be possible, Lenin could not predict. It might be necessary for many years to pass, years during which the process of differentiation of the peasantry would proceed, ultimately creating a rural proletariat that would fight beside the urban proletariat against the bourgeoisie of town and country. Alternatively, favourable conditions might make the socialist revolution possible very soon. Marx himself had considered possible that a revolution in Russia might be a spark that would cause revolutionary explosions in industrial Europe, where economic conditions and social structure made the establishment of socialism possible. If a large part of industrial Europe became socialist, then the gap between the bourgeois and socialist revolutions in Russia could be greatly reduced.

The Mensheviks did not accept this analysis. In their view the bourgeois revolution should be led by the bourgeoisie. The proletariat should support the bourgeoisie against the autocracy, and should then make use of the liberties of bourgeois democracy to build a mass movement of the workers, as in the West. Their task would be helped by the economic development of Russia, by which every year the working class was increasing its numbers by recruiting from the peasantry. The Mensheviks had little enthusiasm for the peasantry as an ally in revolution. They had the traditional contempt of West European Marxists for 'rural idiocy'. In the Mensheviks' view the gap between the bourgeois and proletarian revolutions would necessarily be long, though they also recognised that the establishment of socialism in Europe would accelerate the whole process.

A special point of view was that of L. D. Bronstein—better known as Trotski—who had played an important part in the events of 1905 in St. Petersburg, and in the following years took an independent position between Mensheviks and Bolsheviks. In a pamphlet published in Vienna in 1909,[1] Trotski had argued that if the proletariat were to lead a bourgeois revolution in Russia, it would not be able, as Lenin was suggesting, to limit the revolution to the bourgeois stage. If the proletariat seized power, it would have to carry the revolution on to the socialist stage. But in a country economically and socially so backward as Russia, the socialist revolution would be defeated. Therefore it was essential to the success of the proletarian revolution in Russia that there

[1] Republished in Moscow in 1922 under the title *1905*. Trotski was the deputy chairman of the St. Petersburg Soviet of Workers' Deputies in October 1905. Arrested after the dissolution of the Soviet, he made an impressive speech at the trial. He afterwards escaped from Siberia and went to Vienna.

should be socialist revolutions in industrial Europe. The bourgeois revolution in Russia must be the spark setting off the explosion in Europe.

The opportunity to test these different theories came in March 1917. The March Revolution was a result of the war. It was caused by a combination of dismay at war casualties, economic hardship and general political incompetence. Never perhaps in history had a great nation made such heroic efforts on behalf of such despicable rulers. The immediate occasion was furnished by workers' demonstrations, and the issue was decided when the troops in the capital went over to the crowds. On 15th March the Tsar abdicated, and on the following day a Provisional Government of liberal politicians was formed. Beside the government was the Soviet of Workers' and Soldiers' Deputies. The workers' deputies were elected in the factories, and the soldiers' in army units. At this time the soviets, which were formed all over the country, were genuinely representative bodies. They expressed the pent-up feelings of the long-inarticulate masses, until then almost completely excluded from Russian political life. In St. Petersburg the government and the soviet viewed each other with suspicion. The soviet gave a qualified recognition to the government. For its part the government declared its intention of holding, as soon as possible, elections to a Constituent Assembly. But meanwhile the government was based on no legislative body, and the soviet, being the only assembly in the capital that could claim a representative quality, demanded with increasing success that the government should hold itself responsible to it.

This 'duality of power' in Russia was watched with close attention by Lenin in his Swiss exile. The idea developed in his mind that, whereas the Provisional Government was the organ of the bourgeoisie and the bourgeois revolution, the soviets were organs of the proletariat and the proletarian revolution. The situation in Russia had in fact elements of two revolutions. The duality could not be permanent: one or the other of the revolutions must triumph. The task of himself and his party was to ensure that the second triumphed, and thus that the gap between the bourgeois and the proletarian revolutions should be made as short as possible. The correct tactic for the Bolsheviks was therefore to deny support to the Provisional Government and to do everything to strengthen the soviets in the capitals and the provinces. The correct slogan must be 'All power to the soviets!' This conception of the revolutionary role of the soviets and the jump straight from the bourgeois to the proletarian revolution was linked in Lenin's mind with the ideas that the Russian revolution must become the starting-point for socialist revolutions in advanced European countries, and that a new International, based upon a true vanguard of the international proletariat, must be founded, in place of the now defunct Second International, to co-ordinate the European revolutions.[1] Once he had returned to Russia in April, having passed from Switzerland through Germany to Sweden with the permission of the German General Staff, Lenin immediately and energetically advocated these policies. The Bolshevik leaders whom he found in control of the party—Kamenev, Stalin and Muranov—were astonished at his views, but were soon converted to them.

Lenin's tactics with regard to the soviets must be considered not only on the level of revolutionary doctrine, as summarised above, but also on the level of practical politics. The great practical merit of the soviets from Lenin's point of view was that they represented not the trained politicians but the untrained masses of the factories and the armed forces. Excluded from political life under the old regime, the inexperienced, primitive and largely illiterate masses were being brought for the first time into political life through the soviets. Even in the Petrograd Soviet, whose chief personalities were the known leaders of the three socialist parties, men of definite opinions and considerable experience, the great majority of deputies had no fixed party allegiance, but supported whatever proposals most appealed to their strongly but vaguely revolutionary frame of mind. Socialist Revolutionaries, Mensheviks and Bolsheviks could not count on automatic party discipline by the deputies: these would vote as they felt at the moment. In the soviets of lesser cities this was still more the case. The soviets were thus a forum much more favourable for the Bolsheviks than could be any parliament or Constituent Assembly which would consist of disciplined party groups, each composed of the most eminent leaders of each party. In a parliamentary regime, governments would be formed by agreements between party leaders, men whose political views were already well defined. The Bolsheviks would have to discuss and bargain with the other leaders, or else be driven into ineffective opposition. But if by attractive demagogic slogans the Bolsheviks could capture the soviets, and through them gain control over the masses, they would cut the ground from under the feet of their rivals. Power would be theirs before any parliamentary system had been created.

[1] See below, pp. 50–51.

There was thus a tactical aspect to Lenin's preference for the soviets, as well as a doctrinaire aspect. Lenin's plan was a partnership between the politically trained and well-disciplined conspiratorial Bolsheviks and the politically ignorant and gullible masses. This partnership was to give the Bolsheviks a monopoly of political leadership. In April 1917 the Bolsheviks were supported only by a small minority in the soviets. Lenin set himself to win a majority by unlimited demagogy on the three principal issues of peace, the claims of the workers, and the peasants' demand for land. For three months the Bolsheviks gained ground. In July came a setback, when a mass demonstration in which they were involved was a failure, and the publication of documents purporting to prove that Lenin was a German agent created a popular reaction against him. After this setback, Lenin, who decided to go into hiding in Finland, gave up the slogan 'All power to the soviets!' Opinion in the soviets was predominantly hostile to the Bolsheviks, and it now seemed to Lenin that the best forum for his activities would be the factory committees.[1] But in September, after the unsuccessful rebellion of General Kornilov against the Provisional Government, opinion in the soviets once more turned towards Lenin. At the end of September the soviets of the two capitals had Bolshevik majorities. Possession of these majorities gave Lenin the confidence to make his armed bid for power in November. Thus the soviets, apart from any theoretical significance which Lenin might sincerely ascribe to them as organs of proletarian revolution, had a historic importance as instruments enabling the Bolsheviks to seize power. But in order to understand how the Bolsheviks were able to get control of these instruments, we must consider the political and social issues of conflict during the months from March to November.

FROM MARCH TO NOVEMBER

The most important problem was that of peace. The Russian people were sick of war. The leaders of the political parties wished to make peace as soon as póssible. But to get out of a war is always harder than to get into one. The German government, now in fact dominated by General Ludendorff, was bent on great territorial conquests: it was not going to give Russia a just peace. Russia's Allies believed that the war could be won, and could not consent to a Russian separate peace which would release great German armies to fight them. Meanwhile Russia had to be defended.

[1] See below, pp. 32, 42.

Only some of the Right and Centre supporters of the Provisional Government wished to prolong the war to a victory which would give Russia more territory and influence than she had in 1914. The Socialist Revolutionaries and Mensheviks never faced the reality. By ideology they were passionate pacifists. All arguments based on alleged international facts were suspect to them as manœuvres of the bourgeoisie. They took refuge behind the fine phrase 'peace without annexations and without indemnities'. Constant repetition of this magic incantation was for them a substitute for policy. When forced by events to take some practical decision, they usually gave a three-quarter-hearted support to national defence.

Lenin's mind was clearer but not more realistic. For him, obligations to the Allies did not exist. The Tsar had made agreements with the French and British politicians, puppets of the French and British capitalists, who owned the metallurgical industry of southern Russia and the oil wells of the Caucasus, and required supplies of Russian cannon-fodder to pursue their robber aims at the expense of the German and Austrian capitalists and imperialists. In return for the profits and the cannon-fodder the British and French capitalists had promised the Tsar a few more provinces of Austria, Turkey or Prussian Poland. All talk of liberating Slavs, Armenians or Belgians was completely insincere. Now that the Tsar had been overthrown, all these bargains must be repudiated. Peace must be made at once, without an hour's delay. The troops must at once fraternise on the front. As for the argument that unilateral surrender would only help the German imperialist Ludendorff and the German capitalists, Lenin brushed it away. He was convinced that the German proletariat would overthrow William II and Ludendorff. In his utopian belief in a German revolution Lenin persisted right up to the eve of Brest-Litovsk. Meanwhile the Bolsheviks threw themselves energetically into the campaign of propaganda for immediate peace, especially among army units. Already before the March Revolution army morale was declining: there is no doubt that pacifist and defeatist propaganda speeded the decline. In this propaganda, conducted through the various committees and elected bodies set up in the armed forces, on the initiative of the Petrograd Soviet and with the permission of the Provisional Government, the Bolsheviks played a leading part. Though their contribution to the disintegration of Russia's armies cannot be exactly measured against that of other factors, it was without doubt large.

These months saw a rapid growth of trade unions, which now at last enjoyed all the rights customary in Europe, including the right to strike. Already in March an eight-hour day and the institution of elected factory committees were introduced in Petrograd by agreement between trade unions and employers' organisations, and in Moscow by unilateral decision of the soviet. The trade unions had 1,500,000 members in July and more than 2,000,000 in the autumn. The economic difficulties from which factories had been suffering already in 1916, and which were caused by the effects of the war on supplies, were now enormously increased by labour troubles. Output fell rapidly as time rates took the place of piece rates and working time was spent on meetings in the factories, demonstrations in the streets, and constantly recurring strikes. The strikers demanded shorter hours and higher wages at a time when industry could less afford these than ever. Workers' committees increasingly interfered with management. Some factories were forced to close, and unemployment increased. All this provided admirable opportunities for the Bolsheviks. Economic hardships were ascribed to sabotage by employers. As a remedy for all ills the Bolsheviks demanded 'workers' control' over industry. Their propaganda was conducted principally through the factory committees, in which they soon gained large support.

The Bolsheviks devoted far more effort to the factory committees in the individual enterprises than to the trade unions which grouped workers in many enterprises or in whole branches of industry. Their preference for the factory committee over the trade union exactly corresponded to their preference for soviets over parliamentary forms of government. Leaders of trade unions, like parliamentary leaders, were mostly persons of considerable experience and of definite opinions, and few of them were Bolsheviks. Factory committees, like soviets, consisted of energetic but inexperienced persons with no fixed opinions. The Bolshevik policy of capturing the masses from their rivals, of a partnership between the Bolshevik professional revolutionary and the politically illiterate workers, could be more easily applied in the factory committees than in the trade unions, as it could be more easily applied in the soviets than in a parliament. As for the chaos that resulted from Bolshevik demagogy in the factories, this actually helped the Bolshevik cause. The argument that the economy must not be disrupted as long as Russia was at war, made no impression on them at all. They positively wished to undermine the war effort. Peace should be made at once: if it had not already been made, this was solely due to the fact that the Provisional Government was composed of puppets of the French and British capitalists who wished to prolong the war. Their talk of giving the workers their rights after the war was over, or when the Constituent Assembly met, was simply a trick to postpone concessions and to cheat them in the end of all their rights.

The same imputation of dishonest motives was made by Lenin and his party in the land question. All the parties supporting the Provisional Government regarded the distribution of nobles' land among the peasants as essential, though there were differences of opinion about compensation. The land settlement was to be made by the Constituent Assembly. Meanwhile, in order not to prejudice the Assembly's decisions, and in order not to disorganise the war effort, the peasants were urged to be patient. A hierarchy of land committees was created to mediate in land disputes, and ensure that things were done in an orderly manner. But the peasants were not disposed to be patient. Soviets of Peasants' Deputies sprang up over the country. Many of these, and many of the local land committees, seized landlords' estates. Peasant soldiers began to desert from their units to take their share in the redistribution. Disorders and arson multiplied. In all this revolutionary propaganda played its part, but it came less from the Bolsheviks than from the Socialist Revolutionaries. The Bolsheviks, it is true, did their best. We have already seen that Lenin before the war had taken over the agrarian programme of the Socialist Revolutionaries, though for motives different from theirs. Lenin now urged immediate distribution of the land among the peasants, and imputed to all who urged delay the intention of cheating the peasants of their due. Lenin spoke forcibly to this effect at the First All-Russian Congress of Soviets of Peasants' Deputies in Petrograd in June.[1] Those points in his speech which coincided with the Socialist Revolutionary programme were applauded, but those which introduced new principles—special organisations for poor peasants and farm labourers and creation of state-owned model farms—aroused little interest. In general the Bolsheviks did not at this stage have much influence on the peasants, except in the armed forces. The revolutionary activity among the peasants in their villages was led by Socialist Revolutionaries, whose local organisers were usually much more radical and much more impatient than the party's leaders who sat in the Provisional Government or in the Petrograd Soviet. But though the peasants' revolt was not made by the Bolsheviks, yet by increasing the general

[1] Lenin, *Sochinenia*, 3rd edition, Vol. XX, pp. 403–18.

confusion in the country and in the army it helped the Bolsheviks in their bid for power.

The revolt of General Kornilov in September was a turning-point in the Revolution. Kornilov was not of noble birth, a monarchist or a reactionary. He was driven to desperation by the disintegration of the army. He was a patriot who believed that Russia must be saved from the enemy, and believed that this could only be done by tightening discipline. At the Moscow State Conference, an assembly called at the end of August by the Prime Minister of the Provisional Government, the Socialist Revolutionary lawyer, A. F. Kerenski, in the vain hope of creating a measure of national unity behind a strengthened government, Kornilov became convinced that Kerenski and the politicians of the Left were useless demagogues, consciously or unconsciously destroying Russia. He became convinced that he must overthrow Kerenski if he was to save Russia. He could count on the support of most army officers and of the business men and politicians of the Right and Centre. But Kerenski and his friends he regarded as completely unreliable. For his part Kerenski saw in Kornilov an Imperial officer supported by the forces of reaction who, even if he himself did not wish to restore the Imperial regime, was bound to become a tool in the hands of those who did. Kerenski himself wished almost as strongly as did Kornilov to restore the fighting spirit of the army. But he believed that this should be done, not by Kornilov's method of tighter discipline and extension of the death penalty to breaches of discipline by troops behind as well as at the front, but on the contrary by a further 'democratisation'. The committees and commissars in army units should be strengthened, and should use their powers to explain to the soldiers the necessity of defending the 'revolutionary fatherland'. Thus Kerenski hoped that a new and finer morale could be created.

The distrust between these two men symbolised the conflict between the moderate Right and the moderate Left, from which only the Bolsheviks gained. Kerenski was very quick to decide that Kornilov was plotting against him, and to denounce him as a rebel. Earlier he had shown much greater forbearance to the Bolsheviks. Since July Lenin had been in hiding, but the Bolshevik organisation had been able to operate legally in the capitals and the provinces. When Kornilov marched on Petrograd, the Bolsheviks played a leading part in improvising its defences and in organising delegations of soldiers and workers to harangue the rebel troops. These were successful, fraternisation took place, and the rebellion failed. The Bolsheviks had gained prestige as the most resolute defenders of the Revolution.

Some writers on the Revolution express regret that Kerenski and Kornilov 'could not have united against the Bolsheviks'. But this is to misunderstand the situation. The gulf between the moderate Right and the moderate Left was as deep as between either and the Bolsheviks. To all except the Bolsheviks, it was the only gulf. Kornilov hardly distinguished between Kerenski and the Bolsheviks: both were Red demagogues who were destroying Russia. To Kerenski the real enemy was Kornilov, whom he believed to be the leader of all the forces of counter-revolution. In the face of the counter-revolutionary threat, there could be 'no enemies on the Left'. Kerenski could not give Kornilov the benefit of doubt that he allowed to Lenin. Lenin, he thought, was another socialist, misguided, tiresome and turbulent, but still on the same side of the barricade. He could not be considered an enemy in the same sense as an Imperial general. Kerenski himself was less affected by this sentimental belief in socialist solidarity than were the other Socialist Revolutionary and Menshevik leaders. But he was to some extent affected by it, and to his colleagues and followers, on whose support he depended, it was a dogma. But Lenin did not share it. He exploited for his own purposes the sentimental loyalty of the other socialist parties. But to him Kerenski, or the Menshevik leader Tseretelli, were as much enemies as Nicholas II. To him there were three forces—Right, Left and Bolsheviks. This was no new attitude for Lenin. Ever since 1905 he had regarded the Mensheviks as enemies no less than any other political party. He had shown no less hatred for his rivals within the Marxist movement than for non-Marxist socialists, non-socialist liberals, reactionary monarchists or the Tsar's police. Now he put his hatred into practice.

On 23rd October Lenin finally persuaded the Central Committee of the Bolshevik party to seize power by force. The enemy forces were divided and irresolute. Now was the time to act. If action were further postponed, the opportunity would pass, perhaps never to return. The insurrection was prepared by a Military Revolutionary Committee of the Petrograd Soviet. Its leading figure was Trotski, who had returned to Russia soon after Lenin, had found himself in complete agreement with him on policy and tactics, and had formally joined the Bolshevik party in July. The Committee efficiently performed its task of placing men in key posts in the army units to ensure their obedience to its orders. On

7th November the insurrection took place.[1] The government was defended only by a few hundred soldiers. Not all troops obeyed the Bolsheviks, but those who did not, simultaneously refused to obey Kerenski. The Cossacks hated Kerenski, who had beaten their hero Kornilov, more than the Bolsheviks, whom they did not consider a serious threat. In Moscow there was fighting for four days, in Kazan and Saratov a few shots were fired. Within a few days the government set up by the Bolsheviks was recognised in northern and central Russia, and during November in Siberia.

THE CONSTITUENT ASSEMBLY

The first round had been won, but only the first round. The next problem before Lenin was the Constituent Assembly. He had always urged that the election should be quickly held, and having seized power he could hardly call it off. Besides it seems that he genuinely believed that the Bolsheviks would do very well in it. Polling took place at the end of November. In the big cities there was much intimidation against the liberals, but socialist parties were not on the whole persecuted. The results disappointed the Bolsheviks. Of some 707 elected members, 410 were Socialist Revolutionaries and 175 Bolsheviks. The Mensheviks had 16 seats, Liberals ('Kadets') 17 and various national groups 86.

Lenin never considered respecting the electors' verdict. His only concern was to find arguments to justify ignoring it. He had an important success at the end of November. At an all-Russian Peasant Congress held in Petrograd, the Bolshevik delegates were able to split the Socialist Revolutionary representatives and to detach a left wing led by the woman terrorist Maria Spiridonova. Several of these 'Left S.R.s' were then given places in Lenin's government. This could now claim to be a broad coalition, with peasant as well as working-class support. The S.R. split had taken place, not at any official meeting of an organ of the S.R. party, but at a peasant congress in which the party was strongly represented. Of the 410 S.R. members of the Constituent Assembly, only 40 supported the Spiridonova group, while 370 remained loyal to the old leadership. But Lenin argued that the S.R. party was now split into two parties of at least equal importance, and that the

---

[1] I have used throughout this chapter the dates of the European (Gregorian) calendar. By the Julian calendar, in use in Russia until 1918, the date of the Bolshevik seizure of power was 25th October. It is therefore usually referred to as the 'October Revolution'. The same difference in date causes its predecessor to be known as the 'February Revolution'. I find it more convenient to use the terms 'March Revolution' and 'November Revolution'. Readers are warned, to avoid confusion.

verdict of the polls was meaningless. A day or two before the split at the Peasant Congress, the electors of Russia had voted for a party which, after the split, 'no longer existed'. This manœuvre of Lenin with the S.R.s was to furnish a precedent for the East European Communist parties nearly thirty years later.[1] The manœuvre is one more example of Lenin's technique of undermining the mass support of his rivals, which he had already shown in his use of soviets against parliamentary bodies, and of factory committees against trade unions. As their candidates for the Constituent Assembly the S.R.s, like the other parties, had put up their leading members, persons of proved conviction and loyalty to the party, who could not be swayed away from it to another party by revolutionary demagogy. But the S.R. delegates at the Peasant Congress were of a different calibre. They were mostly simple peasants, elected by their fellows, who could be and were won away by Lenin's arguments and stage-managing. The highly emotional Maria Spiridonova was no less easy game than the peasants.

Lenin's plan of partnership between the gullible masses and the Bolshevik professional revolutionaries, designed to make the masses a weapon in Bolshevik hands against the Bolsheviks' socialist rivals, was working brilliantly in the three fields of Workers' and Soldiers' Soviets, Peasant Congress, and factory committees, but it could not succeed in the forum of the Constituent Assembly. Therefore the Assembly must be dissolved. Lenin prepared a propaganda campaign to justify the Assembly's suppression. He used three arguments: that the S.R. party was no longer the same party since the split; that the soviets, organs of the proletarian stage of revolution, were a 'higher form of democratic principle' than the Assembly, an organ of the bourgeois stage; and that the results of the election were not representative as it had been held on electoral registers made before the insurrection and at a time when 'the people could not yet know the full scope and meaning of the October socialist proletarian-peasant Revolution'.[2] The first argument presumed that the Bolsheviks had the right to decide who represented the S.R. party—Spiridonova or the established leaders of the party. The second argument assumed that Lenin's doctrine about soviets and parliament was an established truth. The third argument is truly remarkable. Organise a military insurrection to overthrow your political rivals. Call this insurrection, conducted by certain military units in the capitals with con-

[1] See below, pp. 249–251.   [2] See above, p. 36, footnote.

siderable backing from the working class of those cities, a 'socialist proletarian-peasant revolution'. It then follows that realisation of the profound changes introduced by this great historic event would have caused the people to vote differently had the polling been not eighteen days after the great historic event, but, say, a month or two. This hypothetical poll, which did not take place, was the true expression of the Russian people's wishes, not the real poll which did take place. The argument would be ridiculous were it not that Lenin was so profoundly convinced of his exclusive capacity to act in the name of great historic forces that he probably believed it.

The Assembly was dissolved on 18th January 1918, after it had rejected by 237 votes to 138 the demand of the Bolsheviks that it should recognise the soviets as a body superior to itself. There was no resistance. The S.R.s were not an effective force. Their party had not the same centralised discipline as the Bolshevik: its strength came from the scattered peasant masses, not from the concentrated proletariat and armed forces of the great cities. Lenin was able to assert that he, not the S.R.s, had the support of the peasant masses, because there was no way of finding out what the peasant masses really thought, apart from the votes they had given at the November election, and because meanwhile he was promising them what they wanted, and what the S.R.s also had promised them, and what they were in any case taking—the land.

Defeat of the Assembly was victory to the Bolsheviks in the second round. The third round was the problem of peace with Germany. This was attained, on disastrous terms, by the Treaty of Brest-Litovsk in March. Not only were the Baltic provinces, White Russia, the Ukraine and the Caucasus lost to the Bolshevik government, but great discontent was caused within the government camp. The Spiridonova group of S.R.s left the government, and several leading Bolsheviks were bitterly hostile. Meanwhile in the south-east, in the Don valley and the Kuban steppes, the first armed anti-Bolshevik Russian forces were being organised. The civil war was beginning.

THE CIVIL WAR

The civil war falls into two phases, divided by the armistice in Western Europe.

In the first phase the Bolsheviks had two dangers to face. The first came from Germany, which controlled vast Russian territories, and also gave some material support to anti-Bolshevik groups operating on territory which the German government officially regarded as being subject to Lenin's government. The most important of these forces were the Don Cossacks. There could be little doubt that if Ludendorff could win the war in the West he would turn back against the East. A victorious militarist monarchist Germany would never tolerate Lenin's Bolshevik regime as a neighbour. From this danger Lenin was saved by the victory of Marshal Foch. The second danger came from the democratic forces which recognised the Constituent Assembly and which believed that by making the treaty of Brest-Litovsk Lenin had shown himself a puppet of the Germans. For these men the democratic and patriotic motives were about equally important. Their leaders had sporadic contact with the remaining representatives in Russia of the Western Allies, from whom they received copious promises but little help.

At the end of May the outbreak of hostilities between the Bolshevik government and the small but well-disciplined Czechoslovak volunteer army on Russian soil led to the capture by the Czechoslovaks of a number of cities from Samara on the Volga across Siberia. In Samara a government of S.R.s was set up, and in July S.R.s made an insurrection in Yaroslavl and other cities near Moscow. The insurrection was crushed by the Bolsheviks, but part of the Volga valley and all Siberia passed out of their hands. In September a State Conference was held in Ufa in the name of the Constituent Assembly. After a compromise had been made at Ufa between the S.R.s and the more conservative groups, a provisional anti-Bolshevik government, or Directory, was formed, which had its seat in Omsk. During the autumn however friction between the Left and Right forces supporting the Omsk government grew. On the front its armies lost ground to the Bolsheviks. In November Admiral Kolchak, the supreme commander of the Directory's forces, seized power in Omsk.

From then onwards the regime in Siberia became increasingly militarist, reactionary and dictatorial. The old conflict between Kerenski and Kornilov had repeated itself, with the victory this time going to the Right. The workers and peasants in general, and persons of Left opinions in particular, lost enthusiasm for the struggle. Moreover when the Germans had been defeated by the Allies, it was no longer possible to regard the Bolsheviks as puppets of a hostile foreign Power. With patriotism no longer dictating resistance to Lenin, with the Omsk regime growing into a dictatorship apparently no less odious than the Bolshevik and increasingly similar to the Imperial regime, and with Bolshevik propaganda busy behind the White lines, it is not surprising that Kolchak's government should lose popular support.

In the second phase of the civil war the threat to the Bolsheviks came from Russian armies, led by professional officers of the Imperial army, holding conservative or reactionary political opinions, and to some extent armed and equipped by the French and British governments. There were two main fronts. One was in Siberia against Kolchak. The danger from Kolchak was greatest in the spring of 1919. By July the Bolsheviks had reconquered most of the Ural region, and in the autumn Kolchak's forces were disintegrating. The other front was in the south. Here the Volunteer Army, a small force of high quality created by Kornilov and Alekseev at the end of 1917,[1] maintained itself with great courage and in the face of great difficulties during 1918, in conflict with both Bolsheviks and Germans. After the Armistice it received supplies from the Allies through the Black Sea, and grew as rapidly in numbers as it deteriorated in quality. During the summer of 1919 the southern armies, led by General Denikin, swept across the Ukraine and turned north towards Moscow. In mid-October they were held by the Bolsheviks between Moscow and Orel, and a retreat began which turned into a rout.

During the civil war there were for varying periods forces of French, British, Japanese, American and Greek troops on parts of Russian soil. Except for the Japanese in the Far Eastern provinces they played only a minor part, but their presence made it possible for the Bolsheviks to exploit Russian patriotism, to represent their rivals as agents of foreign Powers, and to create the legend that by winning the civil war the Red Army had smashed the combined military might of the great capitalist states.

The war went on into 1920. Russian puppets of the Japanese were still active in the Far East, General Vrangel's army operated from the Crimea, and the Poles under Piłsudski invaded the Ukraine in April.[2] By the autumn Vrangel and the Poles had been defeated and the Japanese eventually evacuated the Russian Pacific coast in 1922 as a result of American diplomatic pressure. But already at the end of 1919 the Bolshevik victory was substantially secured. It remains briefly to summarise the causes of the victory.

---

[1] Kornilov was killed at the siege of Ekaterinodar in March 1918. His successor, General Alekseev, former Chief of Staff of the Imperial Army, died in October 1918.
[2] See below, p.72.

CAUSES OF BOLSHEVIK VICTORY

The Bolsheviks won the political struggle for power between March and November 1917 by their uninhibited demagogy and by their skilful use of the best channels through which to influence the workers and soldiers. The choice of slogans and of machinery was Lenin's, and it was here that his genius revealed itself most clearly. The forces with which the Bolsheviks gained victory in November were the working class of the capitals and the military units stationed there. The peasant masses were essentially neutral, a portion of them benevolently so. The enemy forces were irreparably divided. That division was not Lenin's work, but he appreciated its significance more fully than did either faction of his enemies and he used it to the full.

The most important single cause of Bolshevik victory in the civil war was military superiority. The Bolsheviks had a strong central position, based on Moscow and central Russia but also always including Petrograd and most of the north-west. Their enemies were operating on the periphery, and could not easily or quickly communicate with each other. The Bolshevik Red Army began as an unreliable rabble of soldiers whom the Bolsheviks had urged for months to run away before the enemy. But under Trotski as Commissar for War, and with the help both of energetic Bolshevik administrators and of many former Imperial officers who were recruited by patriotism, the offer of good posts, or fear, a powerful and disciplined force was created. Even at the end of the civil war, the Red Army was inferior to a West European army, not only in equipment but in morale and discipline. But it was superior to the White armies it had to fight. The Bolshevik party provided a stiffening element which held it together by a combination of enthusiasm and terror. Despite the general poverty and misery, the army was better cared for than any other group of the nation. Something was also done for the education and cultural welfare of the Red soldiers. All this opened new horizons to thousands of peasant conscripts. Natural abilities and initiatives among the primitive Russian masses, which under the old regime had had no outlet, were able to make themselves felt within the new army. This tremendous release of new forces and genuine new enthusiasm is an important aspect of the Bolshevik leadership. The other aspect is the ruthless terror of the *Cheka* or political police, which exterminated thousands of real and imagined enemies of the Bolshevik regime. The *Cheka's* activities did much harm to the Bolshevik cause, both by the hatred which it created inside and outside Russia, and by the unnecessary waste of human lives and waste of personnel in supervisory and administrative jobs. But on balance the terror probably did more good than harm to those who wielded it, more harm than good to its enemies.

The second group of causes concern the attitude to the Bolsheviks and Whites of different classes and sections of the population, the impact on the masses of the policy known as 'War Communism'.

That the Bolsheviks had won over the bulk of the working class has already been shown. The course of the civil war did nothing to convince the workers that they would fare better under a White than a Bolshevik regime. In fact it is likely that many of those workers who had originally preferred Mensheviks or Socialist Revolutionaries to Bolsheviks supported Lenin by the end of the war. The first months of the Bolshevik regime were marked by the spontaneous and uncoordinated seizure of factories by the workers. It was not easy to give precise meaning to the slogan 'workers' control', which the Bolsheviks had used to gain the support of the workers during the summer of 1917. In practice the workers often ran the factories with little regard either for government directives or for the needs of other enterprises. The government could not long tolerate these 'syndicalist' tendencies which threatened anarchy in production. Most large factories were formally nationalised by the end of June 1918, and at the end of the year this was extended even to small industrial enterprises. A vast new industrial hierarchy was created, headed by the Supreme Council of National Economy.

In problems of labour organisation the Bolsheviks soon after seizing power reversed the policy they had pursued during 1917. While preparing to seize power, they had encouraged the factory committees and opposed the trade unions, just as in the political field they had encouraged the soviets and opposed parliamentary forms. Now that they had power, they preferred trade unions to factory committees, a centralised command over the labour force from above to disruptive influence from below. They now urged the unions to discipline the committees, placed their own men in the unions, and won over some of the existing union leaders. At the first trade union congress, held in January 1918, Zinoviev for the Bolsheviks proposed absorption of the unions into the state machine (*ogosudarstvlenie*), while Menshevik spokesmen—still influential—urged independent status for the unions. A formal compromise was made between these two points of view, but the outbreak of civil war in fact led to the triumph of the Bolshevik policy.

In December 1918 the obligation of labour for all between 16 and 50 was formally decreed. A special committee (*Glavkomtrud*) carried out the mobilisation of civilians for special tasks such as collection of stocks of firewood or building projects. After the defeat of Denikin large armed forces were used for labour under military discipline. When Vrangel and the Poles had been defeated, still more military formations became available for the same purpose. The chief champion of the use of such 'labour armies' was Trotski, but the principle was approved by the whole party leadership and by the heads of the trade unions. That the unions, which played a leading part in the mobilisation of the people both for the army and for civilian labour, were closely interlocked with the state machine, was obvious to all: it remained to see whether this would result in the subordination of the unions to the state, or of the state to the unions.

The peasants supported the S.R.s where and while the S.R.s were an effective force. But after Kolchak's *coup d'état* there was no practical opportunity to support S.R.s: the choice was between Bolsheviks and Whites. Of these two on the whole the peasants preferred the Bolsheviks.

In the first months after the November Revolution the peasants had had no grounds to dislike the Bolsheviks' agrarian policy. Already on 8th November Lenin decreed the confiscation without compensation of all estates of nobility, church and Imperial family. On 19th February 1918 followed the formal socialisation of the land. The government wished both to encourage the formation of model farms and of new types of collective cultivation, and to organise a migration of families from overpopulated to sparsely inhabited areas, in order to equalise throughout the country the amount of land gained by peasants from landowners' estates. In fact however little was done in either direction. Redistribution of land was unsystematic, and considered only immediate local interests. But the fact remained that the Bolsheviks had given the peasants the land: for this they were grateful.

The trouble began in the summer of 1918, when the supplies of food to the army and the non-agricultural population became scarce. From the beginning the government was resolved to obtain food cheaply. The peasants could hardly be expected to increase their output in order to sell at very low prices. As the currency depreciated, and as the supply of manufactured goods which money could buy diminished, they became still less inclined to make a special effort. Since no economic incentive could be offered the peasants to produce for the market, only propaganda and force remained. Propaganda stressed the peasant's interest to defend the revolution, to give his produce to the workers' government which protected him from the White armies that were bringing back the landlords: this argument without doubt had its effect, and was reinforced by the oppressive actions of the Whites in the territories which they held. But force was also needed. It took the form of a complicated hierarchy, under the People's Commissariat of Supplies, whose executive arms were the 'provision detachments' (*prodotryady*) recruited from the urban workers. When the quotas fixed by the provincial Commissars of the Supply hierarchy were not delivered, the detachments were sent to requisition the required amount by force. In this they were assisted during 1918 by 'committees of the poor' (*kombedy*). These were recruited from the poorer peasants, to help the authorities find concealed grain surpluses. They had a direct incentive in the promise that a part of all surpluses found would be sold at an exceptionally low price to their members.

Though the real aim of Bolshevik policy was to extract food from the unwilling peasantry, the doctrinaires could not be satisfied unless the policy were dressed up in 'social' phraseology and a scapegoat were found for failures. The first was provided by a theoretical division of the peasantry into three classes, the second by the alleged wickedness of the *kulak*. The Bolshevik leaders maintained that the obstacle to the organisation of supplies was the hostility of the *kulaks* to socialism, and that this could be overcome by organising the class war in the villages. The tactic at first recommended by the Bolshevik leaders was to make an alliance with the poor peasant (*bednyak*), to ensure benevolent neutrality from the middle peasant (*serednyak*), and to isolate and defeat the *kulak*. During the civil war official emphasis varied between support of the special interests of the poor peasants and efforts to win the friendship of the middle peasants: the first predominated in 1918, the second in 1919 and 1920. In the last part of the civil war the official view was that there must be a 'firm alliance' between the urban proletariat and poor peasants on the one hand, and the *serednyak* on the other.[1]

In practice these doctrines seldom corresponded to realities. There is little evidence that there was ever much class antagonism

[1] See the resolution issued by the party at its 8th Congress in March 1919, published in *VKP (b) v Rezolyutsiah*, Moscow, 1936, pp. 315–17.

within the peasantry. The changes in the peasants' attitude to the Bolsheviks, sometimes friendly, sometimes hostile, but usually reserved and suspicious, cannot be explained by the greater or lesser influence of the *kulak* or the *serednyak*. The fact that the *kombedy* were at times useful to the authorities does not prove that the 'poor peasant masses' supported 'their' government and 'their' party against the village exploiters and the rural bourgeoisie, 'their' class enemy: it proves only that in conditions approaching famine a man with an empty belly will denounce his neighbour if he believes that the neighbour has a hoard and knows that if a hoard is discovered he will get a share of it. Nor did the detachments of hungry workers trouble to distinguish between the three categories of peasants differentiated by the party doctrinaires: they seized what they could find, where they found it. Circumstances stressed rather the common interests of all peasants against the town than the common interests of poor peasants with workers against rich peasants. The food shortage that menaced the towns was caused not by the wickedness of 'speculating' *kulaks* but by the shortage of crops, and this was due in part to military operations and in part to the absence, already noted, of any economic incentive to the peasants either to produce more or to market more of what they produced. Equally, the violence and injustice committed by Bolshevik officials against peasants were caused not by wickedness, which could have been remedied, but by desperate need, which could not.

During the civil war the enthusiasm of the peasants for the Bolsheviks in the territories ruled from Moscow certainly diminished. Even so, patriotism and fear of a return of the landlords in the wake of White armies kept a large part of them loyal, and the *Cheka* was able to deal with the others. In the territories which changed hands—the Ukraine, the south-east and the Urals—the peasants' attitude also changed. After experience of Bolshevik requisitions the Kuban Cossacks were glad to welcome the Whites in 1918, but the policy of the Whites gradually lost them their support. The Bolsheviks antagonised the peasants of the Ukraine in early 1919, but they were more prudent when they returned in the autumn, and the peasants had meanwhile suffered from the heavy hand of Denikin. Taking the whole period of the civil war, one may risk the generalisation that though the Bolsheviks did much to incur the peasants' hatred, both by avoidable mistakes and by unavoidable points of policy, yet at the decisive moments in the struggle they were less hated by the peasants than were the

Whites. The Bolshevik victory in November 1917 owed little to peasant support, but the Bolshevik victory in the civil war was to a large extent due to this relative preference by the peasants.

Much the same can be said of the attitude to the Bolsheviks of the non-Russian nationalities. The practical application of the doctrine of 'self-determination up to the right of secession', accepted by Lenin before 1914 and reaffirmed during 1917,[1] was not easy. Was this right to be recognised to political groups which were not socialist or proletarian, and were even fighting their own proletariat, or should the proletarian groups among the non-Russian nationalities be supported by the Red Army against their rivals, even if they only represented small minorities within their nations? This question never received a clear theoretical answer. In practice, whenever they had the opportunity, the Bolsheviks gave military support to like-minded parties among the nationalities. Their aim was to establish a Marxist—or, as it now came to be called, a Communist[2]— regime among all the former nationalities of the Russian Empire, and to spread the communist revolution into Europe. In practice, the success or failure of the Bolsheviks was decided not by revolutionary theory but by blood and iron. Those nationalities of old Russia which were favourably placed by geography, established independent states, and their governments were not communist. This was the case with Poland, Finland and the Baltic states, while the Transcaucasian republics of Georgia, Azerbaidjan and Armenia were able to survive for more than two years. Those whose geographical situation was unfavourable were subject to Bolshevik rule. This was the case with the Ukraine, White Russia, the Tatars of Volga and Ural, and the peoples of Central Asia. The Bolshevik victory over the nationalist movements of these nations was won by force.

Yet even here consent played some part. The masses, and even to some extent the nationalist leaders, of the non-Russian nations feared and disliked the Bolsheviks less than they feared and disliked the Whites. Kolchak and Denikin were implacably devoted to the idea of 'one indivisible Russia'. They would make no concessions to the national movements on territory under their control. Kolchak suppressed the Tatar nationalists, Denikin the Ukrainians and the north Caucasian peoples. Even the demands for autonomy

[1] See the party resolution of April 1917, published in Lenin, *Sochinenia*, 4th edition, Vol. XXIV, pp. 269–70.
[2] The party was renamed 'Russian Communist Party (Bolshevik)' at the 7th Congress in March 1918. After the formal institution of the Soviet Union in 1923, it became the 'All-Union Communist Party (Bolshevik)'.

of the Kuban Cossacks, perhaps the most loyal of all the supporters of the Whites, were rejected by Denikin, and their leaders imprisoned or even killed.[1] In contrast to this blank hostility was the propaganda of the Bolsheviks, which promised self-determination to nationalities as such. The belief that Bolshevism would not mean subjection to Russia, that there would be Ukrainian Bolshevik, Tatar Bolshevik or Caucasian Bolshevik regimes, caused thousands of members of these nations to support, or at least not to oppose, the Red Army.

The third group of causes of Bolshevik victory concern the divisions in the enemy ranks. The mentalities earlier symbolised by Kerenski and Kornilov survived throughout the civil war. The hatred of the White leaders for democratic parties and ideas could not be overcome even by the blandishments of the Allied military and political missions attached to them. The doctrinaire distrust of the democrats for the generals was increasingly justified by the repressive action of the generals against them. The White officers did not hesitate to arrest, maltreat or kill democrats. The struggle was between three groups, not two. Unfortunately the most numerous group, the democrats, possessed neither the military cadres and international backing of the Whites, nor the resources and ruthlessness of the Reds. Their numbers availed them nothing. They were forced to choose between two evils. The struggle which had at first placed the Bolsheviks alone against the rest of Russia, became what the Bolsheviks had hoped for, a struggle between Left and Right, with the leadership of the Left passing inevitably to the Bolsheviks. In a sense the victory was the victory not of the Bolsheviks alone, but of the whole Russian Left, of all Russians who felt themselves loyal to 'the Revolution'. But the fruits of victory were enjoyed exclusively by the Bolsheviks.

The fourth group of causes of Bolshevik victory concern the international situation at the time of the Revolution and civil war. War-weariness, we have seen, had favoured the Bolsheviks in 1917. The same factor proved dangerous to them in 1918, when the pitiful morale of the army, which Lenin and his party had done so much to make pitiful, forced them to accept a disastrous peace. Lenin's utopian belief in the German proletarian revolution very nearly cost him all that his genius had won. But he was saved, as we have seen, by Foch. In 1919, the Western Allies were far from united

---

[1] On the orders of General Vrangel, troops surrounded the building in which the meeting of the Kuban *Rada* (provincial assembly) was being held on 7th November 1919, dissolved the Assembly, imposed a ready-made 'constitution', and court-martialled and hanged one of the members named Kalabuhov.

on the Russian problem. The picture painted for thirty years by communist propaganda, and accepted to-day by millions who are not communists, of an invasion of revolutionary Russia by the massed armies of the united capitalist imperialist Powers is quite false. The French government was extremely hostile to the Bolsheviks, but its brief attempt at military intervention in the Black Sea was less than half-hearted, while its material help to the White armies was not large. The Italian government was also hostile, but did even less. The British and American governments were never eager to fight the Bolsheviks or even to support their enemies. In the first months of 1919, when swift and massive help to the Whites might perhaps have won the war, Lloyd George and Wilson were both keen to reach agreement with Lenin. In the summer of 1919 Allied policy hardened and became more united. Kolchak was recognised as 'supreme Ruler' of Russia in June. But help did not greatly increase thereafter.

In the Far East the American government was mainly worried by Japanese ambitions, and American policy saved Lenin from the loss of the Maritime Province in which the Japanese were entrenched. The French and British quickly lost interest in the White armies as these lost their battles. This was partly due to support for the Bolsheviks from the French and British labour movements. More important however was the nature of the French and British parliamentary systems. After the war was over elections had to be won. The French and British voters wanted their relatives back home from the army. No politician who tried to keep the armies mobilised could have hoped to win the election. Agreement between government and opposition to keep demobilisation out of electoral politics would have been possible only if all parties had agreed that supreme national interest required the overthrow of Bolshevism in Russia. But no such agreement existed. The French and British publics and politicians regarded Russia as a remote land. They did not believe that what happened in Russia could really matter to them. The parliamentary systems of the West, which Lenin so fiercely despised, saved him from destruction. Not the German proletariat, which did not lift a finger against Ludendorff until his armies were cracking, but the French and British soldier who defeated the Germans, and the French and British voter who prevented the armies of France and Britain from being used to smash Bolshevism, were the saviours of Lenin, from whom they earned not gratitude but savage contempt.

Allied intervention was insufficient to threaten the Bolsheviks, but Allied military supplies were sufficient to prolong the civil war. Thereby the Allies increased the sufferings of the Russian people. They also forced the Bolsheviks to devote all their energies to the struggle within Russia and so prevented a surge of revolutionary communism through Central Europe. The Communist International, desired by Lenin since 1914, had been founded in March 1919, but it had been unable to influence events. By the time that the Bolsheviks had won the civil war, the revolutionary tide had turned in Germany, and the state machines and economies of Poland, the Danubian and Balkan countries had attained comparative stability. To events in these countries, and to the communist movement in Europe, we must now turn.

CHAPTER THREE

The Comintern

INTERNATIONAL SOCIALISM AND THE WAR

WHEN the outbreak of the First World War revealed the ineffectiveness of the Second International, European socialists did not abandon the hope of common action to stop the fighting. But the socialist ranks were split into several groups.

The most obvious division was between those socialists who supported their respective countries' war efforts and those who opposed them. The first group, who were denounced by Lenin with the phrase 'social patriots', derived most of their following from the old right and centre of their parties, but also included men hitherto considered as members of the left—such staunch Marxists as the Frenchman Guesde and the Russian Plehanov. Moreover those who opposed their countries' war efforts included not only the former left wing but also several prominent leaders of the right, such as the German Bernstein and the British Ramsay MacDonald. These men wished simply to end the slaughter and return to the pre-war peaceful struggle for social reforms.

The second division was within the ranks of the opponents of the war effort, between pacifists and revolutionaries. The revolutionaries, though opposed to their countries' war efforts and opposed to war on principle, did not, like the pacifists, simply wish a restoration of peace as the result of a compromise between the Powers. This, they argued, would only strengthen the imperialist ruling classes in their resistance to the proletariat. They believed that the war should be used for the forcible overthrow of the bourgeoisie. The most extreme exponent of this view was Lenin, whose slogan was 'Turn the imperialistic war into an international civil war'. Lenin also insisted that, as the Second International had been proved useless, a completely new International should be set up. It should admit only real revolutionaries, and should have a rigid centralised discipline.

In the socialist parties of the belligerent countries of 1914 the 'social patriots' formed an overwhelming majority, the pacifists of left and right a considerable minority, and the revolutionaries a tiny fraction. In May 1915 Italy entered the war. The Italian government could not claim, like the belligerent governments of 1914, that it had been forced to take up arms by threat of aggression or obligations of honour: its action was determined by cold calculation of state interest. For this reason socialist opposition to the war was stronger in Italy than in the belligerent countries. The Italian Socialist Party as a whole, including its most moderate and conservative elements, opposed the war effort.

In September 1915 the Italian and Swiss socialists together arranged an international socialist conference at Zimmerwald in Switzerland. It issued a manifesto calling for action by the proletariat to stop the war. It rejected Lenin's programme of international civil war and a new International. In the spring of 1916 a further conference was held at Kienthal in Switzerland. Here Lenin somewhat moderated his demands. Though still in a minority, he gained some further support.[1] The Kienthal Conference did not take a clear decision between the alternatives of resuscitating the Second International or creating a Third. The groups represented at Zimmerwald and Kienthal formed together only a small minority in the international socialist movement Their importance however increased, partly because the increasing hardships of war brought a more radical mood to the civil population of all belligerent countries and especially to the workers, and partly because the Russian Revolution seemed to show that governments could be overthrown by the action of the proletariat.

THE GERMAN REVOLUTION

Since its foundation, the Second International's strongest party had been the German Social Democratic Party. Most European socialists expected Germany to be the first country in which socialism would prevail. In particular the Russian Bolsheviks—none more than Lenin himself—put their faith in the German proletariat and the German revolution.

At the outbreak of war all Social Democrat members of the Reichstag voted for the war credits: the minority who opposed the

At Zimmerwald Lenin's minority declaration was supported by Zinoviev and Radek and by two Scandinavians and a Latvian. At Kienthal he was supported, on the immediate tactical issue of the attitude to a proposed convocation of the International Socialist Bureau, by the German Spartakist delegates, but they were not prepared to go so far as he in denouncing the 'opportunists' (that is, the non-revolutionary left wing of the socialist movement). There is a clear summary of the two conferences in B. Lazitch, *Lénine et la troisiéme Internationale*, Paris, 1950.

war effort obeyed party discipline. In December 1915 this unani-
mity ended when twenty members voted against the credits.
During 1916 the gap between majority and minority widened, and
in April 1917 the minority constituted itself the Independent Social
Democratic Party (U.S.P.D.). Among its leaders were both the
theorist of the left, Kautsky, and the theorist of the right, Bernstein. It was pacifist and radical, but not revolutionary. To the left
of the U.S.P.D. were three small revolutionary groups.

Of these the *Spartakus* League was the best known because of
the personality of its leaders, Karl Liebknecht and Roza Luxemburg. Liebknecht had won great popularity when on 1st May 1916,
though a soldier in uniform, he had led a street demonstration
against the war, and had been sentenced by court martial to five
years of forced labour. Roza Luxemburg, who had begun her
career in the Polish labour movement,[1] had agitated against the
war since August 1914, and had been in prison since February
1915. In prison she wrote, under the pseudonym Junius, a pamphlet, *The Crisis of Social-Democracy.* This not only passionately
denounced war and those who supported or condoned it: it also
argued that the war had been caused equally by the imperialists
of all the great belligerent countries and that the class struggle,
far from having been suspended, was being carried on by the
capitalists against the workers, the war itself being a form of
class exploitation. From the end of 1915 the followers of Luxemburg published a series of illegal pamphlets entitled *Spartakus*
Letters. Whereas the U.S.P.D. leaders confined themselves to
protests against the war, the Spartakists, who were nominally
members of U.S.P.D., called for revolutionary action. Their propaganda, secretly distributed, had some influence on German working-class opinion, but they were not an organised group capable of
action.

More important as a potential striking force were the 'Revolutionary Shop Stewards' of Berlin, led by Richard Müller. This
group organised strikes in June 1916 and April 1917. Its most
impressive achievement was to stage a general strike in Berlin in
January 1918. The strike's aims were definitely political, namely
to prevent the German government from imposing crushing terms
on revolutionary Russia. It followed similar strikes in Budapest
and Vienna, and was followed by strikes in other parts of Germany.
Though successfully suppressed by the authorities, it was none the
less a landmark in German labour history. During the second half

[1] See above, p. 19.

of 1918 the Shop Stewards seriously considered plans for revolutionary action, inspired by the Russian example. Like the Spartakists, they were members of the U.S.P.D., but in fact stood far to their left.

The third group, much less important, was in Bremen. It was led by Paul Fröhlich and by a Polish disciple of Lenin named Karl Radek. It is of interest because it was the only German group that fully agreed with Lenin: Fröhlich had supported Lenin on all issues at the Kienthal Conference.

The German revolution began with a naval mutiny in Kiel on 30th October 1918.[1] The sailors found support from the working class of the northern ports. Meanwhile the Chancellor, Prince Max of Baden, was seeking means of coming to terms with the Allies, and especially with President Wilson. Rightly convinced that the removal of the Hohenzollern dynasty was a necessary step to this end, he persuaded William II to abdicate on 9th November. In Berlin the Shop Stewards' group set up Workers' Councils. Workers' Councils also appeared in other cities, and Soldiers' Councils were formed in army units in the rear of the front. For a short time it looked as if there would soon be a Soviet Germany.

The appearance was misleading. The German revolution was the result of military defeat, not of revolutionary propaganda. The leaflets and money distributed by Yoffe and the Soviet diplomatic mission, in which after Brest-Litovsk Lenin had placed such high hopes, had very little effect.[2] The German revolution had some resemblance with the March revolution in Russia. The Emperor was discredited with the majority of the German people as well as with Germany's enemies, and he had to go. New men had to take over. Non-socialist democrats and socialists would be the rival claimants. In Germany, a country far more industrialised and with a far larger and more disciplined working class than Russia, the socialists' chances might be considered extremely good. But if this difference between Germany and Russia might be expected to favour an extreme development in Germany, there were other factors which operated the other way. These factors explain why the 'German February' of November 1918 was not followed by a 'German October'.

---

[1] Already in the summer of 1917 there had been a naval mutiny. It was however in no way inspired by the politicians of the extreme left.

[2] Yoffe was Soviet Ambassador in Berlin after Brest-Litovsk. Knowing that he was giving financial help to German revolutionaries, the German police fabricated a compromising incident with some subversive leaflets, subsequently expelling him and his mission.

In the first place the relations between state and society in Germany were quite different from those in Russia. The German state was not simply imposed from above on the people: it was linked at all levels with German society. It was thus far less vulnerable than the Russian state. Military defeat did not bring collapse of the state. The Emperor abdicated, but the bureaucracy still functioned. The morale of the army at the front was high, and even in units in the rear, which soon became affected by revolutionary slogans, discipline was broken only for a brief period and in certain places. The Soldiers' Councils were not revolutionary bodies. The General Staff asked for their co-operation in carrying out the retreat of the German army from the Western Front and its demobilisation, and on the whole the co-operation was given. By mid-December the demobilisation was almost complete, and it had taken place with very little disorder. Central, regional and local government worked fairly smoothly under the new chiefs. In short, the German state machine had been shaken but not shattered, and its powers of recovery soon proved stronger than its enemies' powers of destruction.

Secondly, there was in Germany no team of ruthless and efficient professional revolutionaries, ready to take over the new machinery of Workers' and Soldiers' Councils, and turn them into an instrument for their own dictatorship. In November 1918 the Spartakist leaders, adopting the same doctrine as Lenin, hailed the Councils as a form of government superior to the parliamentary. But Roza Luxemburg and Liebknecht did not wish to seize power until it was clear that the majority of the working class supported them. They were for the dictatorship of the proletariat, but this must be a real dictatorship of the workers, not a dictatorship by a clique speaking in their name. The first government of the German Republic was a Council of People's Mandatories (*Volksbeauftragte*), of six persons, three Majority Social Democrats (S.P.D.) and three U.S.P.D. It was set up by the Berlin Workers' Councils on 10th November. For the next month it was not clear whether Germany was to be ruled by Councils or by a parliamentary system. The decision was taken by a Congress of Workers' Councils, of delegates elected from all over Germany, which met in Berlin on 16th December. At the Congress the S.P.D. had nearly three-quarters of the delegates, and among the remaining quarter, who mostly supported the U.S.P.D., extreme left influence was negligible. The S.P.D. leaders' proposal that elections be held to a National Assembly, that is, that Germany have a parliamentary and not a soviet form of government, was carried by a large majority. The councils thus voted themselves out of existence.

The importance of this decision was largely symbolic. The German Revolution did not fail because the soviet form was not adopted, any more than the Bolshevik Revolution succeeded because the soviet form was adopted. Soviets never possessed the magic significance which Communists have ascribed to them ever since 1917. Both in Germany in November 1918 and in Russia in March 1917 the moderate socialists controlled the councils, but whereas in Russia the soviets passed under Bolshevik control later, in Germany the moderates kept control of the councils until they dissolved themselves. The main reason for the difference is that external events did not make the German masses more revolutionary, as they had made the Russian masses: and one reason for this is that whereas the period of uncertainty lasted eight months in Russia it only lasted one month in Germany. A further reason for the difference, which has received much more emphasis in the literature of the subject than has the first reason, but is in reality less important, is the absence in Germany of any revolutionary leadership comparable to that of Lenin. During the month between the beginning of the Revolution and the opening of the Congress, Liebknecht and Roza Luxemburg made no attempt to seize power. This has been held against them by communist writers. But the truth is, not only that they did not wish to seize power by force, but that the German workers did not wish to, and that if the attempt had been made it would have been defeated.

The third main difference between the Russian situation of 1917 and the German situation in 1918 lay in the international field. During the summer of 1917 Lenin had been able to exploit the people's longing for peace and the Provisional Government's inability to give it to them. And meanwhile the army on the front kept the foreign enemy back. But in Germany in 1918 the last Imperial Chancellor Max von Baden gave the people peace, the army was withdrawn from the front and demobilised, and Germany was at the mercy of her victors. It was inconceivable that the Allied governments would allow a Soviet Germany to be formed on the frontier of France. The factor of geographical remoteness, which operated in favour of Russia in 1919, did not operate in favour of Germany. Help from the East was unobtainable, for the Red Army was fully engaged in civil war. Communist writers have retrospectively reproached the German socialist leaders for refusing the alliance of revolutionary Russia against Entente imperialism, and so betraying the German workers. This is empty demagogy: in 1919 the alliance was not available.

The belief that a proletarian revolution was possible in the immediate future continued to exist. On 30th December 1918 the Spartakist League and the Bremen group of Fröhlich combined to form the Communist Party of Germany (K.P.D.). They were unable to persuade the Berlin Shop Stewards to join them. The Shop Stewards demanded for themselves half the seats in the political committee of the new party, and they insisted that the party should take part in the forthcoming election to the National Assembly. Luxemburg and Liebknecht were prepared to concede the second point. They were convinced that the conditions of Russia in the autumn of 1917 were not present in Germany, and that nothing could prevent the holding of the election. But the extreme wing of the Spartakists, carried away by enthusiasm for the Bolshevik Revolution—which they were far from understanding—outvoted Luxemburg and Liebknecht. Consequently the Shop Stewards, essentially a revolutionary group, remained within the U.S.P.D., essentially a non-revolutionary party, while the Luxemburg-Liebknecht group were tied to a more or less anarchist wing. This was an important contributory cause of the weakness of what revolutionary forces there were in Germany in these critical weeks.

Tragedy came in Berlin in January. An undisciplined force of revolutionary sailors, known as the People's Marine Division, which had come from Kiel to Berlin in November, revolted against the government at the end of December. It was repelled by regular troops under a regular general. In protest against this 'massacre of the sailors', the U.S.P.D. *Volksbeauftragten* resigned. Their places were filled by Majority Socialists, and the government became an all-S.P.D. ministry. The Chief of Police, a member of U.S.P.D., was then dismissed, but refused to give up his post. The refusal was approved by the leaders of U.S.P.D., Shop Stewards and K.P.D. These three groups did not in fact wish to make a serious attempt at a second revolution: such however was the mood of the anarchist fringe of the Spartakists.[1] Revolutionary crowds seized various public buildings in Berlin on 4th January 1919. For a week the members of the government were besieged in the centre of the city. The situation was saved with the help of the old army

---

[1] Luxemburg and Liebknecht were against any insurrectionary action, but felt themselves bound to join their comrades.

generals and of irregular forces known as Free Corps.[1] On the night of 10th–11th January troops entered Berlin and captured the buildings held by the insurgents. Luxemburg and Liebknecht refused to escape from Berlin: they insisted on sharing the fate of their comrades. Both were captured, and were murdered by Free Corps men. Their death was a deadly blow to the German left. Roza Luxemburg, one of the few who could challenge Lenin both in problems of Marxist theory and in international prestige, was an irreplaceable loss to the whole European socialist movement. The Berlin insurrection was a tragic blunder. It had no chance of success.

Here a further difference between Germany and the Russia of 1917 should be noted. The attitude of the Social Democrat leaders both to the generals and to the extreme left was quite different from the attitude of Kerenski. In 1917 Kerenski considered Lenin a fellow-revolutionary, a comrade even if misguided, but saw in Kornilov an enemy, the representative of all the forces of counter-revolution. He had been swift to break with Kornilov, slow to take action against Lenin. To Ebert, the leader of the German Social Democrats in 1919, Luxemburg and Liebknecht were pestilential disturbers of the public peace, who must be made harmless, while General Groener and the officers of the former Imperial army were the legal forces of order. Not only did Ebert differ from Kerenski, but Groener differed from Kornilov. To Kornilov, Kerenski embodied the revolutionary forces that were destroying Russia: to Groener, Ebert was a sound German patriot, with whom one might disagree on politics but who was entitled to one's help when threatened by subversive elements.

This difference between Germany and Russia is explained, not by the excessive cunning of Groener, or by Ebert's betrayal of the German proletariat, but by the differences between state and society in Germany and in Russia. In Russia the state machine, including the army hierarchy, was something apart from, hostile to and hated by, the people: in Germany the army was part of the nation, linked with each level of society. In December 1918 three-quarters of the German working class had voted for Ebert's policy. Ebert knew that the insurgents in Berlin were supported only by a small minority of the German working class, and by nobody outside the working class. Their adventure endangered the future of the democratic German republic that he hoped to build: it could not be

[1] The Free Corps were bands of volunteers commanded by regular officers, originally recruited for the defence of the eastern borderlands against Poles and Balts. They may be compared, in outlook and in behaviour, with the British 'Black and Tans' in Ireland.

tolerated. In order to suppress it, he had to have recourse to what was left of the army. It is true that the defeat of the Berlin insurrection restored the prestige of the officer class, that in the following years they gained great power, and that in the end their strength enabled Hitler to embark on his career of aggression. But a distinction must be drawn between the failure of all republican governments in Germany, from 1919 to 1933, to curb the influence of the military leaders, and the decision of Ebert and Noske in January 1919 to use the army and Free Corps. The decision of January 1919 was inevitable, and its consequences were not irreversible. In any case the responsibility for the situation in which it was taken lies with the anarchist elements of the K.P.D. who insisted on making the bid for power.

After the Berlin disaster, the best hopes of the German left were in Bavaria. Here for a time the peasants were in revolutionary mood, and supported the socialists. These were not, as in Berlin, quarrelling among themselves, but were united under the left leader Kurt Eisner, first Prime Minister of Bavaria after the overthrow of the monarchy. But on 21st February 1919 Eisner was assassinated, and his regime began to disintegrate. Inspired by the news that a communist regime had been installed in Hungary, and hoping for similar action in Austria, a group of extremists led by an anarchist named Landauer proclaimed a Soviet Republic of Bavaria on 7th April. The Landauer government collapsed after a week. In its place the communists, led in Bavaria by the Russian-born Eugen Levine, assumed power in hopeless circumstances. Regular troops, acting in the name of the legal Bavarian government of the official socialist Hoffmann, but in fact led by men resolved to stamp out socialist rule in Bavaria, took Munich on 1st–2nd May. Their victory was followed by a massacre.

THE HUNGARIAN REVOLUTION

The only European country where communists for a time seemed capable of holding power was Hungary. The social structure of Hungary, as we have seen, was in some respects similar to that of Russia. The pre-war political life of Hungary however differed from that of Russia by the absence of any effective revolutionary movement. For this there were three main reasons. The landowning class, whose power in the countryside had not, like that of the Russian landowning class in 1905, been shaken as a result of defeat in war, had been able to prevent any political activity among the peasants of the districts of pure Hungarian population.

Secondly, to a far greater extent than Russian, Hungarian political life was dominated by the conflict between nationalities rather than between social classes. The 'diversionary' effect of the Polish-Ukrainian, Russian-Jewish and Tatar-Armenian conflicts on Russian politics[1] was negligible in comparison with the effect on Hungarian politics of the national demands of Roumanians, Serbs, Croats and Slovaks. Thirdly, the politically conscious intelligentsia, from whose ranks revolutionary leadership was most likely in such a country to come, was largely Jewish, and as such both distrustful of and distrusted by the Hungarian masses.

During the war however the industrial workers of Budapest became a more united, powerful and politically conscious force. Trade union membership more than doubled. The Hungarian socialists became more and more opposed to the war. The news of the demands made by the Central Powers on Bolshevik Russia at the Brest-Litovsk negotiations caused great indignation, and was mainly responsible for an important outbreak of strikes in Budapest in January 1918. Though the strike collapsed, radical social feeling grew stronger. It was allied both to the liberal opposition of the middle class and to the strong anti-German Hungarian nationalism which, dormant in the decades before 1914, had been revived by the course of the war.

When Austria-Hungary surrendered to the Allies in October 1918, a Republic was proclaimed in Budapest. The first government was led by an aristocrat of left sympathies, Count Michael Károlyi. It was composed partly of radicals from the ruling class and bourgeoisie, partly of Social Democrats. A rival to these groups soon appeared in the Communist Party, which was founded at the end of November and was led by men who had been prisoners of war in Russia and had been indoctrinated by the Bolsheviks.

The situation in Hungary during the winter of 1918–19 in some ways closely resembled that of Russia between March and November 1917. There were the same doctrinaire arguments as to whether this should be a bourgeois or a proletarian revolution; the same unwillingness of the socialists to assume sole power; the same impossibility of ensuring working-class mass support to a non-socialist government. As in Russia in 1917, so in Hungary the revolutionary government was unable to secure a legal basis by holding a Constituent Assembly: the obstacle in Russia had been the continuance of the war, the obstacle in Hungary was that large areas which the government persisted in regarding as part of the Hungarian State were either annexed to the Succession States

[1] See above, pp. 10–11, 20.

or under Allied military occupation. Meanwhile the communists, led by Béla Kun, made violent demagogic attacks on the government, accusing the social democrats of betraying the workers, and, like Lenin in 1917, promising everything to the masses as soon as they should be in power.

The political course of events was also similar to that in Russia. A government reshuffle in December, following an armed demonstration engineered by the pro-communist government commissar attached to the Soldiers' Council, led to the resignation of two conservative ministers: the parallel was May 1917 in Petrograd. A month later, a further government reshuffle led to a strengthening of the social democrats in the government: the parallel was the increased representation of Kerenski and the moderate socialists in the summer of 1917. In February 1919 the communists attempted somewhat half-heartedly to seize power by force: the parallel was the 'July days' in Petrograd. This attempt was followed by the arrest of the communist leaders. Firm action against the communists was however prevented by two factors. One was the hostile attitude of the Allied representative, Lt.-Col. Vyx, whose threats and insults undermined the government's authority. The second factor was that a number of the leading social democrats—the intellectual rather than the trade union elements—sympathised with the communists, while others, like Kerenski and Tseretelli in 1917, were reluctant to consider them as enemies.[1]

The crisis came on 20th March, when Vyx presented further demands for cession of Hungarian territory. The non-socialists, who had hoped against hope for understanding on the part of the Western Powers, saw that their policy of friendship with the West had failed. The only hope appeared to be that Soviet Russia would help Hungary against the West. But the men who had Russia's confidence were the communists: they must be brought into the government. The socialists therefore sent a deputation to discuss with Béla Kun in prison. The resultant agreement represented a capitulation by the socialists to the demands of the communists. The Social Democrat and Communist parties fused in a single Hungarian Socialist Party, and Hungary was proclaimed a Republic of Workers', Peasants' and Soldiers' Councils. Several leading socialists resigned rather than accept these terms, and of those who accepted few were happy. But there seemed no alternative.

[1] Detailed accounts of these events are in W. Böhm, *Im Kreuzfeuer zweier Revolutionen*, Munich, 1924, and E. Garami, *Forrongó Magyarország*, Vienna, 1922.

The first month of the communist regime was disastrous. When discussions with an Allied mission headed by General Smuts had broken down, the Roumanian army marched into the Hungarian plain. The Hungarian army, badly reorganised after the demobilisation of November 1918, and subsequently demoralised by four months of political agitation, offered little resistance. The situation was saved at the beginning of May, when Budapest workers volunteered for service by the thousand, and officers of the old army, preferring even Bolsheviks to Roumanians, accepted the commands that were offered to them. The Roumanians were driven back across the Tisza, and in the north the Hungarian Red Army overran most of Slovàkia. Russian aid, which had been the main inducement for surrender to the communists, was not available. The Bolshevik forces in the south-west Ukraine, which Lenin had intended to send across Roumania to help Hungary, were disorganised by the mutiny of the Ukrainian Ataman Hrihoryev, and the advance of Kolchak from Siberia compelled the Bolshevik leaders to send their best troops eastward.

Hungarian successes were short-lived. The communists failed to win peasant support. In February the social democrats had prepared a law to divide the great estates among the peasants as their property. This was overruled by the communists, who preferred to form great co-operative units in place of the estates, and even made the former owners or their bailiffs government commissars in charge of them. The agricultural labourers did not become owners, but remained paid labourers, often working for the same bosses. The Revolution seemed to have done nothing for them. When the authorities were forced to requisition crops, and were unable to pay for them with adequate supplies of manufactures, peasant disappointment turned to active hostility. Industry also was in a bad condition. Between October 1918 and June 1919 output in the coal-mines fell by half: the same fall of productivity took place as in Russia under 'War Communism'. The workers were hungry and began to turn against the communists. In June there was a railway strike and a peasant rising in the western region. A Commission, modelled on the Russian *Cheka*, led by a certain Szamuély, tried to suppress opposition by reprisals, but only increased it. Kun decided to accept new peace terms offered by Clémenceau. Thereby he lost the support of the nationalist officers, who began to go over to the counter-revolutionary 'government' set up in Szeged under the protection of the Roumanian army. In July treachery in the Hungarian Command enabled the Roumanians to advance by surprise,

and the defence of the Hungarian Soviet Republic crumbled. Kun
fled on 1st August, and those social democrats who had refused
to co-operate with the communists in March now took power.
Their hope of preserving at least a democratic regime within a
small Hungary was disappointed within a few days. The Roumanian army was persuaded by Hungarian reactionaries to occupy
the capital, while a counter-revolutionary conspiracy overthrew
the social democratic government. This was followed by a White
Terror, which gave place to an orderly regime of extreme conservatism. The Revolution had ended in complete failure, and in
essentials the regime of 1914 was restored. The Communist Party
ceased to exist as a serious force until resuscitated by the invading
Russian army in 1944.

The main reason for the defeat of Hungarian communism was
the unfavourable geographic situation. The victorious Allies could
clearly not tolerate a militant communist regime in the very heart
of Europe. The Allies were moreover committed to support of the
Succession States—Roumania, Czechoslovakia and Yugoslavia—
which had territorial claims on Hungary. Defence of these claims,
rather than an ideological crusade, was the justification for the
Roumanian invasion, which had Allied diplomatic support and
would have had military support had that been necessary. The
Hungarian communists could not make the ideological issue clear
to world opinion by accepting the territorial claims, since this would
have lost them all support in Hungary. But there can be no doubt
that the resolute support given by the Allies to the Roumanians
was due less to their conviction that the territorial claims were
just than to their desire to be rid of a soviet regime in Central
Europe.

This unfavourable geographical and military situation would
have ensured the defeat of Soviet Hungary even if Béla Kun had
had ten times the genius of Lenin. Nevertheless Kun's faults did
contribute to the disaster. Much the most important of these was
the doctrinaire treatment of the peasant problem. The failure to
give the peasants the land was rightly criticised by the Russian
Bolshevik leaders both at the time and subsequently. Less convincing is the subsequent communist argument that disaster was
due to 'social democratic treason'. There is no serious evidence
that social democrats were disloyal: on the contrary some of the
republic's best leaders were socialists. Those socialists who had
from the beginning opposed the soviet regime, took power in
August only when the Red Army was demonstrably defeated, in

a last hope of saving democratic government and protecting the Hungarian workers from reprisals. The communists had done far more, both before and after March 1919, to demoralise the nation and the workers, and to undermine their powers of resistance, than did the social democrats. The legend of socialist treachery was invented by Lenin partly because he needed a scapegoat and partly because it suited his general tactics in 1920.[1]

The Hungarian communists had had hopes of help from Austria. The Austrian Social Democratic Party, like the German, had had a right and a left wing before 1914. During the war, however, no split took place. The arguments of the left wing, led by Friedrich Adler and Otto Bauer, persuaded the party's leaders, and in October 1918 the party was united and its official policy was that of its left wing. It was thus able to keep the support of the overwhelming majority of the Austrian working class. The Austrian Communist Party, founded in December 1918 by men returned from imprisonment in Russia, was no more than a tiny fraction. In contrast to Hungary, the Austrian socialist leaders were able to hold their own in the Workers' and Soldiers' Councils, to refute communist demagogy and outwit communist manœuvres. The first government of the Austrian Republic was a coalition between social democrats and Christian Socials. The latter were a Catholic party with democratic tendencies, representing part of the urban middle class and the bulk of the peasants. In 1919 the peasant element predominated, and the Christian Social Party was in radical mood, eager to co-operate with the social democrats. In fact the government was not so much a coalition of two parties as an alliance of workers and peasants, with the workers leading. The Austrian socialists were faced with the hostility of Czechoslovakia, with which they were disputing the German provinces of Bohemia, and with the uncertain attitude of the victorious Western Powers. If they were to retain freedom to organise the Austrian Republic as they wished, it was essential that they should not antagonise the Allies. For this reason they could not risk helping the Hungarian Revolution.[2] They refused any warlike supplies, and the value of peaceful trade was small. The only hope for Kun seemed to be forcible seizure of power in Vienna by Austrian communists. The attempt was made in mid-July 1919, under the supervision of an emissary of Kun named Bettelheim. It was a ridiculous failure, and

---

[1] See below, pp. 73–75. There is an interesting discussion of this question in an article by D. Cattell, *The Hungarian Revolution of 1919 and the Reorganisation of the Cominterm in 1920*, in the *Journal of Central European Affairs*, January-April 1951.

[2] See Otto Bauer, *Die österreichische Revolution*, Vienna, 1923, pp. 136–42.

it was duly disowned, with unconvincing indignation, by the international spokesmen of Communism after it had failed.[1] The Austrian socialists remained strong, but in 1920 the balance of political power turned somewhat against them. The coalition became one of parties rather than of classes, and the urban bourgeois element gained ground within the Christian Social Party. Austria remained for some time a stronghold of working-class democracy, but the prospect of proletarian dictatorship, whether under communist or left socialist leadership, remained remote.

COMMUNISM IN EASTERN EUROPE

In the countries bordering Russia on the west, and in the Balkan countries, the years 1918–19 brought short periods of revolutionary crisis, to which it is worth while to devote a little attention.

The most impressive movement was in Finland, and it had been crushed long before the European War was over. The social democrats were the strongest single party in Finland before 1917, and had a large following among peasants as well as workers. Finnish independence from Russia was proclaimed by the parliament in Helsinki on 6th December 1917. In the following weeks the left wing gained control of the Social Democratic Party, seized the city of Helsinki and proclaimed a Finnish Workers' Socialist Republic on 28th January 1918. For some months the socialists controlled the industrial south, while their opponents, commanded by General Mannerheim, organised an army in the north-west. In the civil war which followed, the main combatants were Finnish armies, the one based on the socialists' political army, the Red Guard, the other on the Civil Guard created from the middle class and peasants. Russian military units stationed in Finland, of Bolshevik sympathy, gave some support to the Reds. The Whites appealed for help to the Germans, who sent first a force of former Finnish deserters from the Russian army, who had been fighting in the German army, and then regular German units. The Reds were caught in a pincer movement by Mannerheim, who moved south to capture the industrial centre of Tampere, and the Germans, who landed on the south coast and entered Helsinki unopposed. By May the Whites were masters of Finland.

Civil war cost the Finns some 25,000 dead, many executed in cold blood. The only serious labour movement on Russia's borders had thus been crushed. The Red defeat was due partly to the success

[1] See the letter by Radek, quoted by Paul Levi, *Unser Weg wider den Putschismus*, Berlin, 1921.

of the Whites in exploiting nationalist sentiment: they were able to convince the Finnish peasants that the Reds were tools of Russian imperialism in Bolshevik form, and that only they stood for Finnish independence. It was also due to the unfortunate military situation. Ludendorff feared that the Allies would advance from Archangel through Finland towards Petrograd, with the aim of reconstituting the Russian front against Germany.[1] To prevent this it was necessary that Finland should be held by German forces or by Finns in whom the Germans could have confidence.

In the Baltic provinces Bolshevik regimes had been proclaimed after the November Revolution, but had been swept away by the advancing German armies early in 1918. On the surrender of Germany, civil war broke out. Non-socialist democratic governments of the Baltic nations were faced with Soviet Russian invasion supported by a section of their own peoples. The democratic nationalists prevailed fairly soon in Esthonia and Lithuania, but in Latvia a three-cornered struggle developed between Latvian nationalists, Latvian communists and German troops. The communists had genuine popular support, as they could appeal to a long socialist tradition based not only on the working class of Riga but also on the revolutionary feeling of the Latvian peasants, which already in 1905 had expressed itself in agrarian risings directed at the local landowners, who were mostly Germans. Many Latvian workers and peasants thus saw in the Soviet Russian forces deliverers from the hated German landowning class, which was still supported by troops of the German army which remained in control long after Germany had signed the armistice in the West. The communists held Riga until May 1919, when the Germans captured it and carried out brutal reprisals. Only when the Western Powers had forced the Germans to evacuate did the democratic Latvian government exercise authority over the whole country. In the new state the socialists were an important party, but the communists never recovered much influence until the invading Red Army placed them in power in 1940.

In Poland there was, as we have seen, a strong socialist movement before 1914, but it was predominantly nationalist and anti-Russian. When the Germans surrendered, the first Polish government formed on Polish territory was headed by the veteran socialist leader Daszyński. This 'People's Government' of Lublin lasted however only a few days. It had to reckon with the hostility not only of the extreme left, the S.D.K.P.L. founded originally by

[1] Ludendorff, *The General Staff and its Problems*, 1920, Vol. II, pp. 548–50.

Roza Luxemburg, but also of the more numerous and formidable National Democrats. This party dominated western (ex-German) Poland, union with which was the wish of every Pole, and its leaders, in exile in Paris, had the support of the Allied governments. A socialist revolution against the National Democrats, against the Polish peasants and against the Western Allies, with only the doubtful possibility of help from the Russian Red Army and from revolutionised units of the German army—from forces of the two countries that were Poland's traditional enemies—was a prospect that could commend itself only to visionary fanatics. The alternative was a compromise with the National Democrats, which would save Poland's independence and restore territorial unity at the cost of postponing the achievement of socialism. In November 1918 Jozef Piłsudski, former socialist and wartime leader of the Polish Legions, was released from imprisonment in Germany and became the first Chief of State of independent Poland. He met the Lublin leaders, and persuaded them that there must be a compromise with the Right. Daszyński was succeeded by a much less eminent socialist, Moraczewski, and in January 1919 Pilsudski was able, after hard bargaining, to effect an agreement between this government and the National Democrats. Piłsudski's action was a historic turning-point, for it removed any threat of revolutionary chaos, to be exploited by communists, on a vital piece of territory lying between Bolshevik Russia and revolutionary Germany. Meanwhile in December 1918 a Polish Communist Party had been founded by the fusion of S.D.K.P.L. with the left wing of P.P.S. During the winter of 1918–19 the communists had a majority in the Workers' Councils of the Dombrowa coal-mining area and were also strong in Warsaw. But the majority of the working class of the country followed the main body of P.P.S., which was strongly anti-communist, and in the countryside the communists made hardly any impression. During 1919, while the Bolsheviks were engaged in civil war, a democratic but non-socialist regime was consolidated, and Piłsudski created a Polish national army.

Russia's remaining western neighbour, Roumania, had a social and political system even more similar to that of the old Russia than was Hungary's. But a combination of statesmanship and good fortune saved Roumania from the fate that overtook Hungary. In 1918 the dominant Liberal Party introduced universal suffrage and decreed a far-reaching land reform. Knowing that the nobles' estates would be distributed among them, and that they would for the first time have a vote, the Roumanian peasants remained loyal to the regime. Even direct contact with the revolutionised Russian armies at the end of 1917 had little effect on their morale. Russia's capitulation at Brest-Litovsk forced Roumania to conclude a separate peace. Though this included oppressive economic conditions, it ex- tended Roumanian territory in the east by allowing the annexation of Bessarabia, formerly a Russian province. During 1918 Roumania was cut off from Bolshevik territory by the German armies of occu- pation in the Ukraine, and after Germany's surrender by the Ukrain- ian nationalist forces of Petlyura. When in the spring of 1919 the Bolsheviks were planning to invade Roumania, Hrihoryev's mutiny once more saved the situation. Meanwhile the government's author- ity had been reasserted over the whole country, and national enthus- iasm had been aroused by the union with Roumania of the formerly Hungarian and Austrian territories of Transylvania and Bukovina. In the belief that they were defending these newly-won provinces from Hungarian counter-attack, Roumanian soldiers marched with- out hesitation against the Hungarian Red Army. Within Roumania the socialist movement was too weak to interfere in any way with government action: a socialist bid for power by force was absolutely inconceivable.

In the Balkans the most promising field for revolution was in Bulgaria. Already in 1903, the year of the Bolshevik-Menshevik split in Russia, the Bulgarian socialists had split into two factions, the left or 'Narrow' and the right or 'Broad'. During the war the Narrow gained ground. In September 1918 the Bulgarian front broke, and the peasant soldiers began to drift home. At this moment the extremely radical Agrarian Union, led by Stamboliiski, tried to make a revolution against the dynasty: a republic was pro- claimed in the south-western town of Radomir. Stamboliiski asked the Narrow socialists to join him, but they refused. The peasant movement, they argued, was essentially reactionary: its policy was 'no struggle of the proletariat against the bourgeoisie, but a struggle within the bourgeoisie'.[1] The peasant movement was the rural branch of the bourgeoisie, King Ferdinand's clique the urban branch. The opportunity was quickly lost, and the republic quickly suppressed. Ferdinand however was forced to abdicate soon after- wards, and Bulgarian public opinion remained in radical mood. In the summer of 1919 the Agrarian Union was by far the strongest force in the country, but the Narrow socialists, who took the name Communist Party early in the year, were the second. Though one

[1] *Kommunismus*, Vienna, of 31st May 1920.

chance had been lost, the situation still offered opportunities for a revolutionary leadership, had such existed.

Of the East European states which had come out of the war victorious and gained territory, Yugoslavia was the only one in which the revolutionary movement was strong. This may be explained in part by the terrible sufferings of Serbia during three years of enemy occupation; partly by the traditional Serbian sympathy for Russia, which now to some extent operated in favour of Communism; but chiefly by the effect of the national factor, which was not the same as in the other countries. Poles, Roumanians and Czechs were delighted to have obtained independence or unity with their brethren formerly subject to other Powers: the Slovaks were on the whole glad to be united with the Czechs. The nations included in the new Yugoslav state were far less enthusiastic. Among Croats and Macedonians only a minority positively desired the new state, and there was considerable though less widespread opposition to it in Bosnia and Montenegro. It was from these discontented nationalists as well as from the small working class of Serbia and Croatia that the Communist Party, founded in April 1919 at a Congress of the pre-1918 socialist parties and groups of the various Yugoslav territories, drew its support. During the first half of 1919 public order was extremely insecure throughout the new state, and revolution did not seem improbable.

THE FOUNDATION OF THE COMINTERN

In all these events the Russian Bolsheviks had been unable to play a part. Civil war had engaged their forces at home, while the triumph of nationalism in the western borderlands had encircled and destroyed the Hungarian Revolution, and in Germany and Austria the workers themselves had freely shown their preference for Social Democracy rather than Bolshevism.

All that the Bolsheviks had achieved was a gesture. In March 1919 there met in Moscow the founding Congress of the Third International, which ever since 1914 Lenin had been determined to create in place of the ineffective Second. When the Congress met, Bolshevik territory was cut off by fighting armies from the industrial countries of Europe, Kolchak's offensive was approaching the Volga, Luxemburg and Liebknecht had been murdered, revolution had been suppressed in Finland and was collapsing in Latvia, and the Hungarian Soviet Republic had not yet been proclaimed. The 'delegates', with two exceptions, were either subjects of

Soviet Russia or European communists who happened to be in Moscow, but had not been sent there by any party or group. The two exceptions were the German Eberlein and the Austrian Steinhardt, both of whom had made their way through the lines of the civil war. Eberlein had instructions from Roza Luxemburg to state that in the K.P.D.'s view the creation of a new International was premature. Luxemburg distrusted Lenin's whole conception of a vanguard of the proletariat and an organisation of professional revolutionaries.[1] She was not convinced that every opportunity had been exhausted of reconstituting the Second International in a better form. But when the Congress opened, Luxemburg was dead, and Eberlein, carried away by the eloquence of Steinhardt, who, supported by Hungarian and Balkan speakers, argued that the foundation of a new International would directly and immediately assist the cause of revolution in Central Europe, withdrew his opposition.

The new organisation, known as the Communist International, or Comintern, issued a manifesto to the 'Proletarians of the whole world', which extolled the soviet form of government and the dictatorship of the proletariat, emphasised the need to support colonial peoples in their struggle against imperialist Powers, and urged a fierce struggle against the non-communist labour movement. Enemies in the labour movement included not only 'social patriots' but also the 'vague unstable tendency of the centre'. As examples of this tendency were specially mentioned the German U.S.P.D., the French Socialist Party, the Russian left Mensheviks and the British I.L.P.

The new International was soon joined by the communist parties of Central and Eastern Europe and by three western parties. These were the Swedish left socialists, the Norwegian Labour Party and the Italian Socialist Party. The tasks before the new International were not yet clearly defined, nor had the principles of its organisation been firmly established. For the time being its main effect was to create a soviet myth. Sections of the European socialist left became convinced that there was some magic quality in the institution of the soviets, which would make the revolutionary movement irresistible. They need only chant the magic incantation 'All power to the soviets', and the walls of the capitalist Jericho would fall down. The best example of this mentality, and of its disastrous effects, is the record of the Italian Socialist Party from 1919 to 1921.

[1] Her views were expressed in trenchant language in her *Die russische Revolution*, published posthumously by Paul Levi in 1921.

During 1919 in Italy there was a general belief that revolution was impending. The machinery of government was tottering, the industrialists were frightened of the workers, and the workers were enamoured of their vision of the soviet paradise. The ruling class had little control over events, but the forces of revolution had no leadership. During the year there were strikes, demonstrations, disorders and little local revolts. In October the Socialist Party held its Congress in Bologna and solemnly declared its faith in soviet government and its adherence to the Comintern. On 16th November a parliamentary election was held, and the Socialists won two-fifths of the poll, thereby becoming the largest single party in Italy. But, having rejected parliamentary government, the socialists could not make use of their parliamentary position: on the other hand none of their leaders was capable of planning a revolution. In April 1920 a meeting in Milan of the National Council of the party, held while a big metal strike was in progress in Turin, produced a further flood of incendiary slogans, but the only practical action the Council found possible to recommend to the party was to make every effort to win the forthcoming municipal and county elections.

The climax came in August. A wages disagreement between the metallurgical trade unions and the employers led to a lock-out in Milan. The union then instructed the workers to take over their factories and operate them themselves. The movement spread through most of the heavy industry of northern Italy. This was the opportunity for revolutionary leaders, had such existed. This was the chance for the Socialist Party to put itself at the head of a revolutionary movement to seize power. But the chance was not taken. On 10th–11th September 1920 the Council of the nation-wide trade union movement, the General Confederation of Labour (C.G.L.), held a conference with representatives of the party leadership. The meeting decided not to make a bid for political power, but to confine the struggle to a demand for a measure of workers' control over the factories. This gave the Premier, the wily Liberal elder statesman Giolitti, the chance to manœuvre and temporise. He did not try to repress the strikes, but set up a mixed Commission of workers and employers to discuss the workers' demands. Meanwhile the occupied factories were running out of raw material, and the workers were becoming bored. The movement fizzled out, an unimportant compromise was made by the Commission, and it was now clear to all that there was no serious danger of a proletarian revolution in Italy. From this time industrialists and landlords, conservatives and counter-revolutionaries recovered self-confidence. The fascist bands of toughs, owing allegiance to Benito Mussolini, began their acts of violence against the Socialist Party, the trade unions and the co-operatives.

One may doubt in retrospect whether a revolution could have been successful at this time in Italy. If revolutionaries had seized the industrial north, they would have had to fight a civil war against the agricultural and conservative south, and they would have had to reckon with the hostility of Catholicism both within Italy and abroad. The victorious Western Powers would also hardly have allowed a Soviet Italy to be created. But certainly big initial successes were within the socialists' reach: their opponents lacked not only material means of defence but the will to resist. That nothing happened was due almost exclusively to the weakness of the socialist leaders, to their pathetic combination of big words and small deeds.

In Germany 1919 and 1920 were bad years. The sporadic fighting between the Free Corps and various groups of armed workers, which took place in many parts of Germany during 1919, amounted to little less than a civil war. The workers had the heavier casualties. The Constitution passed by the Weimar Assembly in July 1919 was democratic but not socialist. This reflected the composition of the Assembly, in which the socialist parties together had less than half the seats. In the month when the official social democrats had held power, they had done none of the things necessary even for preparing the ground for socialism. They had not distributed among the agricultural labourers the landed estates of Eastern Germany; they had not nationalised heavy industry; they had left the personnel of civil service and judiciary unchanged and had restored the authority of the regular army and police. In the summer of 1919 the anti-democratic forces were much stronger in fact than the extremely democratic Weimar Constitution made them seem. This was shown when on 13th March 1920 a Free Corps unit seized power in Berlin and proclaimed a new government under a bureaucrat named Kapp.

While the regular army hesitated between Kapp and the legal government, the trade unions, led by the moderate socialist Karl Legien, declared a general strike which brought the surrender of the rebels within a few days. Legien then proposed that the victory be consolidated by the formation of a workers' government, based on the socialist parties and on the socialist and Christian trade unions.

This was not a plan for revolution, but at least it was a plan to safe-guard working-class interests against further attack from the militarists. The plan was rejected by the U.S.P.D., and, after some hesitation, by the K.P.D.[1] The result was that the victory over Kapp did not improve the position of the German workers. The Free Corps remained a force, and repression of the workers by regular troops and police continued, especially in Westphalia. But though this setback was due to the intransigence of the left, it was the left—both U.S.P.D. and K.P.D.—which profited from the growing discontent of the workers during 1920. Both parties gained some support at the expense of the S.P.D., though the latter still outnumbered the two other parties together.

In Yugoslavia the communists did well at the election to the Constituent Assembly in 1920.[2] But police repression weakened the party, and in the following year the assassination of the Minister of Interior by a communist provided an excuse to dissolve the party. Thereafter the Yugoslav communists quickly lost ground. Those who had supported the communists from national discontent now preferred one of the various nationalist and separatist groups. The working class of Yugoslavia was not numerous, and it was by no means unanimous in support of the communists. In Bulgaria the communists remained a strong party, and enjoyed democratic liberties, but were ineffective. A railway general strike in the autumn of 1919 won material concessions from the government but did not bring revolution nearer. In Roumania the communists had a majority in the labour movement, but this was so small as to be politically insignificant. The Greek Communist Party was also very small and weak.

The last moment when hopes of revolution soared high was in August 1920. In April Piłsudski had made an agreement with the Ukrainian nationalist Petlyura, by which in return for Ukrainian renunciation of Eastern Galicia the Poles undertook to assist Petlyura in the reconquest of the Ukraine from the Bolsheviks. The Polish army advanced in May, but by the end of June it was once more in retreat. The Russian Red Army entered Poland, and set up in Bialystok a committee of Polish communists, led by Dzierzhinski, the founder of the Russian *Cheka* but by birth a Pole, and Feliks Kon, the former leader of the P.P.S. left wing. Hopes

[1] The K.P.D. first expressed itself willing to form a 'loyal opposition' to a workers' government, then went back on this statement. O. Flechtheim, *Die K.P.D.*, Offenbach, 1948, pp. 63–4.
[2] The Communists had 58 seats, the Serbian Radicals 91, Democrats 102, and Croatian Peasant Party 50.

were high that a Soviet Poland would link Soviet Russia with Germany, and that the German communists with Russian help would make a new, and this time successful, bid for power. But the Bolshevik success proved as short-lived as the earlier Polish success. The Polish people rallied round Piłsudski, and the propaganda of the Bialystok committee achieved nothing. Anti-Russian nationalism proved a stronger force than social revolution. Meanwhile in Germany no one stirred. In mid-August Piłsudski made his offensive south of Warsaw and the Red Army in its turn retreated. An armistice was made at Riga in the autumn. The first Bolshevik attempt to revolutionise Poland by military invasion had failed.

THE TWENTY-ONE CONDITIONS

During the Russian advance into Poland, the Second Congress of the Comintern was sitting in Moscow. It was here that the principles of organisation of communist parties were laid down. They were formulated in the Twenty-One Conditions, which all communist parties were thenceforth bound to accept. Of these the following were the most important.

All parties joining the Comintern must resolutely fight against reformism,[1] centre tendencies and pacifism, remove from their membership all persons holding any such views, and break off all friendly relations with such groups.

Communists must form nuclei within their countries' trade unions in order to capture these from within. They must combat the unions' existing leadership and the 'Amsterdam' International of trade unions. They must agitate for the affiliation of the unions to the new Red trade union International (*Profintern*) centred in Moscow.[2]

Communists must make propaganda within their countries' armed forces, when necessary by secret and illegal means.

Communists must make special efforts to win peasant support.

Communists must support the emancipation of oppressed nationalities and colonial peoples. They must develop among their

[1] Communists of course do not object in principle to reforms, but regard them as opportunities to make political gains. In communist terminology 'Reformists' are those who regard reforms not as a means, but as an end and who are content with the prospect of occasional concessions from the ruling class; 'Revolutionaries' assert that reforms can never be more than palliatives and that only revolutionary violence can ensure the interests of the proletariat. The *locus classicus* for a discussion of these issues is Lenin, *Left-wing Communism, an Infantile Malady*, 1921.

[2] The Amsterdam International was the pre-war international trade union organisation, loosely associated with the Second International though independent of it. *Profintern* was devised merely as a trade union subsidiary of *Comintern*.

own workers fraternal feelings towards the workers of colonies or of oppressed nationalities subject to their own nation. They must agitate among their own armed forces against oppression of colonial peoples.

In countries where a communist party is permitted by the laws to function legally, it must nevertheless maintain, parallel with its legal organisation, a 'clandestine organisation capable at the decisive moment of fulfilling its duty towards the revolution'.[1]

In countries with a parliamentary system, communist parliamentary groups must be completely subordinated to the party's central committee, which must give them exact directives as to how to behave in parliament.

Communist parties must support unreservedly all soviet republics in their struggles with counter-revolution, urge workers to refuse to transport arms or equipment destined for the enemies of a soviet republic, and pursue propaganda by legal or illegal means among all troops sent to fight against a soviet republic.

Communist parties must be based on the principle of 'democratic centralism' on which the Bolshevik party had been based since its foundation. They must proceed to 'periodic purges of their organisations, in order to remove interested and petty-bourgeois elements'.[2]

All decisions of Congresses of Comintern were to be binding on all parties belonging to it.

These conditions were intended by Lenin to split the left socialist movement, and they did. During the first months of 1920 a serious threat had appeared to the young Comintern. The Swiss and Austrian socialists, supported by a section of the French party, had revived the plans, which had been discussed at Zimmerwald and Kienthal and had had some sympathy from Roza Luxemburg, of reconstructing the Second International. The initiators of this plan were socialists of the left, not of the right: their aim was a truly revolutionary International, but one not excessively dependent on Moscow. These men could not be accused of revisionism, social patriotism or the other sins of those who had led the Second International at the time of its collapse in 1914. Their proposals might therefore make a strong appeal to the left elements in those parties whose attitude to the Comintern was still unclear, especially in the Italian party and in the U.S.P.D. Lenin decided to meet this threat by forcing a definite split in the left socialist movement. Even more

[1] 2-oy s'yezd kommunisticheskovo Internatsionaka, Moscow, 1920, p. 562.
[2] Ibid., p. 565.

than at Zimmerwald and Kienthal, his attack was concentrated on the non-Bolshevik left—the 'opportunists' as he called them—rather than on the right, whose enmity he took for granted. Just as after 1903 he had deliberately split the Russian movement in the belief that a small party of professional revolutionaries could be made the spearhead of revolution, and could make up by their discipline and revolutionary skill what they lost in numbers, so now he split the international movement in the belief that a spearhead of disciplined revolutionary parties, directed from a single centre, would more effectively promote international revolution than a larger, more representative but less resolute International. The Comintern must perform in the international field the task that the Bolsheviks had performed in the purely Russian field. The experience of the Bolsheviks must be the basis for the Comintern. Lenin was not seeking permanently to subordinate the European communist parties to the Russian party; he wished Moscow to be the Comintern's centre simply because it could give security as the capital of the only communist-ruled country. The parties of the Comintern were to be of the Bolshevik type, but each would be led by its own leaders, and the control which the Comintern would exercise over them, though very strict, would operate through an Executive Committee elected from their number, not appointed by the Russian party.

In the next months the Twenty-One Conditions were considered in turn by the three most important left socialist parties in Europe, the U.S.P.D., the French and Italian socialist parties.

In October the U.S.P.D. held its Congress at Halle. During the summer its delegates had visited Moscow to discuss with the Russian leaders. They urged acceptance of the Conditions, and the Congress supported them by 236 votes to 156. The minority continued to exist under the name U.S.P.D. until September 1922, when it reunited with the S.P.D. The majority proposed to the K.P.D. that it should fuse with it. This proposal the K.P.D. duly accepted, and in December the formal unification was carried out at a joint congress of the two parties. By this fusion the German Communist Party had at last become a numerous and potentially strong working-class party

At the end of December the French Socialist Party considered the Conditions at its Congress in Tours. The situation in France had at no time since the end of the war been revolutionary in the sense in which it had been in Central Europe and in Italy. The socialists were however a strong national party, and within their ranks the left wing had gained ground. This was still more the case with the trade union movement, which was independent of the party but whose membership of course overlapped with it at all levels. The Congress accepted the Conditions by a majority of 3 to 1. Thus at this moment the communists held a majority of the workers, though the majority of the Socialist parliamentary group were against them. In 1921 came the split in the trade union movement. At the Congress of the national trade union organisation (C.G.T.), held in Lille in July, the supporters of the communists had slightly less than half the votes. In the following months the debate continued, between the ideas of trade union independence upheld by the established leaders, and of subordination to political revolutionary leadership, upheld by the communist-dominated *Comités syndicalistes révolutionnaires*. It ended in the formation by the communists of a rival trade union machine, which they saw fit to name the 'unitary' Confederation of Labour (C.G.T.U.).[1]

The Italian party considered the Conditions at the Congress of Livorno in January 1921. Those who had led the party since the Bologna Congress, the 'Maximalists' who had so long and so loudly extolled the virtues of the soviet form of government, felt unable to accept the Conditions. The Maximalist leader Serrati was especially unwilling to force a split and purges in the trade unions. The events of August 1920 had shown that the C.G.L. was a powerful weapon, even if it had been badly managed: this was no time to deprive the Italian workers of the weapon. The party's dislike of the Conditions was increased by the arrogant behaviour of the two Comintern delegates to the Congress, the Hungarian Rákosi and the Bulgarian Kabakchiev, whose assumption of superior wisdom and insults to veteran leaders of Italian labour merely infuriated their audience. About one-third of the Congress votes urged acceptance of the Conditions. This third then split from the party and later constituted itself the Italian Communist Party. More than half voted for Serrati's motion that the Conditions be accepted in principle but interpreted according to the conditions of Italy. A small minority took a definite anti-communist attitude.

For some months Serrati's followers persisted in regarding themselves as members of the Comintern, but were reluctantly obliged to recognise that Moscow would not accept them unless they surrendered unconditionally. During 1921 and 1922 the

---

[1] J. Montreuil, *Histoire du mouvement ouvrier en France*, Paris, n.d. (?1947), pp. 356–369.

divided Italian labour movement suffered one defeat after another. Despite the terror of fascist bands, the workers in the parliamentary election of May 1921 still gave their votes to the socialists. But now there was no hope of socialist revolution: all that was possible was to save democratic institutions, within which the socialists might later hope again to advance. This however required alliance with non-socialist democrats against the fascist enemies of democracy, and this the doctrinaire Maximalists would not accept. Disagreements between trade unions and party, socialists and communists, moderates and Maximalists, paralysed the Italian working class. The C.G.L. and the socialist parliamentary group did what they could on their own: it was not enough. In August 1922 the last attempt at a general strike was broken by fascist violence; in early October the socialists at their Rome Congress finally split into two parties, Maximalists and Reformists; and at the end of the month Mussolini was in power.

CHAPTER FOUR

Communism in Russia 1921-1928

THE NEW ECONOMIC POLICY

THE victory of the Red Army over the Whites was followed by a serious crisis of the Bolshevik regime. Sacrifices that were accepted as long as the Revolution was threatened by White generals supported by foreign 'imperialists', were no longer tolerated when the war was won. At the end of 1920 peasant guerrillas were active in the Ukraine and Central Russia, and in February 1921 the sailors of Kronstadt mutinied. The mutineers accepted the Revolution, but demanded an end to the dictatorship of the Bolshevik party and freedom for workers and peasants to choose their own rulers. Lenin never considered political concessions. He chose to regard the mutiny as a White Guard conspiracy, exploiting 'petty bourgeois elemental discontent'. Under Trotski's direct orders the Red Army suppressed it by force.

But Lenin realised that the time had come for economic concessions. The New Economic Policy (N.E.P.) was introduced at the 10th Congress of the Communist Party, held in March 1921 while the battle for Kronstadt was still on, and was amplified in the following months. Its essence was to restore and confirm private ownership and private initiative in agriculture, retail trade and even in sectors of wholesale trade and industry. Requisitions of foodstuffs were replaced by a much smaller tax in kind. All produce left after payment of the tax could be used by the peasants as they wished, whether to improve their holdings, to trade or to eat. Traders were allowed to buy and sell foodstuffs and consumers' goods. By the end of 1922 three-quarters of the volume of retail trade was in private hands. Private business also accounted for the greater part of small-scale industry, but the great majority of factory workers were employed in large-scale enterprises, which remained nationalised.

These concessions were defended by Lenin, against strong

opposition from doctrinaires in the party, on the ground that only agreement between workers and peasants could save the socialist revolution in Russia until such time as revolution took place in Europe. Russia's economy must be 'adapted to the economy of the middle peasant'.[1] But economic retreat made it all the more essential, in Lenin's view, that the party's control be maintained over the 'commanding heights of the economy'. Here the main challenge to the party came from the trade unions.

At the 10th Congress two extreme positions were taken on the question of the unions' relation to the state. One extreme was urged by Trotski, the organiser of the 'labour armies' of the civil war, the advocate of the 'militarisation of labour'. He proposed more closely to link the personnel and the functions of the trade unions and the industrial managements, until the common sphere of their activities 'swallowed up the whole work, that is, finally fused the trade union and economic organs'.[2] The opposite extreme was urged by a group known as the Workers' Opposition. They wished to subordinate managements to trade unions, to equalise wages, and to entrust the conduct of economic policy to a pyramid of councils elected by the workers, culminating in a national Congress of Producers. This of course was in essence a syndicalist programme. The policy adopted by the Congress was that proposed by Lenin and other leaders (the 'Group of Ten'). It was nominally a compromise, but in practice was much nearer to Trotski than to the Workers' Opposition. The unions were in fact subordinated to the state, but it was admitted in principle that the workers must still possess instruments of class defence, since the state machine, though held at the top by the 'party of the proletariat', still suffered from 'bureaucratic perversion' at the lower levels, and since classes other than the workers still played a large part in the economy. Strikes were not therefore forbidden in principle, but they were condemned in theory and punished in practice. The party's control over the unions was further strengthened by the 11th Congress of the Communist Party in March 1922.[3]

PARTY AND STATE

Lenin's theory of the superiority of soviets over parliamentary forms of government remained official communist doctrine, binding on all Comintern parties. But the doctrine was and is a myth. The

---

[1] *10 s'yezd RKP (b)*, Moscow, 1921, p. 227.   [2] Ibid., p. 359.
[3] *VKP (b) v Rezolyutsiah*, Vol. I, pp. 427–33.

nature of the Bolshevik state was little if at all determined by the fact that its organs of government were soviets.

In 1917 the soviets, representing the inarticulate and inexperienced masses, had been an admirable forum for Lenin's demagogy, designed to disrupt the Russian state. Once in power, the Bolsheviks required not disruption from below but centralisation from above. Just as they subordinated the factory committees to the trade unions,[1] so they subordinated the local soviets, which represented the masses, to the central organs composed of politically conscious persons owing full allegiance to the Bolshevik party.

Under the Constitution adopted on 10th July 1918 by the 5th Congress of Soviets, the supreme political body in the republic was to be the All-Russian Congress of Soviets, indirectly elected on a franchise which gave five times more representation to urban than to rural voters. The Congress itself met only for brief periods: between these meetings its powers were exercised by its Executive Committee (V.Ts.I.K.) of not more than 200 members. The V.Ts.I.K. in turn chose the members of the Council of People's Commissars (Sovnarkom), the national government. In practice not only did the Congress lose power to V.Ts.I.K., but V.Ts.I.K. lost power to Sovnarkom. The growing centralisation of power was caused in part by the necessities of the civil war, in part by the removal from effective influence in V.Ts.I.K. of all political parties other than the Communist;[2] and in part by the highly centralistic nature of the Communist Party itself. Once both Sovnarkom and V.Ts.I.K. had become exclusively communist organs, it was inevitable that the former, composed of leading communists, should control the latter, dominated by communists of lesser though considerable rank.

In peace as in war, the party dominated the political and economic administration. Soviets, factory managements, trade unions and other public organisations were directed by 'fractions' of Communist Party members within their ranks, which took their orders from the party leaders, and were pledged to act unanimously within their organisation. At the same time official doctrine insisted that the functions of the party and of the administrative organs must not be confused. 'The party strives to direct the activity of the

---

[1] See above, pp. 42–43.

[2] The Menshevik and Socialist Revolutionary parties were banned in the summer of 1918, allowed to operate again, with heavy restrictions, in the winter of 1918–19, and driven out of existence by increased administrative pressure in 1920–1. They were never formally outlawed, but ceased to exist.

soviets but not to replace them.'[1] It should lay down directives, but the officials must do the administering. This distinction of functions has remained official doctrine ever since it was first clearly formulated at the 8th Congress of the party in 1919, but it has never been achieved. Ever since then, party press and meetings have been full of complaints that the party was taking over the soviets' jobs for them, that party members were becoming sub-'merged in administrative routine instead of confining themselves to general policy. The reason is not that party members have ignored official doctrine, but that the nature of the regime has made the doctrine unrealisable. Non-party officials have not dared to assume responsibility, but have always referred even details to party members. When the party members strictly confined themselves to supervision and advice, this caused duplication, hesitation and inertia. When they exceeded this role, they became full-time administrators, and neglected their purely party activities. The party and state hierarchies in practice overlapped. But whether this resulted in the transformation of the state administration by the will of the party, or in the imposition on the party of the spirit of the traditional bureaucracy, was an open question, which soon became a matter of bitter controversy among the leaders of the party.

The same process of centralisation which we have noticed in the hierarchy of soviets also took place within the hierarchy of the Communist Party. The nominally sovereign body within the party was the All-Russian Congress, composed of delegates elected by the lower ranks of the party. The Congress met once a year during the first eight years of the Soviet regime, but after 1925 the intervals became longer. Between Congresses, the party was to be led by the Central Committee, which was elected by the Congress. But from 1919 onwards the powers of the Central Committee steadily declined. Firstly, the number of its members increased, and this made it a more unwieldy and less decisive body.[2] Secondly, the Central Committee met less frequently.[3] Thirdly, the Central Committee lost power to three smaller bodies, elected from its members, which had been created at the 8th Congress—the Political Bureau (*Politburo*), Organisational Bureau (*Orgburo*) and Secretariat.

The *Politburo* was intended originally to deal only with such

---

[1] *VKP (b) Rezolyutsiah*, p. 315. Voted at the 8th Congress in March 1919.

[2] At the 7th Congress in 1918 it had 15 full members and 8 candidates (probationary members): after the 13th Congress in 1924 it had 53 full members and 34 candidates.

[3] At the 8th Congress it was laid down that a full meeting ('Plenum') should meet at least twice a month: at the 10th the interval was increased to once in two months.

political matters as required urgent decision, and to report on its actions to the fortnightly Plenums of the Central Committee.[1] By 1923 however it was already clearly the master of the Central Committee. A resolution of the 12th Congress, held in that year, referred to 'planned direction by the *Politburo* of the state administration and especially of economic administration'.[2] The membership of the *Politburo* always to a considerable extent overlapped with that of *Sovnarkom*. These two bodies, closely interlocked, in fact directed party and state.

The *Orgburo* was responsible for the internal organisation of the party, and reported on this to the Central Committee. The Secretariat was intended to carry out its detailed work. In the following three years however the *Orgburo* lost power to the Secretariat, which became responsible for the direction of party members to jobs and appointments in party and state. In April 1922 the post of General Secretary was created, and was entrusted to Stalin, who was a member of both *Orgburo* and *Politburo*. The Secretariat and the *Politburo* were in fact the two supreme bodies of the Soviet state, and Stalin rose to supremacy by his membership of both.

Repressive power continued to be vested in the organs of state security. After the civil war there was a strong demand within the party to restrict the powers of the *Cheka* and to 'strengthen the principles of revolutionary legality'. In February 1922 the *Cheka* was abolished, but was replaced by a 'State Political Administration' (G.P.U.), with subordinate 'political administrations' in provinces and districts. The G.P.U. possessed its own 'special army detachments'. Its powers were in fact greater than those of the *Cheka*. The destruction of all organised political opposition to the Bolsheviks thus brought no relaxation of pressure. The continuance of this type of repression was defended by official spokesmen mainly on the ground that the Republic was encircled by hostile capitalist states, which, even if they did not possess a secret army of agents within its borders, would soon create one if revolutionary vigilance were relaxed. In practice the G.P.U. was a state within the Soviet state, with more far-reaching powers than any police organisation known to history. It was however subject to the same trends as affect all such organisations. In particular, there

---

[1] The original members of the *Politburo* were Lenin, Trotski, Kamenev, Buharin and Stalin. The first 'Political Bureau' in the party's history was nominally created in October 1917, before the insurrection. In fact it never functioned. The *Politburo*, as it is known to history, dates from the 8th Congress.

[2] *VKP (b) v Rezolyutsiah*, pp. 511–12.

arose a vested interest in the manufacture of plots and alarms o. plots. Alleged discovery of treason justified increased repression, repression created hatred and discontent, hatred and discontent strengthened the conviction of the leaders that the danger of plots was real.

To prevent abuses in the administration and in the party, to avoid what Lenin called 'bureaucratic perversion', special organs of 'popular control' were set up. It was believed that the evils of bureaucracy were due to the reactionary outlook of the former bureaucrats, who were still employed in large numbers in the state machine. The reactionary outlook was variously attributed to feudalism or to capitalism. It was believed that it could be overcome if new organisations, composed of persons with the new progressive and proletarian outlook, were set up to watch the bureaucrats at work. The members of the new organisation, known as *Rabkrin*,[1] had wide powers to examine office archives, to watch administrators at work, to receive complaints from individual citizens, and to take action not only to remedy abuses but to improve methods of work. As it was felt that the pernicious influences might penetrate even into the party, it was decided to set up a similar organisation within the party. This was the hierarchy of 'control commissions', instituted in the autumn of 1920 and regularised by the 10th Congress of the party in March 1921.[2]

This experiment did not justify the original hopes. *Rabkrin* was fiercely attacked in April 1922 by Trotski. Its members, he claimed, were persons who had failed in other jobs, and its work was marked by 'an extraordinary development of intrigue which has become a byword throughout the country'. Lenin at first defended *Rabkrin*, but at the end of the year he came round to Trotski's view. In his famous article 'Better less, but better' of January 1923, he wrote: 'The Commissariat of *Rabkrin* now enjoys not a shade of authority. Everyone knows that there is no institution worse organised than our *Rabkrin*.'

The target of Lenin's attacks on *Rabkrin* was of course its Commissar, Stalin. Fortunately for Stalin's career, Lenin had a fatal stroke in March 1923, shortly before the 12th Congress of the party met. At the Congress, Stalin wisely adopted the proposals that had been drafted by Lenin for the improvement of *Rabkrin*. Their essence was closer co-ordination between *Rabkrin* and the

[1] This is an abbreviation of the Russian words for 'Workers' and Peasants' Inspection'. The institution was first called People's Commissariat of State Control.
[2] Provincial control commissions were elected by conferences of provincial party organisations, the Central Control Commission by the Party Congress.

Control Commissions of the party. Stalin remained Commissar, and was now the master of both control hierarchies—state and party—as well as of the regular bureaucracy of the party itself, headed by the Secretariat. At the 13th Congress in 1924 the provincial control commissions were placed under the direction of the Central Control Commission, and its membership was greatly increased. Just as V.Ts.I.K. had lost power to *Sovnarkom* and the Central Committee of the party had lost power to the *Politburo* and the Secretariat, so the Central Control Commission lost power to its Presidium.[1] The Presidium co-ordinated its activities closely with those of the G.P.U. All these machineries of appointment, control and repression were now held by the single hand of Stalin.

Not only was the party increasingly centralised: its internal discipline was made more severe. Here the turning-point was the 10th Congress of March 1921. Two opposition groups appeared at this congress. The Democratic Centralism group pleaded for simpler machinery and smaller numbers of bureaucrats. The Workers' Opposition group, whose views on the trade union problem have already been mentioned,[2] demanded a purge of non-proletarian elements in the party, the reassertion of the supremacy of the working class in the Communist Party and the Soviet state, and much more freedom of opinion within the party. The group denounced 'the ridiculously naive belief that it is possible to bring about Communism by bureaucratic means'.[3]

Lenin not only opposed these views, but objected strongly to the fact that their exponents had formed groups within the party, operating collectively in favour of their views. Lenin insisted that though all members of the party were entitled to discuss theoretical questions freely at party meetings, they were not entitled to organise a political struggle within the party. At Lenin's request, the Congress passed resolutions on the 'syndicalist and anarchist deviation' and on 'unity of the party'.[4] The latter declared 'any sort of fractionalism' within the party inadmissible. Members should put any criticisms they had to make of the party's actions before the whole party, not before any smaller group within the party with some 'platform' of its own.

---

[1] The Presidium was elected by the Central Control Commission from its own members.
[2] See above, p. 79.
[3] A. Kollontay, *The Workers' Opposition*, n.d. (?1923), p. 15.
[4] *10 s'yezd RKP (b)*, pp. 310–11 and 309–10.

THE NON-RUSSIAN NATIONALITIES

Centralisation of government and of the party, and tighter party discipline, affected the practical application of the Bolshevik doctrine on the treatment of the non-Russian nationalities. During the early years of the regime, nationality policy was not uniform in all areas. Official doctrine always mentioned two 'deviations' which should be equally avoided—'Great Russian Great Power chauvinism' and 'local bourgeois nationalism'. The proletariat of each nation must oppose the policy of its own bourgeoisie. Thus, since the Russian bourgeoisie had wished to keep the non-Russian peoples in subjection to Russia, the Russian proletariat must insist on the right of these peoples to independence: since the bourgeoisie of the non-Russian peoples had wished to create separate states under their own domination, the proletariat of those peoples must insist on the necessity of union with the Russian proletariat in one socialist state.

During the 1920's official statements of nationalities policy issued in Moscow usually laid greater emphasis on the struggle against Great Russian chauvinism than on that against local nationalism. In the policy carried out in the non-Russian areas, however, there were considerable variations.

The nationality which enjoyed the greatest measure of self-government was the Ukrainian. The policy of the Ukrainian republic—at first nominally independent, and after 1923 a member of the Soviet Union—was described as 'Ukrainisation'. The Ukrainian language, treated under the Imperial regime as an inferior dialect, was now given priority in public affairs and schools throughout the Ukraine. A new Ukrainian intelligentsia arose. Ukrainian literature and learned publications flourished. The industrial working class ceased to be Russian and became Ukrainian. The cities of the Ukraine became Ukrainian cities. Even in religious life there was relative liberty.[1] This cultural progress to some extent compensated for the lack of political freedom. The progress was the work of Ukrainian Bolsheviks, chief among whom was Skrypnik, who held the Commissariat of Education from 1927 to 1933.

The Transcaucasian republics lost their independence in 1920 and 1921, partly through their mutual quarrels, partly through

---

[1] A Ukrainian Autocephalous Orthodox Church was founded by a congress held in Kiev in 1921. In 1926 it had 29 bishops and more than 10,000 priests. *Entsiklopedia Ukrainoznavstva*, Munich, 1951, p. 617.

lack of support by the Western Powers, partly through Soviet-Turkish agreement. In Azerbaidjan, where the Moslem population was very hostile to the Bolsheviks, and their support came from the Russian or Armenian workers of Baku, Soviet policy had to some extent the character of russification. Armenia and Georgia however were ruled by Armenians and Georgians. But in Georgia, where Lenin himself had wished for conciliation, a brutal policy was carried out by Stalin, Moscow's specialist for Caucasian affairs. Stalin not only repressed the Mensheviks, who had had the support of the Georgian people until the Bolshevik invasion in 1921, but also antagonised the Georgian Bolsheviks. Georgia was ruled by Georgian puppets appointed in Moscow. Their unpopularity was shown in 1924, when there was a mass rising of Georgian peasants, brutally suppressed.

The Bolshevik leaders were especially concerned to win over their Moslem subjects. If Moslems outside the Soviet Union could be made to believe that Soviet Moslems enjoyed freedom, social justice and religious rights, this would strengthen communist propaganda in Asia and the Middle East. But with the exception of the Volga Tatars, the Moslems of the Soviet Union were socially and culturally too backward to be greatly attracted by communist ideas. On the other hand, the Russians who lived in their midst were more willing to support Moscow, in some cases because they genuinely accepted communism, in others merely because they felt that any Russian government must protect them against the hostile Moslems. Thus the exponents of Bolshevism in the Moslem areas were mostly Russians, and the policy carried out in the name of the Communist Party was a policy which favoured the Russian minorities at the expense of the Moslem majorities. This was most unwelcome to Lenin, Stalin (the Commissar for Nationalities) and the other Bolshevik leaders, but they were powerless to prevent it. For all the obvious differences, there is a certain analogy between their position and that of the British or French Colonial Offices in the face of the Kenya settlers or the Algerian *colons*.

The most socially and culturally advanced Moslems were the Tatars of the Volga basin. Already at the turn of the century Tatar schools were growing both in numbers and in quality. Already in 1905 a modernist and democratic movement, similar to Kemalism in Turkey twenty years later, enjoyed support among the Volga Tatars.[1] In 1917–18 the Tatars attempted to

[1] This is described in G. von Mende, *Der nationale Kampf der Russlandtürken*, Berlin, 1936, pp. 44–90.

establish an autonomous, or even independent, Volga-Ural state. Their hopes were crushed first by Kolchak, then by the Bolsheviks, and then by the famine of 1921–2 which ravaged the Middle Volga region. In the early 1920's however the Bolsheviks—and especially Stalin himself—sought to conciliate the Tatars. Those who survived the famine, and were not regarded in Moscow as implacable bourgeois nationalists, were able to make themselves careers. Tatar communists played a part not only in their own homeland, but also in other Moslem areas of the Soviet Union, where their higher level of education made them useful instruments of Moscow's policy. In 1923 however it was discovered that the leading Tatar communist Sultan-Galiev, assistant commissar of Nationalities under Stalin, had kept a secret correspondence with exiled Moslem nationalists, in which he discussed plans to separate the Tatar lands from the Soviet Union.[1] The discovery led to a purge, and to a dominance of Russians in the state and party hierarchies of the Tatar region. Despite constant warnings from Moscow against 'Great Russian chauvinism', this remained the case throughout the 1920's.

In Central Asia Russian domination was still more striking. In the steppe lands inhabited by Kazakh and Kirgiz nomads, the instruments of Bolshevik rule, as of Imperial rule, were Russians. In Turkestan, with a settled population of more advanced social structure, things were no better. The only Bolshevik stronghold was the city of Tashkent, with a large population of Russian railwaymen and bureaucrats. Russian communists in Turkestan were regarded as heirs to the Tsars; non-Bolshevik Russians supported them, while non-Russians distrusted them, and when possible fought them.

In the principalities of Khiva and Bokhara[2] the Bolsheviks found some Moslem allies. The Young Bokhara party resembled the Tatar democrats or the Kemalists. When Tashkent Bolsheviks invaded Bokhara in 1918, it supported them, but its leaders were massacred by followers of the Emir. When in 1920 the Emir fled, Bokhara became a 'People's Republic', ruled by a coalition of Bolsheviks and Young Bokhara, which was soon transformed into a Bolshevik monopoly of power.[3] In 1924 the People's Republics of Bokhara and Khiva were incorporated in the Soviet Union, and the whole of Central Asia was split up into a number of federal or

[1] *VKP (b) v Rezolyutsiah*, pp. 537–38.
[2] These were vassal states of the Russian Empire, not formally incorporated in it, ruled by their traditional potentates.
[3] The left wing of the Young Bokhara party fused with the Bolsheviks.

autonomous republics. The ostensible purpose was to remake frontiers on lines of ethnic division. The real aim was to exalt dialects into languages and tribes into nations, in order to divide the Central Asian Moslems against each other, and link the divided lands separately to Moscow.[1]

During the 1920's communist spokesmen both in Moscow and in Tashkent continued to fulminate against the survival of a 'colonialist mentality' among Russian communists in Central Asia, and preached the necessity to increase the number of Asians in industry, in civil administration and in the party hierarchy. But progress was slow.[2] Modernisation was effected in a brutal and clumsy way, and even such genuinely democratic measures as emancipation of women and land reform were resisted by the population. Land reform and irrigation were designed to benefit Russian settlers. Attempts by the Central Asian republican authorities to limit Russian immigration were frustrated partly by the central government and partly by local Russian communists.[3] Education made progress, but reality was still far behind propaganda. Hundreds of schools existed only on paper: they had not been built, and the children alleged to be taught in them remained illiterate.

Two points should here be stressed. One is that a communist regime was not chosen by the non-Russian nations, European or Asian, Christian or Moslem, but was imposed on them by the superior force of the Russian state, which was in communist hands. The second is that the faults of communist rule in Asiatic Russia were at least in large part due to the primitive condition of the local nations. Bolshevism faced many of the problems that faced the governments of European Powers in their colonies, protectorates and dependencies. The glowing promises of the Bolsheviks could not be fulfilled: the obstacles lay not so much in the wickedness of the Tsar's administrators, the Russian capitalists or the native ruling classes, as in the ignorance and poverty of the peoples. But communists have never admitted this. They have claimed to have brought liberation, progress and complete equality to the formerly downtrodden peoples of Russia. The only way to place

---

[1] Uzbekistan and Turkmenistan became Soviet republics. Kirgizistan, Kazakhstan and Tadjikistan were at first autonomous republics, but became Soviet republics in the 1930's.

[2] In 1927 only one-third of the trade union members in Central Asia were Asians. Of 30,000 railwaymen 2,400 were Asians. Sixty-two per cent of public officials in Uzbekistan were Russians. Figures are quoted from official Soviet sources by Mustafa Chokay-oglu, *Turkestan pod vlastyu Sovyetov*, Paris, 1935, pp. 28–9.

[3] Chokay-oglu, op. cit., pp. 61, 68, gives examples.

the communist achievement in perspective would be to compare the reality of the Soviet Union with the reality of other countries with similar problems. Thus Soviet policy in the Ukraine might be compared with the treatment of the lesser nationalities in Poland or Roumania between the wars, and Soviet policy in Central Asia with British policy in Iraq and French policy in Syria. Such comparisons are made extremely difficult by inadequate information from the Soviet side, and in fact they have never been attempted in a systematic manner. Instead there have been comparisons between two propaganda pictures, between a caricature of European imperial rule, with all negative aspects stressed or magnified and all positive achievements ignored, and an idealised version of Soviet rule in which the promised blessings of the future communist utopia are treated as contemporary facts. This fantastic distortion has long passed for the truth in a large part of the world. Members of persecuted national minorities in Eastern Europe, and of frustrated Asiatic or African nations under European rule, longing to believe that somewhere in the world was a state in which these oppressions and inequalities had been abolished, fell ready victims to this propaganda, which had a high priority in Comintern activity both in Eastern Europe and outside Europe.

STALIN AND THE OPPOSITION

After his stroke of March 1923, Lenin was never well enough to play an active part in Soviet politics. He died in January 1924. During 1923 the disagreements within the Communist Party, which had existed earlier, became really important. The following period marks the rise of Stalin to supreme power. In 1923 and 1924 he combined with Zinoviev and Kamenev against Trotski: between 1925 and 1927 he defeated Zinoviev and Kamenev, who were forced into alliance with Trotski. These fractional struggles, which have both a personal and a doctrinal aspect, had important effects on the world communist movement.

Trotski was the most brilliant figure in Russia after Lenin's death, a fact which brought him more jealousy than devotion from the other leaders of the party. To the Bolshevik bosses, who liked to make parallels between their revolution and the French, Trotski was the obvious candidate for the role of Bonaparte. Trotski himself was resolved that, come what might, he would be no Bonaparte. So keen was he to prove this to everyone that he failed to defend himself, and went to extreme lengths to show how complete was his party loyalty. He was too devoted to principles and dogmas to be a successful politician. He thought always in Marxist theoretical categories, without the suppleness and opportunism of Lenin. Trotski's great achievements in the revolution and civil war were due to his personality, to his courage and eloquence, to his energy and ability to inspire others. Yet he seems hardly to have understood this. It is not that he was modest, but that his vanity consisted in seeing himself as the instrument of never clearly defined historical and class forces. Though his own personality had played a decisive role, he underrated the role of personality in politics. He never understood how Stalin created the power which broke him. Trotski was an efficient administrator at the highest level, but never took the trouble to understand how the lower levels of the administration worked. He associated only with a few friends and disciples: for lesser persons who did not owe direct allegiance to himself he had no patience. The great *prima donna* found it hard to mix with men of lesser clay.

The three who opposed him were united by their fear of him but by little else. Zinoviev was the real boss of the Comintern, a fiery demagogue, easily given to wild optimism but not always reliable in difficult times, a despot and an intriguer in his dealings with subordinates and colleagues, a veteran Bolshevik and master of the party machine in Petrograd.[1] Kamenev was a less dramatic and more likeable figure, not only learned in party doctrine but possessed of a good education in economic and political problems, a more reliable organiser and more solid worker than Zinoviev. Kamenev enjoyed a large following in the party machine in Moscow. Stalin was the least known to the public. To those who worked with him he appeared an amiable and efficient mediocrity, willing to undertake the routine jobs which bored his colleagues: they did not understand that he was thereby building himself an impregnable position.

Stalin proceeded cautiously. Control of the Secretariat, *Rabkrin* and the Control Commissions gave him, as we have seen, a commanding position in the hierarchies of both state and party. The General Secretary appointed the provincial and regional secretaries, the masters of the party machine outside the two capitals. By a combination of charm and threats, kindness and blackmail, discreet use of patronage and creation of an omniscient filing system, by a process that will probably for ever be withheld from the historian's eye, Stalin bound these men to himself. At the same time

[1] An unpleasant picture of Zinoviev is given in A. Balabanova, *My Life as a Rebel*, 1938, pp. 241–9.

he removed friends of Trotski from key positions. Already at the 12th Congress of the party in 1923 Stalin had his solid block of support.[1]

The crisis in relations between the 'triumvirate' and Trotski came in the autumn of 1923. After two years of economic recovery under N.E.P., serious difficulties arose in the exchange of goods between town and country. Trotski criticised the government for its failure to deal with this problem. At the same time political opposition groups appeared within the working class, and there were several strikes during the year.

The main subject of dispute between Trotski and the triumvirate was the role of the bureaucracy. Trotski argued that party members, who during the civil war had cheerfully accepted posting from one place and duty to another, were now insisting on safe permanent jobs. This desire for creature comforts explained the bureaucratisation of the party and the rise of Stalin, who pandered to it. Stalin no doubt still considered himself a Bolshevik revolutionary, but he had become an instrument of the reactionary forces in Russian society, which had not been removed by the mere military defeat of the Whites. 'The dialectics of history have already hooked him and will raise him up,' Trotski said of Stalin in 1924. 'He is needed by all of them—by the tired radicals, by the bureaucrats, by the Nepmen, the *kulaks*, the upstarts, the sneaks, by all the worms that are crawling out of the upturned soil of the manured revolution.'[2]

In this analysis there was truth, but there was also a large dose of utopianism. Trotski imagined to himself the bureaucracy as a loathsome monster to be destroyed, and to be replaced by the abstraction of the proletariat. His hatred of bureaucracy caused him to exaggerate the role played by members of the former ruling class or of former non-Bolshevik parties who held posts in the administration. It is improbable in fact that such persons had any importance as a group, even if as individuals they acted in accordance with the general outlook which they had acquired by their education under the old regime. The misdeeds of the bureaucracy were not caused by the presence of these men. The real causes were two. One was the miserably low level of education, and the lack of any sense of social responsibility among the officials. This was of course, as Lenin had pointed out, a legacy

---

[1] On Stalin's tactics at this stage, see B. Bazhanov, *Avec Staline dans le Kremlin*, Paris, 1930, pp. 26–7. The author was Stalin's personal secretary in 1923–4.
[2] Trotski, *Stalin*, p. 392.

from the old regime: it could only be remedied by what Lenin had called a 'cultural revolution', for which many years were needed. To denounce the bureaucrats for their faults was of small help. The country had to be administered, and this could only be done with the human beings available. The second and more fundamental cause of the trouble was the nature of the leadership at the top. The only remedy against abuse of power by the group of bosses headed by Stalin was to give the people freedom to choose their rulers. In their doctrinaire obsession with the evils of the abstraction 'bourgeois. democracy', the Bolsheviks could not see the simple truth, more fundamental than any truths or untruths about capitalism or socialism, that autocracy corrupts and that only representative institutions can mitigate, though they cannot remove, the evils of despotism.

There could of course be no question in 1923 of granting the Russian people a freedom of choice: this would have ended the monopoly of the Bolsheviks, and neither Trotski nor any other party leader would have accepted that. But freedom of choice within the party, which would at least have reduced the evils, was theoretically compatible with, even theoretically required by, Bolshevik doctrine. This was now demanded by Trotski, but pursued with remarkable clumsiness. Instead of concentrating his attacks on Stalin, he made an undiscriminating frontal attack on the party machine as such, thus rallying all the secretaries and their clients behind Stalin. Instead of trying to separate Zinoviev and Kamenev from Stalin, he tilted against all three at once.

Stalin could count on the support not only of Zinoviev and Kamenev and their disciples, and of his own block of provincial secretaries and their dependants, but also of the millions who sought for a more normal and secure life. These latter had little ground to love Stalin and the party bosses: if Trotski had put himself at their head and opposed the party bosses, they would gladly have followed him, for there was no Bolshevik leader who enjoyed so much admiration even outside the party ranks as Trotski. But Trotski chose to scorn such support. From the lofty moral peak of revolutionary romanticism he looked down with contempt on the 'movement for creature comforts'. His rhetoric, his histrionic talents and his sincere convictions allowed him to offer his followers only further sacrifices, further heroics, further revolutionary miracles. Thus the demand for freedom and the demand for security were not combined: the two potential oppositions to the triumvirate did not unite. Those who put their faith in Trotski as a leader had to swallow his programme of *audace, toujours de l'audace*. Those who wanted a peaceful life had to turn away from him. To these latter Stalin knew how to appeal. To them he appeared not as the party boss, protecting his own well-placed satraps, but as the sensible chap who understood the common man's wish to relax after so many horrors.

The controversy became public in December 1923, when *Pravda* published a letter from Trotski to the party branch of the Moscow district Krasnaya Presnya on the *Politburo's* proposals for the internal democratisation of the party.[1] The triumvirs replied with a campaign of abuse against Trotski and of intimidation against his supporters. Workers who publicly expressed sympathy for Trotski faced dismissal from their factories at a time of widespread unemployment. The universities were purged of students who favoured Trotski's views. The death of Lenin in January 1924 was celebrated by sudden enrolment of 240,000 workers into the party—an increase by about 60 per cent. Persons of little if any political training, they were raw material to be moulded by the party bosses selected by Stalin. In the following year the dispute became still more bitter. An immense amount of rhetoric was devoted to polemics about the respective faults of Trotski in 1908–17 and of Stalin, Kamenev and Zinoviev in March and November 1917. The triumvirs busily mummified Lenin's ideas into a sacred doctrine, against which they accused Trotski of committing sacrilege, of trying to 'replace Leninism with Trotskism'. The struggle reached a climax in January 1925, when Trotski gave up his one remaining position of power, the Chairmanship of the Revolutionary War Council. The Central Committee accepted his resignation, but did not cease to disseminate its accusations and insults through every branch of the party in the country. From this time onwards Trotski was politically powerless, though his name still meant something.

Already in 1923 Zinoviev and Kamenev had discussed with other leading communists schemes to reduce the powers of the office of General Secretary. Stalin however had managed to sidetrack their efforts, and soon afterwards the common fight with Trotski put an end to the friction.[2] The defeat of Trotski, by removing the common enemy, revived dissension: during 1925 the relations of

[1] The letter is published in full in M. Eastman, *Since Lenin Died*, 1925, pp. 145–53.

[2] See Boris Souvarine, *Staline*, Paris, 1935, pp. 359–60. The removal of Stalin from the office of General Secretary had been proposed in Lenin's so-called 'Testament', written in January 1923, which has been much discussed in Trotskist polemical literature.

Zinoviev and Kamenev with Stalin deteriorated. The conflict took the form of growing hostility between the Leningrad and Moscow branches of the party. The former was firmly held by Zinoviev's personal machine: in the latter Kamenev had once had strong influence, but Stalin was now supreme through his nominee Uglanov. The climax of the struggle came at the 14th Congress of the Communist party in December 1925. Here the Leningrad group were outvoted by the delegates from Moscow and from the provinces. At the Congress Zinoviev and Kamenev pleaded for freer discussion within the party, the very demand which they had treated as seditious when it had been put forward earlier by Trotski. Kamenev proposed that the Secretariat should be definitively subordinated to the *Politburo*. He declared: 'We are against the creation of a theory of the Leader.' He also said: 'I have come to the conclusion that Comrade Stalin is unable to fulfil the role of the unifier of the Bolshevik Staff.' These last words provoked an uproar in the Congress hall, with loud shouts of 'Long live the Party! Long live the Central Committee! Long live Stalin!'[1] That the 'theory of the Leader' was well developed could not be doubted. This public demonstration of *Führerprinzip* may be regarded as symbolic of a new phase in the evolution of the Soviet regime and of the Comintern.

Stalin's dispute with Zinoviev and Kamenev was mainly due to personal rivalry. But each contestant was eager to convince the party that his policy alone was right, and his rival's disastrous. And the bitterness of the personal struggle caused each to stress his differences from the other, until really grave divergencies of policy separated the two camps. These concerned economic policy and the role of world revolution.

The economic dispute concerned the speed of industrialisation and the attitude to be adopted towards the peasantry. The opposition's argument, in its extreme form,[2] was that industrialisation could only be paid for at the expense of the peasants, by forced loans, higher taxes and a new price system. Stalin denounced the champions of this policy as 'superindustrialisers'. He remarked that 'the workers and peasants wish to feed like men'. He jeered at the rich imagination of Russian intellectuals who like to think up fantastic plans but forget that 'grandiose enterprises are not possible without a certain minimum of resources and reserves'.

[1] *14 s'yezd VKP* (*b*), Moscow, 1926, pp. 274–5.
[2] In *Novaya Ekonomika* by the economic theorist Preobrazhenski, which appeared in 1925.

He expressed indignation at those who 'consider the toiling peasant masses an object for exploitation by industry, a sort of colony'. The whole controversy was one of emphases and *nuances*. Both sides claimed to be in favour of industrialisation, and both sides professed concern for the fate of the *serednyak*.[1] But the difference between the policies was greater than the difference between the speeches. The Opposition at this stage stressed industrialisation even at the cost of incurring a great deal of peasant discontent: Stalin stressed conciliation of the peasants even at the cost of delaying industrialisation.

The controversy about 'socialism in one country' was also a matter of emphases and *nuances*. Stalin had first expressed the belief that socialism could be built in one country in his *October Revolution and the Tactics of the Russian Communists*, published in December 1924. He quoted out of its context a phrase of Lenin, that the victory of socialism is possible 'initially in a few, or even in one single, capitalist country'.[2] Basing his argument on Lenin's theory of Imperialism and of the 'uneven development' of capitalist countries, Stalin had maintained that 'the victory of socialism in one country, even if this country is capitalistically less developed, at a time when capitalism is preserved in other countries, even if these countries are capitalistically more developed, is perfectly possible and probable'.[3] In the first months of the Bolshevik regime, all Bolshevik leaders had been convinced that the Russian working class could retain power only if it received the direct support of European states in which the working class held power. But experience had shown, Stalin argued, that the efforts of the Russian workers, together with the *sympathy* of the international proletariat, had sufficed to save the Bolshevik revolution from its enemies. For the *complete* victory of socialism, however, and a complete guarantee against the restoration of the old regime by external force, the support of the proletariat of several countries was needed. But meanwhile not only did socialist Russia need the help of the international proletariat, but the international proletariat needed the help of Russia for its own triumph. In the summer of 1925 Stalin wrote: 'We can finish building socialism, and we shall build it together with the peasantry, under the leadership of the working class, for . . . with the dictatorship of the proletariat we have . . . all the factors necessary to finish building an entirely socialist society.'[4]

[1] See above, p. 44.   [2] Lenin, *Sochineniya*, 2nd edition, Vol. XVIII, pp. 232-3.
[3] Stalin, *Sochineniya*, Vol. VI, p. 370.   [4] Ibid., Vol. VII, p. 116.

Stalin's rivals maintained the traditional view that socialism could not be built in a single country so backward as Russia without the victory of the proletariat in several advanced countries. Kamenev denied that the only danger to socialism in Russia was external and military: it was also internal and economic. N.E.P. had been a correct policy, a necessary retreat, but N.E.P. was not socialism. The Russia of N.E.P. was not yet a socialist country. Those who claimed more, called themselves 'optimists', but were actually persons with weak nerves. The Russian workers did not have to be deceived by false pictures: they had enough courage to face the reality. Economic factors would be as important for the future of Russia as military. Russia must speed up her industrialisation, must 'catch up and surpass' the level of the capitalist countries: this was 'as essential a presupposition of the final triumph of socialism in our country as the absence of military intervention'. Trotski maintained his view that revolution in the industrial countries of the West was essential, and he argued that it would surely come. There were no good grounds, he argued, for the view that 'it is easier for us to build socialism with the peasantry than for the European proletariat to seize power'.[1]

The controversy was conducted in an atmosphere of scholastic hair-splitting, each side arming itself with batteries of quotations from Lenin, and arguing about the meaning of 'complete victory' and 'final victory'. The constant references to 'optimism' and 'pessimism' however reflected the true mood of the party members.[2] Stalin was victorious not only because he packed the Congresses and Conferences with his own nominees, but also because he diagnosed the mood of the party, and of the nation, better than did his rivals. The defeats of European Communism in 1918, 1919 and 1923 had caused great gloom. The European workers had not done their duty. Whether they were unlucky, incompetent or cowardly, the fact remained that they had failed. Must the Russian Revolution perish through their failure? Stalin's opponents tried to avoid an answer to this question by insisting that the European revolutions would after all soon come off, but in the last resort their answer had to be negative. Stalin offered a brighter hope. By roundly asserting that, short of overwhelming foreign military intervention, socialism could triumph in Russia by the Russian workers' own efforts, he could appeal to Russian

[1] *15 Konferentsiya VKP (b)*, Moscow, 1927, p. 533.
[2] This is well and clearly argued in Deutscher, op. cit., pp. 285–92. It cannot fail to strike any reader of the minutes of the 14th Congress.

national pride both within and outside the Communist Party. The argument of Kamenev, that Russian workers did not have to be told that the present state of affairs was socialism in order that they should work, was perhaps basically more flattering to the Russian workers that was Stalin's belief that the picture had to be gilded: but Stalin's diagnosis of their mentality seems to have been the wiser.

The victory of Stalin did not mean that the aim of European and world revolution was abandoned: it meant that the reason for it was different. Originally, European and world revolution had been the main aim of all communists, irrespective of their nationality: now these were considered valuable mainly as a means of protecting the socialist fatherland of Soviet Russia, the land of all toilers, from foreign invasion. European revolutions were still regarded essentially as actions to be performed by European proletariats, aided when possible by Soviet Russia: the time when revolutions were regarded as the imposition by the armed force of Soviet Russia of a ready-made blueprint of socialism prepared in Moscow, was yet to come. But to Russian communists revolution in other countries was now not so much an end in itself, as a desirable alteration of the international balance of power that would strengthen the Soviet state in the face of its enemies. The emergence of the Stalin doctrine of socialism in one country thus marked a further stage in the subjection of the communist parties to Moscow. The earlier stages were the Twenty-One Conditions of the 2nd Congress in 1920; the March Action and the expulsion of Levi from K.P.D. in 1921; the events of 1923 in Germany and Bulgaria: and the 'bolshevisation' programme of the 5th Congress in 1924.[1]

The defeat of Zinoviev and Kamenev at the 14th Congress of the Soviet Communist Party was not the end of the struggle: it continued for two years more. In the first weeks of 1926 Zinoviev's party machine in Leningrad was destroyed. In April 1926 the faithful remnant of followers of Zinoviev and Kamenev agreed to make common cause with the faithful remnant of Trotskists. Stalin was more than a match for them. The convenient and mysterious death of the Commissar for War, Frunze, enabled Stalin to put his loyal stooge Voroshilov in his place. In July the Zinovievite Lashevich was removed from the post of Deputy Chairman of the Revolutionary War Council, and the Opposition's last hold on the army was lost. In the autumn meetings of oppositionists in the capitals were broken up by lorry-loads of Stalinist toughs, who

[1] For these events, see below, pp. 99–106.

shouted slogans in chorus or deafened the audiences by the hooters of hundreds of vehicles drawn up near the meeting-place. In October there were fights between supporters of Stalin and of the Opposition in Leningrad factories. On 16th October the six Opposition leaders made a retreat. They declared that, though they still held their opinions, they would accept the discipline of the party, as at all costs a schism must be prevented. Trotski and Kamenev were removed from the *Politburo*, and Zinoviev resigned from the chairmanship of the Comintern: he was succeeded in fact though not in name by Buharin.

During 1927 the struggle was revived by matters of foreign policy. The most important of these was the Chinese Revolution. Events in Britain also played some part in the controversy between the Opposition and Stalin.[1] The complete failure of Comintern policy in China, and a series of diplomatic affronts to the Soviet government in the summer of 1927, produced the conviction in Moscow that there was an imminent danger of war. This war scare Stalin fully exploited to his own advantage. At the July Plenum of the Central Committee, Trotski justified his right to attack the government by the experience of Clémenceau, who had overthrown France's incompetent rulers in order to save his country in the First World War. The Plenum however gave the required overwhelming majority to Stalin. In October the Central Committee and Central Control Commission, using the powers granted under the 10th Congress Resolution, expelled the Opposition leaders from the Central Committee. On the 10th anniversary of the November Revolution, 7th November 1927, a few hundred supporters of the Opposition attempted a counter-demonstration in Moscow at the time of the official celebrations. They were deluged with rotten apples and galoshes, with which the Stalinist demonstrators had thoughtfully equipped themselves beforehand. A week later Trotski and Zinoviev were expelled from the party. The 15th Congress of the party, which met in December, duly confirmed this action. In January 1928 Zinoviev and Kamenev abased themselves before Stalin and showered abuse on Trotski. Trotski remained unrepentant. He was banished to Alma Ata in Central Asia, and a year later he was expelled to Turkey.

[1] See below, pp. 106–107, 146–9.

CHAPTER FIVE

Communism in Europe 1921-1933

T HE twenties were a depressing period for European communists. The revolution seemed to be in retreat in Russia, and in Europe the remnant of the revolutionary fervour of 1919 soon fizzled out. The unsuccessful attempts of 1923 in Germany and Bulgaria were mere undistinguished epilogues. Thereafter the European communist parties, and the Comintern itself, were increasingly dominated by the Russian party, and the internal dissensions in the Russian party were reflected in the main European parties. A brief summary of this dreary story is necessary for an understanding of the evolution of world communism.

The crisis of 1921 in Russia still further increased the desire of the Bolshevik leaders for the spread of revolution to Europe. To expedite this process, the Comintern sent Béla Kun to Germany. The fusion of the majority of U.S.P.D. with the original K.P.D. had at last made the German Communist Party a numerous and important mass organisation. At this time there was a group among its leaders who believed that immediate revolutionary action could succeed, and clamoured that the party should 'take the offensive'. Béla Kun urged the same view with the authority of the Comintern behind him. The stronghold of the K.P.D. was in Central Germany, the only industrial region in which it outnumbered all other working-class groups. In March 1921 the German central government decided to reinforce the police in the Mansfeld mining area The miners decided to prevent this by force, and the K.P.D. in agreement with Kun appealed for a general strike to support the miners' fight. The response was extremely small. Not only did the police prove too strong for the miners, but there were tragic fights between unemployed and employed workers: the former in certain cases burst into factories and tried to compel the workers to strike against their will. The whole affair was fiercely denounced by the most eminent of the K.P.D.'s leaders, Paul Levi. His criticisms of the optimistic illusions of those who had ordered the rising, and of needless provocations of the police and army which could and did only bring suffering to the workers, were to some extent upheld by Lenin at the 3rd Congress of the Comintern, which met in June 1921. But Levi himself fell into disgrace because he had dared to place the blame for the disaster on the leadership of the Comintern and of the Russian party.[1] Levi was expelled from the K.P.D. An important step had been taken in subjecting that party to Moscow.

The 3rd Congress denounced left-wing extremism, and urged closer contact between the communist parties and the masses.

The Comintern recommended a policy of 'united front' with non-communist workers' organisations. This has since become a well-known communist tactic. It has two variations—'united front from below' and 'united front from above'. The first is openly directed against socialist leaders, and aims at winning the socialist masses away from them. It combines general arguments for workers' unity with violent abuse of socialist politicians. The second tactic is more subtle. It ostensibly includes co-operation not only with the socialist masses but also with the socialist leaders. It does not openly denounce the leaders to their followers. Its aim however is to gain positions of influence within the united front, in order at a later stage to undermine the authority of the socialist leaders and tear their followers away from them. This tactic was further developed during the 'Popular Front' period of the mid-1930's. In the early 1920's however the two variations had not yet been so clearly differentiated. The tendency was towards the front from below. But in April 1922 the Comintern pursued the attempt at a front from above so far as to negotiate with the Second International and the Vienna Union ('International Two-and-a-half').[2] No agreement was reached, because the non-communists, at the insistence of the Belgian socialist Vandervelde, asked that the Bolsheviks should grant political liberties in Russia.

In October 1922 the Fascists seized power in Italy. During the two years that passed before Mussolini established a complete dictatorship, the Communist Party, which had found in Antonio Gramsci a leader of real ability and broad vision, fought a gallant rearguard action. Sections of the socialist and liberal movements also made belated attempts to fight the tyranny. The great industrial city of Turin was the centre of this resistance, in which not only the workers but a part of the intelligentsia took part. But too

[1] Paul Levi, *Unser Weg wider den Putschismus*, Berlin, 1922.
[2] *The Second and Third Internationals and the Vienna Union, conference of the executives in Berlin*, 1922. The Vienna Union consisted of various left-wing socialist groups, the most important being the Austrian.

many opportunities had been lost in the post-war years, and the enemy was too strong. By 1925 the once impressive labour movement of Italy was in ruins.

During 1922 and 1923 the difference, and at times the conflict, between the policies of the Comintern and the Soviet government in Germany became very clear. The first aimed at a communist revolution. The second, while wishing for such a revolution, was meanwhile concerned to strengthen the Soviet state by exploiting all differences between potentially hostile Powers. The most promising conflict within what Moscow called 'the capitalist camp' was that between defeated Germany and victorious France. German nationalism, as an enemy of the 1918 victors, whom Moscow regarded as its principal enemy, was a potential ally of the Soviet Union. But any German government that sought friendly relations with the Western Powers was a potential enemy of the Soviet Union. Indeed it is no exaggeration to say that there prevailed in Moscow a dogmatic conviction that no agreement between Germany and the West could mean anything else than a preparation for joint military intervention by the Great Powers of Europe against Russia.

In May 1922 the German and Soviet governments signed a treaty at Rapallo. Its importance lay not in its comparatively unimportant text but in the fact that it ended the isolation of both Germany and Russia. In Moscow it was regarded as a foundation on which to build further. In the next months the conflict between Germany and the West about reparations sharpened. In November a government of the Right was formed. Its Chancellor was Cuno, and it was based on the business class. When it stubbornly resisted French claims, Poincaré decided in January 1923 to occupy the Ruhr. There followed passive resistance by the Ruhr population encouraged from Berlin, a catastrophic inflation, and agitation by the extreme German nationalists of the Right.

In this situation the Comintern for a time adopted the tactic known as 'National-Bolshevism'. The German Communist Party made overtures to some of the ex-officers and fascist groups. Karl Radek, the Comintern's German expert, appealed to what he called the 'honest patriotic masses'. During the spring and summer, economic misery brought increased support to the K.P.D., as the most extreme of the workers' parties. But those German workers who supported K.P.D. did so because in their despair they wanted a revolution against their own ruling class, against the great industrialists who were profiting from inflation. This however was

not the first priority for Moscow. Moscow favoured national unity
in Germany because Germany was anti-French and anti-British.
Moscow's view did not change until mid-August. Then a general
strike in Berlin, caused not by K.P.D. but by working-class discontent, led to the resignation of Cuno. He was replaced by Stresemann, also a representative of big business but a believer in co-
operation with the West, in the so-called 'policy of fulfilment'.

Two reasons can thus be found for the sharp change in Moscow's
policy which now ensued. One is that the August strike clearly
showed the revolutionary mood of the German workers: if the
K.P.D. did not put itself at their head it would forfeit their confidence. This consideration was important for the leaders of K.P.D.
But for the Russian party, and so for the Comintern, the second
reason—fear of the foreign policy of the new government—was
perhaps more important. Seeing the possibility of a reconciliation
between Germany and the Versailles victors, which their minds
were not capable of interpreting otherwise than as a plot to en-
circle the Soviet Union, the leaders in Moscow now decided that
a revolution in Germany was desirable. Soviet experts in guerrilla
and street-warfare were sent illegally to Germany. Military detachments of workers were secretly formed, drilled and to some
extent armed. Comintern strategy was that the K.P.D. should
enter into coalition with the regional governments of Saxony and
Thuringia—then held by socialists whose leaders were willing to
co-operate with communists—arm the workers, and create a
territorial base from which to spread the revolution over Germany.
Workers' risings should be simultaneously organised in Berlin,
the Ruhr and Hamburg.[1]

But the commanders-in-chief of world revolution in Moscow
hesitated as to choice of date. Several times action was postponed
on orders from the Comintern. At last in mid-October, when revolutionary feeling in the country had already diminished, and Stresemann had already achieved some success in his efforts to stop
inflation, K.P.D. entered the Saxon and Thuringian governments,
The central government ordered its army to occupy the two provinces. On 21st October a conference of representatives of Works
Councils met in the Saxon town of Chemnitz. The K.P.D. leader

[1] Details on Soviet advice and assistance for guerrilla action, which cannot be confirmed but seem plausible, may be found in Bazhanov, op. cit., pp. 190–205, and in
W. Krivitsky, *I was Stalin's Agent*, 1939, pp. 60–5. For a discussion of Soviet policy
to Germany, see E. H. Carr, *German-Soviet Relations*, 1952, pp. 73–6. Stresemann
proved much less hostile to Moscow, and much less subservient to the West, than
Moscow had feared.

Brandler asked the conference to proclaim a general strike and to support armed insurrection against the central government's action. Himself one of the moderates in the leadership of K.P.D. and a cautious character, Brandler pleaded his cause with little conviction, and the conference rejected it. The K.P.D. then decided to call off the whole rising. The regular troops quietly occupied Saxony and Thuringia, and the coalitions were overthrown. In the Ruhr and Berlin no one stirred. Only in Hamburg, which by an error had received the wrong instructions from the party leaders, a few hundred communists, unsupported by the city's workers, rose and were defeated by the police after three days of sporadic fighting. Thus the last serious plan by the Comintern to make a revolution in Germany ignominiously failed.

The same year witnessed a communist disaster in Bulgaria. In June 1923 Stamboliiski was overthrown by a conspiracy of army officers, middle-class politicians and Macedonian terrorists. As at the time of the 1918 'Radomir republic', the Communist leaders decided that they would remain neutral in a quarrel between the 'urban and rural bourgeoisie'. While the Macedonians massacred the peasants, the workers of the Bulgarian railways and the Sofia factories carried on their work. But the new government quickly abolished many of the liberties that the Agrarian regime had granted both to workers and to peasants. All left groups, communists as well as Agrarians, were repressed. It was soon clear that the communists had missed an opportunity, if not to make a revolution at least to save their liberties. Moreover, as in the case of Germany, international developments caused Moscow to reconsider the situation in Bulgaria. On 24th July 1923 peace was signed at Lausanne between the Western Powers and Turkey. The peace conference, which liquidated the Greek-Turkish war in Anatolia, had been a defeat for Soviet diplomacy in the Straits Question. Worse still, there seemed a prospect of reconciliation between Turkey and the arch-imperialist Power Britain, Soviet Russia's chief adversary in the Near East and Asia. A revolution in the area bordering on Turkey and the Straits became more desirable than ever. The Bulgarian communists were therefore pressed from Moscow to act. During the summer they planned common action with the shattered remnants of the Agrarian Union. The rising took place on 23rd September in north-west Bulgaria. It had no hope at all of success. It was quickly and bloodily suppressed, and followed by ferocious reprisals.

By the end of 1923 hopes of revolution in Europe had been

crushed. The purpose for which the Comintern had been created had not been achieved. Instead of becoming a spearhead of world revolution, an *élite* of professional revolutionaries capable of leading to victory the masses whom the socialist leaders had muddled or betrayed, it had become just a second international labour bureaucracy. In the interests of international labour, the best policy would now have been to dissolve it. But for the Moscow government the Comintern remained a useful weapon of foreign policy. Communist parties must devote themselves above all to fulfilling the 14th of the 21 Conditions of 1920—to protect soviet republics in their struggle against counter-revolution, that is to say, to support Soviet foreign policy. The March action of 1921 in Germany, and the events of 1923 in Germany and Bulgaria, had already shown that the needs of Moscow must determine the time and place of communist action. During the later 1920's, when Europe had attained relative economic and political stability, the outlook for communist parties became very bleak: they could survive only by the material and moral support of Moscow. The vested interest of their leaders' ambitions tied them to Moscow. Thus during these years Soviet domination over the European communist parties was made still more effective. Not only the state interests of Soviet Russia, but the internal struggles of the Russian Communist Party, determined their policies. Not only did their policies depend on Moscow's wishes, but their leaders were imposed on them by Moscow.

THE 5th CONGRESS AND 'BOLSHEVISATION'

The first effects of the dispute between Trotski and the triumvirs on the Comintern were felt in the German party. The disaster of 1923 had of course been due above all to the strength of the opposing forces: no communist revolution could have succeeded at that time. But in so far as the difficulties were aggravated by the faults of the communist leadership, it was, as we have seen, in Moscow rather than in Germany that these were to be found. Moscow however was determined that Trotski's criticisms of the Russian leaders of the Comintern should be denied: all the blame for the defeat must be placed on the German leaders. Brandler and his friends were made the scapegoats. At the 5th Congress of the Comintern, held in June 1924, a new panacea was announced for the international movement. The communist parties must be 'bolshevised'. This magic word was interpreted to mean that the parties must be re-organised on the model of the Russian party, as moulded by Stalin's bureaucrats. When this solemn incantation had been recited, and the necessary ceremonies performed, by the European parties, the elixir of revolution would be in their hands.

The chief victim of this policy was the French party. Already in 1922 discontent had been expressed within the party at the excessive domination by Moscow. In January 1923 Frossard, one of the party's founders, had resigned after he had been fiercely denounced from Moscow because he was a freemason. A group of intellectuals resigned about the same time, with a public protest against interference from Moscow and a warning against the tendency 'to anaemiate and soon to abolish critical sense and the spirit of discussion'. The reorganisation after the 5th Comintern Congress bewildered the party members. Hitherto the party machine had been based on the traditional regional units of France. This system, which seemed to correspond to common sense, was to be replaced by a different hierarchy, in which the basic units were to be party cells in places of work rather than in places of residence. Communists were to be organised by the factory or office rather than by the district. This formal reorganisation was supposed to possess some magic quality which would regenerate and revolutionise the parties. In France it produced only annoyance. In the words of a working-class *militant* of the time, the party had become *un parti pour les types calés*.[1] The confusion was increased by the outbreak of a conflict within the French party between Trotskists and Stalinists.

In July 1925 Boris Souvarine, formerly the party's representative in the Comintern, was expelled from the party. He was followed by the left-wing trade unionists Rosmer and Monatte. Now few remained of the men who had founded the party at the Tours Congress of 1920. The party, which had then had a majority of the French labour movement, was becoming a small sect of fanatics, far inferior in numbers and influence to the Socialist Party.

In the German party the eclipse of the Brandler group was followed by the victory of the left wing, led by the Russian-born Maslow and the Austrian-born Ruth Fischer. Backed at first by the Comintern, they soon fell into disfavour. They did not hesitate to criticise the policy of the Russian party. Following the line of Zinoviev and Kamenev in their conflict with Stalin, they accused it of making a reactionary compromise with the peasantry. Maslow and Ruth Fischer even dared to question the right of the Russian party as such to lead the Comintern. They had ideas of a more 'western' and at the same time more revolutionary tendency

[1] G. Walter, *Histoire du parti communiste français*, Paris, 1948, p. 176.

for the International. This challenge could not be tolerated. Stalin successfully intrigued with their rivals in the party. In 1926 they were expelled from K.P.D.[1] Leadership was thereafter in the safe hands of Ernst Thälmann, a Hamburg worker, brave and honest but stupid and above all obedient to Moscow.

THE BRITISH GENERAL STRIKE

The most important development in Europe that affected the struggle between Stalin and the Opposition, took place in Britain. The growth of radical trends within the British labour movement in the early 1920's, itself a result of the depressed condition of several major British industries and especially of coal-mining, had raised hopes in Moscow of a revolutionary movement in Britain. The British trade unions established relations with the Soviet trade unions. In 1925 an Anglo-Russion trade union committee was set up. The British union leaders wished to create a single world trade union organisation, including the Russian unions and the Comintern-sponsored organisation, the *Profintern*,[2] but failed to overcome the objections of the socialist ('Amsterdam') trade union organisation, the I.F.T.U. The British unions hoped however that the Anglo-Russian Committee would facilitate indirect co-operation between the Russian and European labour movements, and that ultimately unity could be achieved. The hope of the Comintern and of the Russian Communist leaders was that the Committee would be a useful channel for Communist propaganda among the British workers, designed of course to undermine the position of those very British trade union leaders with whom the Russians were supposed to be co-operating through the Committee.

[The radical trend in British labour grew stronger during 1926, and culminated in the General Strike of May. The General Strike however had never been intended by its leaders as a revolutionary bid for power: it was a means of pressure on the government and the employers, and as such it failed. In Moscow exaggerated hopes had been placed in the strike, and the consequent disappointment produced a flood of invective against the leaders of the British unions and of the British Labour Party, who were declared to be traitors to the working class. Trotski, in his *Where is Britain going?* published in 1926, had expressed his confidence that the British Communist Party would win over the masses of the British

---

[1] Ruth Fischer's version of these events is in her *Stalin and German Communism*, Harvard, 1948, pp. 500–8, 553–4, 571–2.
[2] See above, p. 73.

working class from the reformist petty-bourgeois renegades. Not only did this not happen, but Stalin insisted on maintaining the Anglo-Russian Committee after the failure of the strike. Trotski urged that it be dissolved, as co-operation between Communists and the British renegades was inadmissible in principle and would be sterile in practice. Stalin replied that this was 'left-wing infantilism'. Co-operation was of value, as the Russian trade unions reserved the right to criticise the British union leaders, and they had access to the British masses. The Committee could be especially useful in exposing to the British masses the bellicose plans of the British imperialists, who were preparing war against the Soviet Union.[1] The Committee lingered on through most of 1927. As late as August, Stalin argued that it was a useful means of influencing the British masses. But in September the British union leaders themselves decided to dissolve it. The views of Trotski had been shown to be less far from the truth than those of Stalin.

THE 6th CONGRESS AND 'SOCIAL FASCISM'

The war scare of 1927 had a lasting effect on the European communist movement. During the following years it remained a dogma of all communist parties that the Soviet Union was in immediate danger of invasion. This was repeated by the 6th Congress of the Comintern, which met in June 1928. Its Manifesto stated that the capitalist states 'with England at their head' were preparing war against the Soviet Union. The Congress decided that a 'third period' had begun. The first had been the revolutionary period up to 1923, the second the period of stabilisation of capitalism since 1924. This third period was marked by growing contradictions of imperialism and by a sharpening of the class struggle. The Congress launched the slogan 'Class against class'. In Europe this meant a special onslaught against the Social Democratic parties. Social Democracy and Fascism, the Congress pointed out, were two weapons of the bourgeoisie: the first was used to demoralise the working class from within, the second to strike it from without.[2] In the following years, especially in Germany, Communists stressed the parallel roles of Social Democracy and Fascism to the point where the distinction was almost obliterated. In fact the expression 'Social-Fascist' was invented as a term of abuse against German Social Democrats.

The years 1927–32 were worse for the European communists

[1] Stalin, *Ob oppozitsii*, Moscow, 1928, pp. 299–308 and 664–8.
[2] *Protokollen des 6. Weltkongresses der K.I.*, Hamburg, 1929, Vol. IV, pp. 13–44.

than the years 1923–7. The first important set-back occurred in
Poland. In May 1926 Piłsudski seized power. The government he
overthrew was a coalition of the Right, much disliked by the Polish
workers. The Socialists therefore supported Piłsudski, whom their
leaders had never completely ceased to regard as one of themselves.[1] The Communists, obeying the 'united front' tactic, followed the Socialist lead. Their leaders believed that Piłsudski's
rebellion was the beginning of a revolutionary situation, that Piłsudski would prove a sort of Kerenski. Radek pointed out in
Inprecorr[2] the ridiculous ignorance of Piłsudski, who did not realise
that he was the instrument of social forces that would sweep forward to revolution. Piłsudski, poor fellow, thought that he was just
making an old-fashioned military revolt, and that he would be
able to keep events within the framework of 'legality'. Piłsudski
was 'the last Mohican of Polish romanticism': he was 'a joke of
world history'. But Piłsudski did in fact exactly what he had intended. There was no revolution, and the new regime was a
mixture of parliamentary and authoritarian government: as the
years went by the latter trend prevailed. The Polish Communist
Party had a much harder time than before 1926. And as for jokes
of world history, there was one in store for Radek.

To the south of Poland the communist outlook was dim. In
Czechoslovakia the party was free and influential, but it commanded
only part of the working class. In Austria the communists were a
tiny sect in the working class: their contribution to street disorders in Vienna in 1927 did not strengthen them. In Italy and
Hungary communists were cruelly and successfully repressed. In
Bulgaria an attempt on the life of King Boris in Sofia Cathedral in
1925 by two communists led to mass arrests and to persecution of
communists of a cruelty unusual even in Bulgaria. In January 1929
King Alexander of Yugoslavia introduced a dictatorship, and here
too the principal victims were real or alleged communists. In
Roumania a more democratic government came to power in 1928,
but it did not hesitate to repress, with considerable brutality, a
miners' strike in the Jiu valley in 1929. The growing economic
discontent in Roumania swelled the ranks not of the insignificant
Communist Party but of the fascist Iron Guard.

---

[1] Piłsudski had in fact ceased to be a socialist already before 1914: formally the
breach was complete in 1918. As he himself put it to his socialist ex-comrades, 'You
and I were passengers on the same train. When it got to "Independence" station, I
got off, but you went on.'

[2] *Inprecorr*, 1926, No. 44. 'Piłsudski's victory', by Kark Radek.

It was in Germany that communist imbecility reached its peak. During the last years of the Weimar Republic, while Hitler's Nazis were becoming a power in the land, communist hatred was directed at the 'Social-Fascists'. In this the K.P.D. were only obeying Comintern orders. The 11th Plenum of the Comintern in March-April 1931 stated that the social democrats were the most active of the German parties in the preparation of aggression against the Soviet Union. This curious belief can only be explained by the prevalence in Moscow of the old dogma that co-operation between Germany and the Western Powers must always be designed to organise a joint attack on the Soviet Union. As the social democrats were in fact the German party most eager for good relations with France and Britain, it must follow that the social democrats were preparing such an attack.

The true significance of events in Germany was lost to the communists. This was that the misery of the economic depression was driving the masses not to the communists but to the Nazis. The latter not only appealed to the despairing middle class, which had been ruined once by the inflation of 1923 and saw itself again threatened with destruction, but also enlisted many thousands of unemployed workers, for whom the trade unions had been unable to do anything, and who listened eagerly to the Nazi denunciations of the social democratic bosses (*Bonzen*) and Judeo-Marxist agents of Moscow. The Nazis appeared as a serious force in the election of 1930, with 105 seats to the Communists' 77. But the K.P.D. continued obediently to direct its fire against the social democrats. In April 1931 it told its supporters to vote in favour of the referendum initiated by Nazis and Nationalists for the overthrow of the legally elected government of Prussia, then in social democratic hands. The referendum was not successful. In 1932, when the reactionary Chancellor von Papen arbitrarily dissolved the Prussian government, and the socialists tamely submitted, the Communists made the empty gesture of proposing a general strike. At the parliamentary election of July 1932 the Communist seats increased from 77 to 89, the Nazis from 105 to 230: this the K.P.D. regarded as a triumph for themselves. In October they supported the Nazis in a transport strike in Berlin. At the second parliamentary election of the year, held in November, Communist strength increased to 100 seats, while the Nazis actually lost ground. There was thus a real though slight swing of opinion to the left. This would have been the time to suggest common action by the workers' parties, to smash the fascists and make a proletarian revolution. But the K.P.D. stuck to the Comintern line, and in January 1933 Adolf Hitler peacefully became Chancellor of Germany.

CHAPTER SIX

Nationalism and Revolution in Asia

WHETHER Europe is more than a geographical expression, is a question on which wise men and women can disagree in good faith. Against the diversity of nations, classes and churches may be set the unifying factor of a common cultural heritage. But that Asia is nothing but a geographical expression there can be no doubt. The Chinese, Hindu and Moslem civilisations differ as much from each other as from the civilisation of Europe or of any part of Europe.

This is no place to sum up these civilisations, nor is the present writer qualified to make the attempt. But no account of Asian communism can make sense without some reference to its general background. No doubt the social and political development of Asia in the nineteenth and twentieth centuries has been influenced at least as much by centuries of Buddhist, Hindu and Moslem thought and action as by the impact of the western world. Yet in the relatively narrow field of social and political history in this period the countries of Asia and of Moslem North Africa strikingly resemble both each other and the less developed countries of Europe. The impact of the West has everywhere had a similar effect and it is the impact of the West that forms the background to the rise of communism outside Europe. The similarities were of course noted by the leaders of the Comintern, who reduced them to formulae much simpler than the reality. The formulae deserve careful attention, and something will be said of them in later chapters. But they are an incomplete explanation of the events. Something more is needed. The following brief survey of Asia, and of Moslem North Africa, which is its westward extension, in the early 1920's, is based on much the same principles as the survey of Europe before 1914 in the first chapter. It inevitably underrates, and perhaps even ignores, historical and cultural factors that profoundly affect the social and political mentality of Asian and Moslem peoples. Yet the attempt must be risked, in the hope that it will clarify rather

111

than obscure the significance of the communist movements that
arose in these lands.

SOCIAL CLASSES

The most advanced economy among the states of Asia in the
1920's was that of Japan, which was of the mixed industrial-agrarian
type. In 1920 slightly more than half the population were employed
in agriculture, and about one-third in industry, mining, transport
and commerce. In 1936 these two groups each employed about 44
per cent of the population.[1] In some other Asiatic countries there
were, as in Eastern Europe before 1914, industrial islands which
exercised some influence on the surrounding countryside. Obvious
examples are the great ports of China and India. But away from
these islands Asia remained almost completely agricultural.

In Asia's agrarian society the social class that had most economic
power was that which owned most land. But the wealth, influence and
origin of landowners varied exceedingly. In Japan a form of feudalism, which had points of resemblance with the feudalism of medieval
Europe, survived until 1869. When feudal institutions were swept
away by the Japanese modernisers, the former feudal lords retained
substantial amounts of land. But Japan did not possess vast *lati-
fundia* of the Russian, Hungarian or Spanish type. In China the
largest landowners were members of the class of gentry-officials,
or in more recent times military officers. Their estates too were of
modest proportions, with the partial exception of Manchuria. In
India on the other hand vast estates did exist, and were a result of
British rule. Before the British conquest, Indian rulers had assigned
the tax revenue from whole districts to notables, the *zemindars*,
who paid the government its due and made what profit they could
from the population. These tax-farmers were treated by the British
as legal owners of the land they taxed—a status which they had not
previously enjoyed but now exploited in order to make great fortunes.[2] Another country of wealthy estates was Egypt. Already in
the early nineteenth century the modernising pasha Mohammed

---

[1] The following figures are based on a table in G. C. Allen, *A Short Economic History
of Japan*, 1946, p. 164. The numbers employed in the main categories were as follows
(to the nearest 100,000):

	1920	1930	1936 (estimate)
Agriculture, forestry and fishing...	14,700,000	14,700,000	14,700,000
Mining, manufacturing, commerce and transport	9,900,000	11,500,000	13,080,000
Public services and professions ...	1,000,000	1,000,000	2,100,000

[2] See Zinkin, *Asia and the West*, 1951, pp. 84–7; A. R. Desai, *The Social Background
of Indian Nationalism*, Bombay, 1948, pp. 157–160.

Ali had given to the large landowners more secure ownership than they had had under the previous Ottoman regime, and had enabled them greatly to increase their estates by bringing further land under cultivation in favourable conditions. In the 1920's about a quarter of the arable land was held by large landowners.[1] In Persia most cultivable land belonged to landowners, little to peasant owners.[2] In the Ottoman Empire, in Central Asia under the Russian Empire, and in Moslem North Africa, various types of land tenure existed, including forms of private ownership, communal ownership and tribal property. Large landowners or tribal chiefs were the leading social figures. Religious organisations also owned, or had the use of, considerable areas.

European conquest and the penetration of capitalism into Asian economies produced new forms of wealth in land. The introduction of British law into India and Burma made possible the mortgaging and sale of land, which had been unknown in earlier times, and gave in practice far more effective protection to the moneylender than to the peasant. Millions of formerly landowning Indian peasants became tenants of moneylenders. In Madras province in the depression of the 1930's 40 per cent of the land was sold, and half of this went to non-agricultural persons.[3] In Burma it was found that in 1931 56 per cent of the land in the fertile Delta was owned by non-agriculturists.[4]

In certain regions European landowners were an important element. The earliest of these were the Spaniards in the Philippines, who created *estancias* of the type that became so important during the same centuries in South America. In the nineteenth century appeared the plantations—British tea in India and rubber in Malaya, Dutch coffee and sugar in Java, French rubber in Indochina. In North Africa tens of thousands of Frenchmen settled, not only large landowners but also small farmers.

European influence—direct conquest in the colonies, indirect domination in all the still independent states except Japan—brought very substantial benefits to the Asian peasant masses. Public peace, better transport, and the beginnings of medical services at least weakened their three traditional enemies, war, famine

---

[1] Doreen Warriner, *Land and Poverty in the Middle East*, 1948, p. 35. Owners of more than 50 acres were 0·5 per cent of all landholders, and possessed 37 per cent of the arable land More than 20 per cent of the arable land belonged to owners of more than 200 acres.

[2] See R. N. Gupta, *Iran, An Economic Study*, New Delhi, 1947, pp. 42–7. Also article by G. Hadary, 'The Agrarian Reform Problem in Iran', in *Middle East Journal*, Spring, 1951 issue.

[3] Zinkin, op. cit., p. 84.   [4] Harvey, *British Rule in Burma*, 1946, p. 52.

and disease. But this proved a mixed blessing, for the consequent growth of population pressed on available resources. Undeveloped areas, such as the Deltas of the Irawaddy in Burma and the Mekong in Indochina, or the plains of Manchuria, provided an outlet for a time, and the world economy into which Asia was increasingly drawn has offered many new means of livelihood. But from the end of the nineteenth century the tendency towards overpopulation has been unmistakable. The other evil which western influence has brought to the peasant has been indebtedness. This has been mentioned in connection with India and Burma. It was also a terrible scourge in China. In Japan and Indonesia its effects were not so grave, for the governments of both these countries took steps to prevent the alienation of land, which if by no means wholly successful at least mitigated the evil.

Industrial workers became an important class in Japan by the 1920's. The number employed in factories—which does not include miners, dockers or railwaymen—grew from 400,000 in 1900 to 1,600,000 in 1919 and 2,900,000 in 1937.[1] In India in the same period there was a similar increase—from 400,000 to 2,500,000.[2] This was of course a much smaller proportion of a much larger population, yet was a notable growth. The great majority of the new workers of Asia were unskilled recruits from the villages. Like the corresponding groups in Eastern Europe, they mostly had the outlook of peasants, and returned to the village when employment was scarce. They came to the towns to earn enough cash to pay taxes and buy the few town-made goods that their families needed: the food of their families was provided by the small landholding which they owned or rented. They were therefore content with a wage less than would support their families. They served as a reserve of cheap labour, pressing on the wage level of those who depended entirely on wages. But though the Asian workers were mostly unskilled, and their standard of living was not higher than that of the peasants, they were gradually being transformed into a class distinct from the peasantry. Dockers, miners and agricultural labourers of the plantations were all more concentrated, and thus more accessible to political ideas, than peasant smallholders. The minority of skilled workers provided some of their leaders.

Asian business classes were also emerging, especially in Japan and to a lesser extent in China and India. Industrialisation was part of the modernisation which Japan's new rulers pushed ahead

[1] Allen, op. cit., p. 167.   [2] Zinkin, op, cit., p. 25.

from the 1880's onwards. Even more than Imperial Russia, Imperial Japan regarded industrial growth as a valuable means to strengthen the state. Already before the Meiji Restoration of 1868—which inaugurated systematic modernisation in Japan— there had been a considerable class of wealthy merchants. The new regime used the wealth and the commercial experience of these men to build the new economic machine. They were rewarded for their services by grants or cheap sales of valuable assets. As in Imperial Russia, though industry and trade were closely controlled by the state, the ownership of factories and mines was mostly in private hands. The most successful of the new Japanese businessmen built enormous fortunes, and by the second decade of the twentieth century had attained considerable political influence. At the head of the Japanese business class were the so-called *zaibatsu*, monster concerns with a wide range of industrial, trading and banking interests.[1] In China industry was largely in foreign hands, but Chinese business men were becoming both wealthy and influential. One type of Chinese capitalist was the so-called *compradore*, who acted as a middleman between foreign interests and the Chinese market, and in some cases attained so much wealth and influence as to be a major social factor in his own right. In India the pioneers of modern capitalism were the British, the competition of whose wares at first destroyed much of the industry and trade that India had had in an earlier age. The first mining enterprises and textile factories in India were British, but after a time Indian business men began to compete. A landmark was the foundation in 1911 by Indian capital of the Tata iron and steel works.

The two remaining social groups of importance in Asia were, as in Russia and in eastern and southern Europe, the intelligentsia and the bureaucracy. Their significance can best be explained by a brief discussion of education and of political systems.

EDUCATION

Education in Asia had been traditionally the task of religious organisations. A few words must here be spent on the religious geography of the continent.

The Moslem world stretched from Central Asia—Russian or Chinese—through Afghanistan, northern India, Persia and the

---

[1] The Mitsui and Mitsubishi concerns, the largest and best known of the *zaibatsu*, had a wide range of interests, comprising 'mining, metals, mechanical engineering, electrical apparatus and machinery, textiles, paper, cement, glass, chemicals, shipbuilding, shipping, foreign and domestic trade, banking and insurance'. (Allen, op. cit., p. 127.)

Arab lands as far as the Atlantic. It also included part of the East Indies, especially Java, which had adopted Islam in the fifteenth century. Education was based on the Koranic schools. Some centres of Moslem learning, such as the medieval university of Al-Azhar in Cairo, still enjoyed prestige in the twentieth century by virtue of their great past.[1] In China there was an ancient and well developed system of schools, based on the philosophy of Confucius and his disciples and designed especially to train scholar-administrators. Confucianism had also made an impression on the culture of Japan. The south-east was the main stronghold of Buddhism. In Ceylon, Burma and Siam Buddhist monasteries were important centres of learning, and monastery schools maintained a high proportion of literacy among the people.[2] In India, the birth place of Buddhism, this religion had become extinct about the seventh century. In China and Japan a form of Buddhism more complicated than that of the south-eastern lands became a strong but not a dominant influence. To some extent it modified, and was modified by, Chinese Confucian and Japanese traditional teachings.[3] In Hindu India education was complicated by the caste system, higher forms of learning being reserved for Brahmins. At one time Hinduism was dominant in Java and in Cambodia, but it was replaced in the first by Islam and in the second by Buddhism.[4]

Christianity was the youngest of Asia's religions. Nestorian Christians made some converts in the eighth century in China, but persecution and indifference defeated them. The Christian communities of Armenia, Georgia and the Lebanon were no more than isolated outposts of the Byzantine or Latin world on the fringe of Asia. But the coming of the Portuguese and Spaniards in the sixteenth century brought a serious Christian onslaught on the East. The Spaniards were successful in the Philippines, which have remained to this day a predominantly Catholic country, the only

---

[1] Al-Azhar was founded in the tenth century under the Fatimid dynasty that then ruled Egypt. After more than a hundred years of brilliance it entered on a period of decline, still further accentuated under Turkish rule after 1517. During the nineteenth century it recovered influence throughout the Moslem world. Though the quality of its teaching has varied, it has the advantages of a long continuous history and worldwide prestige.

[2] For a brief discussion of Buddhist education see J. S. Furnivall, *Educational Progr ss in South-East Asia*, New York, 1943, pp. 13–15.

[3] For a brief account of Buddhist influence in China and in Japan, and the interaction between Buddhism and native religions and moral traditions, see C. P. Fitzgerald, *China, a Short Cultural History*, 1935, pp. 270–86; Sir G. Sansom, *The Western World and Japan*, 1950, pp. 122–6, 218–19, 511–13.

[4] For a brief account of Hindu influence in South-East Asia, and of the rise and fall of the medieval kingdoms of Cambodia and Java, see Rawlinson, *India, a Short Cultural History*, pp. 147–54.

large Christian region in Asia. The Portuguese had at first great success in Japan, but savage persecution in the seventeenth century destroyed their handiwork. In more recent times Christianity has made little impression in India or the Far East. The only sign of success was the Taiping Rebellion of the 1850's in China, which was fought in the name of a sort of Christian doctrine.[1] Minor exceptions to the rule of Christian failure were the conversion of the Karens in Burma, and of some hundreds of thousands in Indochina.

The schools of the eastern religions were adequate for the needs of their civilisations. The Moslem, Buddhist and Confucian systems were open to persons of talent from humble families: only the Hindu system was socially exclusive. But none were suited to the needs of the new age of the supremacy of Europe. The impact of the West was bound to bring great changes in education, both in those lands which became colonies of Europe and in those which remained independent.

In the colonies missionary zeal and the desire for economic development favoured change, while the cautious respect of new rulers for old civilisations favoured conservatism. In India a landmark was the Despatch of 1854 which accepted the principle that the government must provide a system of western education for the people of India. After the Mutiny of 1857 policy was more cautious, and in any case the task was so vast that progress could not be rapid. Yet solid foundations were laid. In Burma the Indian model was on the whole followed. In Indochina the chief emphasis was laid on the spreading of French culture: the French had fewer doubts of their cultural superiority over their Asian subjects than had the British. The Dutch in Java were much more cautious. Education of the Javanese was left as far as possible to the native Moslem schools. But the presence of large Dutch and Eurasian populations—proportionately far larger than the corresponding elements in British or French colonies—created a demand for European schools, and these soon affected the education of the Javanese. In the twentieth century western education made great strides in all these territories. Universities were founded at Hanoi in 1907, at Rangoon in 1920, and at Batavia in the 1920's.[2] The Philippines remained far in advance of the other colonies. The Uni-

---

[1] See Fitzgerald, op. cit., pp. 562–79.
[2] The University of Hanoi was more than once closed and reorganised, but was in action from the late 1930's. In Batavia an Engineering and a Law College were founded in 1924, a Medical College in 1926, and a united university at the end of the 1930's. See Furnivall, op. cit., pp. 80, 87.

versity of St. Thomas in Manila dated from the seventeenth century, and the Catholic Church controlled by the end of the nineteenth century an impressive system of schools. When the Philippines were taken from Spain by the United States in 1898 much greater sums were spent on education. The religious schools with instruction in Spanish remained, but state schools, and a State University—founded in 1908—grew up beside them, with instruction in English.[1]

Of the independent countries the first whose ruler attempted to found a western system of education was Egypt. Mohammed Ali took France as his model. His efforts were not very successful, but they formed a first foundation on which later rulers built. He also sent numbers of Egyptians to study abroad, and this produced the first generation of westernised intellectuals. Japan's reformers devoted the same energy to education as to industrialisation: their motive was the same—to strengthen the Japanese state. The landmark was the education law of 1886, on the basis of which was built an efficient system of primary, secondary and higher education. In the twentieth century the Japanese have been a literate nation. In China and the Ottoman Empire less was achieved. Chinese and Turkish subjects studied abroad, and European and American private schools and colleges were founded on Chinese and Turkish territory. Outstanding examples are the Jesuit University of St. Joseph and the American Syrian Protestant College, both established in Beirut in the third quarter of the nineteenth century.[2] In China both Catholic and Protestant missions were important centres of modern knowledge. But the Chinese and Ottoman states did not accomplish much for the modern education of their subjects.

It is important to note that, in independent and colonial countries alike, relatively much more was done for higher than for elementary education.

The country in which this contrast is least striking is Japan, the only Asian country which built a system of modern popular education. Here the motive was clearly political. The Japanese reformers noted the contribution that schools had made to the greatness of Prussia. Japanese school-children were not only taught the 'three R's': they were systematically indoctrinated with the principles of loyalty to the Emperor. It is interesting to note that the leaders of Japan paid so much more attention to education than

[1] See J. R. Hayden, *The Philippines*, New York, 1942, Chapters 21 and 23.
[2] The American mission was established since 1820, and founded the college in 1866. The first Jesuit school in Beirut was opened in 1839, the University of St. Joseph in 1875. G. Antonius, *The Arab Awakening*, 1938, pp. 41–5.

did the rulers of Imperial Russia, whose economic modernisation coincided so closely in time with that of Japan, and was inspired by the same motive—imperial greatness.

The contrast elsewhere in Asia between the relative development of elementary and higher education was not mainly due to any reactionary prejudice of the rulers in favour of the education of the privileged classes. The colonial governments frequently expressed their conviction that more attention should be paid to the education of the masses. The obstacles were of two kinds. One was financial: the cost of creating sufficient elementary schools in India was more than any government, however prosperous, could undertake in a short time. The other obstacle was the indifference of the peasants. In Burma, for example, the state primary schools, founded in accordance with a law of 1871, were miserably attended.[1] Children were needed in the fields, and their parents were unwilling to let them go. Transport was also in many cases a difficult problem. These were the same obstacles that existed in Eastern Europe, where, as we have seen, the same disproportion between higher and elementary education prevailed. In the case of Japan the overriding drive for imperial greatness overcame these obstacles. Colonial governments and decaying Asian monarchies did not feel the drive.

Though the numbers of secondary school and university students enormously increased, the quality of their learning was by no means satisfactory. Higher education in Europe was the product of a long tradition: even modern natural science had its roots in earlier centuries. Western higher education was imported into Asia ready-made. The cultural traditions from which it emerged did not exist in Asia, and the cultural traditions of Asia were not linked to it. Western education, including knowledge of the English, French or Dutch language, was chiefly regarded as a means to get relatively well paid jobs in towns. Secondary schools and universities were thronged by those whose ambition was to become a clerk, a petty official or a lawyer. Education was a preparation not for life but for a job. The best minds of course rose above the narrow materialism and worship of success that these conditions favoured, but in Asia as everywhere in the world the best minds were a small minority.

The same causes that we have already noted for the frustration of the intelligentsia in Eastern Europe,[2] existed to an even greater extent in Asia. The gap between the centuries was even greater.

---

[1] Furnivall, op. cit., pp. 55–8.   [2] See above, pp. 8–9.

If the graduates of modern schools and universities were living at least on the threshold of the twentieth century, their compatriots in the Asian villages were living as their ancestors had lived for a millennium or longer. As the numbers of graduates increased, the competition for jobs became fiercer, and the overproduction of intellectuals and semi-intellectuals became an acute social and political problem. In the colonial countries these two types of dis-content were aggravated by the stigma of alleged inferiority to the white man: resentment of this had both its ideal and its personal aspects. This factor was less important in the independent countries but it played some part there too, even in Japan, whose destiny lay in the hands of its own rulers, not of foreigners.

In Asia still more than in eastern and southern Europe, it was the intelligentsia, the product of western influence, that provided the leadership of national and social revolutionary movements.

POLITICAL SYSTEMS

There is an obvious distinction between independent and colonial countries, but the distinction was less clear in practice than in theory. On the one hand Japan was clearly independent, and by her victory over Russia in 1904 established her status as a Great Power. On the other hand the European colonies in south-east Asia and protectorates in North Africa and Arabia, and the Japanese colonies of Korea and Formosa, were clearly not in-dependent. But several important states occupied an intermediate position. China possessed the largest population, and the second largest territory, in the world, while both the Ottoman Empire and Persia were large states with an ancient and glorious history. Yet all three were subject to constant interference by the European Powers or by Japan. Their peoples were increasingly aware that their independence was more formal than real, and increasingly resentful of the fact. The smaller states Afghanistan and Siam enjoyed greater independence in their internal affairs, though their foreign policy was at the mercy of foreign Powers, the first of Britain or Russia the second of Britain or France.

Japanese government until the Restoration was feudal. The effective ruler since the twelfth century had been the *Shogun*, whose power was of military origin.[1] Bound to him by military obligations were the great lords or holders of fiefs, the *daimyo*, the most important of whom were great territorial magnates. These were served in turn by larger numbers of lesser nobility, or

[1] On the institution of the shogunate, see Sansom, op. cit., pp.191–8.

samurai. Both these categories were supported by the tribute of the peasants. After 1868 the tribute was abolished, and the government's financial support to the *samurai* commuted. They were forced to seek new occupations. The situation of the Japanese *samurai* thus closely resembled that of the smaller nobility of Russia, Poland and Hungary, mentioned earlier.[1] Like their European counterparts, they became army officers and bureaucrats, to some extent intellectuals or business men. Like their European counterparts, their economic position was that of a middle class, but their mentaility was that of rulers. Like their European counterparts, they were the most determined exponents of nationalism, and later imperialism.

Japan adopted in 1889 a Constitution not unlike that of Prussia. The resemblance was due not only to conscious imitation but also to a certain similarity of social structure and of military traditions.[2] The franchise was restricted, government was not responsible to parliament, and the Emperor had a veto power. The most important political body in the country were the *Genro*, or Elder Statesmen, who were consulted by the Emperor on all major issues of policy, and overruled not only parliamentary opinion but also the views of Ministers who were not of their number. The army and navy were beyond the control of civilian ministers.[3] Even so, the habit of parliamentary procedure made some impression on Japanese political life. Political parties were formed. After 1918 the party politicians predominated in the government, and after the death of the leading Elder Statesman, Prince Yamagata, the founder of the modern Japanese army, in 1922, a period of comparatively liberal government began. In this period the business class, especially the *zaibatsu* trusts, played a more active political part. In 1925 universal suffrage was adopted.

In China the traditional form of government was bureaucratic. The administration was conducted by Confucian scholars, who had a high standard of efficiency and honesty. Western influences slowly undermined this regime. The greatest blow was the Taiping rebellion of 1853 to 1860. This was both a religious and a social movement. The Taipings' religion was a form of crude Christianity; their social support came from the impoverished peasantry of the

[1] See above, pp. 3–4, 8.
[2] This point is discussed by Sansom, op. cit., pp. 381–2.
[3] The Ministers of War and Navy could only be members of their Services. If a Minister of War or Navy resigned, and his Service refused to nominate a successor, government became impossible. Army and Navy could use this threat to impose its will on any civilian Ministry in any matter on which they felt strongly.

Yangtse valley. For some years they held the most important provinces of China. The Manchu dynasty finally defeated them, with some help from the European Powers. Though the dynasty survived for another fifty years, the old regime never really recovered. The demand for reform came chiefly from young intellectuals who had received a western education, either at western schools in China or by studying in America, Europe or Japan. For the 'hundred days' of June to September 1898 the Reformers, led by Kang Yu-wei, held power under the young emperor Kwang Hsue. But the emperor was overthrown by his aunt, the Dowager Empress Tze Hsi, and the Reformers were executed or imprisoned. The anti-foreign 'Boxer' movement of 1900 was encouraged by the Dowager Empress, who thus succeeded in diverting popular discontent from reform and against the Europeans. After the European Powers had sent military contingents to suppress the Boxers, the disintegration of the old regime was still more rapid. The competitive examination system was abolished, and public offices were distributed on a sort of spoils system. Military officers began to dominate civil government.[1]

In 1911 the Manchu dynasty was overthrown, and the Republic of China was proclaimed. But this was only the beginning of a long period of anarchy. The republican politicians were enthusiastic democratic intellectuals. Prominent among them was Sun Yat-sen, who had engaged in miscellaneous revolutionary activities since 1895 and had picked up various ideas in Japan, America and Europe. In 1912 he founded the Kuomintang, by combining several groups of different shades of political and social radicalism. The Kuomintang was the strongest party in the Chinese parliament elected in 1913, and supported the candidacy of a reforming general, Yuan Shih-kai, to the Presidency of the Republic. Yuan however soon deprived the Kuomintang of its seats in parliament, and made himself the dictator of China with the approval of the European Powers. After Yuan's death China was divided between different groups of generals, conspicuous for political intrigue rather than military prowess.

In the great periods of China's history, government had always been civilian. Only in periods of anarchy, between the fall of one dynasty and the rise of another, had the military power prevailed over the civil. China had now entered one such period: it was to

_____

[1] For accounts of this stage of Chinese political development, see A. N. Holcombe, *The Chinese Revolution*, Harvard, 1930, pp. 120–55; M. N. Roy, *Revolution and Counter-Revolution in China*, Calcutta, 1948, Chapters 9, 10, 11.

last for many years. At the end of the First World War, one group of generals, based on Peking, dominated the north, and relied on support from the Japanese, who had used the preoccupation of the Powers in Europe to seize territory for themselves. In the south, Canton was for a time the centre of a government based on a compromise between Sun Yat-sen and local warlords.

Both in India and in the Moslem world the traditional form of government had been despotic monarchy based on military power and a machinery of tax collection. This regime survived in Persia and the Ottoman Empire until the twentieth century. In India and south-east Asia the European colonial Powers took over the old machine and adapted it to their own use. Liberal opinion in the home countries exercised ever stronger pressure on them to liberalise the regime in the Asiatic dependencies. The development of a modern economy, at least in the great cities, and the formation by modern education of Indian and south-east Asian intelligentsias, created a local demand for democratic institutions and for an increasing measure of national self-government. The double pressure, from Europe and from Asia, produced results. Landmarks were the Montagu-Chelmsford report on India of 1918, which led to the establishing of a new constitutional regime in the following year; the Burmese Constitution of 1923, which followed similar lines; and the system of *Volksraad* and Regency Councils introduced in Java from 1916 onwards.

ASIAN NATIONALIST MOVEMENTS

Nationalism is an European export to Asia, which hardly has its equivalent in Asian history. The states of Asia were seldom ethnically homogeneous. Surrounded by sea, Japan possessed a natural unity. In China, centuries of centralised government and the use of a single written language had prevailed over racial and linguistic diversity, and had created something that could be described without gross inaccuracy as a Chinese nation. Elsewhere diversity was in most cases stronger than unity. The great empires of India's long history had not ruled the whole sub-continent: this was achieved for the first time by the British. Indochina and Indonesia are European creations. But as young men of these countries acquired a western education, they began to think in terms of Indian or Indonesian nations. The independence from foreign rule which was their aim, must embrace the whole territory ruled by the foreign Power. If the British or Dutch pointed to the diversity, as an obstacle to quick independence, they were accused of a machiavellian desire to divide and rule.

Asia is strewn with religious and linguistic minorities. North Africa has its Arabs and Berbers; Persia its Persians, Kurds and Turks; Burma its Burmese, Karens and mountain tribes. The Arab lands have their Armenian, Coptic and other groups, their Sunni and Shia Moslems, their Orthodox, Catholic and Nestorian Christians. India is divided not only between Hindus and Moslems but also between dozens of different languages. In south-east Asia European colonial rule enabled Asian colonists to establish themselves in commerce—the Indians in Burma and the Chinese in Malaya, Indochina and Indonesia. Independent Siam also had a large Chinese minority of recent origin. Finally in certain areas Europeans had not only provided soldiers and administrators and merchants, but had come to settle in large numbers. The Dutch in Java and the French in North Africa are the obvious examples.

The presence of minorities did not however prevent the development of powerful nationalist movements among the majorities. A few words on these must conclude this survey of the Asian background.

The first form of Moslem reaction against western ascendancy was the Panislamism of the end of the nineteenth century.[1] This however broke up into the three currents of Arab, Persian and Turkish nationalism.

The first stronghold of Arab nationalism was Egypt, which under Mohammed Ali and his successors, and after 1882 under British protectorate, evolved separately from the Arab lands which were part of the Ottoman or French empires. Its exponents were the Arabic language newspapers of Cairo and the Moslem university of Al-Azhar. The intellectual and commercial middle class of Egypt, which included Christian Copts as well as Moslems, was larger and more influential than that of other Arab lands.[2] When the request of the Egyptian nationalist leader, Saad Zaghlul, to lead a delegation to plead for Egypt's full independence at the Paris Peace Conference was refused, widespread strikes and disorders broke out in March 1919. Though suppressed by British

---

[1] The ideological pioneer of Panislamism was the reformer and writer, Djemaladdin al-Afghani, who spent many years in Persia, Turkey and Egypt. Panislamism was exploited, less from conviction than for its tactical utility, by the Ottoman Sultan, Abdul Hamid (1876–1909).

[2] Not only Moslems, but Lebanese Christians, played a part in the movement, especially through their influence on the Cairo Press.

troops, they revealed the popularity of the nationalists. The nationalist party, the Wafd,[1] dominated the Egyptian scene from this time. In Syria and Mesopotamia Arab nationalism, directed during the war against the Turks and afterwards against the British and French mandatory Powers, grew in strength. In French North Africa the earliest nationalist group were the Young Tunisians, formed in 1907. Tunisian nationalism grew during the following decade. In 1920 was founded the Liberal Constitutional Party, or *Destur*.

The origins of Turkish nationalism were in Russian territory. The most advanced, in education and in social structure, of all the Turkish peoples[2] were the Tatars of the Volga. Already before 1905 there had developed a democratic and modernist movement among the Tatars, with its centre in Kazan and with a following in the Crimea, Azerbaidjan and even in the Emirate of Bokhara. But the nationalist movement of the Volga and Ural peoples was crushed first by Kolchak and then by the Bolsheviks; Crimea and Azerbaidjan were conquered by the Red Army; and the 'Young Bokhara' movement, after a short period of co-operation with the Bolsheviks, was also suppressed.[3] Turkish nationalism was confined to Anatolia, where it won mass support only after the Ottoman Empire had lost both its European and its Arab provinces. The Young Turks who made the Revolution of 1908 and overthrew Sultan Abdul Hamid were democrats and modernists, intellectuals influenced by western ideas, but they could not bring themselves to abandon Ottoman imperialism. It was one of their younger disciples, the brilliant soldier Mustafa Kemal, who raised the standard of Turkish nationalism, liberated Anatolia from the Greeks in 1922, and carried through by ruthless means a political and cultural revolution. Though it consciously appealed only to Anatolian Turks, Kemalism by its sensational victories and reforms exercised a great influence on the whole Moslem world.

The Persian reformers were disciples of the panislamic moderniser Djemaladdin-al-Afghani.[4] The movement for a Persian Constitution won a first victory in 1906, when the Shah agreed to institute

[1] Wafd is the Arabic word for 'delegation'.
[2] The languages of Volga, Crimean and Azerbaidjani Tatars, of Uzbeks, Kazakhs and Kirgiz, resemble each other and Anatolian Turkish approximately as languages in the Latin group or in the Slav group. Of the Moslem peoples of Russia, all but the Tadjiks—who have a language akin to Persian—and the North Caucasians—who have numerous unique languages—belong to the Turkish-Tatar group. For an account of Turkish nationalist and modernist movements in pre-1917 Russia, see G. von Mende, *Der nationale Kampf der Russlandtürken*, Berlin, 1936. There is a brief survey in my *Decline of Imperial Russia*, 1952, pp. 163–4, 240, 306–7.
[3] See above, p. 87 and footnote.   [4] See above, p. 124, footnote.

a National Assembly. In July 1909, when he attempted to dissolve the Assembly by force, a revolution took place in Teheran, supported by some of the southern tribes, and the Shah was forced to abdicate in favour of his twelve-year-old son. But in the following years the democrats quarrelled with each other, and the intervention of Russia, which under the Anglo-Russian Convention of August 1907 received a sphere of influence over northern Persia, paralysed their efforts.[1] During the First World War Persian politics were hopelessly confused, and the survival of the country as an independent state remained uncertain.

The Indian National Congress, founded in 1885, at first made moderate demands for self-government, then for Dominion status. Its most radical wing began to speak of complete independence already before the war, but this was not for many years the official aim of the party. The Constitution of 1919 did not satisfy Congress. The growing strength, and the growing radicalism, of Congress was shown in the campaign of 'non-co-operation' organised by its leader Gandhi in 1921.

In Burma and Indochina nationalist movements were only in their infancy in the years following the war. More important was Moslem nationalism in Java. The organisation founded in 1909, which took two years later the name *Sarekat Islam*, pursued at first cultural and economic, not political aims. It was designed both to defend Moslem culture and to protect Javanese merchants against the competition of the Chinese.[2] It soon however became a centre of nationalist politics, and a strong minority within its ranks fiercely attacked Dutch rule. From opposition to local Chinese capitalists it passed to opposition to capitalism in general.

These Asian nationalist movements bore a more or less democratic stamp. The autonomy or independence at which they aimed was conceived in terms of western parliamentarism. They also had slogans of social reform, but the idea of the class struggle within the ranks of the nation was as yet little known. The leaders were intellectuals or merchants. They regarded themselves as leaders of their nations, and their nations as units—including within them the various linguistic or religious groups that had long been established in their countries. There was hardly a trace of Marxism in these movements. But the growing bitterness of their struggles certainly gave them a revolutionary character.

[1] An interesting and detailed account of these events is E. Browne, *The Persian Revolution*, 1910.

[2] G. Bousquet, *La politique musulmane et coloniale des Pays-Bas*, Paris, 1939, pp. 8–10.

CHAPTER SEVEN

Communism in Asia 1919-1935

A T least since 1914 Lenin had paid great attention to the problems of imperialism and colonies. These were insepar-able from the problems of the non-Russian nationalities within Russia, of which something has already been said. One of the main arguments against 'Great Russian chauvinism'—which, as we have seen, was officially regarded during the 1920's as more pernicious than the opposite deviation of 'local nationalism'—was that if the Soviet government gave truly equal status to the non-Russians, and especially to the Moslem nationalities of Asiatic Russia, it could win the confidence of the Asiatic peoples beyond its frontiers, and lead them against the western imperialists. An idyllic but quite unreal picture of Soviet policy in Azerbaidjan and Central Asia was used in propaganda directed to Turkey, Persia and Afghanistan.

The defeats of 1919 in Germany and Hungary, and the subse-quent decline of revolutionary ardour throughout Europe, caused the Bolsheviks to show greater interest in Asia. The proletariat of the West must be reinforced by the toiling masses of the East. The capitalist Powers of the West must be struck at vulnerable points in their colonial empires. Lenin's view was summarised in his often-quoted phrase that 'the result of the struggle depends in the last resort on the fact that Russia, India, China, etc., form a gigantic majority of the population of the world'.[1] Stalin, in his lecture 'On the foundations of Leninism' in April 1924, stressed, among the tasks of communists, 'to convert the dependent and colonial countries from a reserve of the imperialist bourgeoisie into a re-serve of the revolutionary proletariat'.[2]

But the task was far from simple. The Asiatic and Moslem nations were socially backward. Their industrial proletariats, with the single exception of Japan, were small. The leaders of their

---

[1] Lenin, *Sochinenia*, 3rd edition, Vol. XXVII, pp. 416–17.
[2] Stalin, *Voprosy Leninizma*, 11th edition, 1939, p. 47.

nationalist movements were certainly not Marxists: some were even religious 'reactionaries' idealising a pre-capitalist past. What attitude was the Comintern to take? Should it support the forces of social revolution, feeble as they were, at the cost of splitting the nationalist ranks, or should it support the existing nationalist leaders even if they were socially reactionary, in order to cause trouble to the Western Powers, the main forces of world capitalism? A pure communist internationalist would prefer the first policy, a Soviet government official the second. As the control of the Soviet government over the Comintern grew, the second policy predominated. Nevertheless, neither the Comintern nor the Soviet government ever completely committed itself either way. The result was that they lost the confidence of many revolutionaries, without gaining the confidence of many nationalists. Revolutionaries in some cases felt themselves betrayed by Moscow. Nationalist leaders distrusted those who—whether openly, or with attempts at secrecy pursued with the discretion of an angry buffalo—proclaimed their intention to overthrow them by revolution. The result was that the non-communist nationalists merely made use of Soviet and Comintern help as bogeys to frighten the Western Powers. Having established their nuisance value, and thus raised their price, they came to terms with the West at the expense of Moscow and of their own communists.

THE MOSLEM LANDS

The first example was Turkey. In his struggle against the Greeks, the old Ottoman regime and the Western Powers, Kemal Ataturk enjoyed the sympathy of Soviet Russia.[1] The two states took a common attitude to the three Transcaucasian republics. Kemal sacrificed his Azerbaidjani kinsmen to Russia, in return for a free hand to destroy Armenia. When the Bolsheviks annexed Georgia in February 1921, he made no objection. Attempts to develop communism in Turkey were however completely unsuccessful. In September 1920 the Bolsheviks organised in Baku a Congress of the Peoples of the East. The self-constituted 'delegates' allegedly included persons of thirty-seven nationalities.[2] There were rousing cheers, shouts of Holy War (*Jihad*), and much

---

[1] Louis Fischer, in his *The Soviets in World Affairs*, 1st edition, 1930, Vol. I, p. 391, states that Karakhan, then Assistant Commissar of Foreign Affairs, told him: 'We helped Kemal with much cannon, money, arms and military advice.' Absence of any serious independent confirmation suggests that this was an empty boast by Karakhan.

[2] Fischer, op cit., Vol. I, p. 283.

firing of pistols in the air and brandishing of swords, but little if any-thing came of it all. The Turkish 'delegates' returned to Turkey, where they were arrested and killed. Communist activities have been savagely suppressed since then. Turkey experienced a cultural, and to some extent a social revolution. But this was the work of Kemal, and was done in the name not of Marxism but of Turkish nationalism. Moreover, having beaten the Greeks in Anatolia, and having alarmed the West by his association with Soviet Russia, Kemal came to terms with the West. The Conference of Lausanne ended, in July 1923, in a compromise between the Turkish and British points of view, and defeat for the Russian proposals concerning the Black Sea Straits.

In Persia too there was a brief period of success followed by failure. The Bolsheviks made a good impression by declaring in January 1918 that they renounced all privileges previously held by Imperial Russia, under the Anglo-Russian convention of 1907 and subsequent agreements. In May 1920, after the Bolshevik conquest of Azerbaidjan, Russian warships appeared off the Persian Caspian port of Enzeli, and Russian troops were landed in the area. By agreement between the Russian commander Raskolnikov and a local Persian rebel named Kuchik Khan, a soviet republic was proclaimed in the province of Ghilan. An Azerbaidjani communist named Pishevari became Commissar of the Interior, and organised a dictatorship modelled on the Russian *Cheka*. In June 1921 the Ghilan troops marched towards Teheran, with some reinforcements from Soviet Georgia, and in July a few more Soviet troops landed at Enzeli. During this time the Soviet Minister in Teheran, T. A. Rothstein, maintained that his government knew nothing of the independent activities of Persian communists, and could in no way influence them.[1] In February 1921 Reza Khan, the commander of the only effective military force in Persia, seized power in Teheran, and soon afterwards defeated Kuchik Khan. Britain, which still had troops in southern Persia, put pressure on the Soviet government to withdraw. By the autumn of 1921 both British and Russian forces had been evacuated, and Reza was able quickly to reoccupy Ghilan. Pishevari fled to the Soviet Union, where he played some part in Comintern affairs.[2] Like Kemal, Reza was a moderniser, but had no mercy for communists. Like Kemal, once in power he established good relations with the European Powers, including Britain, and they recognised him as

[1] G. Lenczowski, *Russia and the West in Iran*, New York, 1949, pp. 65–7.
[2] Under the name Sultan-Zadeh. See also below, p. 320.

Shah when he assumed that title in 1925. His relations with Moscow remained correct.

Elsewhere in the Moslem world neither the Soviet state nor communism achieved much. For a time the anti-British ruler of Afghanistan, Amanulla, flirted with Moscow. But the Bolshevik annexation of Bokhara, and suppression of any Panislamic or Pan-Turkish trends in Central Asia, reduced his enthusiasm. His own westernising policy provided no openings for Marxism, to which his backward country was in any case unreceptive. In the end his reforms cost him his throne. His successor, Nadir, was pro-British.[1]

In the Arab lands there was much hostility to the Western Powers but small opportunity for communists. For a time the Comintern had hopes of Egypt. The conflict between the Wafd and the British, and the outbreak of violence in March 1919, seemed to offer a favourable environment. Small communist groups were formed in the main cities in 1919, but their members were mostly European workers or middle-class intellectuals of European or Levantine origin. The war had stimulated the growth of Egyptian industry, and a working class was beginning to emerge. From 1921 onwards the communists made greater efforts to recruit Moslem Egyptian workers. They organised a trade union group, the Egyptian Confederation of Labour, which claimed 50,000 members and was affiliated to the *Profintern*. In 1922 the Egyptian Communist Party had 2,000 regular members, and was accepted as a member of the Comintern.[2] In 1924 it organised a sit-in strike in an Alexandria factory, which was suppressed by troops. In 1925 the government of the Right which replaced that of Zaghlul took severe measures against communists. The party appears to have been well penetrated by police spies, and in May 1925 all its leaders and a large number of lesser members were rounded up. All this was a small if gallant beginning, and in the following years no appreciable progress was made. In French North Africa too in these years communist influence was negligible.

JAPANESE COMMUNISM

As the most industrialised country in Asia, Japan might have been expected to offer the best prospects of communist action.

---

[1] Soviet sources assume that British intrigues were responsible for the overthrow of Amanulla. It would be interesting to know whether there is any basis in fact for this belief. Some details on Soviet relations with Afghanistan may be found in Fischer, op. cit., Vol. II, pp. 785–94, and in G. A. Agabekov, *Die Tscheka bei der Arbeit*, Stuttgart, 1932, pp. 181–4.

[2] Article by Avigdor in *Revolyutsionny Vostok*, 1934, No. VI, entitled *Ob osnovnyh etapah egipetskoy kompartii* (The Basic Stages of the Egyptian Communist Party).

During the war Japanese industry had grown rapidly, and the workers had not only become more numerous, but had begun to organise themselves. The first trade unions were extremely moderate. Their leaders believed in co-operation between employers and workers, not in class struggle. Strikes were still forbidden by the laws. This did not however prevent strikes from taking place with growing frequency.[1] The first post-war years were marked by growing influence of Marxist socialism both in the trade unions and among the university students. There were thus the first beginnings of that combination of revolutionary intellectuals with a small but growing working-class movement, which had formed the basis of Russian Marxist action at the turn of the century. In July 1922 was founded the Communist Party of Japan. For a short time the greater political freedom, which accompanied the change from the domination of Elder Statesmen and army chiefs to a more or less parliamentary regime led by liberal politicians and business men, enabled the Japanese communists to make a certain progress.

The freedom did not last long. The Japanese police was both efficient and ruthless. In June 1923 most leading communists were arrested. The disorders and mass hysteria that followed the disastrous Tokyo earthquake of 1st September 1923 were used by the police to make large-scale arrests of trade unionists and of persons suspected of left sympathies. Later in the year the communist leaders were released. But they were now extremely pessimistic about the prospects of communism in Japan. A section of them urged that the party should be temporarily dissolved, and this decision was taken, with the support of a majority of those party members still at liberty who could be consulted, in the spring of 1924. The Comintern opposed, but could not prevent, the decision.[2]

During the next two years communist influence was expressed through two organisations in which individual communists had direct or indirect control—the Japanese Trade Union Council[3]

[1] H. Eydus, *Yaponiya ot pervoy do vtoroy mirovoy voiny*, Moscow, 1946, pp. 59–60. The most important strikes of these years were of railwaymen in Tokyo in July 1919, and of dockers in Kobe in September 1919. The first important expression of popular discontent were rice riots in several cities and country districts in 1918. They were the result of rising food prices.

[2] R. Swearingen and P. Langer, *Red Flag in Japan: International Communism in Action, 1919–1950*, Harvard, 1952, pp. 19–21.

[3] This was formed in May 1925, by the former left wing of the General Federation of Labour, which had been expelled from it. The leading personality of this left wing was the communist metal-workers' leader, Watanabe Masanossuke, who in October 1928 committed suicide when on the point of arrest, or, according to the communists' version, was killed by the police.

and the Workers' and Peasants' Party of Japan. The latter was founded in December 1925, in accordance with a directive of the 5th Congress of the Comintern, held in June 1924. Already in 1923 had been set up in Moscow a Peasant International (*Krestintern*), designed like the trade union *Profintern* as a subsidiary of the Comintern. It was hoped that the tactic of workers' and peasants' parties, indirectly controlled by communists, would achieve results in Eastern Europe,[1] and still more in Asia. The Japanese party made little impression on the peasants, but some on the workers. The authorities almost immediately banned the party, but in March 1926 a reorganised party with less communist influence was permitted, and survived for two years. At the end of 1926 the exhortations of the Comintern and or exiled communist leaders[2] bore fruit, when a secret conference re-founded the Japanese Communist Party. That Marxist ideas or slogans commanded some support was shown when at the general election of February 1928, the first held in Japan with universal suffrage, nearly half a million votes were cast for various 'proletarian' groups.[3]

The election results alarmed the government. On 15th March 1928 most leading figures of the party's subsidiary organisations, and several leaders of the party itself,[4] were arrested. From this time police repression became really efficient. In July 1928 was set up a special anti-communist counter-intelligence department, the Special Higher Police, generally known as 'Thought Police'.

During the next three years, despite arrests and killings, an illegal communist organisation continued to exist. In 1932 misery resulting from the economic depression, and discontent with the war in Manchuria and China, provided a more favourable atmo-

[1] The leader of the Croatian Peasant Party (of Yugoslavia), Stepan Radić, paid a visit to Moscow early in 1924 and conferred with the leaders of *Krestintern*. Nothing came of it. The *Krestintern* was extremely unsuccessful as far as Eastern Europe was concerned. The peasant movements of Poland, Roumania, Yugoslavia and even Bulgaria, were little influenced by communist propaganda, direct or indirect, at least until the Popular Front period, and then any sympathy they felt for communists or for Russia was due not to the activity of communists but to the broad anti-fascist and patriotic appeal of Popular Front slogans. See below, pp. 188–90.

[2] The most eminent of these was Sen Katayama, a pioneer of socialism in Japan at the beginning of the century, who left Japan in 1910, spent nine years as an active member of the labour movement in the United States, and went to Russia in 1919. For many years a member of the Presidium of the Comintern, Katayama stayed in the Soviet Union until his death in 1933.

[3] The Workers' and Peasants' Party won 193,000 votes, the Right Socialists 120,000 and the Centre Socialists 85,000. Eydus, op. cit., p. 116

[4] These included the two most eminent leaders of the post-Second World War period, Kyuichi Tokuda and Sanzo Nozaka. Tokuda remained in prison from March 1928 to October 1945, Nozaka was released for reasons of health in 1930, escaped to Russia and became the successor to Katayama in the Comintern. In 1940 he went to China, and worked with Mao Tse-tung until his return to Japan in 1946.

sphere for revolutionary activity. The Comintern, concerned above all to create the maximum opposition to a foreign policy which seemed likely to threaten the frontiers of the Soviet Union, adopted, in its 1932 Thesis on Japan, a new policy calculated to appeal to wider sections of the population. But the communists made only small and short-lived gains. The police had spies within the party, and were able to arrest almost the whole leadership in October and November 1932. New leaders sent by the Comintern were successivly arrested. From 1933 to 1945 the Japanese Communist Party was a negligible force.[1]

The obvious immediate cause of the failure of Japanese communism is the ruthless efficiency of the police. But the Comintern could not be content with this: it must find a 'social' explanation. Hence the long discussions, accompanied by the customary 'left' and 'right' deviations, as to the nature of the Japanese economy. One school held that Japanese capitalism had reached the monopolist, imperialist and decadent stage, and that Japan was therefore ripe for a proletarian revolution. The other school held that 'feudal' remnants still impeded the development of Japanese capitalism, and that Japan still had to experience her bourgeois-democratic revolution.[2] The facts could not easily be fitted into either framework. Japan was an imperialist Power, Japanese industry was largely controlled by monopolies, yet the country was ruled not by capitalists but by a civil and military bureaucracy whose leaders either were descended from former feudal families, or had been intellectually moulded by feudal traditions.

To the non-Marxist student, the notions that Japanese political development could be scientifically predicted, once it had been definitely established whether Japanese society was monopoly-capitalistic or semi-feudal, and that there was a 'correct line' for

---

[1] The only noticeable activity was the organisation by Nozaka of anti-war propaganda among Japanese troops in China, and the creation from prisoners of war of a few Japanese units which fought side by side with Mao's men. See Swearingen and Langer, op. cit., pp. 72–83.

[2] The chief exponent of the left deviation was Kazuo Fukumoto, who, like Trotski in relation to Chinese society (see below, pp. 147–8), stressed the capitalist element in Japanese society, and minimised the 'feudal' element. In July 1927 Fukumoto's doctrines were refuted by the Comintern, then led by Buharin. The disgrace of Buharin in 1929 led to a change in the Comintern 'line' for Japan, as for other countries. The 1931 Thesis of the Japanese party argued that Japanese society was fully capitalistic, and ripe for proletarian revolution (Swearingen and Langer, op. cit., p. 44). Only a year later however the 1932 Thesis—dictated, as explained above, by the needs of Soviet foreign policy—reversed the position, and once more argued, as had Buharin, that feudal remnants must still be fought in Japan, and the bourgeois-democratic revolution was the next stage. The new Thesis was accepted with alacrity by Jokichi Kazama, the General Secretary of the party, who only a year earlier had brought back from Moscow the diametrically opposite Thesis of 1931.

the communist party, ascertainable by a truly Bolshevik leadership, appear rigidly doctrinaire, and at best not more than one-third true. More important, as causes of communist failure, than any 'social' hypothesis of this standard type, are the hierarchical nature of the Japanese political and social systems, the strength of the state machine, and the persistence of traditional loyalties.

The slump of the early 1930's brought mass discontent, but the use made of it by the communists was negligible in comparison with the gains of the extreme nationalists. These used violent methods, especially the assassination of politicians, business men and even senior service officers. Their aims, like those of the German Nazis in the same years, were nationalist and imperialist. But they were to some extent also social revolutionaries. They were inspired by intellectuals but led chiefly by army officers.[1] The officers were in many cases of peasant origin. They sympathised with the peasants' resentment at their poverty and with their distrust of the towns. They hated the capitalists, partly because they considered them to be exploiters of the peasants, and partly because the methods and the achievements of the business class were the very antithesis of the old military virtues of traditional Japan, to which they wished to return. Despite the difference of cultural background, there is a strong resemblance between this Japanese military nationalism and the popular fascist movements of Eastern Europe, especially of Roumania and to a lesser extent of Hungary. Common features include the combination of frenzied nationalism and vague social slogans; the idealisation of peasant virtues; the use of assassination and the unwillingness of law courts to condemn assassins who acted from 'patriotic' motives;[2] and the role of army officers or bureaucrats who either themselves came from the small nobility (Japanese *samurai*, Hungarian gentry, Polish *szlachta*) or adopted through their professional training the ethical standards and outlook of that class.

INDIA AND JAVA

The social structure of India was even less suitable for communist activity than that of Japan, but the much greater freedom of

[1] There is much interesting material on these groups in Hugh Byass, *Government by Assassination*, 1943.

[2] The Roumanian Iron Guardists were more than once acquitted of political murders that they had committed or inspired. The Moslem Brotherhood in Egypt, in its early days, seems to be an example of the same pattern. The Roumanian Iron Guard, Hungarian Arrow Cross, Moslem Brotherhood and Japanese Young Officers had very different doctrines and different fates. But in the social conditions from which they emerged, the social origin of their leaders, and the slogans and methods of their political struggle there are striking resemblances. The present work, which is devoted

speech and organisation permitted by British 'imperialist exploiters' was a more favourable factor. During the war the numbers of industrial workers greatly increased. In 1920 was founded the All-India Trade Union Congress. This was closely connected with the Congress Party, but was also influenced by Marxist groups. In 1924 some Marxist intellectuals founded the Communist Party of India, and in 1926, in accordance with the Comintern policy mentioned above, communists organised a Workers' and Peasants' Party. In 1927 at the congress of the A.I.T.U.C. held in Kanpur, the communists gained control of the unions. These developments alarmed the British authorities, who began to take special measures against communists. In 1929 they arrested several communist leaders, including some Englishmen, and tried them at Meerut for conspiracy. In the same year the trade union movement split, with the communists retaining only a part. Indian communism remained weak as an organised force, with a little influence in some industrial centres and universities but hardly affecting the main stream of Indian political life.

For a short time communist prospects seemed fair in Indonesia. The first socialist party of Java (I.S.D.V.) was founded before the war by Dutch railway workers.[1] Trade unions made their first appearance around the same time. At the end of 1919 a Congress set up a Trade Union Centre for the whole labour movement. In the following year the I.S.D.V. transformed itself into the Communist Party of Indonesia (P.K.I.), and was accepted as a member of the Comintern. The trade union movement split, the communists forming their own separate Revolutionary Trade Union Centre.

The Javanese communists became for a time an important force not through their influence over the small working class but through their penetration of the nationalist movement. *Sarekat Islam*, as we have seen, began its career as a defence of Javanese interests against Chinese merchants. It thus had anti-capitalist features from the beginning, and was accessible to socialist propaganda. Its third congress, held in the autumn of 1918, adopted demands for far-reaching social reforms, and elected the socialist—later communist—Semaoen to its Central Committee.[2] *Sarekat Islam* gave its

---

to communism, cannot adequately discuss these phenomena. But a comparative study of revolutionary organisations of a fascist or obscurantist type in backward societies would be a very interesting and useful enterprise. See also below, pp. 190, 340.

[1] Article by P. *Eyquem* in *Revue du Monde Musulman*, LII, pp. 55-83. The leading Dutch socialist involved in the foundation of I.S.D.V. was Sneevliet, a former teacher, who was chairman of the Railwaymen's Union. His chief Javanese assistant was Semaoen. Two other Javanese socialists trained by Sneevliet, who became prominent in the communist movement, both in the 1920's and after the Second World War, were Tan Malaka and Alimin.   [2] Eyquem, loc. cit.

support to the formation of the Trade Union Centre, and allowed the P.K.I. to join its ranks as a body.

Soon however co-operation was replaced by friction. The loyalty of the P.K.I. to the Comintern, and its ideological incompatibility with Islam, were insuperable obstacles. At the 6th Congress of *Sarekat Islam*, held in October 1921, P.K.I., being unable to accept a new regulation on internal discipline and acceptance of Islam, seceded, taking with it about one-quarter of the organisation's membership.[1] P.K.I. and S.I. continued to co-operate theoretically, for example in support of the pawnshop workers' strike in January 1922,[2] and Semaoen on instructions from Moscow made efforts to ensure a common front with the nationalists. Co-operation finally broke down early in 1923. After this the P.K.I. tried to carry out the Comintern directives on Workers' and Peasants' Parties[3] by forming a new mass organisation, to be directed by the communist nucleus, under the name *Sarekat Rakjat*. As a rival to *Sarekat Islam* it was not successful. The climax of revolutionary action in Indonesia came at the end of 1926, with an armed revolt in Batavia and in western Java, followed early in 1927 by a revolt in Sumatra. These were anti-Dutch risings, caused by a combination of economic discontent and exasperated nationalism. But the communists provided the leadership.[4] After the suppression of the revolt the communist party declined, but the nationalist movement continued to be influenced by the anti-imperialist slogans and doctrines of the Comintern.[5]

THE ORIGINS OF CHINESE COMMUNISM

Far the most important communist movement in Asia developed in China. It developed in spite of the fact that the industrial working class was relatively very weak. There are two main reasons why communism was so much more successful in China than elsewhere in Asia. One was the exceptional prestige enjoyed in China

[1] Seven out of 30 of the 'sections' in which *Sarekat Islam* was organised voted that the communists should be exempted from this regulation.

[2] The state pawnshops were important institutions, as they provided credit to the poor on more favourable terms than almost any other organisation in Eastern Asia, where the moneylender was usually supreme. Their employees formed an important part of the small Javanese working class and clerical class.

[3] See above, p. 132.

[4] Communist accounts of the rising are Kjai Samin, *The Uprising in Java and Sumatra* in *Communist International*, issues of 15th April 1927 and 30th May 1927; and A. Gubei, *Revolyutsionnoe dvizhenie v Indonezii na sovremennom etape* (The present stage of the Indonesian revolutionary movement) in *Revolyutsionny Vostok*, 1933, No. 5, pp. 32–46. Gubei takes the story up to 1933.

[5] The nationalist leader Šoekarno was for a time connected with the *Liga gegen Kolonialgreuel und Unterdrückung* in Berlin, a Comintern subsidiary. See Bousquet, op. cit., p. 63.

by intellectuals—exceptional even in Asia, where, as we have seen, intellectuals played a dominant role in political movements. This exceptional prestige was due to the ancient Chinese tradition of rule by scholar-administrators. The second factor was the breakdown of the machinery of government, the anarchic condition into which China had relapsed after the overthrow of the Manchu dynasty. The other factors obviously relevant to Chinese communism—peasant poverty, nationalist feeling and desire for political change—existed in other countries of Asia. But not being combined with these two special factors, they did not produce the results that were seen in China.

The founders of the Chinese communist movement were two professors of Peking university, the Head of the Department of Literature, Chen Tu-hsiu, and a historian, Li Ta-chao.[1] Both men were profoundly impressed by the Bolshevik revolution. The great attraction of Bolshevism, and especially of Lenin's doctrine of imperialism, was that it could reconcile admiration for western civilisation with resentment against western policy in China. It provided the means of 'judging and criticising the capitalist West from a western point of view'.[2] The two men began in 1918 seriously to study Marxism. By 1920 both had been converted to the new faith. Meanwhile the development of social and political forces in China was becoming very favourable for the creation of a Marxist revolutionary movement.

North China in 1919 was ruled by a government of warlords who were at the mercy of the Japanese. Japan put forward claims to further Chinese territory, and these were accepted by the victorious Powers at Versailles. This provoked a widespread nationalist campaign, led by the intelligentsia, and directed against Japan and the European Powers. It was known as the May Fourth Movement, from a big demonstration organised by the students in Peking on 4th May 1919, which was followed by similar action in other cities, in all cases led by the intellectuals and supported by the urban masses.

The other important social development was the emergence of

---

[1] B. L. Schwarz, *Chinese Communism and the rise of Mao*, Harvard, 1951, discusses at some length the background of these two men and their intellectual influence. This admirable work, by a scholar who not only knows China and the Chinese language, but also understands the nature of communism, is the first really serious analysis of the Chinese communist movement that is free from pro-Chinese or anti-Chinese bias, Marxist or ex-Marxist or anti-Marxist blinkers. The main interest of the book lies in the years 1928–32, but its account of the foundation of the party, and of the personalities of Chen and Li, is also indispensable to students.

[2] Schwarz, op. cit., p. 15.

organised industrial labour. The workers supported the May Fourth Movement, and there were several big strikes. Trade unions grew rapidly in the next two years. In 1922 a Labour Conference met in Canton, with delegates of workers' groups from many parts of China. A Central Trade Union Federation was founded. In October there was a strike in the Chili coal-mines in northern China, and troops of the warlord Wu Pei-fu fired on the strikers. At the end of the year a railway strike on the Peking-Hankow line resulted in further clashes between troops and railwaymen, and further casualties.

This situation was of interest to both Comintern and Soviet government. Their aims were however different, and at times threatened to conflict.

The Comintern in June 1920 sent an emissary, Voitinski, to Shanghai. He met both Li and Chen, and played a part in bringing the various Chinese Marxist groups together. In July 1921 they held a congress in a girls' school in the French Concession of Shanghai, and founded the Communist Party of China.

Already in July 1919 the Soviet government had made a general statement, similar to that concerning Persia, renouncing all privileges extorted from China by Imperial Russia. Its language was conveniently ambiguous about the status of the Chinese Eastern Railway through Manchuria, which had been Russian-owned since its construction in the 1890's.[1] Of the various groups disputing power in China at this time, Moscow at first preferred the warlord Wu Pei-fu, who was in conflict with the so-called Anfu clique of warlords subservient to the Japanese. Civil war was still raging in Siberia, and the Japanese occupied the Russian Far East: the main concern of the Bolsheviks was to strengthen anyone who was hostile to Japan. But when Wu defeated the Anfu clique, he showed himself well disposed to Britain, which Moscow regarded with little less hostility than Japan.

Meanwhile in the south Sun Yat-sen, the democratic revolutionary of 1911 and founder of the Kuomintang, had established himself, with the support of local warlords, in Canton. In the spring of 1921 an emissary of the Comintern, Maring, met him in Kwangsi province. Maring became convinced that Sun represented the most important trend of Chinese nationalism. During a visit to Canton in 1922 the Comintern emissary was impressed by the good relations that existed between Sun and the trade unions, and by

---

[1] On this obscure and controversial question, see the interesting article by Allen S. Whiting, 'The Soviet offer to China of 1919', in *Far Eastern Quarterly*, August 1951.

the help which Sun's authorities had given to the Hongkong strike.[1] He therefore recommended strongly to Moscow that the Comintern should co-operate with the Kuomintang. At the same time Sun's hopes of American or European protection were disappointed by the course of the Washington Conference of 1922. He was the more ready to look for help to Russia. The departure of Japanese troops from the Russian Far East brought the Soviet Union into direct geographical contact with China, and so enabled Moscow to influence Chinese events. In January 1923 the eminent Bolshevik diplomat Yoffe arrived in Shanghai and met Sun Yat-sen. The two men issued a statement full of revolutionary rhetoric, and the period of the Kuomintang's co-operation with the Soviet Union and with the Chinese communists began.

Chen Tu-hsiu was much less enthusiastic about the Kuomintang than were the Russians. He knew Sun and the nationalists of old, and disliked them. Even to co-operate with them and with the Chinese bourgeoisie against the foreign imperialists or the warlords was distasteful to him: a still closer association was utterly repugnant. But this was what the Comintern ordered. The Chinese Communist Party had joined the Comintern at its second congress, held in July 1922. In the following month, at a plenary meeting of the party's Central Committee held in Hangchow, Maring proposed that the party should fuse with the Kuomintang. He himself undoubtedly had in mind his own experience in Java, where, as we have seen, the communist party belonged to *Sarekat Islam* and operated within its ranks as a revolutionary nucleus.[2] But the Comintern's main motive was undoubtedly to unite as broad a front as possible against the Western Powers, the enemies of world revolution in general and of the Soviet Union in particular. In order to make this tactic doctrinally acceptable, Maring propounded the view that the Kuomintang was 'not a bourgeois party but a coalition party of all classes'. By entering this coalition party, the proletariat would transform it into a spearhead of revolution. The view of Chinese society proclaimed in the following years by the Comintern was that there were four classes hostile to imperialism—proletariat, peasantry, petty bourgeoisie and national

[1] Dockers on strike in Hongkong received material aid from Canton, and some found a refuge there.

[2] Maring is the same person as Sneevliet (see above, p. 135 footnote). He had been expelled from Java by the Netherlands authorities. For some years he was one of the Comintern's main Far Eastern experts. That the Java experience was quoted at the Hangchow Plenum is stated by H. Isaacs, *The Tragedy of the Chinese Revolution*, 1938, pp. 61–2.

bourgeoisie. Against them were the 'feudal' warlords,[1] the compradores, and their common masters the foreign imperialists. The
Kuomintang, by the participation of the communists, would be
made into a 'bloc of four classes'. As a social analysis, this was
highly dubious. But it had always been Lenin's way to dress up
his political aims in a tattered garment of social phraseology, and
the Comintern was following in the master's footsteps. The social
phraseology did not impress the Chinese communist leaders, but
they accepted the Comintern's demands. They agreed that the
party should enter the Kuomintang, and in 1923 this decision was
carried out.

The decision was subsequently interpreted by Trotski and his
disciples as a capitulation by the communists to the Kuomintang.
But this accusation is hardly justified. The agreement made with
Sun Yat-sen, on the advice of the 'political adviser' sent by
Moscow, Michael Borodin, was very favourable to the communists.
They were allowed to enter the Kuomintang as individuals, but
the Communist Party continued to exist as an independent body,
with its own internal organisation and political programme. The
communists in fact set to work to infiltrate both the Kuomintang
and the various military, civil and economic organisations on
Kuomintang territory. Communists held key positions in the trade
unions, the peasants' associations and the officer corps of the new
army. The Soviet military adviser to Sun Yat-sen's government,
Blucher, founded a Military Academy at Whampoa, and this was
well infiltrated by the party. The new army, like the Red Army
in the Soviet Union, had political commissars, and a high proportion of these were communists. The communists' aim was—to use
the terminology of Russian Marxism of 1903–5—to secure the
'hegemony of the proletariat' within the revolutionary alliance.
They were to impose their leadership on the machinery of the
Kuomintang, as in 1917 Lenin had imposed his leadership on the
machinery of the Russian soviets.

But the leaders of the Kuomintang were not fools. Moreover
Borodin made a good job of organising the Kuomintang itself on
the principles of 'democratic centralism'. He taught the Kuomintang leaders the communist technique of power, and they did not
intend to let it be used against them by the Chinese communists.
The Kuomintang itself was divided into right and left wings, the

---

[1] The word 'feudal' has been so misused by Marxists that it has lost any meaning
it may once have had. In Stalinese it is used to qualify anything that is (*a*) pre-
capitalist, and (*b*) bad.

former influenced by Canton merchants and conservative bureaucrats and deeply suspicious of the communists, the latter more radical and willing at first to accept at their face value the communists' assurances of co-operation. In October the right wing attempted a rising against the government, with anti-communist slogans, but was defeated by the Whampoa cadets and the communist-controlled Workers' Militia. This was followed by a trend towards the left which lasted throughout 1925. A special Workers' Guard enjoyed a semi-autonomous status within the army. In August one of the two leaders of the left wing of the Kuomintang, the political director of the army Liao Chung-hai, was assassinated: the crime was followed by a purge of right-wing sympathisers. The other leader of the left, Wang Ching-wei, became head of the government.

The triumph of the left did not last. In March 1926 the commander of the armed forces, Chiang Kai-shek, arrested communist political commissars in the army, and disarmed the Workers' Guard. Chiang had not been a prominent member of either the right or the left groups. His main motive was to end the confusion of competing military and political groups and to create a single disciplined military and political authority. But as it was the communists who most strongly insisted on maintaining their own authorities side by side with the recognised official hierarchy, it was they who suffered from Chiang's action.

The communists did not reply to force with force. Moscow was determined to maintain the alliance between communists and Kuomintang. This was too valuable to the foreign policy of the Soviet Union to be thrown away merely in the interest of the Chinese revolution. The communists were instructed by the Comintern to seek a compromise with Chiang. For his part Chiang could not afford at this stage to lose his Russian military advisers. The quarrel was therefore patched up. Chiang himself succeeded Wang as head of the government. The number of communists among the cadets of the Whampoa academy was limited. Communists were excluded from high civil administrative posts. Communist agitation among the peasants was to be reduced: 'social peace' was to be preached instead of class war, incitement against the landlords as such was to be replaced by denunciation only of 'bad landlords',[1] the slogan of land redistribution was to be re-

[1] Another 'social' catchword that recurs in Chinese communist literature. In fact Chinese communists differentiate between good and bad landlords by the same means as the late *Reichsmarschall* Göring differentiated between Jews and Aryan—*Wer Jude ist, bestimme ich.*

placed by that of a mere 20 per cent reduction in rents. Finally, unity between communists and Kuomintang was to be restored in practice by both parties taking part in the military expedition which was being planned to the north of China.

THE DISASTER OF 1927

The northward march, which began in July 1926, was a brilliant success. The Kuomintang armies were greeted by the peasants as their liberators, and opposing armies retreated or deserted to the victors. In the liberated cities the workers poured into the trade unions, which claimed to have 2,000,000 members at the beginning of 1927. In the countryside the peasants poured into the Peasants' Associations: early in 1927 they claimed to have nearly 10,000,000 members in four south-central provinces only.[1] Chiang Kai-shek set up his headquarters at Nanchang, capital of Kiangsi province, but the Kuomintang political leaders decided to make their capital at Hankow, further up the Yangtse river. Relations between the two centres became strained.

The first disaster to the communist cause took place in Shanghai. Not only was this by far the largest and most modern city in China, but its workers were the most efficiently organised. In February 1927, as the armies of the national revolution approached, the workers of Shanghai rose, led by their communist trade union chiefs. They drove out the forces of the local warlord, and set up a City Council, which in its rough and ready way genuinely represented the city masses, rather as the soviet in St. Petersburg had represented its masses in 1917. But Chiang Kai-shek, whose army was within a short distance of Shanghai, held back his forces and waited, while the enemy warlord reassembled his troops, re-entered Shanghai, and massacred the workers. Meanwhile tension between Chiang and the Hankow government had gone so far that the latter in March relieved him of the post of commander-in-chief. At the same time in Hankow the communists increased their influence, and were given the Ministries of Labour and Agriculture.

Chiang had not yet however lost the support of the Comintern. On 21st March the Shanghai workers made a general strike, followed by an insurrection. Three days later Chiang was on the outskirts of the city, and the communists in Shanghai asked the Comintern for advice. They were told to treat Chiang as a revolu-

[1] Estimate quoted in explanatory notes to Trotski, *Summary and Perspectives of the Chinese Revolution*, Selected Works, ed. Max Schachtman, New York, 1936, Vol. I, pp. 338–41.

tionary leader, and to regard all suggestions that he might be their enemy as 'provocations by the imperialists'. The official press of the Comintern took the same line. On 5th April in Moscow Stalin himself declared that Chiang was submitting to the discipline of the Kuomintang, that he could not do otherwise than lead his army against 'the imperialists', and that Chiang must be used to the end by the communists, then 'squeezed like a lemon and thrown away'.[1] When Chiang's troops entered Shanghai, the Comintern representative, Mandalian, told the workers not to provoke Chiang or fight him, nor to surrender their arms to him, but to bury them. This pedantic instruction was no solution to the problem: it deprived the workers of the means of self-defence without satisfying Chiang. The municipal government set up by the insurrection was not recognised by Chiang. He waited for a few days, and then on 12th April arrested the communist leaders. Those who were still at liberty ordered a general strike and demonstration. Chiang's troops fired on the demonstrators, the trade union buildings were seized, and thousands were imprisoned or executed, some with horrible cruelty.

The Shanghai rising was the only great revolutionary effort ever made by the Chinese industrial workers under communist leadership. Thereafter the Chinese proletariat remained a passive factor for more than twenty years. The tragedy was emphasised by the imbecility of Comintern policy. The military balance of power was such that no combination of wisdom and heroism could have enabled the communists to hold Shanghai. But the Comintern leaders could have enabled their followers to remain alive, and probably even to maintain their trade union machinery for use at a later time, if they had made a realistic appraisal of the situation.

The centre of the political struggle was now in Hankow. Three forces were in play—the Communist Party; the left Kuomintang, led by Wang Ching-wei, who had returned from exile in response to a popular demand largely organised by the communists; and a warlord named Tang Shen-chi, who hoped to take Chiang's position as military commander in the Kuomintang regime.[2]

The left Kuomintang leaders had the choice of allying themselves with a strong combination of warlords against Chiang, in which case they would sooner or later have to break with the communists, whom the warlords would not tolerate; or of putting themselves at the head of a revolutionary movement, together with the com-

[1] Trotski, op. cit., explanatory note 44, pp. 331-2.
[2] On the role of Tang and other warlords at this stage, see Roy, op. cit., Chapter 18.

munists, in which case they would have had against them not only Chiang but also the other warlords.

The communists had the choice of preserving the alliance with the left Kuomintang, at the cost of a very moderate social policy which must disillusion both the more radical members of their party and the worker and peasant masses who had recently thronged to their standards; of or boldly leading a social revolution, in the hope that the support of the masses would give them victory against the combined forces of the whole Kuomintang, Chiang and the warlords, who would be driven together by the threat of revolution, and who would probably be supported by the 'imperialists'. Comintern advice was consistently in favour of maintaining the alliance with the Kuomintang, even at the cost of social concessions.

For a time the crisis was postponed by an attempt to continue the northern march as far as Peking, a project which could temporarily unite left Kuomintang, communists and Tang Shen-chi. But this failed when the Hankow forces found their road to Peking blocked by a warlord with whom they had hoped to co-operate. This man, the 'Christian General' Feng Yu-hsiang, demanded that he be given the command against Peking, and that the Hankow government reopen negotiations with Chiang. Hankow, wishing neither to accept these terms nor to fight Feng, withdrew the expedition.[1]

The communists still clung to their alliance with the left Kuomintang, and discouraged mass revolutionary action. Their leaders expressed disapproval of 'excesses' committed by peasants against landlords. In May 1927 a Kuomintang general suppressed the trade unions and the Communist Party branch in the large city of Changsha. The Peasant Associations, which were especially strong in this province, mobilised their forces and prepared to march on Changsha, but were ordered by the provincial committee of the Communist Party to retire. The communist leaders in Hankow accepted the assurance of Tang Shen-chi that he would discipline the Changsha rebels, but in fact he took no action against them, and they took the initiative, pursued and massacred the peasant detachments. For months there had been sterile arguments in Hankow as to what kind of land reform should be made, and what kind of landlords should lose what kind of land, but nothing was

---

[1] Roy, op. cit., pp. 474–6. Feng in later years flirted with the communists. At the end of the Second World War he went to Moscow. His career ended mysteriously in a Soviet ship on the Black Sea.

done to satisfy the peasants' demands. Moscow continued to urge that the alliance with the Kuomintang be preserved, but at the same time demanded 'the deepening of the agrarian revolution'. The Comintern's directives to the Chinese party were pedantic, contradictory and divorced from Chinese reality. They were to confiscate, and give to the peasants, land belonging to 'landlords' but not land belonging to army officers—two categories that could not be separated from each other. They were to 'destroy unreliable generals', create eight to ten divisions of revolutionary peasants and workers with 'absolutely reliable communist composition', and 'put new worker and peasant elements into the Central Executive Committee of the Kuomintang'.[1] How this was to be done without antagonising the leaders of the Kuomintang, without causing a breach between the two parties, Stalin's directives did not explain. As Chen Tu-hsiu sadly observed, 'The International asks us to implement our own policies. On the other hand it will not allow us to withdraw from the Kuomintang. Thus there is no way out.'[2] Meanwhile Feng had met Chiang, and then had once more urged the Hankow government to break with the communists. In July the government demanded that the communists should publicly denounce the peasant movement. The communists refused, and resigned from the government. In Peking the Manchurian warlord Chang Tso-lin raided the Soviet Embassy, seized documents, and arrested and executed Chinese communist leaders who were in hiding there, among them Li Ta-chao. Kuomintang authorities and warlords outdid each other in the persecution of communists and of rebellious peasants.

Thus both Comintern and Soviet government had failed in China. Like Kemal and Reza, the Kuomintang leaders had used Soviet support long enough to raise their nuisance value in the sight of the Great Powers, and had then come to terms with the Great Powers at Moscow's expense. Borodin and Blucher were now sent back to Russia. Britain and the European Powers made to the Kuomintang government concessions which they had refused to the earlier regimes.[3] In November 1927 Chiang resumed his post as Commander-in-Chief of Kuomintang forces, and thereafter was the dictator of nationalist China. His regime was much less revolutionary than that of Kemal, or even than that of Reza. The victory

[1] Stalin, *Ob Oppozitsii*, pp. 661–2; Schwarz, op. cit., p. 67; Isaacs, op. cit., pp. 294–6.
[2] Schwarz, op. cit., p. 67.
[3] The first step was the British surrender of the concessions in Hankow and Kiukiang, in February 1927. Holcombe, op. cit., pp. 207–8.

of Chiang was not a victory for the original Kuomintang, a movement of both national and social revolution: it was a result of a
compromise between these new forces on the one hand and the old
warlord regimes on the other. Some warlords, it is true, were
finally eliminated, but others merely recognised the new leaders,
and carried on their old practices under a new name. Chiang no
doubt wished to be a Chinese Kemal, and he did achieve something
to modernise China. But his resources continued to be strained by
civil war against the communists, which as we shall see dragged
on for years, and from 1931 onwards he had to face aggression or
the threat of aggression from Japan.

As customary in Comintern practice, the blame for the disaster
was removed from the infallible leaders in Moscow, and placed
firmly on the shoulders of the Chinese leaders. At an Emergency
Conference held on 7th August 1927 Chen Tu-hsiu was blamed for
his 'opportunism'. The crimes imputed to him were that he had held
back the peasant movement and that he had feared to pursue a
revolutionary policy out of excessive regard for the wishes of the
Kuomintang. In fact of course these errors were not Chen's but the
Comintern's. This did not prevent Buharin from writing that the
Chinese communist leaders had 'sabotaged the decisions of the
Comintern . . . had not stood the test of fire . . . had suffered ship-
wreck'.[1] The Comintern however still hoped that victory was near.
Another 'revolutionary rising tide' was imminent.

On 1st August communist forces occupied Nanchang, but were
soon forced to abandon it. They made their way south, and in mid-
September took the port of Swatow. This city too they had to
evacuate. In the same month Hunan province was the scene of
'Autumn Harvest Risings' organised by Mao Tse-tung, who had
distinguished himself as a leader of peasants during and since the
northward march from Canton. In December 1927 the communists
made a last sensational attempt. Led by a German communist,
Heinz Neumann, they seized power in Canton for a few days.[2]
The rising was quickly defeated, and was followed by the usual
orgy of torture and massacre.

TROTSKI AND STALIN ON CHINA

The events in China were a subject of fierce controversy between
Stalin and Trotski.

[1] *Inprecorr* of 14th July 1927, quoted in Isaacs, op. cit., p. 323.
[2] It has been alleged by Trotskists that the Canton rising was timed to coincide
with the 15th Congress of the Soviet Communist Party (see above, p. 98) in order
to disarm criticism of Stalin's China policy by news of a 'revolutionary victory'. The
news of the rising was in fact so presented to the Congress.

The controversy was obscured by the usual doctrinal hair-splitting, and the usual loose use of social phraseology in what was a political, or even more a personal, quarrel. It is impossible to see with certainty when personal issues decided policy, and when political decisions caused or intensified personal disputes. Yet something must be said about Stalin's and Trotski's views of the Chinese tragedy, and about its real significance as it appears to a non-communist critic.

The essence of Stalin's argument was that the Kuomintang was worthy of support because it was anti-imperialist. His aim was to concentrate as large forces as possible against the European Powers and Japan, the enemies of the Soviet Union. But this policy had to be dressed up in the right garment of social phraseology. Hence the doctrine of the bloc of four classes. When Chiang Kai-shek suppressed the Shanghai workers and quarrelled with the Hankow government, a 'social' explanation had to be found. The formula chosen was that the national bourgeoisie had betrayed the revolution, and that Chiang was its instrument: the Hankow government represented a bloc of only three classes—petty bourgeoisie, peasants and workers. These three classes must fight together against the combination of feudal elements, militarists, compradores and national bourgeoisie. The communists must remain in the Kuomintang, for if they abandoned it they would simply make a present of the whole Kuomintang machine to its right wing and to the bourgeoisie. The present stage of the Chinese revolution was bourgeois-democratic. The participation of the communists in the Kuomintang would make possible the hegemony of the proletariat in the bourgeois-democratic revolution, and would help to accelerate the progress towards the next stage, the socialist revolution. When this stage had been reached, then the communists must set up soviets and thus create a 'duality of power', as in Russia in 1917. But to launch soviets in the bourgeois-democratic stage of the revolution would frighten the petty bourgeoisie, represented by Wang Ching-wei and the left Kuomintang, into the camp of the national bourgeoisie and the feudal elements.[1]

Trotski maintained that Stalin exaggerated and misunderstood the anti-imperialist character of the Kuomintang.[2] He denied that feudal elements represented a class distinct from the bourgeoisie. Landed interests were inextricably intertwined with urban capital,

---

[1] Stalin, *Ob Oppozitsii*, pp. 423–35, 551–7, 583–605.
[2] Trotski, op. cit., pp. 182–6.

both Chinese and foreign. Chinese rural society was dominated by capitalism to a far greater extent than Stalin admitted. The Chinese revolution must regard capital, both foreign and Chinese, as its principal enemy, and must expropriate bourgeois property in city and village at an early stage: there could be no 'democratic period' such as existed in Russia from November 1917 to July 1918. In fact Trotski, who in 1909 had prophesied that the Russian proletariat could not halt the revolution half-way at the bourgeois stage—as advocated in Lenin's *Two Tactics*—but would have to go on to the socialist stage,[1] was now arguing that the nature of Chinese society made it equally inevitable that the Chinese revolution should pass straight to the socialist stage. The Chinese revolution should in fact move even faster and further than had the Russian. Trotski argued in 1928 that the 'mass movement of workers and peasants was on a scale entirely adequate' for the seizure of power by the communists. If workers and peasants were in fact following the national bourgeoisie, this was only because the Comintern had dragged them into such a course. 'If at the beginning of the northern expedition we had begun to organise soviets in the liberated districts . . . we would have rallied round us the agrarian uprisings, we would have built our own army, we would have disintegrated the enemy armies.'[2] After the defeats of the spring and summer of 1927 the Comintern had made one blunder after another. Finally in December they had made the Canton commune, and proclaimed a 'soviet', with complete disregard of the nature of soviets. 'The soviet is not a talisman with omnipotent powers of salvation.'[3]

Neither Stalin's nor Trotski's social analysis fits the Chinese scene, but Trotski's is perhaps less unreal than Stalin's. He was certainly right in objecting to the excessive use of the word 'feudal', and he was right to stress the role of the village capitalists—moneylenders and merchants—and the connections between landlords and urban bourgeois. But both he and Stalin underrated the role of warlords and bureaucrats, whose power over the masses was not chiefly due to their economic strength.

But though Trotski's social analysis is partly wrong and partly irrelevant, his main political argument, that a revolutionary policy could have given the communists power, cannot be so easily dismissed. In the first months of 1927 central China was seething with unrest. The machinery of government had been extremely feeble ever since 1911, now it hardly existed at all. The communists domi-

---

[1] See above, pp. 27–28.   [2] Trotski, op. cit., p. 186.   [3] Trotski, op. cit., p. 205.

nated trade unions and peasant associations. During the northward march the communists had not in fact obeyed the self-denying ordinances of the May compromise with Chiang, but had urged confiscation of landlords' estates, non-payment of rent and formation of peasant guards. This radical policy had won them mass support. It is true that the armed forces on which the communists could count were fewer and not so well armed as the forces either of Chiang or of the northern warlords. They had however a few elite formations, such as the 'Iron Army' which captured Hankow. And this was perhaps one of those historic moments when morale is more important than armaments. In a situation of mass revolutionary enthusiasm, a combination of resolute leadership with good propaganda might have won the day: the warlords' troops might have deserted them. In March 1917 the Tsar's soldiers had refused his orders and gone over to the demonstrating workers. In September 1917 Kornilov's soldiers had refused his orders and fraternised with the Petrograd workers. The same thing might have happened in China in 1927. It is of course clear that the communists could not have hoped to win and hold all China: the foreign Powers would have defended Shanghai and Peking and Tientsin, and the Japanese might well have taken Manchuria. But the communists might have held a vast area which would have become a base for the long civil war that would have followed, and which did in fact follow in circumstances much more unfavourable' for the communists. That this did not happen, that the attempt was not made, may in part be due to inadequate leadership by Chen Tu-hsiu and his colleagues, but it was to a much greater extent due to hamstringing directives issued by the Comintern, that is, by its 'leader and teacher of genius', Stalin.

THE RISE OF MAO TSE-TUNG

During the following decade little was heard in the outside world of the Chinese communists. Yet it was a decade of great importance for communism both in China and elsewhere. It was in China in these years that techniques were evolved which were not only to prevail in China but to produce results in other lands of Asia and Europe.

During these years the Chinese communist movement had two distinct branches. On the one hand was the Central Committee of the party, which was usually located in Shanghai, attempted to direct action among the Chinese industrial workers, and was subject to constant and detailed supervision by the Comintern. On

the other hand were the Chinese soviets and Red Army, located in
the countryside, which largely developed on their own lines. The
first was almost completely unsuccessful, but the second achieved
great results.

After the Canton disaster some communist units took refuge in
the mountains of Kiangsi province. In the first half of 1928 Mao
Tse-tung and Chu Teh established in the Chingkanshan district
a base for guerrilla action. Mao already had great experience as
an organiser of revolutionary peasants. Already in February 1927
he had written a *Report on the Peasant Movement in Hunan*,[1] which
contained some views that could hardly be accepted by an orthodox
Marxist. He had treated the peasants as a revolutionary vanguard,
a role which in orthodox Marxist doctrine is reserved for the proletariat.[2] 'The peasants', he wrote, 'have fulfilled a long unfulfilled
revolutionary mission, performing a major task in the national revolution.' He stressed the role of the poor peasants in contrast to the
rich peasants, but he did not even mention the industrial proletariat.
He assigned 70 per cent of the credit for the revolution to the peasants, and 30 per cent to 'urban dwellers and military units'.[3] In
September 1927 Mao had led the unsuccessful Autumn Harvest
Risings, and had been blamed for their failure. His reputation was
not high in 1928 either with the party's official leaders or with the
Comintern. Yet his activities were the only communist achievements
in China at this time. He had a military force, which he called a
'Red Army', and in the areas which he controlled he set up local
government bodies which he called 'soviets'.

The 6th Congress of the Chinese Communist Party was held
in Moscow in July 1928, coinciding with the 6th Congress of
the Comintern. This congress recognised the value of peasant
guerrilla, but gave less importance to it than to working-class
action. It was approved only 'on condition that it is carried out in
alliance with a new revolutionary wave among the proletariat in
the cities . . . The consolidation of working-class leadership among
the peasantry is a prerequisite to the success of the agrarian
revolution.'[4]

For two years after the 6th Congress the leading personality
in the Chinese Communist Party was Li Li-san, who had made his
name as a labour organiser in Shanghai in 1925. Under constant

---

[1] This is quoted in full in Fairbank, Schwarz and Brandt, *Documentary History of
Chinese Communism*, 1952, pp. 80–9.
[2] Tito committed the same sin. See below, pp. 263 ff.
[3] Fairbank, Schwarz and Brandt, op. cit., p. 83.
[4] Ibid, p. 164.

pressure from the Comintern, Li did his best to revive revolutionary spirit among the industrial workers. His efforts were completely unsuccessful. Ever since the Shanghai disaster of 1927 the Chinese proletariat had remained deaf to communist blandishments. It was interested only in immediate economic issues, in which it followed the leadership of the non-communist trade unions permitted by the Kuomintang government. Meanwhile Mao's guerrilla forces gained in strength, but official doctrine did not change. At a 'conference of delegates from soviet areas', held in May 1930 near Shanghai, the leading role of the proletariat was once more stressed. The conference 'repudiated the incorrect line of neglecting the leadership of the city and of concentrating exclusively on "encirclement of the city by the country" through attacks on the cities by Red Army forces'.

But Moscow's demands on Li Li-san were not moderated. The only forces available to him were the guerrillas, yet Moscow was implacable in its insistence that action must be led by the workers. In a letter of 11th June 1930 to the party, Li for the first time mentioned the Red Army, and tried to find a verbal formula that would compromise between doctrine and reality. 'It must be the Red Army's aim', he wrote, 'to create a proper co-ordination with armed uprisings in important urban centres, capture them, and establish a national revolutionary government.'[1] He thus evaded the question whether the Red Army should wait until a rising had taken place in a city before attacking. In fact Li decided to attack first, and on 28th July 1930 Red Army troops captured Changsha, without any workers' rising to assist them. They were however obliged to abandon it after a few days in the face of Kuomintang government troops.

This failure cost Li Li-san his leadership. A scapegoat had to be found on whom was to be placed the blame for all previous failures: it could only be Li Li-san. Though he had faithfully endeavoured to carry out the impossible orders of Moscow, Moscow's mistakes were attributed to him. He was accused of disobedience to the Comintern, of both right and left deviations, of opportunist passivity, petty bourgeois chauvinism and Greater Chinese nationalism (*velikokitaizm*).[2] At a meeting of the party's *Politburo* held in November 1930, Li was forced to resign.

Li's discomforture was not at once followed by Mao's triumph. Of the various groups that aspired to the succession, the victor was the 'returned student clique' sponsored by the Comintern delegate

[1] Schwarz, op. cit., p. 142. [2] Schwarz, op. cit., p. 157.

Pavel M!f. The leading figure for the next period was Wang Ming, the most subservient to Moscow of all the leaders that the Chinese party has had. But Mao's authority was also increased. During the winter of 1930–1 Mao successfully eliminated his rivals to leadership of the soviet areas. In November 1931, with the approval of Wang Ming and of the Comintern, a First All-China Conference of Soviets was held at Juichin, and set up the Provisional Central Government of the Chinese Soviet Republic, of which Mao was elected chairman. Meanwhile the party grew still weaker in the cities. Its illegal organisation was crippled by arrests and executions. Mao politely invited the remnant of the Central Committee to join him on 'liberated territory'. When it hesitated he threatened to cut off its financial supplies. At last the Committee came, in the autumn of 1932. Wang Ming went to Moscow, where in the following years he played a considerable part in Comintern affairs.[1]

The Japanese invaded Manchuria in the autumn of 1931, and it was clear that this conquest would not satisfy them. But the prospect of further Japanese aggression did not prevent Chiang Kai-shek from fighting the growing menace of the Chinese soviets. The communists accused Chiang of neglecting the country's peril in order to make sure his own dictatorship. Chiang accused the communists of disrupting national unity at a time of national danger: only when the communist rebels had been destroyed could a united China face the foreign invader. Chiang's attacks became so dangerous during 1934 that Mao decided to take his forces to the north-west, where they would be close to Soviet-dominated Mongolia and far from the main centres of Chiang's power. The epic Long March lasted from October 1934 to October 1935. The army covered some 8,000 miles, and had very severe casualties. It established itself in the north of Shensi province, and the communists made their capital in the town of Yenan.[2]

Mao and his faithful comrade Chu Teh were brilliant guerrilla leaders, and they were brilliant organisers of the peasant masses. The peasants provided the soldiers for Mao's Red Army and the administrators for the liberated territories. The communists' success with the peasants was largely due to their policy of land reform. The Land Law of the Soviet Republic, decreed in November 1931,[3] provided for the confiscation, without compensation,

---

[1] He made one of the main speeches at the 7th Congress of the Comintern of 1935, which introduced the Popular Front. He even became an expert on Latin America (see below, p. 198).
[2] The classical account is Edgar Snow, *Red Star over China*, 1937.
[3] Fairbank, Schwarz and Brandt, op. cit., pp. 224–6.

of 'all lands of feudal landlords, village bosses, gentry, militarists, and other big private landowners', regardless of whether they worked or leased them. The land of rich peasants was also liable to confiscation, but some land was to be left to them. Red Army men were each to receive a plot of land. Redistribution of land among the poor peasants was to be on an equal basis, but this principle would only be applied when the majority of peasants in each area had been persuaded that this was right. Confiscation of land belonging to temples or religious bodies was also to be made dependent on the support of the majority in each area, 'so that their religious feelings may not be offended'.

The emphasis on peasant interests, which not only appeared in communist statements from the early 1930's onwards, but was confirmed by the observations of western correspondents who visited the soviet areas, caused many western commentators to regard the Chinese communists as 'agrarian socialists', who were 'not real communists at all'. This was a profound error. The Chinese communist movement was a movement of peasants, but not a peasant movement. The masses among whom the communists lived, on whose support their political aims and their very lives depended, were peasants. The communists had to get peasant good-will, as Lenin in 1917 and 1918 had had to get peasant good-will. The only way, for Mao as for Lenin, was to give the peasants what they wanted—the use, on more favourable terms, of the land. But in the 'liberated territories' the political and military hierarchy was firmly controlled by communists. The only political propaganda permitted in these areas was communist, a simplified form of Marxism suited to the peasant audience.

The peasants were drawn into the political machine as they had not been for centuries, if ever. It was agreeable to them to be wooed by the communists, to be treated as if they were worth consulting and persuading and 'educating'. The officials of the Manchu dynasty or the warlords had never paid them such flattering attention. The communists reaped rich dividends from their policies of 'mass enlightenment'. Enormous human reserves, never before touched, were now fully exploited. Peasant men and women of natural ability, with a talent for organisation, could make careers and could feel that they were serving their people. Lenin's tactic of the partnership between the disciplined communist conspirators and the illiterate masses[1] was carried even further in China than it had been in Russia. But in

[1] See above, pp. 29–30, 32, 37–8, 41.

China as in Russia all the controls were held by the party. Those Chinese peasants who rose in the hierarchy of the 'liberated territories' learned the principles of democratic centralism, accepted the leadership of the party, and became members of the party.

The leaders of the Comintern, and the earlier leaders of the Chinese communists, genuinely believed that the industrial proletariat must lead the revolution, and were perplexed and tormented by the party's failure among the industrial workers. But the truth is that neither the Russian nor the Chinese communist party was a party of the industrial workers. Successful communist parties are power machines, political elites that draw their members from all social classes, but themselves stand outside social classes. The raw material for the elites can be drawn as well from a peasantry as from a working class, in fact can in a sense be more easily drawn from a peasantry, because peasants are less likely than workers to have formed for themselves ideas that may conflict with communist doctrine. The more primitive the country, the more is the peasant mind a clean slate, on which communists may write their message. This does not mean that communists will always be successful among backward peasants. They can be prevented by either or both of two factors—a strong machinery of power that is hostile to communists, or a strong religious loyalty. But neither of these things was present in China. The machinery of government had disintegrated, and religion had less hold on the Chinese than on any other people of Asia or Europe.

CHAPTER EIGHT

Stalin's Revolution

LENIN's Revolution had been essentially political. It had completed the destruction of the Imperial regime initiated by
the March Revolution; had suppressed all Russian socialist
parties other than the Bolshevik; and had set up a Bolshevik dictatorship over the whole Russian people. It had also accomplished
great social changes: it had destroyed the economic power of the
landowners and of business men. But the most numerous class in
Russia, the peasants, having received their share of the landowners'
confiscated estates, continued to live according to the social pattern
of the past. Stalin's Revolution, which began in 1929, had more
drastic social consequences than Lenin's. It destroyed the independent peasant small-holders as a class. It created vast industries
by massive mobilisation of man-power and systematic exploitation
of the working class. It also had political consequences, for it
completed the subjection of the party to the will of Stalin, which
had begun already in the 1920's. Finally it affected every field of
cultural life, subordinating literature, the arts and the sciences not
only to a negative censorship—which had existed under Lenin—
but to detailed positive direction by the autocracy. Lenin's regime
had been a strict dictatorship: Stalin's was totalitarian.

Stalin's Revolution began as a result of shortages in the food
supply to the towns. The peasants, having more land than before
1917, ate more food. Scarcity of consumer goods deprived them
of incentive to grow more crops or to sell more of what they grew.
With each year the growth of the total population and the inevitable variations of crop due to weather, made the supply of the
urban population more insecure. The Soviet leaders, resolved both
on general grounds and for military reasons to develop Russian
industry rapidly, had to face the problems of agricultural output
and marketing.

Two alternative policies could be adopted towards the peasants.
One was to give them economic incentives. Better prices would be

paid for farm produce, a larger share of Russia's industrial capacity would be given to production of consumers' goods, and if this would still not fill the gap, further supplies of consumers' goods would have to be imported, if necessary at the cost of imports of raw materials for industries producing capital goods. Measures of this sort would encourage the peasants to work harder, produce more and sell it to the towns. They had however serious disadvantages. They would retard the growth of heavy industry, which the ruling group in the party considered more necessary than ever as they claimed to believe that Russia was in real danger of military attack.[1] A second objection was that increased trade with the 'capitalist world' would be necessary, and that this would place Russia at the mercy of her enemies. Thirdly, the increased agricultural production would above all enrich the wealthier peasants. Communist dogma taught that the wealthy peasants were exploiters, enemies of the working class and of the Soviet system. These three theoretical objections ruled out a policy of economic incentives.

The alternative was a policy of coercion. Supplies must be taken from the peasants at low prices, and force must be used against the wealthier peasants, the *kulaks*. This course had obvious theoretical advantages. The state would acquire great wealth without having to pay for it. A fatal blow would be struck at a group of persons whom the Communist leaders regarded as the one remaining dangerous 'class enemy'. Cheap food supplies would feed the industrial population, whose numbers would further be increased by recruits from villages. Production could be concentrated on heavy industry, without any need to divert consumers' goods to the countryside.

The policy adopted by Stalin lent itself well to Marxist rhetoric. Enemies, scapegoats and puppets had to be found. The supply crisis of 1927–8, like the supply crisis of 1918, was attributed to sabotage by *kulaks*. These enemies of the people were trying to starve the Soviet government into submission. The remedy was to organise the class war in the villages. The slogan was the same as under War Communism—rely on the poor peasants, win over the medium peasants, isolate and destroy the *kulaks*. Accounts written some years after the period of collectivisation by official Soviet writers give the impression that this correct line of comrade Stalin was in fact carried out. The broad popular masses of the poor peasants, it is claimed, led by the valiant Communist Party, rose in a class war against the *kulak* exploiters and destroyed them. The truth is quite different.

[1] See above, pp. 98, 107

There were few rich peasants in Russia in 1928.[1] There is little evidence that they exploited the rest of the peasantry, or engaged as a group in political opposition to the regime. Nor was there any more evidence than in the War Communism period that a sense of class division existed in the villages.[2]

In the summer of 1928 houses of alleged *kulaks* were searched, their crops were confiscated, and peasants were encouraged to denounce each other. In the autumn of 1929 the attack on the *kulaks* rose to a climax. At the end of December Stalin announced that the party would pass from a policy of 'limitation of the *kulaks*' to a policy of 'liquidation of the *kulaks* as a class'. A directive of 1st February 1930 authorised the complete expropriation and deportation of *kulaks* and their families. In practice this policy was carried out by emissaries of the party who knew little if anything of Russian rural life, used the most violent methods long before the February directive sanctioned them, and used them against thousands of peasants, regardless of whether they belonged to the economic category defined as *kulaks* or not. In many areas whole villages were treated as enemies. There were clashes with troops and massacres of peasants. It was a war of the Communist Party and its armed forces against the Russian and non-Russian peasantry.

The liquidation of the *kulaks* was a preparation for the mass collectivisation of agriculture, which began at the same time. The reason for collectivisation most frequently stressed in official Soviet statements, and best known in the non-Soviet world, is the long-term aim of improvement of agricultural output by mechanisation and by farming in large instead of small units. It had however short-term aims of greater practical importance to the Soviet leaders. These were to ensure that a much larger share of the existing output should be marketed, and to ensure a regular supply of recruits from the countryside to the new industries and new construction schemes that were being created under the Five Year Plan. These two aims were to be secured by creating a centralised administrative apparatus for the countryside, firmly controlled by the Communist Party. The apparatus was the double hierarchy of collective farms and machine-tractor stations (M.T.S.).

[1] *Kulaks* were defined as those who (*a*) owned means of production to the value of more than 1600 roubles, and hired labour for more than 50 days in the year; (*b*) owned to a value of more than 800 roubles and hired labour for more than 75 days in the year; or (*c*) owned to a value of more than 400 and hired for more than 150 days in the year. According to the census of 1926, those falling into these categories formed 4 per cent of the peasants. For a discussion of these peasant incomes, see N. Yasny, *The Socialised Agriculture of the USSR*, Stanford University Press, 1949, pp. 161–82.
[2] See above, pp. 44–5.

Collective farms were managed by committees, nominally elected by the members. The committees were ruled by their chairmen, who were in fact appointed by the emissaries of the Communist Party By a decision of the party's Central Committee of November 1929 not less than 25,000 industrial workers were sent to the villages to conduct collectivisation. During the first years of the new system nearly half the collective farm chairmen were members of the party, and a majority of all chairmen were not peasants. The M.T.S. had a monopoly of agricultural machinery. Their task was to plough the collective farms' land in return for a portion of the crop. By 1932 about half the collective farms were ploughed by M.T.S., by 1937 nearly 90 per cent. Each M.T.S. served about 30 collective farms. In 1933 were created special 'political departments' of Communist Party members in each M.T.S. The head of each M.T.S. political department was in fact the dictator of the whole rural area served by his station. At the end of the following year the departments were abolished, but the same powers were given to a 'Political Assistant-Director', nominally subordinate to the technician who was appointed Director by the People's Commissariat of Agriculture but in fact exercising powers over the M.T.S. similar to those exercised over a Red Army unit by a political commissar.

The process of collectivisation occupied the years 1929 to 1933. In the first months of 1930 peasants were forced into collective farms by the million. As news of disorders and dislocation came in, the government decided to call a halt. Stalin's letter on 'Dizziness from success' was published in *Pravda* on 2nd March. In the preceding months Stalin himself had most frantically clamoured for speed.[1] Now he placed all the blame on his subordinates. If innocent peasants had suffered that was the fault of over-zealous officials. In the next months peasants left the collective farms in large numbers. But the 16th Congress of the party, held in July, made it clear that the aim was still complete collectivisation. In 1931 pressure was again used. The harvest of 1931 was bad, and the authorities seized all the peasants' grain reserves. In 1932 the harvest was again bad, but the government's demands for grain were not reduced. Troops were sent to collect it, and in the Ukraine and North Caucasus some millions of peasants starved to death. Not till 1934 were more or less normal conditions restored. In that year the government fixed the exact amounts of grain to be delivered, and the surplus was left to the peasants. The collective

[1] Stalin, *Voprosy Leninizma*, 11th edition, Moscow, 1939, pp. 268–74, 275–94, 295–8, 299–304.

farms thus had an incentive to increase their output. The concession of 1934, following the horrors of 1929–33, resembled the concession of 1921 following the horrors of 1918–20. The difference was that the bulk of the peasantry had now been forced into collective farms.

Collectivisation was dearly paid in human and animal lives. At least five million alleged *kulaks* were deported in 1929–30 and in 1932. Of these about a million perished, and many of the remainder succumbed in the next years to the hardships of forced labour at the new industrial sites in the east. The victims of the 1933 famine were still more numerous. The losses of livestock were between a third and a half of the total number of animals in the Soviet Union in 1929.[1]

The chief economic gain to the government from collectivisation was that the portion of the crop that was marketed was increased about two and a half times. The increase in the total crop was not large, and was of course diminished by the subsequent constant growth of population. Of the social consequence—the creation of a new class structure in the countryside—more will be said later.[2] The most important result of all was political. A new administrative hierarchy was created, more centralised and more efficiently gripping the peasantry, than any that had ever existed in an agrarian country. This the government could use to bend the peasantry to whatever economic or political purposes it had.

The collectivisation of agriculture was accompanied by industrialisation on a scale and at a pace never yet known in human history. This had obvious economic aims—to increase the national wealth, to raise the standard of living, and to find employment for the surplus rural population. It also had a military aim—to increase heavy industry, the basis of modern war, at a time when the Soviet leaders professed to believe that their country was threatened with invasion by the encircling capitalist Powers. It also had more specifically Marxist aims—to increase the numbers of the working class, officially regarded as the class that supports socialism, and to diminish first relatively and then absolutely the number of

[1] Horses numbered 33 million in 1928, 15 million in 1933. The figures for these two years for the other main categories of livestock are: Horned cattle 70 million and 34 million; pigs 26 million and 9 million; sheep and goats 146 million and 42 million. In Central Asia the losses were much higher than in European Russia. In Turkmenistan cattle were reduced from 5·8 million in 1929 to 1·2 million in 1933. In Kirgizia sheep and goats were reduced from 5·3 million in 1927–8 to 1·2 million in 1934. H. Sahat-Muradov, *10 let turkmenskoy SSR* and A. Zorin, *10 let sovyetskoy Kirgizii*, in *Revolyutsia i Natsionalnosti*, 1934, No. 6.

[2] See below, pp. 237–238.

peasants, living in the petty bourgeois swamp of 'rural idiocy'. Ever since the beginning of the First Five Year Plan the military and Marxist motives have taken precedence over the normal economic motives. Increase in the power of the state machine has been the first aim, the standard of living has always come far behind. When conditions have been favourable, crumbs have been thrown to the consumers, in difficult times they have borne the full burden. The permanent war scare has been a useful whip with which to drive the people.

For industrialisation three factors are usually required—natural resources, man-power and skill. Skill includes both skilled workers and machinery—the accumulated skill of the labour of others. Of the first two factors Russia had abundance, but the third was scarce. Stalin's solution was to substitute force for skill. Workers were regimented, mobilised and directed. Orders were given to achieve predetermined production targets. If these were not achieved, the managers were treated as saboteurs. Knowing this, the managers drove their workers pitilessly. In every difficulty Stalin had two sovereign remedies, scapegoats and rhetoric. For disasters and hardships scapegoats had to be found, at all levels except the very highest—the infallibility of the 'teacher of genius' himself and of the abstraction in whose name he exercised his genius, the Party, could never be questioned. In rhetoric the fashion was set by the teacher of genius, whose soap-box phrases about the moral superiority and invincible Bolshevik will-power of Soviet man were repeated by hundreds of thousands of party agitators at hundreds of thousands of party meetings.

The most important feature of the industrial policy in the Five Year Plan periods was mobilistion of labour. Jobs which in an advanced industrial country would be done by one skilled worker with a machine, could only be done, in the shortage of skilled workers and machines, by several pairs of bare hands. The bare hands could come only from the countryside. Rural overpopulation had been the greatest weakness of Russia's economy: now it could be a source of strength. Recruitment of labour armies for the new factories and public works schemes was the second task of collective farm managements, no less important than their first task of extracting food supplies from the peasants.

To fit the millions of unskilled rural labourers, whose numbers increased even more rapidly than had been expected, into the new industrial framework, was the task of the trade unions. The process deprived the unions of their last remnants of independence. The

8th Trade Union Congress, held in December 1928, was a turning-point. The old leader, Tomski, who had agreed in the past to a very large measure of control by the government, nevertheless objected to the scale of sacrifices now demanded of the workers. He was replaced by the faithful servants of Stalin, Shvernik and Kaganovich. Since then the unions have been docile instruments in the hand of the party. This result was not due to wickedness on the part of the party bureaucrats in the unions. It was an inevitable result of economic conditions which were determined by Stalin's own decision. If vast masses of unskilled peasants had to be turned into factory workers in a few years, they had to be brutally regimented. The proportion of skilled workers was too small, and the experience of trade unions was too recent, to make possible a working class with a solidarity and an independent outlook of its own. The few skilled men were in the position of overworked sergeant-majors confronted with hordes of raw recruits. They had not time or strength to explain and persuade: they could only bellow and bully. Stalin's decision to force the pace of industrialisation put an end to the possibility that the Soviet Union could be a workers' state.

Much has been written of the convulsions wrought in Russia by the First Five Year Plan. Output of consumers' goods was sacrificed to output of heavy industry. The destruction of small craftsmen's workshops deprived the people of its main source of clothing, and this was not compensated by increased factory production.[1] The food supply was precarious. Housing was pitifully inadequate. The old industrial centres were overcrowded, and in the new centres of the Urals and Siberia no serious attempt was made to accommodate the hundreds of thousands of new workers. The result was constant movement of workers from one place to another in search of a job in somewhat less inhuman conditions.[2] This habit of 'flitting', much denounced in the Soviet press, was, as has been rightly pointed out, a substitute for strikes, which the regime prevented.[3]

As Stalin refused to slacken the pace of construction, social problems could not be solved. The only course was repression. Great efforts were also made to increase the number of women and adolescent workers in industry. Both were employed in heavy labour and at night. Piece rates were substituted for time rates in the greater part of Soviet industry. 'Socialist competition' and

[1] Manya Gordon, *Russian Workers before and after Lenin*, New York, 1941, p. 397.
[2] A good account of these conditions may be found in J. Scott, *Behind the Urals*, 1942.
[3] I. Deutscher, *Soviet Trade Unions*, 1950, p. 88.

Stahanovism were devised to speed up workers' output. 'Shock workers' and Stahanovites earned enormous wages as long as they kept up the pace. The most important result of the system was, however, to enable managements from time to time to increase the minimum standard outputs ('norms') on which wages were calculated. When one Stahanovite record was surpassed by a new record, the old Stahanovite output became the 'norm'. The purpose of the whole policy was to get more out of the workers for the same pay. The cost to the state of the special prizes, medals and decorations, and of the very high wages earned for brief periods by the record-breakers, was more than compensated by the increased gains in the output of state industry, made at the expense of the working class.

The plight of managers was hardly more enviable. They were ordered to produce fantastic outputs, but a host of restrictions limited their ability to obtain raw materials, equipment or labour. Managers or engineers who had been trained before the Revolution were suspect. They were watched both by their workers and by the younger engineers and administrators, trained under the communist regime, who coveted their jobs. If the target were not achieved, the managers would be accused of sabotage. They could hope to survive only if they would break the impossible laws, barter their products for those of other factories, entice workers away from rival factories by promises of higher wages or better dwellings, demand far larger supplies of men and material than they really needed, hoard reserve stocks, make constant journeys to Moscow at the factory's expense and keep permanent representatives in important centres to form a lobby in influential government institutions. All these things greatly increased the general inefficiency, raised the cost of production throughout the country, and were contrary to the laws. But the alternative was ruin for the manager, and probably for most of his assistants as well. The abuses could have been avoided if the pace had been slackened, and if the plans had been made, not in order to win glory for the planners but in order to make the best use of resources that were really available. But anyone who had suggested this would have incurred the wrath of the teacher of genius, who, as has been well said by a recent biographer, 'seemed to live in a half-real and half-dreamy world of statistical figures and indices, of industrial orders and instructions, a world in which no target and no objective seemed to be beyond his and the party's grasp'.[1]

.   .   .   .   .

[1] I. Deutscher, *Stalin, A Political Biography*, 1949, pp. 321-2.

Economic sufferings produced discontent, and knowledge of discontent caused the police to fear conspiracy. At the same time the government sought to appease the suffering masses by liberal use of scapegoats. It could not be admitted that the breakdown of supplies was due to the political decisions of the leaders: it had to be explained by the wickedness of saboteurs and foreign spies. In the early 1930's were staged the first show trials, the rehearsal for the still more sensational spectacles of 1936–8. The victims of these trials were engineers, scientists, historians and former members of the Menshevik and Socialist Revolutionary parties. These years also brought increased religious persecution, and the party tightened its grip over literature and the arts.

The same general trend affected policy towards the non-Russian nationalities. At the 16th Congress of the party in 1930 official emphasis was still on the harmfulness of 'Great Russian Great Power chauvinism'. At the 17th Congress, held in 1934, Stalin declared theoretical discussion as to which of the two deviations were the more dangerous to be unreal. The more dangerous was 'the deviation which they have stopped combating, and thus enabled to grow until it becomes a danger to the state'. The rest of his speech made clear that at the moment he considered the 'local nationalism' deviation the more dangerous. The truth is that between the 16th and 17th Congresses a trend towards russification set in, which has remained strong up to the present day.

The change was most marked in the Ukraine. In March 1930 a trial was held in Harkov of a group of non-communist Ukrainian intellectuals, accused of organising a clandestine 'League for the liberation of the Ukraine'. The famine of 1932–3 was regarded in Moscow as a result of sabotage by peasants influenced by Ukrainian nationalism, and in the Ukraine as an attempt by Muscovites to starve the Ukrainian nation. In January 1933 Stalin appointed Pavel Postyshev as Second Secretary of the Ukrainian Communist Party, and in fact as dictator of the whole Ukraine. Postyshev purged both party and administration, paying special attention to the Commissariat of Education, whose chief, Skrypnik, committed suicide in May 1933. The purge removed about a fifth of the members of the party, and some 60 per cent of secretaries of party district committees.[1] Though russification of the pre-1917 type was not reintroduced, the extreme subordination of the Ukraine to the

[1] According to Postyshev himself, quoted by M. Kowalewski, *Polityka narodowościowa na Ukrainie sowieckiej*, Warsaw, 1938, p. 147, 237 out of 390 district party secretaries and 249 out of 390 chairman of district soviet executive committees were purged.

central government, and the extreme suspiciousness of the central authorities towards any manifestation of Ukrainian national feeling, deprived of any real value the official formula of 'culture national in form but socialist in content'.

Central Asia was also radically changed during the Five Year Plan years.

The losses of livestock were heavier in the Kazah steppes than anywhere else in the Soviet Union. Doctrinaire arguments as to whether nomads should be collectivised before they were settled as permanent agricultural communities, or be settled before they were collectivised,[1] concealed the tragedy of the death by hunger of nearly half the Kazah people, and of the destruction of the way of life of the surviving half who had no desire to be drawn into the whirlpool of Russian industrialisation but asked only to be left alone.[2] Deprived of their traditional livelihood, they were swept into the new industries of the Urals and Siberia, where they led an exceptionally miserable existence as unskilled workers, not only materially destitute but also spiritually uprooted.

In the settled regions south of the steppes, in Uzbekistan and Tadjikistan, there were also great changes. The Five Year Plan required an immense increase in cotton production as well as rapid development of mineral resources as yet barely exploited. The minerals were worked, under the supervision of Russian foremen, by unskilled Uzbek, Tadjik or Turkmen workers, as poor and as uprooted as the Kazahs and Kirgiz in the Urals and Siberia. The planners imposed a drastic reorganisation of the agriculture of Central Asia. Less land was to be cultivated for cereals and more for cotton. Grain was to be imported from Siberia or Russia, and this placed in the hands of the government in Moscow the powerful weapon of famine. The destruction of livestock made the weapon more formidable. Central Asia is naturally suited for cotton growing, and specialisation in cotton increased the wealth of the region. But the wealth went not to the local people but to the state

---

[1] This is discussed in doctrinal terms in the Soviet journal, *Revolyutsionny Vostok*, 1934, No. 5, article by P. Pogorelski, *K voprosu o teorii i praktike osedlania kochevnikov* (Theory and practice of the settlement of nomads).

[2] Between the censuses of 1926 and 1939 the number of Kazahs in the Soviet Union dropped by 869,000. During this period the normal natural increase of population should have produced more than 600,000 more Kazahs than there were in 1926. There is thus a discrepancy of about 1,500,000 Kazahs. The total number of Kazahs in 1939 was about 3,100,000. The 'missing' Kazahs probably include many thousands who emigrated to Chinese Turkestan, but the bulk of the deficit must be explained by starvation and disease resulting from collectivisation. For the demographic facts, see F. Lorimer, *The Population of the Soviet Union*, Geneva, 1946; Walter Kolarz, *Russia and her Colonies*, 1952, p. 268.

machine whose centre was Moscow. There is some similarity between Moscow's insistence on cotton production in Uzbekistan and British encouragement of cotton production in Egypt. The difference is that the economic power of Moscow was reinforced by ruthless political dictatorship, while that of the British was not. Egyptian politicians could denounce British imperialism in all its aspects, and agitate and organise for independence. Uzbek or Turkmen leaders who criticised any important aspect of Moscow's policy were regarded as plotters of treason and treated accordingly.

THE *YEZHOVSHCHINA*

Within the Communist Party the years 1929–34 brought some friction and discontent, but the number of persons affected, though it included some eminent people, was not large. The new industrial and agricultural policy, which represented a greatly exaggerated version of the policy earlier recommended by Trotski, could not be carried out with the 'Right' leaders Buharin, Tomski and Rykov at the helm. By the summer of 1928 the breach between them and Stalin was imminent. In July Buharin met the disgraced Kamenev, and confessed to him his horror at Stalin's policy and methods.[1] Buharin's views on economic policy were formally disapproved at the November Plenum of the Central Committee as 'Right deviation and conciliationism'. In January 1929 an account of his conversation with Kamenev became known to the authorities, and in February he was removed from the editorship of *Pravda*. At the same time Tomski, who had been replaced as Chairman of the Trade Union Council by Shvernik after the 8th trade union congress of December 1928, was removed from membership of the Council. In July Buharin was removed from the Bureau of the Comintern, and his theoretical writings were withdrawn from circulation. In November he was expelled from the *Politburo*. Unlike the 'Left' Opposition of 1926, the three leaders of the 'Right' had never built themselves a faction within the party. They had no hope of organising resistance to Stalin. Perhaps for this reason, they were more mildly treated in the next years, and continued to be consulted as advisers on economic policy and administrative problems.

Stalin's leadership was now complete, and was so rigorously enforced that there could be no open challenge from within the party. During the following years several clandestine 'factions'

---

[1] B. Souvarine, *Staline*, Paris, 1935, pp. 444–9, quotes, from documents secretly circulated at the time by supporters of Trotski, an account of this interview.

were however 'unmasked'. Their leaders, who had circulated
memoranda criticising Stalin, were followers neither of Zinoviev
nor of Kamenev: they were men who had made their careers as
henchmen of the General Secretary.[1] Their punishments were
however made occasions to banish Zinoviev and Kamenev to
Siberia, from October 1932 to May 1933, and to issue severe
reprimands to Rykov and Tomski.[2]

The year 1934 was marked by better economic conditions and
slightly less political pressure. Hopes of a milder regime were
associated with the person of S. M. Kirov, Secretary of the party for
Leningrad and at this time second only to Stalin in the country.
But in December 1934 Kirov was assassinated. The circumstances
of this crime have never been cleared up. Stalin of course attributed
it to Trotski and Zinoviev; the Trotskists accused Stalin of mur-
dering Kirov; while a third version, possibly the most likely, claims
that the assassination was an act of personal hatred.

Zinoviev and Kamenev were arrested soon after the crime,
together with known former followers of these two or of Trotski,
and a large number of Leningrad factory workers. Early in January
1935 Zinoviev and Kamenev were secretly tried by a tribunal of
the security police[3] and sentenced to long prison terms. Plans were
made rigorously to scrutinise party membership and to tighten
security measures. But arrests were not yet on a vast scale. Early
in 1936 Stalin even considered measures to liberalise the regime.
As a test of public opinion, steps were taken to arrange genuinely
free public discussions on two questions—the draft of the new Constitution that was being prepared, and a draft law on the prohibition
of abortions. The results of both sets of discussions were highly
discouraging. Public opinion was strongly opposed to the abortion
law, and free ballots at party conferences in Moscow and Leningrad,
held to discuss the Constitution, revealed large numbers of votes
cast against members of the *Politburo* and even against Stalin himself. For an explanation of these defeats of his policy Stalin sought,
as usual, some group of counter-revolutionary conspirators that
had influenced the people against him. The Zinovievites and
Kamenevites, already under arrest, could not be responsible: the

[1] They included a chief of the Central Committee's propaganda department, Ryutin,
and a premier of the Russian SFSR, Syrtsov.
[2] *VKP (b) v Rezolyutsiah*, Moscow, 1941, Vol. II, pp. 531–2.
[3] The OGPU was abolished, and its functions handed to the People's Commissariat
of the Interior (NKVD) in 1934. Within this Commissariat the functions of political
police were handled by the Chief Administration of State Security (GUGB). In fact
the name and some of the personnel had changed, but the organisation remained
essentially the same.

guilty men must be Buharin, Tomski and Rykov. The preparation of a case against these men, designed to show not only that they opposed Stalin's policy, but that they were planning his overthrow by force, was entrusted to Stalin's special confidant, N. I. Yezhov, who about this time replaced Yagoda as head of N.K.V.D.

Zinoviev and Kamenev were publicly tried in August 1936. They confessed that they had formed in 1932 a *bloc* with Trotskists in Russia and had received instructions from Trotski from abroad. They had planned to overthrow the government and murder Stalin, and they had arranged the murder of Kirov. In January 1937 took place the trial of another group of prominent communists, including Pyatakov, Radek and Serebryakov. They also confessed that they had prepared the assassination of Stalin and other party leaders. They had formed a Trotskist-Buharinist 'parallel centre', and had organised sabotage in mines and factories in the Donets Basin, Urals, Siberia and Moscow. The evidence of the prosecution consisted of confessions by the accused and testimony of other persons also under arrest. Where it could be checked against the evidence of persons at liberty it was proved false.[1] Trotski himself maintained that ever since 1928 he had had no dealings with Zinoviev and Kamenev, and that he had broken with those of his own former following who in the subsequent period had capitulated to Stalin. In particular, Radek, represented at the trial as a Trotskist, was his enemy, responsible for the death of one of his loyal friends.[2]

In fact no Trotskist or Zinovievist organisation existed in Russia. More serious opposition might however be feared from the moderate elements of the party, from those who sympathised with the person or the ideas of Buharin and disliked the increasingly ruthless methods of Stalin's regime. To destroy 'Buharinism' was the main task of Yezhov and his men. Before they died, Zinoviev, Kamenev and Radek were induced to 'implicate' Buharin, Tomski and Rykov. According to one circumstantial account[3] the alleged plot by these three was discussed by a

[1] The hotel in Copenhagen in which emissaries of the *bloc* were alleged to have met Trotski, had been demolished some years earlier. On the day when Pyatakov was alleged to have flown to Norway to meet Trotski, no aircraft landed at Oslo airfield, and Trotski's movements were completely accounted for by witnesses. See *Not Guilty*, report of commission of inquiry into the charges against Trotski, chairman John Dewey, 1936.

[2] Radek was believed to have betrayed to the OGPU in 1929 Trotski's friend Blumkin who had visited him in Turkey and returned to Russia with messages to his friends. Blumkin was executed. He was the first person killed for intra-party factional activity.

[3] A. Ouralov, *Staline au pouvoir*, Paris, 1951, pp. 37–41. The author at this time had access to confidential documents of the Central Committee, and writes from memory. His account cannot be accepted as certain until corroborative evidence is available, but it is not improbable, and fits facts that are known.

Plenum of the Central Committee in September 1936. Yezhov made his report, and Buharin made a vigorous defence. After speeches had been made by many of those present, two-thirds of the Central Committee voted against the acceptance of Yezhov's report. Among the two-thirds were five members of the *Politburo*.[1] Stalin nominally accepted this decision and made more thorough preparations. In February 1937 he had Buharin and Rykov expelled from the Central Committee without formally consulting the Committee. In March 1938 they were tried, together with the former Head of Police, Henrik Yagoda. During the year 1937 the mass purge got under way.

Western comment on the purge has concentrated on the big figures—Zinoviev, Kamenev, Pyatakov, Radek, Serebryakov, Rykov, Buharin, Tomski, Krestinski and Rakovski, the closest collaborators of Lenin. All serious observers must agree, both that the detailed criminal accusations were false, and that the political background depicted in the trials—in particular, the allegation that Trotski and Zinoviev were allies—is untrue. But some explanation is required. Two complementary hypotheses have become widely accepted, and seem convincing as far as they go. The first is that these men confessed to crimes which they had not committed because they were persuaded both that their actions and criticisms had indeed constituted a threat to the party, the Soviet state and the Revolution which were to them the only ultimate values, and that to make in public these concrete false confessions was the best last service they could render to the cause.[2] The second is that Stalin's motive for removing these men was to destroy any potential alternative leadership to his own, which in time of war might take his place. Trotski's 1927 reference to Clémenceau had not been forgotten.[3]

These two hypotheses do much to explain the removal of the most eminent old Bolsheviks and the extraordinary spectacle of the show trials. But these were only a small part of the purge which became known, after the name of its executor, as the *Yezhovshchina*, and raged throughout 1938 and 1939. Within the party machine there were thousands of victims at all levels. In the *Politburo* itself there were six.[4] These men had never joined the

---

[1] Kossior, Postyshev, Rudzutak, Eihe, Chubar.
[2] This view was first expressed in a novel by Charles Plisnier, *Faux passeports*, Paris, 1938. It was later elaborated in Arthur Koestler's brilliant novel, *Darkness at Noon*.
[3] See above, p. 98. This view is ably presented in Deutscher, *Stalin*, pp. 375–8.
[4] Rudzutak, Kossior, Chubar, Petrovski, Postyshev, Eihe.

Trotskist or Zinovievist or Buharinist oppositions, but had been devoted supporters of Stalin until the Plenum of September 1936, when they had opposed Yezhov's attack on Buharin, not because they shared the latter's doctrines but because they objected to the use of such methods within the party. None of the six were brought to public trial. The overwhelming majority of the purged party officials simply disappeared without publicity. Whether they were shot or sent to forced labour, whether they were subsequently pardoned and whether they are still living to-day cannot be ascertained. Three-quarters of the members of the Central Committee disappeared.[1] Many hundreds of secretaries of provincial or district committees of the party, and thousands of party officials of still lower rank, were swept away.

But the purge was not only directed at those party members who held posts in the party machine. Its victims included thousands of party members holding posts in the armed forces, the administration and the economic hierarchy of both the central government and the governments of the non-Russian national republics, and many thousands more who were not members of the party at all. Vast numbers were also affected who were neither party members nor responsible officials, but belonged to some group regarded as actually or potentially hostile to the regime. Members of the families of arrested persons, and their friends, acquaintances or business connections were also liable to arrest and imprisonment. Wives of those arrested were often given the alternatives of divorcing their husbands or suffering their fate, separated from them and from their children. Children were persecuted at school if their parents were accused as 'enemies of the people', unless they publicly denounced them. Infants were sometimes left to die untended, sometimes removed to special 'children's colonies' managed by the police.

The army purge naturally attracted more attention outside Russia than any other part of the *Yezhovshchina*. Tuhachevski, the Chief of General Staff, hero of the Polish war of 1920 and maker of the Red Army, was shot. His trial was secret but the Soviet public was informed that he had conspired against the state in

---

[1] Every Congress of the party from 1918 onwards normally re-elected nearly all of the members of the Central Committee elected by the previous Congress, and added some new persons. The exception was the 15th Congress of 1927, which excluded followers of Trotski, Zinoviev and Kamenev. But even then, most of the members of the 1927 Committee had belonged to the Committee of 1925. Contrast with this the break between the 17th Congress (1934) and the 18th (1939), separated by the years of the *Yezhovshchina*. Of 71 full members of the Central Committee of the 17th Congress, only 16 were members of the Central Committee elected by the 18th.

league with Nazi Germany. 'Implicated' with him was the chief of the hierarchy of political commissars, Gamarnik, a member of the party's Central Committee, who committed suicide. A massacre of senior officers ensued.[1]

In the civil administration certain Commissariats were purged with special severity. One was Heavy Industry, of which Pyatakov had been Assistant-Commissar.[2] There were severe casualties among engineers in heavy industrial plants and scientists whose work was connected with heavy industry. Another special target were the railways.[3] Another was the Commissariat of Foreign Trade, whose Commissar, Rozenholz, was implicated in the Pyatakov trial. The officials of the Commissariat of Finance suffered after the arrest of their Commissar, Grinko, who was tried with Buharin in March 1938.

The impact of the *Yezhovshchina* on the non-Russian peoples is of special interest. The purge of 1933 in the Ukraine was now far exceeded. The dictator of 1933, Postyshev, and his nominal superior Kossior, were removed, and Hrushchov was appointed by Stalin as First Secretary and real dictator of the Ukraine. The purge went on throughout 1937.[4] A radical purge also took place in the Uzbek Communist Party. It was initiated by a special commission sent from Moscow under the Stalinist *Politburo* member Andreyev. The Prime Minister Faizulla Hodzhaev and the secretary of the party Ikramov were tried with Buharin and shot, and a purge of

---

[1] The purge removed 3 out of 5 Marshals; 13 out of 15 Army Commanders; 57 out of 85 Corps Commanders; 110 out of 195 Divisional Commanders; 220 out of 406 Brigade Commanders. Lower ranks of the Officer Corps were also drastically purged, but many of these officers were later released and returned to the service. Of the guilt or innocence of Tuhachevski, it can be said only that, in the mass of German archives made available since 1945, no trace can be found. A plausible hypothesis is that the story was 'planted' on the Soviet authorities by the German Gestapo leader Heydrich, through Czechoslovak channels. A renegade G.P.U. official Krivitsky, believes that Stalin used German 'evidence' against Tuhachevski, knowing it to be false, and that this was connected with plans to make an agreement with Hitler already in 1937 (W. Krivitski, *I was Stalin's agent*, 1939, pp. 248, 255–66). But even if the accusation of plotting with the Germans is—as is reasonably certain—false, it does not follow that there was not some sort of plot by some generals to overthrow Stalin. The truth will perhaps never be proved.

[2] Pyatakov's superior, the Commissar for Heavy Industry, Sergo Ordjonikidze, Stalin's old friend, died in mysterious circumstances early in the purge.

[3] Kaganovich, the Commissar, an intimate friend of Stalin, escaped by sacrificing his subordinates. An extraordinary category were the former employees of the Chinese Eastern Railway in Harbin. When the railway was sold to Japan in 1935, these people, who had always had Soviet passports, were repatriated. During the *Yezhovshchina* they were arrested almost to a man as Japanese spies.

[4] The purge removed all 9 members of the Ukrainian *Politburo*, all 12 members of the Ukrainian Council of People's Commissars, and 45 out of 57 members of the Ukrainian Communist Party's Central Committee. For details see Ouralov, op. cit., pp. 69–72; *Entsiklopedia Ukrainoznavstva*, pp. 554–5; Kowalewski, op. cit., p. 167.

the party and state machine followed. In the other Central Asian republics the purge was more discreet but no less thorough.[1] In Transcaucasia all the leading personalities except the Georgian Beria and the Azerbaidjani Bagirov were swept away.[2] A specially victimised category were the small groups of persons living in cities far from their national territory, for instance Greeks in Odessa, Armenians in Ukrainian towns, Tatars in cities of Central Russia. In some cases these were arrested almost to a man. The incidence of the purge on the Jews, much the most numerous of the scattered minorities, was exceptionally high.

The persecution of non-Russian peoples and of minorities was connected with a panic suspicion of foreign espionage. This led to mass arrests both of foreign subjects living in the Soviet Union and of Soviet citizens who had either been abroad or had contacts with foreign subjects within the Soviet Union. Among the first group an important category were employees of the Comintern. Here there was a significant distinction. Communists of western democratic countries were treated with caution, because their governments might take an interest in their fate, and Soviet policy now sought closer relations with those governments. Communists of countries ruled by fascist or dictatorial governments were treated without mercy. The Polish communists were almost all either shot or imprisoned, and in 1938 the Polish Communist Party was formally dissolved by the Comintern. Austrians who had escaped to the Soviet Union after Dollfuss had smashed the workers' organisations, were arrested as fascist spies. The same happened to many German communists.[3] The Yugoslav leaders mostly disappeared.[4]

The last victim of the *Yezhovshchina* was the security police itself. Yezhov was removed from his post in 1938 and disappeared. Many of the police chiefs, heads of forced labour camps, and

<hr/>

[1] See the interesting articles by O. Ahmeddjan, *Predposylki i podgotovka k provedeniyu 'Yezhovshchiny' v Turkestane* (Preliminaries and preparation of the *Yezhovshchina* in Turkestan) and by Dr. A. Gokdepe, *Natsionalnaya politika Moskvy* (Moscow's nationality policy), part 3, both in *Türkeli*, 1952, No. 3–4 (published in Munich).

[2] According to Ouralov (op. cit., pp. 161–171), in the North Caucasus and the three Transcaucasian republics, between 3 per cent and 4 per cent of the total population were arrested. The author's assertion, which cannot at present be checked from other sources, is based partly on his own experience of the North Caucasian organisation of the party, and partly on Soviet archives captured during the war by the Germans.

[3] Among the victims were Eberlein, the KPD delegate to the 1st Congress of the Comintern, and Heinz Neumann, the organiser of the Canton Commune of 1927 (see above, pp. 69 and 146).

[4] They are mentioned in A. Ciliga, *Au pays du grand mensonge*, Paris, 1950, and in B. Lazic, *Titov pokret i režim*, 1946. The purge is also mentioned, in obscure and unconvincing terms, in V. Dedijer, *Tito speaks*, 1953, pp. 108–9.

examining judges who had conducted the purge found themselves sharing the fate of their victims.

The causes of the purge remain a subject of speculation. Why should Stalin destroy his own supporters, the men whom he had placed in key positions since the 1920's and on whom his power had been built? Why should he destroy so many of the best technical experts of the Soviet Union, and cripple the army which had been created with such care by Trotski, Frunze and Tuhachevski?

Genuine fear played some part, especially in the case of charges of espionage. Soviet police officials' ignorance of the world outside the borders of the Soviet Union no doubt magnified their fear. Twenty years of propaganda had built a frightening picture of infinitely wily and treacherous foreign capitalists. There is also evidence that the N.K.V.D. makes little distinction between a hostile state of mind and hostile actions. One who hates the regime, and would like to see it overthrown, is capable of acting for its overthrow: the fact that he has done nothing to that end is irrelevant. If it is a crime to have a hostile attitude to the regime, as this makes one capable of active treason, then one who might in certain circumstances have a hostile attitude is dangerous, as he is capable of holding the views that would make him capable of a criminal act. With the extraordinary capacity for pursuing a thought to its logical conclusion, and for applying it universally without regard for any other realities, which has long been a characteristic of the Russian political mind, the N.K.V.D. were able more or less sincerely to regard as potentially guilty almost the whole population of the Soviet Union.

A second motive was the need for scapegoats. The Second Five Year Plan period (1933–7) did not require such sacrifices from the people as the First. Nevertheless economic hardships were still very severe. Moreover the people had been led to hope, in 1934 and again in 1936, that their life would be easier, not only that their standard of living would improve but that there would be greater freedom of speech. These hopes were disappointed, partly because Stalin was discouraged by the results of the limited free discussion of early 1936, partly because the now genuine threat of war made further sacrifices necessary. Disappointment when a real improvement is not sustained is often politically more dangerous than discontent with unrelieved misery. The consequent tension calls especially for scapegoats. Stories of espionage in high places were designed to increase the people's contributions for defence. Stories of systematic sabotage by Pyatakov and his fellow-accused were intended to divert rage from the failures of the government's economic policy.

Two factors deserve mention which may have played little part in initiating the purge, but gained importance as it gathered momentum.

One was that every N.K.V.D. official had an interest in making as large a number of arrests, and producing as large a number of confessions, as possible. To some extent of course this phenomenon exists in any state ruled by police methods. It had certainly existed in Imperial Russia. There the promotion of high officers to the highest posts depended on their ability to persuade the Tsar and his closest advisers, both that sedition was seething everywhere, and that only their own vigilance and courage stood between the monarch and destruction. The same general consideration applied to the relations of the N.K.V.D. bosses to Stalin and the party leaders. Lower in the police hierarchy the same was the case. Every petty informer's chance of a better job depended on his ability to convince his superiors that he had unmasked a number of counter-revolutionary plots. But all this was intensified in an unprecedented degree during the *Yezhovshchina*. The principles of Stahanovism and socialist competition were applied to the extraction not only of coal from the pits but of confessions from enemies of the people. Any police investigator who conscientiously examined evidence, and hesitated to pursue a 'case' where no guilt appeared to exist, risked being himself unmasked as a protector of counter-revolutionary saboteurs: too many of his colleagues and subordinates envied his job to make the risk worth taking.

The second factor was that, as the numbers of those sentenced to forced labour increased by millions, these slaves began to play an important part in the national economy. The N.K.V.D. became a vast employer of labour. Its slaves were put to the most unpleasant tasks that needed to be done, in the most unpleasant climates and most remote regions, to which in the past even unusually high wages had not attracted sufficient man-power. The state had already found a method of getting food supplies cheap by creating the hierarchy of collective farms and M.T.S. The mass of industrial workers were being driven to produce more in proportion to their wages. Now, perhaps as much by chance as by design, yet another way had been found to save the government expense, at the cost of the people. Foreign commentators have pointed out that slave labour is not efficient, and that it is wasteful to make skilled engineers or professors of physics build roads beyond the

Arctic Circle. This is perfectly true, but is less relevant than it would be in a western state. The communist rulers have never thought in terms of individual human wastage: the *cliché* that Russian man-power is inexhaustible has been repeated far in excess of the truth. The communist rulers have never been the cold, clear-minded rational master planners that western observers—both friendly and hostile—imagine them to be. They have always been emotional and vindictive: their hatred of those who disagree with them, or appear to threaten their power, especially of those who can in any way be regarded as bourgeois intellectuals, has always far outweighed their capacity to provide the most useful employment for the small amounts of human skill at their disposal. And even if at times Stalin and his colleagues may have seen that slave labour is poor material, the vast complex of vested interests that was the N.K.V.D. stood in the way of a remedy. By 1939 releases did take place, and the number of forced labourers was greatly reduced. Nevertheless very large numbers still remained, and the places vacated by death or by release were filled by others. Ever since the *Yezhovshchina* the N.K.V.D. has had a conscious interest in maintaining a high supply of 'state criminals'.[1]

One final hypothesis deserves brief mention. It is that the purpose of the *Yezhovshchina* was to keep Soviet society fluid, to prevent the formation of a stable ruling class.[2] No evidence can of course be found to show that this was the deliberate purpose of Stalin or Yezhov, and it is not indeed likely that this was so. But that the purge in fact to some extent performed this task, that it was its 'historical function', is a plausible theory. The essence of the purge was that it was conducted on the orders of the very highest authorities, and affected those who stood between them and the masses. In fact the masses too suffered—persons of religious beliefs and of non-Russian nationality especially—but relatively they suffered less than the intermediate strata. The main lesson of the purge was that there was no security for those who administered the political, economic, cultural and military machines. These officials might enjoy privileges denied to the masses as long as they performed their functions, but they could be broken at a moment's notice. 'How are the mighty fallen!' is

---

[1] Article 58 of the Criminal Code (*Ugolovny kodeks SSSR*, Moscow, 1938) can be widely interpreted. Grumbling can be treated as counter-revolutionary agitation, accidental damage to factory property as sabotage, a casual conversation as espionage. These 'counter-revolutionary' crimes involve larger sentences, and thus provide the N.K.V.D. with much-needed cheap labour.

[2] This view is ingeniously expounded in F. Beck and W. Godin, *Russian Purge*, 1950, pp. 217–26.

a reflection that is always popular among the humble and meek. Stalin showed those who could not hope to rise that there were at least compensations in being poor and obscure, while to the ambitious at the bottom of the social ladder he showed that there were plenty of good jobs to be seized from the hands of those that he had cast down.

The Five Year Plans and the *Yezhovshchina* transformed the Soviet Union, and greatly influenced the communist parties *in partibus infidelium*. Of the totalitarian society that emerged in the Soviet Union more will be said later. Of the effect on the communist parties two points may be mentioned here. One was the acceptance of Stalin's type of heresy-hunting. Those who disagreed with the party line were henceforth not misguided comrades: they were enemy agents, 'Trotskist-Buharinist wreckers and bourgeois-landlordite lackeys of international capitalism'. The other is the acceptance of the Stalin cult. For British or Paraguayan communists alike, Stalin was now the teacher and leader of genius of all progressive humanity, the father of all peoples, the infallible pontiff of Marxist-Leninist science.

CHAPTER NINE

The Popular Front

THE significance of Hitler's triumph was at first lost on the communist leaders in Moscow and their German subordinates. Neither Comintern nor K.P.D. would admit that the German working class had suffered a disaster. On 15th February 1933, Radek wrote: 'A party that receives six million votes, deeply linked with the whole history of the German working class, cannot be dismissed from the balance-sheet of history.' The Comintern organ *Rundschau* declared on 1st April 1933: 'The momentary calm after the victory of fascism is only a passing phenomenon. The rise of the revolutionary tide will inevitably continue. The resistance of the masses against fascism will inevitably increase. The open dictatorship of fascism destroys all democratic illusions, frees the masses from the influence of the social democrats, and thus accelerates the speed of Germany's march towards the proletarian revolution.'[1] This eloquent April-foolery was poor consolation to the communist leaders in Hitler's prisons and concentration-camps. The Reichstag fire, the expulsion of the Communists from the cowed assembly, the mass arrests and the Brown Terror made little impression on the Comintern. Refusing to admit defeat, Moscow ordered the party to ignore the terror and act openly, to hold street demonstrations and distribute leaflets as if a revolutionary situation still existed. Thus hundreds of party organisers who might have been saved for underground work were exposed and arrested. Within a few months the once impressive K.P.D. ceased to be a force of any importance. Small illegal groups continued to exist under the Nazi regime, but their efforts, however heroic, had not the slightest effect on German policy. Not until 1945 was a German Communist Party created from nothing by the Soviet military authorities.

Communist policy changed only after the policy of the Soviet

[1] Quoted in Max Beloff, *The Foreign Policy of Soviet Russia, 1929–1941*, Vol. I, p. 67.

government had changed. This did not happen for some time. Hitherto, as we have seen, it had been a dogma in Moscow that the only kind of German government it need fear was one friendly to the Versailles victors. Hitler was clearly hostile to the West: therefore Hitler, for all his persecution of communists, might be useful to Moscow. During 1933 public speeches and newspaper articles in the Soviet Union stressed the desire for friendly relations with Germany. During 1934 however relations deteriorated. Soviet hopes received a shock when Hitler made a non-aggression pact with Poland. In view of the traditional Soviet view of Poland, and especially of Marshal Piłsudski, it was not surprising that Moscow should believe—though wrongly—that these two states could only have come to terms at the expense of Russia. Hereafter it seemed probable that Hitler was even more hostile to the Soviet Union than to the West. Soviet policy kept the same aim—to exploit the hostility between Germany and the West. But whereas hitherto its method had been to encourage Germany to resist the Western Powers, it was now to encourage the Western Powers to resist Germany. Bolshevik blandishments were now addressed not to Berlin but to Paris. Meanwhile in France, not only on the left but among the disciples of Poincaré, alliance with Russia became attractive. In May the French Foreign Minister, Louis Barthou, suggested that the U.S.S.R. should join the League of Nations. Moscow decided to agree, and on 10th September was formally admitted. In the following year Soviet collaboration with the West formally reached its climax with the signature of the Franco-Soviet pact (2nd May) and the Soviet-Czechoslovak pact (16th May).

The new course in Soviet foreign policy required a new 'line' for the Comintern. This was provided at the 7th Congress, which met in Moscow in July-August 1935. It proclaimed the tactic of the Popular Front, the most perfect form yet devised of the 'united front from above'. In order to resist the threat of fascism at home and abroad, and especially the threat of fascist Germany to the toilers' fatherland, the U.S.S.R., communists were to combine not only with the masses but also with the leaders, not only of the social democrats but also of any non-socialist or even right-wing groups that were opposed to the fascists and to Nazi Germany or Japan.

The Popular Front policy brought the communists, whose prestige and influence had reached a low ebb by 1933, great popularity among the more or less non-political masses in many European and

even Asiatic countries. The Comintern's new slogans expressed
the genuine feelings of millions of workers, intellectuals and
peasants in countries misruled by dictatorial cliques or menaced by
German, Italian or Japanese aggression. Judged by its propaganda
appeal, the Popular Front was the most successful tactic ever
adopted by the Comintern in peacetime. Its adoption was in fact
a concession made by Moscow to the mood of the masses, which
Moscow for once accurately diagnosed. It may in fact be argued
that the Popular Front was imposed not by the communist parties
on the masses but by the masses on the communist parties.[1]

Nevertheless the period of the Popular Front was a period of
defeats for international communism.

This was in part due to the failure of the governments of France
and Britain to offer political resistance to the three aggressive
Powers at a time when political resistance could still have achieved
results. The weakness shown in London and Paris caused many
smaller states to choose the attractive but disastrous policy of co-
operation with the fascist Powers. The years 1935–9 were a period
of bloodless victories for Hitler and Mussolini and of cheap military
triumphs for Japan. Millions of persons throughout the world—
from politicians and intellectuals to simple peasants and workers—
were convinced that fascism was the 'idea of the future'. The greatest blow dealt by the Western Powers to the will to resist fascism
was, of course, the 1938 surrender at Munich.

But the failures of the Popular Front tactic were also due to
internal disunity, to the mutual suspicion between the communists
and their partners. Retrospectively it has of course become a dogma
in communist circles that this suspicion was solely due to the
treason of the social democrats. The truth is that the communists
themselves were principally to blame. They were determined to
enjoy both the pleasures of leadership and the pleasures of opposition. They could not bring themselves to cease their demagogic
agitation against the socialists and democrats whom they were
supposed to support. They never gave up their aim of winning the

[1] The new tactic was associated with George Dimitrov, who introduced it in his
speech at the Congress. Dimitrov had won world-wide admiration by his defence at
the Leipzig trial in 1933 of those accused of burning the German Reichstag. He was
released by the Germans and went to Moscow. (For a suggestion that he knew he
would be released, and that therefore his defence was less heroic than it appeared, see
Ruth Fischer, *Stalin and German Communism*, 1948, pp. 308–9). On arrival in Moscow
he was made Secretary of the Comintern. There is however no ground for believing
that Dimitrov initiated the new tactic: it is far more likely that he was used by Stalin
as a reliable mouthpiece who happened to enjoy world-wide prestige. The only non-
Russian communists who appear to have a *prima facie* claim to be considered initiators
of the Popular Front policy are the French. (See below, p. 180.)

socialist and democratic masses away from their leaders. Though appearing in public as allies and colleagues of these leaders, they took every opportunity to undermine their authority. One may doubt whether mass agitation can be conducted by discreet means, even when the agitators are steel-hard Bolshevik conspirators equipped with Marxist-Leninist-Stalinist methodology. Certainly there was nothing discreet about the methods of the communist agitators in Western Europe during the Popular Front period. The socialist and democratic leaders soon became aware of the communists' disloyal behaviour, which inevitably diminished their enthusiasm for the Popular Front and weakened the common resistance to fascism and to the enemies of the Soviet Union.

A third cause for the failures of the Popular Front was the course of internal policy in the Soviet Union. The vast purges of party, administration and armed forces in 1937–8 bewildered the potential friends of the U.S.S.R. among the masses—and even among the members of communist parties—of other countries. They also made the political and military leaders of the Western Powers doubt the value of Soviet Russia as an ally. This doubt of course strengthened the arguments of the 'appeasers' in the West.

The first important success of the Popular Front was in France.[1] Since the 6th Congress of the Comintern relations between French socialists and communists had been extremely bitter. The socialists were supported by the bulk of the French workers, while the communists were a small implacable faction. The economic depression, which came somewhat later to France than to most other European countries, had two important political effects. Economic hardships fell with special severity on the workers, who were less well protected by social legislation than the workers of most West European countries, and created a more bitter class feeling than had been known in France for many years, perhaps ever. At the same time, exploiting the discontent in all classes of the population but perhaps especially in the lower middle class, and pointing to the examples of Germany and Italy, fascist organisations made their appearance in France and won considerable support.

The danger signal was given by the riots of 6th February 1934, when fascist-inspired demonstrators attempted to march on the

---

[1] A useful account of France in these years is Alexander Werth, *France in Ferment*, 1938. The political and economic trends are well covered in François Goguel, *Les partis politiques sous la 3e République*, Paris, 1946, Vol. II. On the origins of the French Popular Front there is some interesting speculation in F. Borkenau, *European Communism*, 1953, pp. 115–62.

Chamber of Deputies. This incident was followed by a communist counter-demonstration on 9th February, and a big demonstration by the C.G.T. on 12th February, in which the communists instructed their followers to take part. After this, though the communist leaders continued to denounce the socialists, a spontaneous movement for unity between all working-class parties and organisations developed, with mass support from within both socialist and communist ranks. In June 1934 socialist and communist leaders made a pact of common action in defence of democratic liberties, opposition to rearmament and hostility to fascism in Germany and Austria. When, during the visit of Prime Minister Laval to Moscow to sign the Franco-Soviet pact, Stalin and Laval issued on 15th May 1935 a joint statement to the effect that Stalin approved French measures of defence, the French communists dropped their opposition to rearmament. In this they were followed more hesitantly by the socialists, who still had an important pacifist wing. In the first months of 1935 co-operation of the parties of the left became a reality. A *Comité national de rassemblement populaire* was created to formulate a common programme. The unity of action of socialists, communists and radicals was formally asserted on 14th July 1935. The traditional commemoration of the fall of the Bastille was held in common. A great procession marched from the Place de la Bastille to the Place de la République, headed by the chief socialist and communist leaders and by the Radical Party leader Daladier. Negotiations for reunification of the two trade union organisations, socialist-led C.G.T. and communist-controlled C.G.T.U., had begun in October 1934, had been broken off, but were resumed with greater energy after the 14th July demonstration. In September 1935 congresses of both organisations approved the principle of reunification, and this was achieved in March 1936. The C.G.T.U. representatives argued fiercely for the specific communist points of view on trade union organisation, and on the internal and international political affiliations of the future united body. But on all three points they were outvoted by two-thirds majorities. Such was the determination of Moscow to secure unity of action that the C.G.T.U. was allowed to accept reunion on the old C.G.T.'s terms rather than on its own.[1]

The essential preliminary work for the formation of the French Popular Front had thus been accomplished, in response to the needs of the French political situation, before the 7th Congress of the Comintern met in Moscow. At the Congress in fact the agree-

[1] Montreuil, op. cit., pp. 460–71.

ment reached in France was held up as a model to other communist parties.

At the parliamentary election of 3rd May 1936 the parties of the Popular Front won 386 seats, and the various groups of the Right 222. Of the three parties the socialists had 149 seats, the radicals 109 and the communists 72. Whereas the number of votes cast for the socialists was almost exactly the same as at the last general election in 1932, the communists almost doubled their poll—from 800,000 to 1,500,000. A Popular Front ministry was formed on 5th June, with the socialist leader Léon Blum as Premier. The Communist Party however decided that its leaders should not accept cabinet office: the party pledged its support provided that the government would carry out the Popular Front programme. This equivocal and distrustful attitude of the communists weakened the Blum ministry from its first day.

The left were now in power, and the communists were stronger than ever before. But the new government's relations with its working-class supporters soon proved extremely delicate. The workers awaited great social changes. Already before the Blum ministry was formed they began to strike, and the movement did not stop when Blum took office. In mid-May 'sit-in' strikes took place in several provincial industrial centres, and at the end of the month they spread through the Paris region, especially affecting metallurgical and engineering plants. At the beginning of June the movement spread back to the provinces. At its peak it affected not much less than a million workers. The 'sit-in' strike, by which the workers occupied their factories, was a new phenomenon in France. The only historical parallel was the occupation of factories in north Italy in August 1920. But the circumstances of France in 1936 were different from those of Italy in 1920. In Italy the socialists had been in at least verbally revolutionary opposition to the government: in France the socialists were in power. In Italy the internal situation was foremost in all minds: in France the internal situation was overshadowed by the dangers of the international situation. The most important difference of all, however, was that whereas the Italian strikes had been ordered by the trade unions, those in France were the result of spontaneous movement, and the trade unions' main concern was to get them under control. The origins of the 1936 strike wave still remain a mystery.[1] The most probable explanation is that they were a genuine popular reaction: none of

[1] A recent work on the subject is J. Danos and M. Gibelin, *Juin 36: masses et militants*, Paris, 1952.

the hypotheses attributing them to secret and sinister influences are convincing. They were certainly not a bid for dictatorial power by the communists. The communists in fact were placed in an embarrassing position. As usual they tried to have their cake and eat it. Communist deputies made speeches in the occupied factories, and communist spokesmen declared on all possible occasions that the correct way to solve the crisis was to grant all the demands of the workers. But at the same time the communists were pledged to minimise class hatred and to maintain French national unity, in alliance with Soviet Russia against Nazi Germany.

The strike wave came to an end when the government imposed arbitration on employers and workers by the 'Matignon agreements' of June. These were however modest gains. In the following months prices rose and there were important exports of capital. In October it became necessary to devalue the franc. In March 1937 Blum announced a 'pause' in his reform programme. This disappointed his working-class supporters without reconciling his business-class opponents. In June Blum resigned when the Senate refused his request for exchange control, designed to stop the continuing export of capital. This was really the end of the Popular Front. The governments led by the radicals Chautemps and Daladier were supported by the left until the autumn of 1938, but their policy was cautious and conservative. The hopes of an increased influence in policy for the working class in general and the communists in particular were not fulfilled.

The failure of its social and economic policy was not however the only reason for the Popular Front's defeat. Equally important were its defeats in foreign policy, and especially in the Spanish Civil War. Sympathy for the rival forces in Spain greatly widened the breach between left and right in France. It gave to French internal politics in these years a quality of ideological fanaticism such as had not been seen in France for a long time. It helped to undermine the democratic foundations of French government and morally to disarm France in the face of fascist aggression.

Though a country of indisputably western culture, Spain had, as we have seen, a social structure and political traditions which resembled those of Central, or even Eastern, rather than Western Europe.[1] In many parts of the country great estates belonged to aristocratic landowners, who employed numbers of landless labourers. The Catholic Church had great wealth—not so much in

---

[1] The best account of the political and social background of twentieth-century Spain is Gerald Brennan, *The Spanish Labyrinth*, 1943.

and as in money—and dominated education and cultural life. The army was always an important political force, and usually though not always acted to the advantage of the political right and the ruling class. The bureaucracy was powerful, corrupt and arrogant.

Spanish political life was fairly evenly divided between right and left. The social forces that supported the right included not only the landowners and the Catholic hierarchy, but also the greater part of the middle class of Castile and the bulk of the peasantry in certain regions. The political left was divided into four sections.

First were the republican section of the Castilian business and professional classes, concerned above all to break the stranglehold of the Church over intellectual life and to limit the power of army and bureaucracy. Second were the Catalan nationalists, who drew their support from the business and professional classes and peasants of Catalonia. Their general political outlook was similar to that of the Castilian republicans, but for them the first priority was regional autonomy for Catalonia. Third was the socialist movement, strongest among the workers of northern Spain and of Madrid. The socialists controlled the largest trade union movement of Spain, the General Union of Labour (U.G.T.). From the party's left wing a group had broken off in 1920 to form the Communist Party. But the Spanish communists had always been less numerous and less influential than the socialists. The fourth element was the anarchist and anarcho-syndicalist movement, supported by the industrial workers of Barcelona and of some other Mediterranean ports, and by the agricultural labourers of Andalusia. The anarcho-syndicalist trade union organisation, the National Confederation of Labour (C.N.T.), was a powerful rival to the socialist U.G.T. If the C.N.T. was the mass organisation, the elite group, which controlled it politically, was the Federation of Iberian Anarchists (F.A.I.).

In April 1931 the moderate left had won a victory when King Alfonso XIII abdicated and a Republic was proclaimed. The moderates however wasted the opportunity of serious social reform, especially of redistribution of land, and in 1933 the right won a majority at the polls. A year's government by the right showed an unmistakable trend towards fascism, not unlike the Austrian clerical fascism of Dollfuss. In October 1934 the socialist workers of Asturias and Madrid and the Catalan nationalists in Barcelona rose in armed rebellion. They were defeated, not without heavy fighting and heavy casualties in Asturias. An important cause of defeat had been the refusal of the anarcho-syndicalist workers of Barcelona to support the Catalan nationalists. After the disaster the demand for unity of all the forces of the left became very strong. In 1935 a new agreement was made, for common action at the parliamentary election of 1936, between republicans, Catalans, socialists and communists. This was the Spanish Popular Front. The name and the policy coincided with the Comintern's new tactics, but the agreement owed little to the influence of the Spanish Communists—far the weakest of the four parties. It was a product of Spanish conditions, of the conviction that only unity of the left could save Spain from a fascist regime. Most important of all, the anarchists, whose principles would not allow them to put forward parliamentary candidates of their own, told their supporters to go to the polls and to vote for the candidates of Popular Front parties. The election was held in February 1936, and the Popular Front won a substantial majority.

During the first half of 1936 the republican leaders, once more in power, showed no more determination to tackle Spain's fundamental social problems than they had shown in 1931. The hopes of the masses, especially of the landless peasants, remained unsatisfied. On the other hand the right, realising that if it observed the rules of constitutional government, it was doomed to defeat, decided to reverse by force the verdict of the polls. Army generals and fascist politicians prepared for rebellion. There were minor riots, and assassinations were committed on both sides. The most important victim was the leader of the right, Calvo Sotelo, killed early in July. Sotelo's death precipitated the generals' revolt, which took place on 18th July.

Military revolts were an old institution in Spain: there was nothing surprising about this one. The republican politicians of the Madrid government wavered, and even opened negotiations with some of the generals. But at this point policy was taken out of the republican politicians' hands by the masses. A workers' rising burst forth in the main cities, led in Madrid by the socialists and the U.G.T. and in Barcelona by the anarcho-syndicalists and the C.N.T. Determined not to be cheated of their hopes by militarists or by bourgeois liberals, the workers made their own bid for power. In the next days republican forces were improvised, both from those regular units which remained loyal to the government and from the 'militias' or private armies created by socialists, anarchists, communists and dissident Marxists (P.O.U.M.). These motley forces quickly beat the rebels in the east and part of the south, but were unable to reconquer the north-west, west and south-west. Behind the government's front uncoordinated acts of social revolution took place. Many factories were seized by workers, and various types of agricultural collectives appeared. Republican politicians continued officially to form the government, but all real power was held by the workers' organisations.[1]

The Comintern was thus faced with the first genuine revolutionary situation in Europe since 1919. At the same time it had to take into account the strategic importance of Spain for any future war in which the Soviet Union might be engaged against the fascist Powers. The first triumphs of the revolution were followed by a series of disasters as Italian and German aid to Franco in supplies and in troops rapidly increased. In the autumn of 1936 Madrid itself was in danger.

The Spanish communists were few, and their influence in the trade unions was inconsiderable. In Catalonia they somewhat improved their position by fusing with the socialists to form the United Socialist Party of Catalonia (P.S.U.C.). But as in Catalonia both socialists and communists were far weaker than anarchosyndicalists, even the united party was not at first important.

The communists became an important force in Spain as a result of the assistance given by Soviet Russia to the Republic in its hour of danger. The Soviet government sold arms, equipment and civilian supplies to the Spanish government for hard cash. Secondly, the Comintern recruited volunteers from all over Europe to fight for the Republic in the International Brigades. These were at first composed almost solely of communists. As they expanded, the number of non-communists increased, but the senior officers and political commissars were always communists or persons obedient to communist political orders. The Brigades went into action on the Madrid front early in November 1936. They were at that time the best troops on either side in the civil war. They saved Madrid from the attack of Franco and his Italian allies. They were commanded by 'General Kléber', a Soviet citizen of Roumanian origin whose real name was Stern: their real organiser was the Soviet general Berzin, who headed a Soviet military mission that remained carefully in the background. As Italian and German aid to Franco increased, and the French and British governments persisted in the 'non-intervention' policy, which all the Powers had officially adopted but only they were carrying out, the Republic became increasingly dependent on Soviet and international communist aid, and the in-

---

[1] The most impressive analytical account of this first, revolutionary, stage in the civil war is Franz Borkenau, *Spanish Cockpit*, 1938.

fluence of the Spanish communists in the counsels of government grew.

In return for their help the Soviet leaders and their Spanish disciples demanded three things. First, the irregular militias must be replaced by a regular disciplined army. Secondly, social revolution must be postponed until after victory. Factories and estates whose owners had been killed or had fled to the enemy, were to be administered by the public authorities while the war lasted, but their ultimate disposal was not to be decided. Experiments with new types of social organisation, in industry or in agriculture, must be dropped. Thirdly, the enemies of the communists within the Republican camp must be removed from all power or influence. These enemies were not on the right but on the left. The republicans in Madrid and the Catalan nationalists (*Esquerra*) in Barcelona, both bourgeois parties, supported the communists' drive for a regular army and social stability. They found the communists moderate and efficient allies in defence. With the socialists the communists had uneasy but outwardly correct relations. The anarcho-syndicalists opposed the communists' military and social policy, and the communists cordially disliked them in return. The communists' greatest hatred however was reserved for the P.O.U.M., which they accused—not entirely correctly—of being a Trotskist party, and whose main leader, Andres Nin, had long represented the Spanish Communist Party at the Comintern in Moscow, until he had broken with it in the late 1920's.

During the first half of 1937 the P.S.U.C. in Catalonia gathered under its banner most of the moderates, and also gained some ground among the workers at the expense of the anarcho-syndicalists. It was generously helped by the Soviet consul, and the head of the Soviet trade delegation.[1] The crisis came in May 1937 with street-fighting in Barcelona, apparently started by the anarchists. The anarchist and P.O.U.M. forces were defeated, and the central government resigned. The left socialist leader, Largo Caballero,[2] whom the communists did not trust, was replaced as Premier by the more accommodating Dr. Negrin. In the new ministry the communists had greater influence. During the Barcelona fighting the unfortunate Nin was mysteriously killed,

---

[1] The consul, Antonov-Ovseenko, had been head of the Military-Revolutionary Committee of the Petrograd soviet which had prepared the November Revolution of 1917.

[2] Caballero had become Premier in September 1936, succeeding the republican ministry. The change was formal rather than real. Already in the summer of 1936 real power lay not with the republican politicians but with the socialists.

and Negrin obligingly banned the P.O.U.M.[1] By this time the communists, strongly entrenched in the army, also had considerable control over the Security Police. There were even special prisons managed by communists, with advice from experts of the Soviet N.K.V.D., in which the chief victims were those suspected of Trotskism.

The communists' 'conservative' political attitude has been much criticised by left writers as a betrayal of revolution. This criticism is probably misplaced. There can be little doubt that the communists' tactics were justified by the military situation. Their policy was the right policy to win the war. There are no grounds for believing that they intended, once the war was won, to content themselves with conservative policies. On the contrary, having won prestige as 'saviours of the Republic', and having got the military and police machines into their hands, it may be assumed that they would have used their power to set up in Spain a Stalinist state. The experience of Eastern Europe since 1944 confirms this view. That they did not succeed was due to the fact that the enemies of the Republic were too strong.

Franco received more help from the Axis Powers than the Republic received from Russia or from international communism. Spain was strategically more important for Italy than for Russia, and it was physically easier for Italy to intervene than for Russia. The Western Powers, under British leadership, blindly pursued the tragic farce of non-intervention. Meanwhile Russia had her own preoccupations elsewhere. The Japanese armies in Manchuria formed a direct and serious menace to Soviet territory. In Central Europe the German danger was growing. Russia was also weakened by the *Yezhovshchina* of 1937–8. Among its victims were several of the most prominent Soviet emissaries in Spain, including Kléber-Stern, Berzin, and Antonov-Ovseenko. Militarily weakened, Russia could not risk war for the sake of a country of secondary importance to her. Soviet help to Spain dwindled during 1938.

As Russian interest in Spain diminished, the Spanish communists declined. They still energetically supported the war effort, but their arrogance and their tyrannical methods had lost them many friends. In the spring of 1938 Franco's forces reached the eastern coast and cut off Catalonia from Valencia. Nearly a year more passed before Barcelona fell to them (January 1939). Even after this disaster the

[1] These events are described in George Orwell, *Homage to Catalonia*. The author was a volunteer in an anarcho-syndicalist unit.

communists still wished to fight on. But war-weariness was now widespread on the Republican side. Continuation of the war was increasingly regarded as a private policy of the communists, designed to achieve aims concealed from the Spanish people. A group of officers led by Colonel Casado, and supported by the right-wing socialist Julian Besteiro, seized power and surrendered to Franco. Before this had been achieved there had been fighting between Casado's men and the communists, and some communists had been executed in cold blood on Casado's orders.

If the Popular Fronts of France and Spain had ended in defeat, the first in confusion and the second in tragedy, in other West European countries there was not even temporary success. In Britain and Scandinavia, though Popular Front anti-fascist slogans made an impression on liberal and socialist intellectuals, the socialist parties refused to make common cause with the communists, and no Popular Fronts were formed. In Germany and Italy all anti-fascist groups were helpless.

In the Balkans the Popular Front period brought a small but substantial increase of strength to the communists. In Yugoslavia, where the Communist Party was still illegal, it recruited numerous and courageous members among university students and graduates, and enjoyed a measure of vague sympathy from a much wider section of the population. No Popular Front was formally created, but members and sympathisers of the Communist Party played a part in bringing together various democratic bourgeois and peasant parties in opposition to the dictatorial and increasingly pro-Axis government. The association of communism with Russia and France, the two foreign states most popular among the Serbs, assisted the communist cause. In Bulgaria the same tendency existed on a smaller scale. The international background was less favourable, for although most Bulgarians loved Russia there was much less fear of Germany than in Yugoslavia. The dictatorship of King Boris was however about as unpopular with the Bulgarians as was that of Milan Stojadinović with the Yugoslavs. There was no formal Popular Front in Bulgaria, but the left wing of the Agrarian movement co-operated more closely with the communists. Both parties were illegal and persecuted, and both attracted support from the intelligentsia as well as from peasants and workers. In Greece the Communist Party became for the first time an important factor during the brief period of free parliamentary government which followed the restoration of King George II in November 1935. In the parliament elected in 1936 the communists had fifteen seats, and held a commanding position as the two major parties were almost exactly equal. The communists drew most of their support from industrial workers, especially in the north of Greece. They gained wider sympathy not only from economic discontent and from fear of the fascist Powers, but also from growing disillusionment among the younger intellectuals with the sterile quarrel between royalists and republicans that had bedevilled Greek politics since 1922 and made social progress impossible. No Popular Front was formed in Greece, and in August 1936 the establishment, with the King's consent, of General Metaxas' dictatorship, deprived the communists of all legal means of activity.

In Central Europe communism was weaker, and Popular Front tactics were more unsuccessful, than in the Balkans.

In Poland there was closer co-operation between the socialist and peasant movements. This was an example of greater unity on the left, but it owed nothing to communist influence. In 1937 the peasant strike in Galicia and 'sit-in' strikes in the factories of Cracow were signs of growing social discontent. The government's benevolent neutrality towards Nazi Germany was unpopular with the Polish people. The growth of fascism, both on the government side and in the ranks of the right wing of the opposition, though confined to a section of the middle class—business, bureaucratic and intellectual—and deprived of mass support, was nevertheless alarming. There was no Popular Front in Poland, but the trend of public opinion was in that direction. This was the result of conditions in and around Poland: it was not due to communist influence. The Polish Communist Party was very weak. As we have seen, its leaders in exile in Russia fell victims to the purge of 1937–8, and the party was formally disbanded by the Comintern in 1938.

In Czechoslovakia, where the Communist Party could function legally, it had the support of about half the working class and of some intellectuals. The political parties did not create a Popular Front, but the idea of anti-fascist unity was popular among Czechs, though much less so among Slovaks.

In Hungary and Roumania communist influence was negligible. Both countries were ruled by Whiggish oligarchies, the Hungarian decked in quasi-liberal trappings, the Roumanian in quasi-fascist. Both regimes were evolving towards a more genuinely fascist form of bureaucratic dictatorship. In both countries the democratic forces were on the defensive. In Hungary the social democrats stood solidly for democracy, but they were unable to influence more than the working class of the capital and a few other towns. The Hungarian peasants had no effective representation: the Independent Small Farmers' Party was a curious assortment of peasant tribunes, bourgeois radicals and romantic reactionary nationalists. In Roumania the main democratic force, the National Peasant Party, had disintegrated under the pressure of the economic depression and the intrigues of King Carol II. In both countries the rising revolutionary movement was fascist. The anti-semitic pro-Nazi Iron Guard in Roumania used slogans of both national and social revolution to attract both the university youth and a large part of the peasants and workers. Though subsidised by Roumanian industrialists and landowners and by emissaries of Nazi Germany, it cannot be regarded as a mere tool of capitalists or of Berlin: it enlisted much genuine revolutionary enthusiasm. In the autumn of 1938 its leaders were shot by Carol II's police, and its supporters were fiercely pursued. Fascist groups in Hungary appeared later, and were at first too disunited to be strong. But in August 1938 the two main groups fused to form the Arrow Cross Party. Subsidised from Germany and mildly combated by the Hungarian government, this party made some appeal to discontented peasants and miners, though it could not shake the hold of the socialists on the factory workers.

The first communist experiment with a Popular Front tactic thus proved a failure in Europe. The Popular Front was successful only where a genuine and effective demand for unity of democratic forces already existed, and where national resistance to the fascist Powers was a real issue. The communists did not create the demand, but yielded to it. Having thereby won much popularity for themselves, they tried to exploit the Popular Front for their party aims, and failed. One is tempted to conclude that the Popular Front would have been more successful if the communists had had nothing to do with it. This conclusion however misses the point. It would be justified if the communists had been mainly concerned to ensure the triumph of the democratic forces in countries threatened internally or externally by fascism. For most members of communist parties in such countries this was no doubt the principal aim, but for Moscow it was only a secondary consideration. Moscow's aim was to strengthen the position of Soviet Russia. Alliance with the Western Powers was one possible course: another was alliance with Nazi Germany. When the first did not produce results, the second was adopted.[1] The Popular Fronts were intended, if circum-

[1] There is something to be said for the view that Stalin was trying to do a deal with

stances were favourable, to give the communists—and so Moscow —a share, perhaps even a major share, in the government of their countries: if circumstances were unfavourable they could pursue useful rearguard actions. Democratic unity and resistance to fascism would have gained if the communist parties had dissolved themselves. But this would have deprived Moscow of an instrument of policy that might prove valuable later. Moscow never considered giving it up, and subsequent events showed that from the point of view of its own interests Moscow was right. The experience gained during the Popular Front years, especially in Spain, proved valuable in 1944–8, when the opportunity came to do what the Soviet leaders had come to understand by the notion 'spreading world revolution'—to export the ready-made Stalinist regime by force of arms.

UNITED FRONT IN CHINA

The Popular Front policy achieved more substantial success in China. While the communists completed their Long March, and defended their newly-won territory in the north-west against Chiang Kai-shek's attacks, the Japanese, who had seized Manchuria in 1931, were steadily encroaching on northern China. To Chinese patriots it became increasingly clear that the civil war between Chiang and the communists was a tragic waste of lives and resources. From all sides the demand grew that civil strife be replaced by national unity against the invader. In the cities, businessmen, intellectuals and workers shared hatred of the Japanese. As on earlier occasions, university students played a leading part in the anti-Japanese movement. Chiang's armed forces were affected. The troops of the 'Young Marshal', Chang Hsueh-liang,[1] which occupied some of the territory nearest to the communist region, were especially affected. They were mostly recruited from Manchuria, and passionately wished to see their homeland freed of the Japanese. They were ever more reluctant to be used by Chiang against the communists. In southern China too leading warlords urged Chiang to resist Japan.[2]

Hitler as early as 1937, and that the obstacle was Hitler's reluctance. This is the opinion of Krivitsky, op. cit., who gives some scraps of evidence that fit this hypothesis, though they do not prove it.

[1] The son of the warlord Chang Tso-lin, who had dominated Manchuria in the 1920's, and had raided the Soviet Embassy in Peking in 1927.

[2] Generals Li Tsung-jen and Pai Tsung-hsi, of Kwangsi province, allowed the National Salvation movement to operate in their territory, and in May 1936 issued an appeal for resistance to Japan (L. K. Rosinger, *China's Wartime Politics*, Princeton, 1944, p. 17).

The communists made much better use of the new patriotic mood of the people than did Chiang. Soon after the 7th Comintern Congress, at which the Popular Front policy had been forcibly defended by Wang Ming, now the party's delegate in Moscow, on 1st August 1935 the Chinese Communist Party launched an appeal for a united front of Communists and Kuomintang against the invaders. Chiang ignored the offer, and persisted in his plans to destroy the communists. In his view, the admittedly desirable aim of unity against Japan could only be achieved when the 'Red Bandits' had been wiped out. He professed to believe that this could soon be done. The historian may recognise that there was much to be said for Chiang's basic attitude: he was head of the legal government, the communists were rebels, and they, not he, were obstructing national unity. But Chiang's tactics and propaganda were foolish. By refusing to begin resistance to Japan, he enabled the communists to appear as the true patriots, and made himself appear the obstacle to unity and the persecutor of patriotism.

The patriotic movement gathered strength despite Chiang Kai-shek. On 9th December 1935 the Peking students organised a demonstration which demanded an end to civil war, restoration of civil liberties and resistance to Japan. Similar demonstrations took place in other university towns of China in the following weeks. In a speech to Communist Party 'activists' on 27th December 1935 Mao Tse-tung formulated in greater detail the united front policy. 'The task before the Party', he said, 'is to integrate the activities of the Red Army with all the activities of the workers, peasants, students, the petty bourgeoisie and the national bourgeoisie of the whole country and to form out of this integration a united national-revolutionary front.'[1] During the first half of 1936 the communists helped to form a 'National Salvation' movement. This was designed to enlist persons of all social classes, and of most political opinions and of none. Its greatest successes were won among workers and students in the towns. On 31st May it held a meeting in Shanghai to found an 'All-China Federation of National Salvation Unions'. This movement, in which communist influence was strong, was persecuted by Chiang, but won some public sympathy.

On 12th December 1936, while Chiang was visiting the headquarters of Chang Hsueh-liang at Sian, he was arrested by his host. He was visited in his captivity by the leading communist Chou En-lai, who joined the Young Marshal in urging him to resist Japan, promising if he would do this that the communists would

Quoted in Hu Chiao-mu, *Thirty Years of the Communist Party of China*, 1951, p. 42.

accept him as their supreme commander. The communists were at this time convinced that only Chiang could lead the Chinese people. His person was essential for the short- and long-term policies of the communists, and he must therefore not be harmed. The communists, who for some time had been on fairly good terms with Chang Hsueh-liang, agreed with him that Chiang should be allowed to return safely to Nanking, even though he had given no formal pledge to change his policy. Chiang was undoubtedly impressed by the evidence of popular feeling that had been put before him. He consented to negotiate with the communists early in 1937.

Agreement between the communists and Chiang was achieved by the action of the Japanese, who began large-scale military action against China on 7th July. The announcement that agreement had been reached was issued from communist headquarters on 22nd September. In their manifesto the communists formally accepted the Kuomintang programme and the 'Three People's Principles' of Sun Yat-sen; promised to stop confiscation of land from landowners; renamed the Red Army 'National Revolutionary Army'; and recognised the authority of the Military Affairs Commission of the Nanking government. The land policy in the communist regions was really changed: landowners kept their property, and were obliged only to lower rents to a fixed maximum. But the Communist Party's military and political hold was not relaxed in the regions it controlled. The communists continued to build the cadres of their own military and civil administration, disciplined and indoctrinated on communist principles. Nevertheless relations with Nanking improved, and the Chinese united front worked fairly well during the year that passed between the Japanese attack and the fall of Hankow in October 1938.

MIDDLE EAST AND FAR EAST

Faint echoes of the Popular Front were heard in the Arab lands. The *coup d'état* of October 1936 in Iraq was the joint work of discontented officers and the *Ahali* group of left intellectuals. Soon after the seizure of power, however, the military dictator Bekr Sidki broke with *Ahali*. In French North Africa and in the French mandated territories of Syria and Lebanon, the victory of the Popular Front in France encouraged hopes of reform and somewhat strengthened the influence of those members of the Arab intelligentsia who were attracted by the ideas of the left. But this was only a passing phase. After the general failure of Blum's government, the French parliament rejected the proposed reforms, and in France's Moslem territories nationalism triumphed over left trends, and to some extent sought inspiration from fascist Italy or Nazi Germany. Nowhere in the Middle East or North Africa was communism a force of any importance.

In the Far East outside China communist influence was very small but perhaps increasing. Young Indian intellectuals were attracted by the anti-fascist slogans of the Popular Front. In Japan a Japan Masses Party was formed in February 1937, with a Popular Front tendency, and undoubtedly influenced by communist tactics. The social democratic Social Masses Party rejected proposals for a Popular Front. At the March 1937 election to the Japanese parliament, the two parties together polled twice as many votes as the socialists had won at the preceding election in 1936. The Japan Masses Party was however banned in December 1937, while the Social Masses Party came under militarist and nationalist influence, and dissolved itself in July 1940.[1]

In Indonesia a small illegal communist party was organised in 1935. There was also a small heretical communist group which supported Tan Malaka, a Comintern veteran who since 1928 had been regarded by Moscow as a Trotskist. In April 1937 was formed a legal party of the left, the Indonesian People's Movement (*Gerindo*). Its leaders, who included the socialist Sjarifoeddin, followed the Popular Front line, regarded fascism and Japanese imperialism as the main enemies, and were even willing to cooperate with the Dutch.[2]

LATIN AMERICA

During the 1930's the Comintern began to pay attention to Latin America. Great contrasts in wealth, racial differences and habits of dictatorship and palace revolution made this vast region seem attractive ground for revolutionary activities.[3] The Spanish civil war naturally made an impression on the Spanish-speaking peoples of America. Fascist movements made their appearance on the continent, and were strengthened both by the growing economic influence of Germany and Japan and by the presence of large communities of German, Italian and Japanese origin that had been hardly or not at all assimilated by their new homelands. Thus internal conflicts offered an opportunity to communists, while the strategic importance of Latin America was an incentive to Moscow

[1] For details see Evelyn S. Colbert, *The Left wing in Japanese politics*, New York, 1952.
[2] For details see G. Mc T. Kahin, *Nationalism and Revolution in Indonesia*, Cornell, 1952.
[3] A brief and clear introductory survey of the continent, giving the main geographical, historical and political facts, is R. Humphreys *The evolution of modern Latin America*, 1946.

to press the local communist parties into a more active policy. The years of the Popular Front did achieve some small successes.

Latin America was overwhelmingly agricultural. Industry was principally based on mineral resources—Mexican and Venezuelan oil, Chilean nitrates and Bolivian tin. Only in a few big urban centres—Buenos Aires, Rio de Janeiro, Sao Paulo, Mexico City —had some progress recently been made in manufacturing industry. Agriculture was mostly based on great landed estates, which owed their origin to the Spanish conquest. The dominant social problem was the peasants' need for land. The conflict between industrial labour and capital was in an early stage, overshadowed by the conflict between landowner and agricultural labourer. This social conflict was complicated by the racial issue, which deepened the gulf between rich and poor but also made the poor less capable of defending their interests.

The racial composition of the Latin American countries varied. Bolivia, Peru and Ecuador were essentially Indian states: only the ruling minority were European or of mixed origin (*mestizo*). In Mexico, Paraguay, Colombia, Venezuela and most of the Central American states the Indians were an important minority, but the most numerous element were the *mestizos*, while the more or less pure Europeans provided the ruling group. Chile and Brazil differed from the second category in that the European and mixed merged into each other, while the pure Indians were a relatively unimportant minority. In Brazil European stock was mixed with negro even more than with Indian: the same was true of some of the Central American and Caribbean republics. Finally in three states— Argentine, Uruguay and Costa Rica—the great majority of the population was pure European.

The normal type of government in Latin America was an oligarchic dictatorship, more liberal in the more European states, more despotic in the more Indian. In the Argentine there was a certain habit of Whiggish liberalism, as in England before 1832 or in Hungary in 1900. Bolivia and Peru somewhat resembled European colonies of the nineteenth century: great landowners or mine-owners held in their hands the lives of thousands of Indian semi-slaves. Throughout the continent the army and the Catholic Church played an important part. Neither was necessarily identified with conservatism. There were liberal generals, and the church had at times fought fiercely and successfully to protect the Indians from exploitation. But by the twentieth century both were usually on the side of the ruling class.

The exception that did not fit this pattern was Mexico. Here in 1910 an armed revolt by an upright and moderate constitutionalist against the long dictatorship of Porfirio Diaz had let loose a social revolution. The peasants had fought a long and cruel guerrilla for the land. The assassination of the peasant leader Zapata in 1919 marked the defeat of the extremists. The new rulers settled down to enjoy the fruits of power. Like the colonels who had made their career under the revolutionary banner of Piłsudski in Poland, the victors of the Mexican revolution lost much of their fervour and almost all their purity. Yet the revolution had done more than replace one ruling clique by another. The political power of the landlords and of the Catholic Church was broken: the process involved years of cruel religious persecution. Some land was redistributed to the peasants. The industrial workers began to play a part: the government created trade unions and gave them a privileged position in the state. A Mexican bourgeoisie was in formation, and differed fundamentally from the former ruling class by its fierce nationalism. Whereas the old rulers had felt themselves Europeans, and had never been quite sure whether Mexico was their home, the new leaders and the *mestizo* masses who supported them were quite sure that they were Mexicans, were fiercely 'anti-imperialist' and distrustful of Europe and especially of the United States.[1] In short, in Leninist terms, Mexico had made her bourgeois revolution. Mexico was a sort of democracy, turbulent and tough, but with the same sort of freedom as, for instance, the Serbia of 1903–14.

In the mid-1930's the three most interesting countries from the point of view of communist opportunities were Brazil, Mexico and Peru. In Brazil Getulio Vargas had established a dictatorship in 1930. His regime was something new. The old oligarchy of wealthy magnates from Sao Paulo state had been defeated. Vargas appealed to the middle class and to some extent to the poor. His social demagogy had a mildly fascist flavour. The economic hardships of the world depression brought him both his supporters and his enemies. In Brazil there was a small Communist Party. Its leader was Luis Carlos Prestes, formerly an army officer, who already in 1924 had made a small revolt and led a small force on a Long March through the wilds of the western provinces, and had later spent some years in Moscow. General economic misery, peasant

---

[1] For a discussion of these issues, see F. Tannenbaum, *Mexico: The Struggle for Peace and Bread*, New York, 1950.

land hunger, and discontent with Vargas within the army, offered the Brazilian communists some opportunities.

In Mexico the process of revolution, which had been very slow if not quite stationary from 1928 to 1934, gathered speed again when General Lazaro Cárdenas became President in 1934. Cárdenas greatly accelerated the distribution of land to the peasants, and favoured a semi-communal form of cultivation known as the *ejido*. Already in the Mexican Constitution of 1917 ownership of land had been defined in a manner that recalls the Russian Populist conception of 'labour-ownership'.[1] The rights of individuals were limited by an overriding right of the nation and the state to dispose of land. This conception was emphasised under Cárdenas. In 1940, at the end of his term of office, 51 per cent of the agricultural population of Mexico lived in *ejidos*, and owned 47 per cent of the country's arable land.[2] Cárdenas also gave greater powers and greater independence to the trade unions, and within these communist influence began to make itself felt. Cárdenas expropriated the oil-fields in 1938, and this brought him into conflict with the United States and Britain. The nationalist and anti-imperialist trend of Cárdenas' policy was very acceptable to Moscow. In general, though Cárdenas and his closest collaborators were not communists, or even Marxists, there were better opportunities of communist action in Mexico than elsewhere on the continent.

In Peru the new factor was the appearance in 1931 of a movement called *Alianza Popular Revolucionaria Americana* (A.P.R.A.), led by Haya de la Torre. This was a socialist movement, of a Populist rather than Marxist type. Its leader had been much influenced by the Mexican revolution. The special feature of A.P.R.A. was that it stressed the rights of the Indians. It aimed not only at social justice for the people of Peru but at a new order for the Europeans, *mestizos* and Indians of the whole continent. The continent, in the A.P.R.A. view, was not Latin America but *Indoamerica*. The enemy of all Indoamericans was foreign imperialism. In its first years A.P.R.A.'s wrath was directed mainly at the United States, but later the Axis Powers became its chief bogey. A.P.R.A. has some slight resemblance to such movements as Kemalism, the early Kuomintang or the early Wafd: political democracy, social revolution and nationalism were combined in its programme.[3]

---

[1] Tannenbaum, op. cit., pp. 140–52. See above, pp. 25–6.
[2] Tannenbaum, op. cit., p. 149.
[3] These ideas are authoritatively expressed in Haya de la Torre, *El Antimperialismo y el APRA*, Santiago de Chile, 1936.

The attitude of the communists to A.P.R.A. was similar to their attitude to the Kuomintang in the 1920's: they considered it a petty bourgeois movement capable of serving the interests of the proletariat and in particular capable of damaging the imperialist enemy of Soviet Russia.

In the autumn of 1934 a secret conference of Latin American communists was held in Montevideo.[1] The conference made the diagnosis that could be expected. It noted three main conflicts. The first was the internal class struggle, of workers against capitalists and especially of peasants against landowners. The second was the conflict of the Indians and *mestizos* with the European ruling classes. The third was the conflict of the bourgeoisies of the Latin American nations with foreign imperialist interests which were dictating to them unfavourable conditions of trade, and were hindering their industrialisation. The conference expected that, in their struggle with the imperialists, the bourgeoisies would be compelled to conciliate the masses, and that this would make the task of the communists easier. The conference produced the well-worn Leninist phrases on the land question and the national question, and its slogans about the struggle of the masses and the national bourgeoisie against the imperialists and their latifundiary-compradore agents recall the experience of China. It is not without significance that at the 7th Congress of the Comintern in July 1935 it was Wang Ming who spoke on the Latin American situation.[2]

The first attempt at a Popular Front in Latin America was the National Liberation Alliance formed in 1935 in Brazil. This was inspired by communists, included non-communist trade union and army officer groups, and had Luis Carlos Prestes for its chairman. The Comintern's hopes of this movement were however quickly destroyed. The Brazilian dictator Vargas claimed to have unravelled a communist plot of rebellion, arrested the Alliance's leaders and imprisoned Prestes for ten years. Vargas used the plot to strengthen his own legal powers, and in 1937 illegally prolonged his presidency and introduced a more or less fascist constitution. He made use in 1937 of a fascist movement called *Integralistas*, led by Plinio Salgado, but having won complete power he broke with them. The *Integralistas* in some ways resembled the Roumanian Iron Guard: their fascist doctrines included both social revolution-

[1] V. Cortes, *Etap obyedinyonnovo natsionalnovo fronta v revolyutsiah v stranah Latynskoy Ameriki* (The stage of the united national front in the revolutions in the countries of Latin America), in *Revolyutsionny Vostok*, 1935, No. 3.
[2] Wang Ming's speech is given in full in *Revolyutsionny Vostok*, 1935, No. 4.

ary demagogy and an emphasis on religion.[1] Vargas' tactics towards them also recall the tactics of King Carol towards the Iron Guard: Vargas was less brutal and more successful than Carol, but this must be attributed at least as much to his more favourable geographical situation as to his superior wisdom or virtue.

The second Latin American Popular Front appeared in Chile. It was formed in 1936 in opposition to the measures of repression adopted by President Alessandri, formerly a man of the moderate left but now both conservative and dictatorial. The Front included radicals, socialists and communists.[2] In 1938 the parties of the Front agreed to support the Radical Party leader Aguirre as presidential candidate. The Front was strengthened by a breach between the conservative candidate and the fascists. The election was held in December 1938, and Aguirre won by a small majority.

[1] An account of the Integralists by a German (Nazi) admirer is K. H. Hunsche, *Der brasilianische Integralismus*, Stuttgart, 1938.
[2] See J. R. Stevenson, *The Chilean Popular Front*, Philadelphia, 1942.

CHAPTER TEN

The Nazi-Soviet Pact

Moscow's acceptance of a treaty with Nazi Germany, which called itself a non-aggression pact and was in fact an aggression pact directed against Poland and the Baltic states, was an act of foreign policy by the government of a Great Power.[1] The Soviet government had its reasons. One was that it had no confidence in MM. Daladier and Chamberlain. Since Munich, it had been convinced—though wrongly—that these two were using all the arts of diplomacy to persuade Hitler to attack the Soviet Union. When the evidence of hostility between them and Hitler became undeniable, the Soviet leaders believed—perhaps somewhat less wrongly—that if they aligned themselves diplomatically with the Western Powers, and war broke out, the Soviet Union would bear the brunt of the German onslaught, while the French and British sat behind the Maginot line and watched. The second reason was that the *Yezhovshchina* had reduced the armed forces and civil administration of the Soviet Union to such a pitiful condition that it could not face war. The third reason was that the Soviet leaders believed that the Anglo-French and German forces would be sufficiently well balanced to ensure a long and mutually exhausting war. While 'the imperialists' exhausted each other, 'the land of socialism' would grow stronger in peace. Later on, a chance would come to intervene in favour of world revolution, in favour, that is, of the extension of the Stalinist system to a large part of the world. Meanwhile eastern Poland, the Baltic states and Bessarabia would be substantial gains.

These arguments could carry conviction to intelligent people, though in fact they were unsound. They were unsound because based on an unsound military appreciation. The effective military strength—as opposed to the long-term war potential—of France

[1] The German documents bearing on the treaty have been published by the United States government as *Nazi-Soviet Relations, 1949*. For comment, see M. Beloff, *The Foreign Policy of Soviet Russia*, Vol. 2; A. Rossi, *Deux ans d'alliance Germano-Soviétique*, Paris, 1949; on its implications for South-Eastern Europe, my *East European Revolution*, 1950.

and Britain was far inferior to that of Germany in 1939–40, as it had been in 1914. France had been saved in 1914 by the fact that the Germans had had to fight on a second front against Russia. By depriving France of a second front in 1939–40, Russia gained a breathing-space, but ensured that when the German attack did come, there would be no second front to help her. The terrible sufferings of the Russian people in 1941–4 were in large part due to Stalin's blunder of August 1939.

But this new twist in Soviet foreign policy, adopted for serious even if unsound reasons of Russian state interest, was quickly made binding on all communist parties. There was not even the formality of a Plenum of the Comintern Executive Committee, let alone a Comintern Congress to reverse the decisions of the 7th Congress of 1935. The new line was simply given out by the Soviet government and party. All communists were to praise the 'peace policy' of the Soviet Union, which had 'prevented an extension of the war'. Communists of belligerent countries were to denounce their country's war effort as 'imperialist'. As the German communists were completely silenced, this meant in practice that communist defeatism damaged only the Western war efforts: 'objectively' the new Comintern line benefited Hitler.

The French party, until 23rd August proudly claiming to be in the forefront of patriotic defence against the Axis imperialists, was now suddenly obliged to concentrate its hatred on the Polish landlords, to justify Soviet occupation of eastern Poland, and to agitate for peace with Hitler. On 26th September the party was dissolved by the French government. The C.G.T. expelled communists from its ranks. The Communist Deputies in the Chamber kept their seats as individuals, only changing the name of their faction to 'groupe ouvrier et paysan français'. On 1st October the leader of the group, Arthur Ramette, addressed a letter to Edouard Herriot, President of the Chamber, urging that Parliament be specially summoned to debate the conclusion of peace. The letter referred to 'peace proposals due to the initiative of the U.S.S.R.' No Soviet proposals had in fact been made to the belligerent governments. The only Soviet action had been the signature by Molotov of a joint statement with Ribbentrop on 28th September, to the effect that the German and Soviet governments would undertake a common effort to put an end to hostilities, and that if the effort should fail it would then be clear that 'England and France are responsible for the continuation of the war'.[1] It was Hitler's policy that the

[1] *Nazi-Soviet Relations*, p. 108.

French communists were now supporting, on instructions from Moscow. The letter to Herriot was followed by the arrest of those who supported it.[1] On 4th October the Party's leader, Maurice Thorez, who was serving as a N.C.O. in the army, deserted from his unit. He fled clandestinely to Belgium, thence later to Switzerland, and in the summer of 1940 reached Moscow, where he remained until 1944. At the end of March 1940 the forty-four communist Deputies were tried before a military tribunal of the Paris area for illegally reconstituting the Communist Party in contravention of the decree of 26th September.[2]

The communists were now an illegal organisation, hunted by the police. They did their best to spread defeatist propaganda. They were able to exploit the disillusionment of the French working class, which ever since the collapse of the Popular Front had felt itself to be cheated of its rights. The alleged need to purge the factories of communists, on the ground that they might commit sabotage, was probably abused by employers who wished to revenge themselves on the French workers for the mental discomfort which they had caused them under the Popular Front. Anti-communist action became to some extent anti-working-class action, and to that extent helped the communists' subversive efforts.

However it would be a mistake to exaggerate the importance of communist defeatism in army or factories. The defeat of France in 1940 was a military defeat. The speed of the French collapse was due to the inferiority of the command, equipment and strategy of the French army to those of the German, but the outcome of the conflict was due to the fact that France had to face a power with twice her man-power and more than twice her industrial power, without a considerable ally on land. The British forces did their duty, but—as always in the early stages of a war fought by Britain —their numbers were far too small. In September 1914 it had been the Russian army which, by engaging a great part of the German forces, had enabled the French to win on the Marne. In 1940 the Russian army held aloof. Stalin himself, rather than his French stooges, dealt France her death-blow.

Once France had been beaten, however, the French communists tried to make the best of the situation. With a curious naivety they sought to make a parallel between 1940 and 1917. When the German army smashed Russian imperialism, the result had been

---

[1] The action of the French Communist Party during the winter of 1939–40 is minutely analysed in A. Rossi, *Les communistes français pendant la drôle de guerre*, Paris, 1950.

[2] Thirty-six were sentenced to five years' imprisonment, eight to four years'.

the Bolshevik Revolution. Now the German army had smashed French imperialism: therefore the result must be victory of the French communists. On 25th June the communists even sent a letter to the propaganda section of the German command in Paris, in which they requested permission for their paper *Humanité* to appear legally. They claimed to have been the only French party that resolutely opposed the war against Germany. They promised to denounce British imperialism and to pursue a policy of Franco-Soviet friendship which 'would be the complement of the German-Soviet pact and so would create the conditions of a durable peace'.[1] The Germans, not wishing to strengthen the influence in France of their unreliable Soviet ally, refused this request, but during 1940 they treated the communists mildly. In their illegally published paper, the communists denounced De Gaulle as an 'agent of English finance'. One of their former Deputies wrote to Marshal Pétain, asking to be allowed to testify at the Riom trial against Léon Blum for his 'warmongering' policy. This request too was refused.

The communists pursued a similar policy in Czechoslovakia. Their underground propaganda denounced the Czech leaders of the Nazi 'Protectorate' as reactionaries and capitalists, but it denounced still more fiercely the activities of the exiled ex-President Beneš and other 'British imperialist agents'. As long as Hitler and Stalin were allies, Czech communists refrained from urging resistance to Hitler. There must even be no incitement against the German army of occupation. The crime of Beneš's supporters in Czechoslovakia was that they were 'sowing hatred of the Czech population towards German workers clad in military uniform'.[2]

In the Balkans too communist activities 'objectively' benefited Hitler. The Yugoslav communists, who since 1936 had been the spearhead of the anti-fascist movement, especially among the intelligentsia, now concentrated all their venom against France and Britain.[3] This cost them the sympathy of that section of the

---

[1] A. Rossi, *La physiologie du parti communiste français*, Paris, 1948, pp. 402–10, 431–2.

[2] Statement by the leadership of the Communist Party of Czechoslovakia, dating from the autumn of 1940, quoted in Dr. E. Beneš, *Paměti, od Mnichova k nové válce a k novemu vitězství*, Prague, 1948, pp. 213–16.

[3] In the autumn of 1939 the death of the French Admiral Guépratte, who had evacuated Serbian civilians from Albania to Tunis after the occupation of Serbia by the Central Powers in 1916, was commemorated in Belgrade. The Yugoslav communist students saw fit to insult the memory of a man who had saved hundreds of Serbian lives by breaking up the commemoration with a demonstration against French imperialism.

Serbian intelligentsia which earlier had followed their lead. The Bulgarian communists, by the same policy, probably gained support. The average Serb regarded Russia and France as his country's best friends among the Great Powers, the average Bulgarian, Russia and Germany. The Franco-Soviet pact had been popular with most social and political groups in Yugoslavia: the Soviet-German pact was similarly popular in Bulgaria. The communist following among the Bulgarian intelligentsia possibly increased between 1939 and 1941.

The indirect help thus given by the Comintern to Hitler was believed in Moscow to be compensated by Soviet territorial gains. The first of these was the eastern half of Poland. The Polish lands annexed to the Soviet Union were inhabited mainly by Ukrainians or White Russians. Though these national groups were glad in principle to be reunited with their kinsmen to the east, the overwhelming majority was strongly anti-communist. Though they had fought for twenty years a bitter struggle against Polish nationalism, they detested the rulers of Moscow with equal vigour. The gain to Moscow was not so much that it achieved the ancient aspirations of the Ukrainian nation to unity, as that it destroyed an Ukrainian 'Piedmont', where even under the rule of the Polish 'colonels' clique' Ukrainian nationalism could be openly proclaimed. The Soviet liberators lost little time in supressing Ukrainian political parties and cultural organisations. The large Polish minority suffered even worse. Hundreds of thousands were deported in the usual inhuman conditions to the interior of Russia.

The attempt of the Soviet leaders to subject Finland was unsuccessful. At the beginning of the Soviet-Finnish war the Soviet authorities set up, in the border town of Terijoki, a 'Democratic' government under the old Comintern veteran Otto Willi Kuusinen. Finnish resistance forced them to abandon their hope of conquering the whole country. When peace was made with the true government of Finland, Kuusinen's 'government' was forgotten. Kuusinen himself received a consolation prize by being appointed to the presidency of the Karelo-Finnish S.S.R., which was composed partly of lands now ceded to Russia by Finland, and partly of the north-western corner of European Russia.

The three Baltic states were obliged to sign treaties of mutual assistance with the Soviet Union, and to lease bases on their territory to be manned by Soviet troops.[1] In mid-June the Soviet

[1] Esthonian-Soviet treaty of 28th September 1939; Latvian-Soviet treaty of 5th October 1939; Lithuanian-Soviet treaty of 10th October 1939. Lithuania acquired the city of Vilna, seized from Poland by the Soviet invasion.

leaders decided to exploit the collapse of France to grab some more territory before it was too late. Ultimatums were addressed to all three governments with trumped-up charges of anti-Soviet action, and with the demands that Soviet troops be admitted in unlimited quantities and that 'governments friendly to the Soviet Union' be set up.[1] The Red Army marched in even before the governments surrendered. In each country a puppet acceptable to the communists was made Premier, the former presidents and ministers were arrested or fled,[2] parliaments were dissolved and new elections announced. Slightly more than a week was allowed for the election campaign, and on the first day ready-made Working Peoples' Leagues appeared, composed of a number of organisations never heard of before and including the tiny communist parties. At first the fiction was maintained that independent candidates could stand against the Leagues, though the procedure adopted made this extremely difficult. When despite the obstacles, independent candidates were nevertheless found for every constituency in Estonia, they were either forced to withdraw or declared disqualified.[3] On 14th July the elections were held, and the Working People's League in each country duly obtained an overwhelming majority. On 21st July the parliaments met, and voted for the incorporation of their countries in the Soviet Union. Not only was this incompatible with the constitutions of the three countries, but the proposal had not even been put forward until four days before the parliaments met, when the local organs of the communist parties had suddenly announced that this was the wish of the toiling masses. Incorporation had been preceded by a wave of arrests. It was followed by the rule of the secret police, directed in part by Baltic communist *émigrés* returned from the Soviet Union, and in part by Russians. A year later, and about a week before Hitler attacked the Soviet Union, began a wave of mass deportations of Estonians, Latvians and Lithuanians to the interior of Russia.[4]

The annexation of the Baltic states was an act of state imperialism. As such it belongs rather to the history of Power politics than of communism. It deserves a place in these pages however as a

---

[1] Ultimatum to Lithuania of 12th June 1940, to Latvia and Esthonia of 16th June 1940.

[2] President Smetona of Lithuania escaped to Germany, Presidents Ulmanis of Latvia and Päts of Estonia were deported to unknown destinations.

[3] Ants Oras, *Baltic Eclipse*, 1948, pp. 64–8.

[4] During the period up to the occupation of all three Baltic countries by the Germans, it is estimated that 45,000 persons were deported from Lithuania, 34,000 from Latvia, and 50,000 from Esthonia. See Casimiro Verax, *Lituania entre fuego cruzado*, Buenos Aires, 1944, pp. 299–305; Dr. A. Bilmanis, *Latvian-Russian Relations*, Washington (D.C.), 1944, pp. 227–33; A. Oras, op. cit., pp. 151–78.

dress rehearsal for the Stalinisation of Eastern Europe which followed the Second World War, and which was carried out with
equal ruthlessness but in a somewhat less crude and clumsy manner.

CHINA

In China the Soviet-Nazi pact did not substantially affect communist policy. This was partly because Mao Tse-tung enjoyed
considerable autonomy from Moscow, and partly because Japan,
not Germany, was the enemy. The Chinese party duly denounced
the western imperialist warmongers, but continued to fight the
Japanese. Relations between communists and Kuomintang deteriorated, but this was due not to European politics but to Chinese
conditions. After the loss of Canton and Hankow Chiang's armies
were confined to the western provinces. The Japanese made no
serious effort to conquer this area, and Chiang made no serious
effort to recover the great cities. The front stagnated. In these
conditions the only effective action against the Japanese was guerrilla warfare, at which the communists were far more skilled than
the nationalists. The communists increased their prestige and
popularity throughout China by their guerrilla exploits, while the
nationalists grew ever more jealous.

During these years the administrative machine of China, which
had been in dissolution from 1911 to 1927, and had been to some
extent restored during the decade of Chiang Kai-shek's supremacy,
once more disintegrated. The Japanese conquerors were unable to
replace it. In March 1940 they persuaded Wang Ching-wei, who
had broken with Chiang at the end of 1938 and gone into exile, to
form a 'government' under their protection in Nanking. Wang
was not able to win a large body of opinion, and his administration
worked poorly. In the south and south-west Chiang controlled a
political apparatus. But it was ever more dependent on local landowners and warlords. It had lost almost the last remnants of the
revolutionary and popular character that the Kuomintang had once
had, and resembled the corrupt and despotic regime of the last
decades of the Manchu empire. This degeneration of the Kuomintang benefited the communists. In their liberated areas they built
their own state machine, including civil bureaucracy, propaganda
organisations and schools. Their social policy continued to be
moderate. Even the 'national bourgeoisie' was treated as a progressive class. During these years the communists held a solid
territory in Shensi province, with Yenan as their capital. They also
organised 'anti-Japanese war bases' in other parts of China north

of the Yangtse valley, especially in Hupeh, Shantung and Kiangsu provinces. In these areas the communists held all but the main cities and main lines of communication: it was their administration, rather than that of the invaders, which the population obeyed. There were also smaller communist guerrilla bands in more distant areas, even in the south.

In the territory controlled by the Kuomintang or by the Japanese, the communists gained popularity, especially among students in the universities of cities nominally administered by Wang Ching-wei. There was a steady stream of volunteers from these territories to the 'anti-Japanese war bases'. Even among business men there were well-wishers. Most Chinese capitalists disliked the Japanese. On the other hand the restrictions placed by Chiang's regime on business, in his territory, augured ill for the future, while the dominant position of wealthy families connected by marriage with the Generalissimo[1] caused resentment. To the merchants of Shanghai or Tientsin it did not appear certain that after the defeat of Japan Chiang would be a better master than Mao, whose pronouncements on the future position of the 'national bourgeoisie' were benevolently vague.

Communist successes alarmed Chiang Kai-shek. In Kuomintang territory the growing inflation increased the hardships of the population, increased their discontent, and increased the repressive measures of Chiang's security police. The more dictatorial and unpopular his regime, the more Chiang feared his communist rivals. By the end of 1939 they had ceased to co-operate. In 1940 there were armed clashes between Kuomintang and communist troops in several areas, and early in 1941 Chiang's forces made a large-scale attack on the communist 'New Fourth Army', with serious losses to the latter. After this a large part of Chiang's best troops were occupied in a blockade of the communist territory in Shensi, to the detriment of the joint war effort.

In April 1941 the Soviet government signed a non-aggression pact with Japan. Just as the pact with Hitler in 1939 had diverted German aggression from the Soviet frontiers and against the West, so the pact with Japan in 1941 diverted Japanese aggression from the Soviet frontiers and against the territory of the Western Powers in the Pacific and south-east Asia. This pact did not have time to affect the policy of the Chinese communists, for only two months later the Soviet Union had been kicked into the war and was thus the ally of Britain and Holland, and six months later of

[1] The Soong and Kung families.

the United States as well. Once it had become important for Moscow
to have good relations with the Anglo-Saxon Powers, she could
no longer have an interest in preventing the Chinese communists
from engaging the forces of a Power which, though at peace with
Russia, was holding down the troops of Russia's allies, and thus
making more difficult the launching of the 'second front' in Europe.[1]

During the Hitler-Stalin honeymoon, communist parties in
colonial territories in Asia—for instance, in India and Malaya—
intensified their 'anti-imperialist' agitation, but were too small to
have much effect. One country where the position of the communists
was adversely affected by Russia's pro-Nazi policy was Chile. In
1940 the Comintern line was that Soviet policy was the main
factor for peace, or at least for a limitation of the war, while the
main factor for an extension of the war was the United States.
The Chilean communists, members of the Popular Front which
in 1938 had elected Aguirre to the presidency, were committed to
a policy of hostility to the United States. As this was not acceptable
to other Chilean parties of the left, the Popular Front disintegrated.[2] The Chilean communists ceased to have any effect on
Chilean policy.

THE END OF THE ALLIANCE

It was in the Balkans that the Soviet-Nazi alliance broke down.
The last Soviet success was the annexation of Bessarabia from
Roumania in June 1940. It was followed by deportations of Bessarabian Roumanians into the interior of Russia, and by the formation, from about two-thirds of Bessarabian territory,[3] of a
Moldavian S.S.R. The future of the Balkan states was now a source
of friction between Hitler and Stalin. Molotov's journey to Berlin
in November 1940 did not solve the problem. The Bulgarian and
Turkish questions were the stumbling block which led to the re-
jection by Moscow of the Axis proposals for co-operation.[4] After
this it was only a matter of time before the Germans attacked.

In the first half of 1941 the Balkan communist parties slightly
changed the tone of their propaganda. Hitherto their denunciations
of the 'imperialist war' had been directed solely against France and
Britain: now they denounced also the aggression of Germany

[1] The attitude of the Chinese communists to the European belligerents up to June
1941 is a little-known subject, on which more evidence would be welcome.
[2] Stevenson, op. cit., pp. 107–110.
[3] Northern and Southern Bessarabia, where Roumanians formed only a comparatively small part of the population, were annexed directly to the Ukrainian S.S.R.
[4] *Nazi-Soviet Relations*, pp. 255–9. I have discussed this in my *East European
Revolution*, pp. 63–5.

and Italy. The Greek communists did not preach defeatism in November 1940: while attacking the dictatorship of the King and Metaxas, they also expressed disapproval of Mussolini's invasion. The Bulgarian communists opposed the decision of King Boris to admit German troops in March 1941, which the Soviet government had also officially criticised.[1] The Yugoslav party did not denounce the *coup d'etat* of 27th March, whose anti-German character was obvious to all:[2] rather they tried, with little success, to exploit the new situation to their own advantage. When invasion came, the party's attitude was obscure. Some individuals at least among the party's members or sympathisers did their duty in the armed forces during the few days before the army surrendered.

During May 1941 Stalin made strenuous attempts to appease Hitler, but it was too late. Hitler's suspicions and ideological hatred could no longer be overcome. The Nazi-Soviet honeymoon, which had almost exclusively benefited the Nazis, was brought to an end. While the honeymoon had lasted the Soviet leaders had been sweetly subservient. As poor Molotov remarked on 22nd June 1941, 'we had not deserved this'.[3]

[1] Broadcast statement by Assistant Commissar of Foreign Affairs, A. Y. Vyshinski, 3rd March 1941.
[2] The *coup d'état*, organised by air force officers, reflected the anti-German mood of the Serbian people. This does not necessarily mean that the Simović government wished to go to war with the Axis. Once in power, the new ministers understandably tried to appease the wrath of the dictators, but with no success.
[3] G. Gafencu, *Préliminaires de la guerre à l'Est*, Fribourg, n.d. (?1944), p. 247.

CHAPTER ELEVEN

Communism and the Resistance Movements

W HEN Hitler, rejecting Stalin's last attempts at conciliation and flattery, invaded the Soviet Union, the imperialistic war was changed overnight into the Great Patriotic War of the Soviet Union, and the duty of every communist
everywhere in the world was to contribute to the war effort of
Soviet Russia, or, if geographic conditions made this more possible,
to the war effort of the Soviet Union's allies. The communists
therefore made great efforts to organise resistance in occupied
countries, or to assume the leadership of those resistance movements which had begun without them. In Yugoslavia, Greece and
Albania the communists built strong armies of resistance, and while
fighting the invaders also succeeded in crippling or destroying non-
communist resistance groups. In Italy the communists created the
largest of the resistance forces, and maintained relatively good
relations with other lesser groups. In France the communists had
some success in infiltrating existing movements, and also created
their own separate movement. In Poland communist resistance
was of negligible importance. The Polish Home Army was welded
into an efficient force while the communists, in obedience to Moscow, were still urging Poles to submit to the Partition of 1939,
and after June 1941 the belated attempts of the few Polish communists to resist achieved little. Polish resistance was essentially free
from communist influence: it was broken partly by the Germans,
who destroyed insurgent Warsaw while the Red Army watched
from the right bank of the Vistula, and partly by the Russians,
who disarmed Home Army units and arrested their commanders
as they advanced into Poland. In Asia the communists led powerful
guerrilla armies in China, and a small but brave force in Malaya.
Apart from these major efforts, communists made their contribution to such resistance as was done in Slovakia, Bulgaria, north-
west Europe, Burma and Indochina.

The obvious aim of the resistance was military. The communists were concerned to tie down enemy troops, and so relieve pressure on the Russian front. From this point of view the resistance movements undoubtedly achieved results, though probably smaller than has been generally believed. They were paid at terrible cost in human lives and material destruction. The casualties were not confined to battle, but included many thousands executed in cold blood, hostages and wives and children: the destruction included thousands of humble village hovels burned down as reprisals. Enemy casualties were usually smaller than those of the resisters, but fear of guerrilla raids tied down large enemy forces, and sabotage seriously damaged enemy communications at times when Allied armies were preparing decisive actions. The glamour of a heroic legend that surrounds the exploits of the resisters is deserved. The movements made a strong appeal to the patriotic pride of conquered nations, and to the desire of injured or humiliated individuals to strike back at the powerful and arrogant invaders. Their deeds won the sympathy of public opinion in the belligerent Allied countries, and the movements received not only a flood of verbal encouragement but also substantial material aid from Allied military commands. Thus the Allies helped to build the movements into serious political forces.

From the first the political significance of the resistance was clearer to the communists than to the others. The communists used the resistance to get power into their hands. They realised that patriotic slogans in time of national oppression would win them more popular support than their social revolutionary slogans had ever brought them in time of peace. When liberation came, they hoped to establish their own dictatorship, and if not, then at least to play a far greater part in their country's politics than before the enemy invasion. Key military and civil posts in the areas liberated by resisters must be held by communists. The soldiers of the resistance must, when possible, be indoctrinated with the basic slogans of the communist party. The party must strengthen itself by recruiting into its ranks as many as possible of the new officers and new civil administrators thrown up by the war itself.

As the struggle became more bitter, the social consequences began to be important, and gave the communists further opportunities. Guerrilla war inevitably brings reprisals, and these fall most heavily on the propertied, both in town and in country. Destruction of property weakened the communists' future rivals, and drove many of those who feared reprisals to collaborate with the invaders or the quislings, in order to 'maintain law and order'. This tendency was welcomed by the communists, who were able increasingly to argue that the former ruling classes, and even a large part of the middle classes, were helping the enemy. This enabled them to turn the war of liberation into a civil war, and to fight against the bourgeoisie and part of the peasantry in the name not of the class struggle but of patriotism. At the same time, as the resisters suffered more, and lost what possessions they had had, they became more willing, even eager, to turn the resistance into revolution.

The period of resistance is thus an extremely important one in the development of international communism. The various 'people's liberation fronts' were a more efficient form of the pre-war Popular Fronts. In the face of an ever-present foreign invader, differences of ideology or of party programme are more easily forgotten than in peace. The communists' ruthlessness, which had gained them more enemies than friends in prewar France, now won them more admiration than hostility. They also showed more ability to conciliate, to make concessions which seemed generous yet in fact did not diminish their power, than they had shown in Spain in 1937–8. The use of the 'liberated area' as a training-ground for communist administrators was an extremely important aspect of this period. It had already proved valuable in China since the early 1930's, and to some extent in the Spanish civil war. But during the resistance period it became far more important. It provided numerous cadres to the communist cause not only in Yugo-slavia and China, where the communists were in the end victorious, but also in Greece, Malaya, Indochina and even Western Europe, where victory in war did not bring them power.

THE BALKANS

Communist resistance in China between 1941 and 1945 followed the lines already briefly described: no more need be said of it here. The conditions of Balkan resistance were not unlike those of Chinese. In Yugoslavia, Albania and Greece physical conditions favoured the same kind of guerrilla as in China. In these countries, as in China, the armies of occupation held the main cities, railways and roads, and part of the plains, while the resisters held the mountains, and raided enemy garrisons and lines of communication. Here too a fourfold relationship existed between communists, nationalist resisters, quislings and invaders—in the case of Yugoslavia further complicated by the multiplicity of quislings and of invaders. Here too 'liberated areas' were a training ground for the military and civil cadres of the new communist-directed state machine.

The Yugoslav communists began resistance in Serbia and in Montenegro, after the German invasion of Russia.[1] Driven out of Serbia at the end of 1941, they reorganised their forces during 1942 in the mountains of Bosnia. They survived two very severe enemy attacks in the spring and summer of 1943, and held a considerable territory at the time of the Italian surrender. This was the turning-point in their struggle, for it enabled them to acquire large stocks of weapons. Though in the following year the Germans frequently attacked them, and caused heavy losses, they could never spare sufficient forces to attempt their complete destruction. In Greece the communist-led National Liberation Front (E.A.M.) was founded in September 1941, and its People's Liberation Army (E.L.A.S.), nominally formed in April 1942, was making its presence felt by the end of 1942.[2] By the autumn of 1943 E.L.A.S. controlled large areas, especially in Macedonia and the Pindus, and it too acquired large supplies of arms from the surrendering Italians. The Albanian National Liberation Front (L.N.C.) was founded in September 1942. The collapse of Italy a year later not only provided the Albanian resistance with arms, but enabled its forces to liberate most of the southern provinces. Thus the development of the three movements was very similar. The Yugoslavs however were faced with far greater and more efficient enemy forces, and their sufferings and their military achievements were thus much greater.

The conflict between communist and nationalist resisters came earliest in Yugoslavia. Colonel Mihailović, a Serbian officer of the old Yugoslav army, had formed a resistance group which had begun to fight the Germans before Hitler invaded Russia, that is before the Yugoslav communists took the field. For a time communists and Mihailović were allies. But political, ideological and tactical disagreements were unbridgeable, and they were fighting each other at the moment when the Germans attacked in force. After this Mihailović, who had meanwhile been appointed Minister

---

[1] The best single account of the Yugoslav resistance is S. Clissold, *Whirlwind*, 1949. V. Dedijer, *Tito speaks*, 1953, a semi-official biography, is of considerable interest. A good analysis of the communist technique of power can be found in B. Lazié, *Titov pokret i režim*, 1946. This book's value is however reduced by its strong Serbian nationalist bias. Further references can be found in the bibliographical note of my *East European Revolution*.

[2] An authoritative first-hand account of the Greek resistance movement is C. M. Woodhouse, *Apple of Discord*, 1948. A recent American study is L. Stavrianos, *Greece*, Chicago, 1952.

of War of the Yugoslav government in exile, commanded a somewhat equivocal allegiance from Serbian nationalist forces in various
parts of the country, which were drawn into close military collaboration with the Italian, and in some cases the German, occupation
forces. In the spring of 1943 Mihailović's men took part in the
enemy operations against the communist forces, or Partisans.
Thereafter the Serbian nationalists, or Chetniks,[1] were represented
by the communists' propaganda, with much justification and with
growing effect, as quislings. In Croatia and Slovenia too, sections
of the prewar democratic parties gave varying degrees of support
to the Germans or to the Croatian fascists, believing that the communists would at the end of the war be a serious menace, and that
the Germans, whom the Great Allies would defeat, were less
dangerous. All this helped the communists to fight a civil war in
the name of patriotism.

In Greece the same conflict broke out after the Italian surrender.
Possession of Italian arms made E.L.A.S. less dependent on British
supplies, and emboldened them to risk British displeasure by
attacking the nationalist resistance forces, with whom they had
previously promised the British that they would co-operate. In
October 1943 E.L.A.S. attacked the most important of these, commanded by General Zervas. Only British supplies saved Zervas
from annihilation. The civil war went on until February 1944, when
it was temporarily stopped by British mediation.

In Albania the same occurred. The nationalist *Balli Kombetar*
and communist L.N.C. came to blows, and several leading *Balli*
collaborated with the Germans. A third group, led by Colonel
Abbas Kupi, which was supported by the British, maintained an
independent position until June 1944, when L.N.C. forces attacked
it.[2] In all three countries the British policy of reconciling all who
wished to resist the invaders was unsuccessful.

The social composition of the communist resistance movements
was various.

In Greece the working class of Athens played an important part,
both providing recruits to the guerrilla groups and conducting
underground work in the city. There were some impressive
strikes in Athens. In Yugoslavia the workers played little part,

[1] There is no space here to give a more precise definition of a Chetnik. See Clissold,
op. cit., pp. 55–8.
[2] An excellent work on Albania is Julian Amery, *Sons of the Eagle*, 1948. Though
mainly concerned with Abbas Kupi and with the northern and eastern tribes, it throws
much light on the general social background of Albania. *Illyrian Adventure*, 1952, by
Brigadier 'Trotsky' Davies, for a time Head of the British Mission to the Albanian
Partisans of L.N.C., recounts his experiences.

except in so far as many of the communists who first took the field in 1941 were, or had been, workers. In Albania there hardly existed an urban working class.

In all countries the great majority of the resistance soldiers were peasants. But, as in China, the predominance of peasants in the ranks did not mean that the communist resistance movements were 'peasant movements'. The leaders were, as in China, professional revolutionaries, of whom a large proportion were former university students, but some of whom had once been peasants or workers. As in other countries and at other periods, so now in the Balkans the communist professional revolutionary was a category outside social classes.

The political origins of members of the communist resistance movements were also diverse. The communists encouraged splinter groups from old parties to join the Liberation Fronts. E.A.M. included socialist and agrarian groups, and the Yugoslav movement several moderately prominent individual members of prewar democratic parties. But no non-communist political group had any independent existence within the Fronts, whereas the communist parties themselves preserved their organisation and discipline intact. Essentially the Fronts reproduced the partnership between the politically inarticulate masses and the politically experienced professional revolutionaries first conceived by Lenin in 1917 and later successfully adopted by Mao Tse-tung in the 1930's.[1] The great majority of members of the movements in all three countries were persons of no fixed political ideas, who may have voted for one party or another in prewar elections but had never exercised any political influence. Now through the Liberation Fronts they were brought into political life for the first time, but their political energies were successfully canalised by the communist parties' cadres.

Finally, in the case of Yugoslavia only, the communist-led resisters were also nationally diverse. The first year of Axis occupation and partition of Yugoslavia was marked by a fratricidal war between Croatian and Serbian nationalists, with appalling massacres. The horrors were started by the Croatian fascists, but crimes were also committed on a lesser but still vast scale by Serbian Chetniks against both Moslem and Croatian villages. In the face of this mutual destruction the communists from the beginning proclaimed the slogan of unity of all peoples of Yugoslavia against the invaders, and against their puppets, whether

[1] See above, pp. 29, 32, 37, 153–4.

these be Serbian, Croatian, Slovene or Macedonian. They argued that the petty nationalism of these puppets was as harmful to the nations in whose names they acted as to their victims, and benefited only Hitler. By 1943 this view was being proved right by events. Sickened by the senseless national hatreds, more and more people saw in the communist movement the only way out. This positive policy in the national question—which was of course based on the Soviet doctrine on nationalities—was one of the main reasons for the communists' success.

After the surrender of Italy the Balkan communist movements put forward more serious political demands. Already in November 1942 the Yugoslav communists had held a meeting in the Bosnian town of Bihać, and had formed a provisional legislative body called the Anti-fascist Council of National Liberation of Yugoslavia (A.V.N.O.J.). A year later, in another Bosnian town Jajce, they formed a provisional government, entitled Committee of National Liberation. It denounced the government in exile, forbade the King to return until 'the people had decided', and announced that Yugoslavia would be reorganised as a federal republic. In Greece, after discussions between emissaries of E.A.M. and the exiled King and government in Cairo had broken down, a Committee of National Liberation (P.E.E.A.) was formed early in 1944. Its authority was recognised by all E.A.M. 'liberated areas', which by this time included a large part of the area of Greece. In May 1944 the Albanian communists did the same. At a meeting at Permet they announced the formation of a Council and a Committee of the same type as A.V.N.O.J. and the Yugoslav Committee. These bodies, like their Yugoslav counterparts, forbade the exiled King of Albania to return until 'the people had decided'.

By this time all three movements held considerable areas, in which an elementary civil administration had to be set up, and supplies had to be organised both for the armies and for the civil population. As in China, local persons of ability were recruited for administrative tasks. Among the mountaineers of Bosnia, Montenegro, Albania and central Greece men—and perhaps even more, women—of initiative and efficiency, who had never before had responsibility, who had never before been thought worth consulting, were given opportunities of which they had never dreamed. Great new energies and talents were released, but they were firmly harnessed to the chariot of the communists, who never dropped the reins.

The international situation in the last stages of the war was

COMMUNISM AND THE RESISTANCE MOVEMENTS 217

favourable to the Yugoslav and Albanian communists, but un-favourable to the Greek. By agreement between the three Great Allies a nominal compromise was made between the exiled government and the government of the communist leader Tito, which since the capture of Belgrade by the Red Army in October 1944 was installed in the Yugoslav capital. The evacuation of German troops from Albania enabled the communist leader Enver Hoxha to seize power throughout the country at the end of 1944, and this too was accepted by the Allies. In Greece however the communists were defeated. A joint Greek government was formed in September 1944, in which the communists held several ministries but did not hold the key posts. After the German evacuation however most of Greece was in communist hands. The communists did not attempt to seize Athens, but allowed the government to return, with a British force, in October. Disagreements about the disbanding and disarmament of E.L.A.S. and the regular Greek troops, and the formation of a National Guard, could not be bridged, and in December 1944 hostilities broke out in Athens. The first shots were fired by the enemies of the communists, but the communists were ready, and had overwhelming force. Only the intervention of regular British troops—which had to be reinforced at the expense of the front in Italy—prevented E.L A.S. from capturing all Athens. The fighting was ended by an agreement signed at Varkiza on 12th February 1945. This obliged E.L.A.S. to disarm, but promised democratic liberties for all parties. This was a defeat for the Greek communists, and it was due not to factors within Greece but to British intervention: without British action Greece would have had the same regime as Yugoslavia.

Elsewhere in Eastern Europe communist-led resistance was much less effective. A Partisan movement developed in Bulgaria from the summer of 1943. It fought bravely against Bulgarian police forces, but its numbers were small and its achievements modest. In Slovakia a national uprising occurred in September 1944. Communist-led Partisans and a section of the regular army of the Slovak State together fought for some weeks against the Germans, but the rising was crushed.

In Poland the communist party, dissolved by the Comintern in 1938, was revived in 1942 under the name Polish Workers' Party. Its resistance force, the 'People's Army', played a small part in the Warsaw Rising of August 1944. Communist resistance only began in 1942, and was negligible in comparison with the national effort of the Home Army and Underground Government, controlled by the great democratic parties of Poland, recognising and recognised by the Polish government in exile. This national movement the advancing Russians treated as an enemy: they disarmed units which declared themselves to Russian commanders, in some cases they shot their officers. When Warsaw rose, they did nothing to help until the Germans had almost completed their destruction of the flower of the Polish resistance. In July 1944 the Russians set up a Committee of National Liberation on Polish soil. It was composed of communists and stooges. As its temporary seat of government was chosen Lublin, where in 1918 the first revolutionary government of free Poland had been formed.[1] But the Lublin Committee resembled not the Lublin government of 1918, but the Bialystok Committee of 1920, which the Red Army had set up under Dzierzhinski when Tuhachevski was sweeping into Poland.[2] In 1944 however Poland was at Russia's mercy. The attempts of the Western Powers to ensure representation for the democratic forces of Poland failed. Poland was simply conquered by the Russians: the Polish communists were not an independent political factor, but mere instruments of the occupying Power.[3]

FRANCE AND ITALY

In Western Europe powerful resistance movements developed in France and Italy, in which communists played an important part. Good communications and scarcity of remote mountainous or forest terrain favoured the invaders, and made guerrilla action less easy than in the Balkans or Asia. Instead sabotage, espionage and subversive propaganda were well used. The political results of the resistance movements were not the same as in the Balkans, as both France and Italy were liberated not by Soviet but by Anglo-Saxon armies, which required them as bases from which to pursue the Germans in the later stages of the war.

In France several conspiratorial groups were formed early in 1941, both in the zone of German occupation and in Vichy territory. These established contact with General de Gaulle's Free French Committee in London, though their relations with it were not always smooth.[4] It was not until the German invasion of Russia

---

[1] The 'people's government' of 1918 was headed by the veteran Galician socialist, Ignacy Daszynski. It was replaced, after discussions with Piłsudski, by the more moderate government of Moraczewski. See above, p. 65.

[2] See above, p. 73.

[3] The most authoritative work on the Polish resistance movement is General Bór-Komarowski, *Secret Army*, 1950.

[4] There is a brief account of the early stage of the resistance movement in H. Michel, *Histoire de la résistance*, Paris, 1950.

that the communists became active resisters. The prestige of the Soviet Union made the party once more attractive to the workers, and it was able to enlist recruits. The communists participated in other organisations, but kept their cadres distinct from those of their allies. The most important body which came under communist control was the *Front National*. This included individuals of conservative opinions and bourgeois social origin as well as workers and men of the left, but it was created on communist initiative, and the key positions in it were held by communists. Its main strength was in the zone of German occupation. Its military organisation was called *Francs-Tireurs et Partisans*, and in it the communist control was still stricter than in the Front. On Vichy territory too the communists entered the existing resistance groups.

The communists and the F.T.P. were not content with mere underground organisation and preparation for action in the future when military circumstances would be favourable, which had been the policy of the older resistance movements: they urged immediate military action against the invaders on as large a scale as possible. This of course corresponded to the communist tactic in the Balkans. It could be expected to draw into the struggle large numbers of more or less non-political persons, who could be captured for the Communist Party by patriotic slogans. It would lead to reprisals and atrocities which would embitter all patriots and create an extremist mentality. It would drive the conservative and the propertied into collaboration with the Germans, or at least with Vichy, and so facilitate the communists' aim of identifying national liberation with social revolution. Finally it would increase German military commitments in the West, and so relieve pressure on the Soviet Union. This difference in tactics between communist and other resisters remained throughout the war. The Allied military authorities preferred the more limited tactic of sabotage combined with training for a future rising, because they believed that this would do most to help Allied military operations and would spare French lives. The communists however asserted that the Allies urged this tactic for sinister reactionary motives, because they planned to impose on France a despotic government of the Right, and wished meanwhile to prevent 'the arming of the people'. Allied dealings with Admiral Darlan and General Giraud appeared to support this interpretation.

During the resistance years the communists won an important success in the trade unions. Under German and Vichy rule unions had been dissolved, but the former leaders of the C.G.T. maintained some personal contact with each other. During 1941 and 1942 they also established better relations with the remnants of the former Christian trade unions (C.F.T.C.), which were an independent body but were loosely connected with the left Catholic political group of Popular Democrats. From June 1941 onwards the C.G.T. was wooed by the communists, who urged that the unity between the left trade unions, broken by the C.G.T.'s expulsion of the communists in September 1939,[1] be restored. The undoubted courage and efficiency of communist resistance, and the prestige of the Soviet war effort, created a genuine demand for unity among the workers, and ultimately overcame the reluctance of the C.G.T. By the agreement of Le Perreux, of May 1943, the communists were readmitted to the C.G.T. A new central committee of the reunited trade unions was formed, of nine members of whom three were to be communists.[2] Profiting by the prestige of Russia, the divisions in the ranks of the socialists, and their own experience of conspiracy and infiltration, the communists soon got the key positions into their grasp. The C.G.T. emerged from the war under communist control. Meanwhile relations between C.G.T. and C.F.T.C. became cooler, and the latter drew close to the Catholic democrats.

German actions helped the communist tactic of resistance. The introduction of compulsory labour service, which involved the deportation of thousands of Frenchmen and Frenchwomen to Germany, led to mass desertions. The deserters had to live, and live illegally. They were natural recruits to the resistance. They formed the *maquis* that appeared in various relatively remote areas. Supplies of arms were provided by aircraft based on Britain. Another important category of recruits were officers and soldiers of the Vichy army who had loyally served Pétain until November 1942, but whom the German occupation of the southern zone, and the successes of Allied arms, had convinced that resistance was both honourable and possible. Though these professionals played an important part in the leadership of the *maquis*, political command was to a considerable extent in communist hands. During 1943 and 1944 several strong *maquis* centres were created. There were no permanent liberated territories, for communications were too good and enemy forces too strong. But areas were held for

[1] See above, p. 201.
[2] G. Lefranc, *Les expériences syndicales en France de 1939 à 1950*, Paris, 1950, pp. 118–20.

some days at a time, and substantial enemy forces engaged. When the odds became hopeless, the *maquisards* would try to abandon their positions in good order. In this they were not always successful, and casualties were often very high. At the beginning of 1944 there were said to be some 30,000 Frenchmen in the *maquis*.[1] In June and July the *maquis* of the Vercors plateau engaged large enemy forces, at great cost, while the Allies were establishing themselves in Normandy.

Both in the general interest of the struggle, and in order to impress the Allied governments at a time when they were favouring General Giraud at his expense, De Gaulle was eager to unify the resistance groups under his command. In May 1943 his delegate, the former prefect of Chartres, Jean Moulin, succeeded in creating the National Council of Resistance (C.N.R.). This represented six political parties, including the communists; eight resistance groups, including *Front National*; and both trade unions, C.G.T. and C.F.T.C. In June disaster overtook the organisation. Both Moulin and his military commander were arrested by the Germans. Thereafter the relations between C.N.R. and the French Committee of National Liberation (C.F.L.N.) in Algiers, led by De Gaulle, became looser. The communists gained influence within the key organisations. Of the five members of the C.N.R.'s permanent Bureau, set up to conduct current business, three were communists. In the C.N.R.'s Committee of Military Action (*Comac*) of three, two were communists. When early in 1944 were formed the French Forces of the Interior (F.F.I.), *Comac* became their General Staff.[2] Both F.F.I. and the *maquis* made a substantial contribution to the Allied victory in France in the summer of 1944. Paris itself was liberated mainly by its own resistance forces, together with the Free French division of General Leclerc which formed part of the Allied armies.

It is not easy to estimate the communist share in the achievement of the resistance. The communists were the most influential of the political parties, they controlled their own F.T.P. to the end, they took a leading part in the *maquis*, and they also penetrated other groups. But when victory came, far less real power was in communist hands in France than in the Balkan countries. The C.N.R. was to have been the apex of a pyramid of national liberation committees at the various levels of government. As communist

---

[1] J. Soustelle, *Envers et contre tout*, Vol. II, *D'Alger à Paris*, Paris, 1950, p. 321.
[2] For the role of communists in C.N.R. and F.F.I., for the technique of communist infiltration, and for communist attitude to the Algiers Committee, see Soustelle, op. cit., pp. 301–4, 375.

influence was strong in the C.N.R., it might have been expected
that the local committees would be controlled by communists. No
doubt the communists intended the committees to play the same
role, of organs through which the Communist Party would capture
the masses, which the soviets had played in Russia in 1917 and
the people's committees in Yugoslavia in 1942–4. This hope was
not fulfilled, for two reasons. Despite obstruction by the Allied
governments, whose support for the politically inexperienced
General Giraud was of considerable help to the communists, De
Gaulle succeeded, not only in building a Provisional Government
in Algiers, but also in making himself respected inside France.
He was helped by Moscow's Popular Front policy, which caused
the communists to enter his government in the spring of 1944,
and made them his prisoners rather than him theirs. The 'regional
military delegates' sent from Algiers to the resistance forces
were in most cases able to withstand communist manœuvres.
After the liberation, civil 'commissioners' sent by De Gaulle
established their authority, and in the local committees in most
of France the non-communists prevailed.[1] The second reason for
the failure was that the war was still on, and Allied military
commanders had to be obeyed. This was as important for Moscow
as for Washington or London, and the leaders of the French communists were obliged to order their followers to give whole-
hearted support to the war effort. Thus the course of the war in
1944 prevented the French communists from using the strength
that they had gained through resistance as a means of seizing
power. The state machine was rebuilt by De Gaulle's men, and
the forces in French society—very different from Balkan—which
opposed communism were able to reassert themselves. After the
autumn of 1944 the communists' only remaining hope was to
obtain power by constitutional means.[2]

In Italy the first major act of resistance was the wave of strikes
in the industrial north in March 1943. This was the result of
economic hardships and of the Tunis disaster. It reflected both the
extreme discontent of the workers and the irresolution of the
authorities, who a year or two earlier would have suppressed such
action more promptly and more severely. The illegal communist

[1] See Soustelle, op. cit., pp. 425–35.
[2] There were outbreaks of violence by communists in various regions, especially
in the south, but they did not last long. I cannot agree with Borkenau, op. cit.,
pp. 441–9, who takes these outbreaks very seriously, and regards them as an indication
of major divergences of policy within the Soviet *Politburo*. Such divergences may
have existed, but the outbreaks do not prove it.

and socialist groups played some part in organising the strike. The overthrow of Mussolini on 25th July was a great encouragement to the anti-fascists, who at this time were commanders without troops, intellectuals who had had no opportunity of organising the masses. The armistice of 8th September brought a few days of free speech and movement. Political leaders came into the open. But the obvious intention of the Germans to reconquer and hold Italy made it essential to prepare for underground resistance to German occupation. A Central Committee of National Liberation (C.L.N.) was formed in Rome from eminent representatives of the communist, socialist, liberal, Christian Democratic and Action parties. The former socialist Ivanoe Bonomi was its chairman. Subordinate committees were quickly set up in other parts of the country, especially in the north. The Italian armed forces, lacking clear orders and communication with each other, offered no effective opposition to the Germans. But as in France in 1942 and on a larger scale, individual officers and men, and even individual units, took to the mountains with their arms and awaited an opportunity to fight back. The communists organised bands of workers, especially in Turin, and soon built an organisation of Partisans under their control which became known as *garibaldini*. The Action Party created another effective fighting force under the name *Giustizia e libertà*.[1] The communists were mainly responsible for the organisation of the general strike of March 1944, which affected most of German-occupied north Italy, and was the most impressive action of its kind that took place at any time in Europe under Hitler's rule.

Meanwhile in the south, whose inhabitants were the least politically-minded of Italians, the government of Marshal Badoglio exercised such power as was not in the hands of the Allied military commanders. The political parties which, in German-occupied Italy, were represented in the committees of liberation, were here in opposition. In April 1944, however, Palmiro Togliatti, the leading Italian communist in exile, returned from Moscow to Italy, met Badoglio, and announced that his party was willing to serve in a government under the Marshal and to postpone until after the war the decision whether Italy should be a monarchy or a republic. This was of course perfectly consistent with the new form of the Popular Front tactic pursued at this time by all communist parties, and with the Soviet foreign policy of 'Big Three unity'. But it shocked the other anti-fascist parties, which took their republican-

[1] The Action Party, a non-Marxist left group of socialist tendency, was derived from the former exiled group run by the brothers Rosselli (murdered by fascist agents in France in 1937), whose paper had had the name *Giustizia e libertà*.

ism seriously and abhorred co-operation with a man who had once commanded Mussolini's armies. They had however no alternative but to follow the communist lead. The Badoglio government thus became a government of the political parties, united in a coalition. After the liberation of Rome, Badoglio was replaced as Premier by Bonomi. Within the coalition the communists grew steadily stronger. They were able both to take credit with the Allies for having been the first anti-fascist party to end doctrinaire abstention and co-operate with the authorities on a common-sense basis, and also to point with pride to the achievements of their followers in occupied northern Italy.

In the summer of 1944 was set up in Milan a secret political headquarters for the resistance—the Committee of National Liberation of Upper Italy (C.L.N.A.I.)—composed of representatives of five parties. In practice the communists and the Action Party, which controlled the two most efficient resistance groups, were much more important than the other parties. Politically subject to C.L.N.A.I. but militarily subject to the Allied Command was the Command of Volunteers of Liberty (C.V.L.), whose chief was the regular army general Raffaele Cadorna. In practice Cadorna's two assistants, the communist Longo and the Actionist Parri, who controlled respectively the *garibaldini* and the *Giustizia e libertà* forces, held most of the power, and often gave scant consideration either to Cadorna or to his Anglo-Saxon military superiors.[1]

The same disagreement on resistance tactics that we have noted in France, appeared also in Italy, and for the same political and military reasons. The communists favoured maximum armed resistance at once, with maximum participation of the civil population. This was discouraged by the Allied command, which preferred limited sabotage by small units and preparation for a rising at a later stage. As in France, the Allies' discouragement of mass resistance was attributed by the communists to reactionary political plans.

The culmination of Italian resistance was the insurrection of April 1945 in the northern cities. The victory was won partly by workers who took over factories and public buildings, and partly by Partisans who marched on the cities from outside. As in the case of Paris in August 1944, the German commanders surrendered when they saw that the situation was hopeless, and did not carry out Hitler's orders to massacre and demolish to the last. This does

[1] Cadorna's own account is in his book *La riscossa*, Milano, 1948. Longo's account is *Un popolo alla macchia*, Verona, 1947.

not diminish the merit of the resisters, who showed both courage and organising ability, and among whom the communists predominated.

Immediately after liberation, the local committees, dominated by communists, held power in a large part of northern Italy. But, as in France, the presence of the Allied armies and the need to preserve order behind the front deprived the communists of an opportunity to seize by force the key positions in the state. They had to hand over to the Allied military government, which was the more free to interfere as Italy, unlike France, was not an ally but merely a co-belligerent. Neither government machine nor factories remained in communist hands, the police was not theirs, and their armed forces were disbanded, with some material rewards and many speeches of thanks. Hopes of power for the Italian, as for the French communists depended on their ability to win support by constitutional means.

SOUTH-EAST ASIA

South-East Asia provided two of the conditions required for resistance. The physical terrain was suitable for guerrilla warfare, and the Japanese victory had either destroyed—in Malaya, Burma and Indonesia—or fatally discredited—in Indochina—the state machines of the former colonial Powers. But the third condition, a revolutionary leadership, was lacking until the later stages of the war. Under Japanese rule the masses remained, as ever, passive, but the politically conscious intelligentsia was to a large extent pro-Japanese. The Burmese and Indonesian nationalists hoped that the Japanese would give them their independence. Even when they began to dislike the Japanese, they were not keen to help their former rulers. Only when they saw that the Western Powers were beating the Japanese did prudence suggest a change of attitude.

The exception to the above was the communist attitude. As soon as the Soviet Union was attacked, the communists were obliged to help her, and her allies Britain and Holland. For a time the communists, once the fiercest enemies of the colonial Powers, made great efforts to persuade non-communist nationalists to join them in resisting the Japanese.

The most impressive resistance movement in South-East Asia, which fought longest and hardest, was in Malaya. The Malayan communists were almost exclusively Chinese. After June 1941 they at once supported the war. Their imprisoned leaders were released shortly before the Japanese attack. When Malaya had been overrun, the communists organised a Malayan People's Anti-Japanese Army and a political body called the Malayan People's Anti-Japanese Union. The M.P.A.J.A. was led and organised by communists throughout its career, but it attracted non-communists into its ranks. Though its numbers were never very large, it made itself a considerable nuisance to the Japanese. It had its small liberated areas in the jungle, and used the resistance to train cadres for the future. It received supplies from the Allied South-East Asia Command.

In Burma, Indonesia and the Philippines the communists achieved much less, but even the small resistance effort they did make gave them valuable practice in insurrection, and helped them to create some cadres. In the Philippines the communists played a leading part in the formation of an Anti-Japanese People's Army. In Indonesia, though the principal nationalist leaders collaborated in various degrees with the Japanese, some resistance was offered by communist or left socialist groups, whose best known leader was the socialist Sjarifoeddin.[1] In Burma not only conservative politicians but also younger nationalists, who had been influenced by Marxism and at least professed some sort of socialism, supported the Japanese and took part in the puppet government which they set up in August 1943. Early in 1945 however Aung San, a young left nationalist who as minister of Defence in the puppet government commanded the Japanese-sponsored Burmese National Army, agreed to join the communists in resisting the Japanese. With communist help, contact was made between the B.N.A. and the Allied Command, which sent supplies and liaison missions. On communist initiative, a political body of Popular Front type was formed to direct resistance. It was given the name Anti-fascist People's Fighting League (A.F.P.F.L.), and included communists, socialists and peasant organisations. Communist control was in fact less effective than in the Malayan M.P.A.J.A. or in the Balkan resistance movements.

In Indochina the French administration, loyal to Vichy, ruled under Japanese military control. On Chinese territory an Annamite resistance group was founded in 1941 by a Comintern veteran named Nguyen Ai Quoc, who took the name Ho Chi-minh. It has become widely known since then as the Vietminh.[2] From the first it was dominated by communists, but it co-operated with

[1] See above, p. 194.
[2] The organisation hereafter referred to as Vietminh is the Vietnam Independence Front. Vietnam is the traditional name for the three Annamite provinces of Tonkin, Annam and Cochin China. The people of these provinces are henceforth described

other Vietnamese nationalist groups. When in March 1945 the Japanese overthrew the French administration, resistance developed more quickly. Free French, Vietminh and Chinese efforts were to some extent co-ordinated. The Japanese proclaimed Vietnam an independent state, under the emperor of Annam, Bao Dai. This official Vietnamese government was of little help to the Japanese: it had neither physical power nor moral authority, and it even connived to some extent with the actions of the resisters.

Thus Japanese occupation had provoked some armed resistance by the peoples of South-East Asia, and this had given the small communist groups that had existed before Japanese invasion a chance to make propaganda, to build cadres, and to acquire prestige. At the end of the war the South-East Asian communist movements were still small and weak. Their further prospects would depend not only on their own political skill but also on the attitudes that the returning colonial Powers would adopt to the nationalist movements.

---

as 'Vietnamese'. As a result of Kuomintang pressure, Vietminh made an agreement in March 1944 for common action with two other Vietnamese parties. One was the old nationalist party, the V.N.Q.D.D., which had led a rebellion against the French in 1930, but whose exiled leaders had for some time lost contact with the homeland. The other was a Kuomintang-sponsored party, the *Dong Minh Hoi*, created in 1942. For details of Vietnamese party politics, see P. Devillers, *Histoire du Vietnam de 1940 à 1952*. Paris, 1952.

CHAPTER TWELVE

Stalinism in Russia

THE crushing defeats suffered by the Red Army in the summer of 1941 were above all military defeats, and the advance of the Red Army from 1943 onwards was above all a military success. But in both stages of the Russo-German war political factors played their part. The morale of the Red Army in 1941 was extremely low. Many soldiers felt no desire to fight for Stalin, and a large part of the civil population, both Ukrainian and Russian, welcomed the German forces as deliverers. This immense advantage of Russian goodwill the German political bosses threw away. Nazi Gauleiters oppressed and exploited Russians and Ukrainians alike. Hundreds of thousands of Soviet prisoners of war were allowed to perish from starvation or disease.[1] Hundreds of thousands of others, deported to forced labour in Germany, lived in miserable conditions. In the occupied regions guerrilla forces gained popular support, and when the Red Army again advanced, it in turn was welcomed as a deliverer. Yet even in spite of Nazi blunders and cruelty, hundreds of thousands of Russian and non-Russian soldiers served the Germans, some as civil auxiliaries and some even as fighting units. The project of a Russian Liberation Army, under the former Red Army General A. A. Vlasov, though obstructed until it was too late by the Nazi bosses, met with a genuine response from Russian prisoners and civilians.[2]

Behind the Soviet front, official propaganda laid its main stress on patriotism—especially on Russian patriotism. The party retained its political grip, but it paid little attention to Marxist-Leninist ideology, and it courted popularity by throwing open its ranks to soldiers.[3]

In Russia, as in all belligerent countries, the people hoped that victory over the enemy would bring a new and better world. These hopes were disappointed. The immense task of reconstructing the

---

[1] During the first year of the war nearly three million prisoners died.
[2] A full account of the Vlasov affair, and a penetrating analysis of German policy in occupied Russia, is given in J. Thorwald, *Wen sie verderben wollen*, Stuttgart, 1952.
[3] The party had 3,400,000 members in January 1940, 5,700,000 in January 1945.

devastated land was bound in any case to require great material sacrifices. But the Soviet leaders were not content to ask their subjects to tighten their belts: minds too had to be tightened. The supremacy of the party, and the need for ideological orthodoxy, were once more emphasised. Not only were those who had served the Germans—almost all of whom the Western Allies forcibly repatriated to the U.S.S.R.—punished with death or long terms of forced labour. Returning prisoners of war and deported labourers, and persons who had remained in their homes under German occupation, were treated as suspects. Even troops returning from service in Europe had to undergo an 'ideological decontamination' on their return to Soviet territory. Not gratitude to the heroes, or sympathy for the sufferers, but concern for the elimination of any influences that might directly or indirectly challenge the supremacy of the party, was the guiding principle of policy.

The sum total of suffering, injustice and disorganisation caused by this process of shifting and reindoctrination was very considerable, though it cannot compare either with the convulsions caused by collectivisation of agriculture and the *Yezhovshchina*, or with the human and material losses of military operations themselves. There was however one new form of horror which deserves a brief mention. This was the deportation of whole nations or ethnical groups believed to be either guilty or capable of treason.

The first victims were the Volga Germans.[1] By a decree of 28th August 1941 their 'autonomous republic' was abolished, and some 400,000 persons were deported. No evidence was provided that these Germans had taken any action against the Soviet regime, nor could they have hoped to achieve anything if they had.

In June 1946 it was announced that the Crimean Tatar A.S.S.R. and the Chechen-Ingush A.S.S.R. in the North Caucasus had been dissolved, and their populations deported. The decree stated that members of these nations had assisted the German invaders, and that 'the main mass of the population took no counter-action against these betrayers of the fatherland'. These small nations were deprived of their homes, scattered throughout the vast Soviet Union, and annihilated as nations.[2] They had been conquered by

[1] A German community established in the Volga in the area of Saratov since the eighteenth century. For a brief summary of their fate, see W. Kolarz, *Russia and her colonies*, 1952, pp. 68–76.

[2] The fullest account of the Chechen tragedy is by a Soviet refugee, himself a Chechen and a professional historian, A. Avtorhanov, *Narodoubiistvo v SSSR*, Munich, 1952. The deportation actually took place in February 1944, two years before the publication of the decree.

Russian arms in the past, had struggled in 1918–20 to achieve national independence, and had been reconquered by Bolshevik Russian arms. When another foreign invader appeared, some of them again attempted to free themselves, and the majority failed to attack and destroy those who did this.[1] For failing to sacrifice themselves to reimpose a foreign yoke which they had always hated, and which now appeared to be crumbling, the Crimean Tatars and Chechens were doomed to national extinction. It is relevant to compare this with the treatment by the reactionary British imperialists of the Burmese 'national army' which fought on the Japanese side against the British army. If the British government had followed the example of 'anti-imperialist' Soviet Russia, it would not only have executed or imprisoned all members of this force, but deported the whole population of Burma to the wastes of Arctic Canada.

Somewhat less drastic action was taken against the Kalmyks of the west Caspian steppes and the Balkars and Karachays of the North Caucasus. Their autonomous status was abolished, and many of them were deported, but this was done quietly, without a formal announcement or formal justification.

Very severe deportations took place in the three Baltic states, which were reincorporated in the Soviet Union when the Germans had been driven from their territory. By 1949 about one-quarter of the population of these three countries had been deported to the interior of Russia, and their places had been largely filled with Russian colonists. Like the Nazis in Czechoslovakia and Poland, the Bolsheviks paid special attention to the intelligentsia. The million and a half Baltic deportees included the majority of persons with a secondary education, and of the Protestant and Catholic clergies. The best way to exterminate a nation is to exterminate its brains. The Soviet government wished to make sure of the Baltic littoral and of such industries as existed or were to be created in the Baltic countries. Therefore Russians had to be settled there, and the ancient and civilised Baltic nations had to be destroyed. This was done in the name of socialism and anti-imperialism.

STATE AND PARTY

It will be convenient at this stage to summarise the main features of the political and social structure of Stalinist Russia, whose regime

---

[1] The Chechen revolt broke out before Germany attacked the Soviet Union, and it was in no way directed by the Germans. German forces never reached Chechen territory. Avtorhanov, op. cit.

is, for all communists beyond the Soviet Union's frontiers, a blueprint of the policy and society to which they aspire.

The formal political framework is still supplied by the Constitution of December 1936, associated with the name of Stalin and heralded as 'the most democratic in the world'. It introduced several formal modifications of the 1923 Constitution. The pyramid of soviets, from the village, district and town level up to the Supreme Soviet or national parliament, were now directly elected. Constituencies for the main Chamber, the Council of the Union,[1] were equal: the franchise was thus no longer weighted against the rural population. Persons of bourgeois origin and priests were no longer deprived of a vote. In practice these changes were of no importance. The electors had no choice: they were confronted in every constituency and at every level with a single list composed partly of communists and partly of non-party candidates selected by the communist party.

The Supreme Soviet thus elected only meets for a few days in each year, to ratify decrees and to hear laudatory speeches from selected orators. For the rest of the year legislative business is handled by its Presidium, a smaller body elected from its members. According to the Constitution, the Supreme Soviet elects the government—Council of People's Commissars in 1936, but since 1946 renamed Council of Ministers. Since the war the Council of Ministers has become an unwieldy assembly of departmental chiefs which probably seldom meets as a body.[2] The real equivalent in the Soviet system of a Cabinet were the Premier and Vice-Premiers. In 1952 these numbered thirteen. After the death of Stalin, an inner cabinet of five was set up—Malenkov as Premier, assisted by Beria, Molotov, Bulganin and Kaganovich, each of whom holds the title of 'First Deputy Premier'.

The judiciary is as dependent on the party as are the executive and legislature. Judges of the different levels of courts of law are elected by the soviets or by the same electorate as the soviets. This of course means that candidates for election as judges must be acceptable to the corresponding level of the party hierarchy. Wide powers are exercised by the Procurator of the U.S.S.R., an officer appointed by the Supreme Soviet, that is in effect by the leaders of the party. He in turn appoints the subordinate procurators. The function of this hierarchy is to ensure that decisions of the courts

[1] The Second Chamber, the Council of Nationalities, represents the Republics, autonomous Republics, and autonomous Regions as such.
[2] At the time of Stalin's death it had more than fifty members. The recent amalgamation of ministries reduced their number by nearly half.

of law are not harmful to the interests of the state. When he deems this to be the case, a procurator may cancel a court decision. Parallel with the hierarchy of procurators is the hierarchy of the Ministry of State Control, the successor to *Rabkrin*.[1] Its functions include not only the auditing of public accounts but also the supervision of the whole machinery of government in action.

The powers of the courts are limited still more by those of the security police (M.V.D.-M.G.B.).[2] Counter-revolutionary crimes, defined in the most elastic manner in Article 58 of the Criminal Code, remain the preserve of the M.V.D., which has authority to decide whether or not a given case comes under the provisions of this Article.[3] Where there is suspicion of a counter-revolutionary crime it is the M.V.D., not the procurator, that orders an arrest. If it sees fit, the M.V.D. can by its own special tribunal sentence an arrested person to death or imprisonment, without trial. In the face of these powers the liberties guaranteed in the Constitution appear meaningless.

The M.V.D. is however much more than a police force: it is, physically and territorially, a state within the state. It has its own elite army—the Interior Troops and the Frontier Guards—its own air force and aerodromes, its own factories and railways, its own territories worked by penal labour. But its power is by no means confined to its own territory or its own formations. Most government offices and economic enterprises have their 'special departments' or 'secret departments'—the cells of the M.V.D. within their doors, centres of espionage, provocation and denunciation directed against all persons working there.

In the armed forces there are three separate hierarchies. First is the normal military chain of command. Second is the Political Administration, headed by a special department in the Ministry of War and served by political commissars and political directors (*politruk*) down to company level.[4] It is mainly concerned with the ideological welfare of the troops, that is to say with communist indoctrination and propaganda. The third hierarchy is that of the organs of security, responsible to the M.V.D. and served by 'special departments' down to regimental level and by informers from all ranks.

[1] See above pp. 83–4.
[2] M.G.B. was the Ministry of State Security, which managed most of the secret political work of the Soviet police. The delimitation of functions between M.V.D. (Ministry of Interior) and M.G.B. was not absolutely clear. The reorganisation which followed Stalin's death merged M.V.D. and M.G.B. in a single Ministry of Interior (M.V.D.). [3] See above, p. 174 n.
[4] Commissars at present hold the title 'assistant-commander (political)'.

The party controls the civil, judicial, police and military hierarchies in the sense that the key positions in each are held by members of the party, that the party's doctrines are the official creed for all, and that the leaders of the party impose their will on all subordinate authorities. But the party itself is no less subject than are the civil, judicial, police and military machines to the will of the same leaders. The authority of the leaders so much overshadows both party and bureaucracy that the old primacy of the party has lost most of its meaning. Official doctrine still lays down that the party is the 'directing nucleus'[1] and that the various hierarchies and 'mass-organisations' are 'transmission belts' between the party and the masses. But the party itself has become a transmission belt. It has become one of several instruments of power wielded by the leaders.

The trend in this direction was already visible at the 14th Congress of the party in 1925. It was reinforced by the economic changes wrought during the Five Year Plans, by the *Yezhovshchina*, and by the Second World War.

The 19th Congress, which met in October 1952, thirteen and a half years after the 18th,[2] made some important changes in the party's organisation. The *Politburo* was abolished, and its membership merged in a newly-created body, a Presidium of twenty-five full members and eleven candidates. The *Orgburo* was also abolished, and the membership of the Secretariat doubled. The new Central Committee has 125 full members and 111 candidates. In March 1953, after Stalin's death, these changes were partly reversed. The Presidium was reduced to ten full members and four candidates. Of the ten, eight were former *Politburo* members. The Secretariat's membership was reduced and changed.

The creation of the Presidium of thirty-six, in October 1952, had looked like a blow at the authority of Stalin's immediate subordinates, the top bosses of the party. In the new and larger body, a number of second-rank leaders were associated with them on nominally equal terms. The Presidium seemed to be a testing-ground for new leaders, whom Stalin could play off against his veteran companions. The changes of March 1953 reasserted the supremacy of the top bosses, and firmly pushed the second-rank men out of the inner circle of party leadership.

These events also have some relevance to the relationship

---

[1] Soviet Constitution, article 126.

[2] The Statute of the party then in force provided that congresses should meet at least once every three years. Under the Statute adopted at the 19th Congress the interval has been raised to four years.

between party and state. The October changes, by depriving the party of its small supreme political organ, the *Politburo*, and by doing away with the time-honoured title of 'Bolshevik[1], lowered the party's prestige and relatively strengthened the state hierarchy. The ten former *Politburo* members who had been Vice-Premiers, remained Vice-Premiers. The government kept its inner cabinet, the party had none. Since March 1953 the supreme organs of state and party are again more closely interlocked, but this does not prove that the party has reasserted its old authority. The supreme body in the Soviet Union now appears to be the super-inner cabinet of five (Premier and four 'First Deputy Premiers'),[2] which is an organ of the government, not of the party.

This does not of course mean that the party has ceased to be an important factor. The party is the means of recruitment to high office in the state. The party also controls the whole vast machinery of propaganda. It issues instructions to press and radio, and directives to writers and artists. It conducts the mass campaigns of exhortation and vituperation which penetrate every household in the Soviet Union. But the party is subject to the same leaders who control civil administration, economy, armed forces and police. The party does not control all other organisations: it is the most important of several hierarchies wielded by the same bosses.

Future events will of course largely depend on whether the top bosses, at first apparently drawn together in common resistance to the men whom Stalin, in the last months of his life, was elevating at their expense, will hold together or will quarrel. And this will be decided not only by their personal qualities and ambitions, but also by the development of 'the social contradictions of Stalinism'.

SOCIAL CLASSES UNDER STALINISM

The social class in whose name Stalin ruled was the industrial proletariat. Since the 1930's its numbers have enormously increased. The quality of its labour is still well below western standards, but it has greatly improved during the last decade. The training schools established under the Five Year Plans have turned out hundreds of thousands of more or less skilled workers. Stahanovism and socialist competition have continued. Piece rates have been almost universal since the late 1930's and the gap be-

---

[1] Since October 1952 the party has assumed the name 'Communist Party of the Soviet Union'. The word 'Bolshevik' has been dropped.
[2] See above, p. 231.

tween the highest and lowest wages remains wide. At all times the fulfilment of the Plan has priority over the worker's welfare, and even over his safety. Labour discipline, of a savagery that no west European working class would tolerate, is jointly enforced by manager and trade union. The unions exist to protect, not the worker, but the boss-state.

The standard of living of the workers is a controversial and obscure subject, befogged by propaganda. It certainly improved from 1933 to 1939, deteriorated under war conditions, and recovered rapidly between 1945 and the present. Stahanovites earn extremely high wages as long as they can maintain their exceptional outputs. Skilled workers probably enjoy better material conditions in 1953 than they had under the Tsar in 1913. At the bottom of the Soviet social pyramid, the inmates of forced labour camps, who number some millions, fare worse than any citizen of Imperial Russia. A serious comparison between the material situation of the average worker in 1953 and 1913 is not possible on the scrappy evidence available. The Soviet system of social security is less impressive in reality than in theory. Old age pensions are miserably low. Medical services have improved since 1930, but are still poor, and doctors are compelled by the authorities to treat with suspicion workers who report sick in the factories. Official emphasis is on the need to protect state interests from malingerers rather than on the need to protect the workers' health. There is a general tendency to spend a disproportionate part of the insurance funds on luxurious facilities which are available only to a few privileged workers rather than to improve the welfare of the majority of workers. Magnificent rest centres on the Black Sea coast, and mountaineering and sporting organisations for the elite of Soviet athletes, receive much publicity within the Soviet Union and abroad. But these are things from which the average worker can hardly hope to benefit. As the general level of economic output rises, there no doubt are, and will be, improvements. But two basic causes of exploitation of the workers seem inextricably bound up with the essence of the regime. One is the obsession of the rulers with output targets, which causes them—free as they are from any moral or religious inhibitions—to regard human beings as instruments of production. The second is the absence of any element of choice in the hierarchy of political or economic life. The worker cannot choose his trade union representative, or the officials of the social services. He is placed at their mercy. The system gives the petty bureaucrat little pieces of absolute power, and he can abuse or exploit them as long as he thinks he can get away with it.

The collectivised peasants occupied a position intermediate between that of the urban workers and that which they themselves had had as individual smallholders. Government policy aimed to turn the peasants into agricultural workers, their *kolhozes* into agricultural factories. But this policy met with strong passive resistance from the peasants and was only partly successful. The sytem that emerged was a compromise between the collective and individual principles. Members of *kolhozes* were obliged to work on the collective land but also possessed private plots. These constituted in 1938 nearly 4 per cent of the cultivated land of the Soviet Union, and produced an appreciable portion of the needs of peasant families in vegetable foods. But they were much more important for the rearing of livestock. In 1938, 49 per cent of the cattle of the Soviet Union, 46 per cent of its sheep and goats and 50 per cent of its pigs belonged to private owners. Thus a large part of the milk and meat products that were consumed by the urban population came from the plots. Part of these products the peasants had to deliver to the state at fixed low prices: the rest could be consumed or sold at 'free' prices. It was of course obviously the interest of every peasant to spend as much time as possible developing his plot and as little as possible working on the *kolhoz* lands. Not only was he personally interested in his plot, but it paid him more for his effort than the *kolhoz*, a large part of whose income had to be spent on deliveries of produce at low prices or in kind to the government and to the M.T.S., in addition to other lesser purposes, before it could be shared among the members. The conflicting claims on the peasant's time of the *kolhoz* and of his plot recalled the conflicting claims of the landlord's estate and the peasant's holding in the days of serfdom before 1861. The Soviet press was full of complaints about the peasants' failure to fulfil their obligations to the *kolhoz*. In 1939 special regulations were introduced defining the minimum number of days to be worked for the *kolhoz* per year, and these were supplemented in 1942. During the war *kolhoz* discipline became very loose. The Soviet authorities needed what goodwill they could get from the peasants, and they were in no position to insist on strict observance of the principles of 'socialist agriculture'. The peasants used their more favourable situation to make money on the free market, to encroach their plots on the communal land, and to reduce the time worked for the *kolhoz*. In 1946 came the party's counter-offensive. 'Infringements of the *kolhoz* statute' were fiercely denounced, and officials of party and state were instructed to remedy them and to prevent their repetition. The 'currency reform' of 1947 deprived the peasants of most of their wartime savings.

On the *kolhoz* attempts were made already in the 1930's to introduce methods of labour organisation and discipline derived from the factory. Standards of output were adopted which corresponded to the 'norms' of the factories. These standards were known as 'labour days' (*trudodni*), for which a fixed wage was granted. The number of days of work required to earn one 'labour day' varied according to the type of work performed. The gap between the wages of the more and less skilled forms of *kolhoz* labour widened in the late 1930's. Some attempt was made to introduce shock labour, prizes and decorations, as in industry. Breaches of labour discipline were punished with increasing severity. In general the attempt was made to subject the peasants to the regimentation of industrial life without its compensation of shorter hours: in the busiest seasons the peasants toiled from dawn to dusk as from time immemorial. In some areas at least some of the benefits of social security and welfare were brought into rural life. Electric light was extended over great areas that had never known it. The rural population received better medical services and more schools. Some at least of the *kolhozes* had cinemas, concerts or other cultural amenities. But in the Soviet Union, as in other large countries, the areas close to important urban centres fared better than the remoter districts. The model *kolhozes* in the neighbourhood of Moscow, to which foreign tourists were taken, were not typical of Soviet rural life.

One conclusion that may be drawn with some confidence is that class stratification is more clear-cut in rural society than it has been since the abolition of serfdom. In the years before collectivisation, though there were economic differences between sections of the peasantry, there was no serious evidence of conscious class conflicts between them. Under the new order however a privileged class clearly emerged. It consisted of the officials and skilled workers of the M.T.S., the chairmen and accountants of the *kolhozes*, and to a lesser extent the foremen and lesser officials of the *kolhoz* committees. The powers exercised over the peasants by the heads of this hierarchy were no less absolute than those once wielded by the serf-owners and their bailiffs. Moreover they were largely townsmen, alien to rural life and its values. It is at least a plausible hypothesis that against these new rulers are combined the two forms

of social antagonism that are deeply rooted in the history of
the Russian peasant—distrust of the townsman and hatred of the
landowner.

Many of the *kolhozes* formed in the 1930's were small, both in
area and in the number of families that belonged to them. Indeed
it is likely that in the remoter areas of northern Russia the *kolhoz*
differed little in its economic—as opposed to its political—organisation from the pre-revolutionary commune. The aim of vast,
modern, mechanised estates—agricultural factories—was still
remote. In 1950 the Soviet leaders decided to push ahead with old
plans. *Kolhozes* were to be amalgamated into larger units, and the
old villages were to be replaced by 'agricultural cities' (*agrogoroda*)
to be constructed at the centre of the new giant farms. The press
painted a rosy picture of blocks of flats and social amenities that
would now accrue to the peasants: less was said of the fact that the
peasants would have to give up their private plots. In practice only
part of this programme was achieved. During 1950 and 1951 the
total number of *kolhozes* in the Union was reduced two and a half
times.[1] The project of *agrogoroda* was however abandoned as un-
realistic. It is likely that the main obstacle was not that the proposed social amenities would have cost the state too much (they
would not in any case have been carried out), but that the opposition of the peasants to the loss of their plots would have been
dangerous.[2] As a long-term project the *agrogoroda* have probably
not been abandoned.

The third social group, which Soviet doctrine does not recognise
as a 'class' but calls a 'class stratum', is the 'toiling intelligentsia'.
This phrase covers all who are not workers or peasants. It thus
includes industrial managers, bureaucrats, technicians and clerks,
as well as those who follow what in the West would be called the
'free professions'. Soviet figures dating from 1937 showed
9,600,000 persons as belonging to this group, in a total population
of nearly 170,000,000. This probably did not cover all persons
engaged in non-manual labour, for many full-time officials of the
Communist Party and of the trade union bureaucracy were probably entered as 'workers'. Since 1937 economic development and
territorial expansion will certainly have increased the numbers of
the 'toiling intelligentsia' both absolutely and proportionately.[3]

[1] The number fell from 254,000 in January 1950 to 97,000 in October 1952 (Malenkov, speech to 19th Congress of the party).

[2] In 1953 the peasants still have private plots. The development of livestock on state
and collective farms has, however, reduced the proportion of privately-owned livestock to total livestock population.

[3] The 1937 figures are now obviously completely out of date. They date from

The 'toiling intelligentsia' includes persons of quite humble status and modest means. Clerical workers have a less favourable material position than Stahanovite workers, at any rate for as long as the latter can keep up the pace. But even clerical jobs appear to attract workers and peasants, for the Soviet press is full of complaints about the excess of administrative staff in factories and even in farms. The higher ranks of the 'toiling intelligentsia' include both the ruling caste and the decorative aristocracy of Soviet society. The former are the top managers and bureaucrats, the latter the writers and artists, who enjoy even greater material comfort than the rulers but possess no power.

These men and women are the product of the post-revolutionary system of education. Their training has been narrow, crude and hurried in comparison with the higher education of Imperial Russia, let alone Western Europe or North America. Nevertheless the Soviet regime has succeeded in enormously increasing its supply of qualified persons. The official attitude to managers and intellectuals changed already in 1931. Stalin himself gave the word.[1] The *Yezhovshchina* was partly a set-back and partly an encouragement. It devastated the remnants of the pre-revolutionary experts and technicians. But on those members of the post-revolutionary intelligentsia who were only junior members of the party, or were not members at all, it was less severe. It is even possible that the removal of so many high party officials increased the experts' authority.

The most interesting and most obscure problem of contemporary Soviet society is the relationship of the 'toiling intelligentsia' to the Stalinist regime. Under this regime they enjoy privileges and suffer frustrations.

The privileges include not only a relatively high standard of living and—in the case of top managers and bureaucrats—a sense of power, but also special opportunities for their children. Already

---

before the *Yezhovshchina*, let alone the war. But no more recent figures of professional distribution have been made available. Therefore the 1937 figures are still worth quoting, to show proportions in different categories. The 9,600,000 can be roughly divided into four groups: (*a*) 1,750,000 were managers, great and small (of whom 450,000 were 'heads of administrative institutions'; 350,000 'directors and managers of state industrial enterprises, workshops and departments, and their deputies'; and 580,000 chairmen of *kolhozes* and their deputies). (*b*) 1,500,000 were army officers and officials of various kinds. (*c*) 2,600,000 belonged to the equivalent of the western professional class (of whom 132,000 were doctors; 969,000 teachers; and 550,000 students at institutions of higher education). (*d*) 3,630,000 were clerical workers of various kinds (of whom 1,600,000 were book-keepers and accountants.).

[1] Stalin, *Voprosy Leninizma*, pp. 340–44 (from a speech of 23rd June 1931 to a conference of economic experts).

in 1938, 42 per cent of all students at higher educational establish-
ments were children of 'employees and specialists', while children
of workers, who had formed 50 per cent in 1933, formed only 34
per cent. This trend was reinforced by two decrees of 1940. The
first introduced fees for pupils in the top three classes of secondary
schools and in higher institutions. The fees were high enough to
exclude children of workers and peasants who could not win state
scholarships. At the same time the number of state scholarships
was reduced. The second decree, on 'Labour reserves', provided
for the mobilisation of boys between 14 and 17 years of age, for
compulsory industrial training and labour. The number in fact
called up under this decree appears to have been between a third
and a half of all boys in the relevant age-group. Boys thus mobilised
were arbitrarily excluded from any hope of a higher education. Of
the method of selection used, little is known. But it is clear that
children of the 'toiling intelligentsia' were better placed, both to
avoid mobilisation and to pay the fees of higher education, than
the children of workers or peasants. The tendency towards making
the upper class hereditary is obvious, though it should also be
stressed that it is only a tendency, not an accomplished fact.

The causes of frustration are lack of security and lack of liberty.
The manager must at all costs achieve the plan target that is
assigned to him, but for which often he receives neither enough
equipment nor enough manpower. If he fails, no excuses will be
accepted: at best he will be demoted, at worst punished as a
saboteur. The party organiser's position is similar. If the plan
targets for his region are not achieved, he will be blamed. Both
know that if they obey the laws they are doomed. Their only chance
is to cheat and lie and bribe and intrigue. If they still fail, their
irregularities will be exposed and they will be punished, but if they
succeed nobody will bother about what means they used. Those who
can stand the strain will make brilliant careers. But they cannot
fail to be aware of the appalling and unnecessary wastage of men
and materials that the system involves.[1]

Lack of liberty and lack of leisure are a constant cause of frustration. The manager's time is wasted in an endless series of political
meetings and demonstrations, at which the same ritual speeches
are made, of praise and thanksgiving to the infallible leader and of

[1] The nepotism, corruption and formation of cliques, that were so eloquently
denounced by speakers at the 19th Congress in October 1952, are a result of the
Stalinist system of planning (not of course of planning as such). Punishment of individuals can alter nothing. Not individual wickedness, but the social system produces
these results.

threats and hate for foreign enemies. Even the party organisers must weary of these ceremonies. For intellectuals it is even worse. It is not enough that they should refrain from criticising official policies: they must be told exactly what to say and think. Literature and art are subject to positive directives as well as negative censorship.   Artists and writers must deal with 'contemporary Soviet realities'. They must write, paint or compose as 'the people'—that is, the Communist Party—wishes. The speeches of Zhdanov on literature, philosophy and music, and the dictatorship of Lysenko in genetics, exceeded any regulations that existed in the 1930's. Historians are watched with a special vigilance. It is their task to show that at all times the Russian nation has been in the van of human progress, and to find in the Russian past justification of every aspect of present policy.[1]

There are two possible types of discontent in Soviet society—that of the exploited workers and peasants and that of the frustrated upper caste. If the two were combined, they might be deadly. But this is infinitely more difficult under the Stalinist regime than it was under the Tsars. The Stalinist police is more efficient, more ruthless and more comprehensive. It prevents any association, however innocent its purpose, that is not controlled by it. It penetrates private as well as public life. Unlike the Tsars, the Stalinist leaders know the importance of propaganda. They are not content to keep out all hostile ideas: they set out positively to mould the minds of their subjects. In particular, they lose no opportunity of exciting the envy of the masses against the privileged group, at the same time as they grant to the privileged great power over the masses. A combination of aristocracy and people against the autocrat is not only technically difficult but psychologically improbable.

As long as the two types of discontent are isolated from each other, neither is an immediate political danger to the regime. Of the two, the frustration of the privileged is probably the more important. The historical experience of other lands and other periods shows that material improvements in the position of a social group do not necessarily make it more contented. The better their food and clothes and lodgings, and the more they learn and understand, the more they are aware of what they lack—social status and mental freedom and personal security for themselves and their children. The obstacle to these things is the totalitarian regime. It is likely that many non-party managers and intellectuals blame the

[1] The best discussion of this subject available in English is Klaus Mehnert, *Stalin versus Marx*, 1952.

party for all their sufferings, that they see in the party officials a host of parasites who deprive them of the rightful reward for their labour, and prevent them from working as well as they could for the greatness of their country. But though they may think this, it does not necessarily follow that they are right. In fact it is likely that thousands of party officials share their frustrations. The real conflict of interest is not so much between the intelligentsia and the party, as between the overwhelming majority of the upper caste—within and without the party—and the regime of the autocracy which exploits them all.

THE NATIONALITIES

After the war the tendency, already visible in the 1930's, to emphasise in policy towards the non-Russian nationalities the fight against 'local nationalism' rather than against 'Great Russian chauvinism', was reinforced by two factors. One was the upsurge of Russian national pride during the war. The other was the government's desire to counteract the impression, left on the minds of soldiers who had been in Europe, that western civilisation was superior to Soviet. The party's propaganda extolled the greatness of Russia, in past and present, decried western achievements, and represented the West as both declining and corrupt.

In nationalities policy, two crimes were now stressed— nationalism and cosmopolitanism. A non-Russian was guilty of nationalism if in any way he stressed the differences that separate his nation from the Russian nation: of cosmopolitanism if he stressed any cultural links that bind his nation to any nation whose country is outside the Soviet Union. To these two vices corres- ponded the two virtues of internationalism and patriotism. To be an internationalist is to stress solidarity with, or servility to, Russia: to be a patriot is to stress superiority to nations of similar culture living outside the Soviet Union, and when possible to put forward, on behalf of the Soviet Union, territorial claims directed against neighbour states. Thus, Ukrainians must mini- mise Polish influences in the history of Ukraine and stress Russian influences. Azerbaidjan Tatars must minimise the common cul- tural heritage of Islam, and of Arabic and Persian literature, which they share with the whole Moslem world, and must champion the 'liberation' of Persian Azerbaidjan. Georgians and Armenians must claim Turkish territory, Turkmens Persian territory, Uzbeks and Tadjiks Afghan territory.

In Western Ukraine, armed resistance to the Soviet regime continued long after the Red Army had reoccupied Galicia. Collectivisation of agriculture was forced through in Galicia and in the Baltic states in 1949 and 1950. Party and civil administration was thoroughly purged in the whole Ukraine, and a careful watch was kept on any signs of nationalism in Ukrainian intellectual life.[1] In Central Asia the trends already apparent in the 1930's continued. Industrialisation created new jobs, but also undermined national traditions and culture, dispersed the Central Asian populations, and brought massive colonisation by Russian technicians, workers and peasants. Education and social welfare improved in the urban centres, but in such a manner that the best facilities were available for the Russian colonists. Purges of party and government personnel continued after the war.[2] Of the three Transcaucasian republics it was Azerbaidjan, with its great industrial city of Baku, which suffered most from Russian colonisation and cultural domination. The Armenian and Georgian republics were managed by Armenians and Georgians. But the communists of these two republics did not enjoy greater security than their Russian comrades. An especially severe purge took place in Georgia early in 1952.[3]

Thirty years of Soviet rule have created many thousands of intellectuals, technicians, bureaucrats and managers among the non-Russians. Even if the quality of their education has not been high, the quantitative achievement is impressive. Here at least there can be no doubt that there has been progress in comparison with the Imperial Russian past. The new intelligentsia owes everything to the Soviet regime. It does not however follow that it is grateful to it. The experience of other empires does not suggest that it is likely to be. The Indian intelligentsia owed its education to the British, the Indochinese to the French, the Slovak to the Hungarians. But Indian, Indochinese and Slovak intellectuals were not content to merge themselves in the educated class of the British or French empires, or of the Kingdom of Hungary. Instead of acting as exponents among their own people of the foreign dominant nation whose culture they had acquired, they acted as spokesmen of their submerged peoples in their struggle against

[1] Kolarz, op. cit., pp. 143–4.
[2] Kolarz, op. cit., pp. 269–70; *Türkeli*, 1951, No. 1, article by Uluktuk, '*Natsionalnoosvoboditelnie dvizhenia v Turkestane v novoy sovyetskoy otsenke*' (Fresh Soviet light on national liberation movements in Turkestan); A. Ahmeddjan, '*Novoe nastuplenie bolshevizma na natsionalnuyu intelligentsiyu i kulturu v Turkestane*' (New Bolshevik offensive against the intelligentsia and culture of *kulturu* Turkestan).
[3] The first secretary and other members of the Secretariat of the Communist Party of Georgia were removed from their posts in March 1952. Other victims of the purge were the President of the Supreme Soviet and the Prime Minister. After the death of Stalin, the Georgian purgers were themselves purged.

the dominant nations. Under totalitarian Stalinism there can of course be no nationalist resistance. But that the inclination of Uzbek or Tatar or Georgian intellectuals is to serve their own nations rather than the 'socialist fatherland' whose capital is Moscow, is suggested by the widespread defection of the nationalities to the Germans in the war, by the recurrent purges of party and government in the republics, and by the systematic falsification of these peoples' histories that has recently been ordered from Moscow. Soviet historians now show that the Imperial Russian conquest of Kazahstan and the North Caucasus was 'progressive', and that the armed struggle of Kazahs and Caucasians against Russia—praised by earlier Soviet historians as a fight for 'national liberation'— was the work of reactionary beys and mullahs instigated by British or Turkish imperialists. It would seem that the Moscow rulers are afraid of the dead heroes of the non-Russian nations.

In the non-Russian republics and provinces, the Soviet regime faces a dilemma. It needs educated and skilled persons from these nationalities, yet every intellectual its education produces is a potential nationalist. In the non-Russian areas, the social tension mentioned in the previous section takes on a special form. Here the discontent of the privileged group and the discontent of the masses are more likely to fuse with each other than in the Russian areas. The obstacles to the fusion are only physical—the power of the police—not, as in the Russian areas, both physical and psychological.

THE STALINIST REGIME

The political and social and imperial system described above bears little resemblance to 'socialism', as conceived by generations of men and women in Europe. It is true that the means of production have been nationalised, and that great new industries have been created. But 'socialism' has never meant merely industrial construction plus nationalised industry.

The achievements of the Soviet regime, which are considerable, are the achievements of early capitalism in Western Europe and America. The Soviet worker can achieve a high standard of living if he becomes a Stahanovite, and maintains his output for a considerable time. The American worker could achieve a still higher standard of living in the nineteenth century by exceptionally hard work and skill. The Soviet citizen of humble social origin but unusual ability can make himself a brilliant career: so could the penniless but brilliant American. It is important to understand that the values of the dominant group in the Soviet Union are the values of the rising capitalist class in the Britain of 1830 or the United States of 1870. The Soviet manager displays an individualism more rugged than that of any Rockefeller or Ford. The dangers in his path are far greater: he acquires greater self-reliance and fewer scruples. The aesthetic values of the rising Soviet caste are also those of the rising capitalist class of the West fifty or a hundred years ago. There is the same hatred of originality, the same preference for solid, pompous and ornate palaces, the same love of nice catchy tunes. The directives of Zhdanov to writers and musicians reflected not only the personal whims of himself or his master, but the wishes and prejudices of the whole social group to which he belonged. The attitude of the Soviet rulers to the non-Russian nationalities is also similar to that of our Victorian grandparents. The arguments with which Soviet historians explain to Kirgiz or Tatars how lucky they were to be conquered by the Tsars, are the Marxist-Leninist equivalent of Kipling. In short, the Soviet industrial revolution has produced much the same social phenomena as the European and American industrial revolutions. Everything is the same except that private profit and private ownership of means of production are absent in the Soviet Union. This difference, which to Marxists is the most important imaginable, seems in fact to be rather unimportant. Most of the unpleasant phenomena—exploitation of the proletariat, aesthetic philistinism, imperialism—which were regarded by Marx as products of capitalism, seem rather to be products of early and rapid industrialisation.

But if the economic and social pattern of the Soviet Union resembles that of Europe and America in the industrial revolution, the political pattern is quite different. Soviet totalitarianism has no parallels in nineteenth-century Europe or America, and probably none in human history. Totalitarianism is not the same thing as dictatorship. The essence of totalitarianism is that it is unlimited. The state's control over its subject is positive as well as negative, affects his private as well as his public life, and is restrained by no moral or religious inhibitions whatever. Under past dictatorships— of which of course Russia had had many during her history—there were sections of private and social life in which the state did not interfere, and there were things which, on traditional or moral or religious grounds, rulers could not do. All such obstacles have been swept away under Stalinism.

The economic, political and moral aspects of Stalinist totalitarianism are inseparable from each other. The immediate causes of the misery of the masses and the insecurity of the managers are economic. The hardships result from the frantic pace at which the government has decided that the programme of industrialisation must be achieved. The decision is political, and the successful imposition of the intolerable pressure is a result of the political system. The people of the Soviet Union have no choice of leaders. This is a simple and vitally important matter. Arguments as to whether western parliamentarism is or is not suited to Russia are not so much true or untrue as irrelevant. Not the constitutional form, but the presence or absence of choice is the crux of the problem. This every Russian worker or peasant can understand. He knows that he cannot choose who is to lead him— in his *kolhoz*, in his factory, in his trade union, in his city or provincial council, or in his national government. The rulers have absolute power. In the exercise of this power, however, they are held back by absolutely no scruples whatever. There is nothing that they may not do to men or women or their children, or to the population of whole provinces or countries, to bend them to their will. Anything that serves the Plan is permitted, and whether anything serves the Plan is decided in the last resort only by the autocrat. Rulers and intellectuals of past ages have talked of *raison d'état* as the supreme consideration, but in fact they or their advisers were inhibited to an important extent by moral or religious scruples or superstitions. The Stalinist regime is the first systematically to apply the criterion of state interest to absolutely every part of its subjects' lives.

The Stalinist regime thus combines all the horrors of early industrialism, Victorian imperialism, political tyranny, and ideological infallibility into a single totalitarian whole. The individual writer and artist could defy the tastes of the Victorian bourgeoisie: the 'formalist' in the Soviet Union who persists in his errors is prevented by the police from pursuing his art, and if necessary deported to forced labour. The Nigerian politician can denounce British rule: the Uzbek guilty of 'nationalist deviation' will not deviate for long. Any organised action by workers or peasants against exploitation is a counter-revolutionary conspiracy, punishable by long terms of forced labour or by death.

But to Stalinists in all lands, this regime *is* 'Socialism', and in fact is already well advanced towards transformation into 'full communism', perfection in human society.[1] No other regime is

[1] There was some public discussion in the post-war years in the Soviet Union as

socialist, and no party or politician, calling himself socialist, is entitled to the name unless it or he recognises the supreme authority of the Soviet Union and of its leader and teacher of genius. The so-called socialists of the West are lackeys or paid agents of the capitalists, deliberately deceiving and betraying the working class.

World revolution remains the aim of Soviet policy, both as an end in itself and as the only effective guarantee of the 'fatherland of socialism', which must be in danger as long a there is 'capitalist encirclement'. The arguments used by Stalin in 1925 remain valid. But 'world revolution' since the 1930's has meant something different. If there is only one blueprint of socialism, then world revolution can be achieved only by its imposition on other lands. It can only be the 'extension of the area of sovietisation'.[1] The implications of this became apparent after the Second World War, first in Eastern Europe and then in the Far East.

---

to the nature of 'full communism' and the prospects of achieving it. This is no place for a discussion of problems of Stalinist metaphysics. It is enough to note that the only essential difference between 'socialism' and 'communism' was in the level of economic output. Under 'communism' as under 'socialism' the party and the security police would still prescribe what every citizen was to do, say and think. There would however be more food and clothing, and eventually refrigerators and television sets for everyone. But this pie was still in the sky, as Stalin himself reminded his subjects in his September 1952 article *Economic problems of socialism in the U.S.S.R.* The toiling masses must work much harder for a long time before the necessary output could be achieved.

[1] Beloff, op. cit., Vol. II, p. 394.

CHAPTER THIRTEEN

The Stalinisation of Eastern Europe

THE prefabricated revolutions which between 1945 and 1948 brought nearly a hundred million Europeans under Stalinist rule, were the first considerable triumph that could be claimed for the communist cause since the Bolsheviks seized power in Russia. As we have seen, native communist forces obtained power mainly by their own efforts in Yugoslavia and Albania, but were defeated by foreign intervention in Greece, while in Poland the native revolutionary movement, which was not led by communists, was also suppressed by foreign intervention. By the summer of 1945 Soviet Russian military forces occupied all Poland, Roumania, Bulgaria, Hungary and Czechoslovakia, and the eastern half of Germany.[1] In these territories, and for some years also in Yugoslavia, a similar type of regime emerged, which was officially described as 'popular democracy'.

Three distinct phases may be traced in the establishment of this regime. Not all countries passed through all phases, and the timing of each phase was different in each country.

In the first phase government was by a genuine coalition of parties of left and left centre. The coalitions in all cases included communist and socialist parties. In Hungary, Roumania and Bulgaria they included peasant parties; in Czechoslovakia, where there was no specific peasant party,[2] its place was taken by non-socialist democratic parties which drew their support partly from peasants and partly from the urban middle class. Yugoslavia, Albania, Poland and East Germany never passed through this stage at all. In Roumania and Bulgaria it existed from the autumn of 1944 to the spring of 1945. In Hungary it lasted until the spring of 1947, and in Czechoslovakia until February 1948.

[1] Soviet forces were withdrawn from Czechoslovakia in December 1945, and from Bulgaria in 1947. In the other countries they remain to the present day, on the ground that this is required for communication with their forces in their zones of Germany and Austria.
[2] The old Agrarian Party was banned on the ground that its former leaders had collaborated with the Germans after Munich. All Czech parties hoped to capture its former supporters. In fact the communists were the most successful.

In the second phase government was by bogus coalition. Several parties still nominally shared power and possessed independent organisations: but their leaders were in fact chosen not by them but by the communist leaders, and the policies of the coalitions were determined by the communists. Political opposition was however still tolerated, although attended with physical risks for those who practised it. Yugoslavia and Albania never passed through this stage. Poland and East Germany began their post-war history in it.

In the third phase the bogus coalitions were transformed into what the communists like to call a 'monolithic block'. The communist leaders not only laid down the lines of policy, but centrally controlled the organisation and discipline of the non-communist groups that were still left in the governments. Socialist parties were forced to 'fuse' with communist parties. No more political opposition was tolerated in parliament, press or public meeting. In Poland, Roumania and Bulgaria the transition from the second to the third phase began in the autumn of 1947, and was marked by the flight of Mikołajczyk to the West and the trials for treason of Maniu and Petkov—that is, by the political destruction of the leading non-communist statesman of each of these three countries. In Hungary the transition began in the spring of 1948, with the flight or arrest of those socialist leaders who opposed 'fusion'. In Czechoslovakia the second and third phases were merged into one, and both were complete by the end of 1948. In East Germany the third phase was completed in 1949, if not even earlier.

This is no place to recount the story of Stalinisation. It is however important to mention certain aspects of the process. These are the attitude of the communists to the peasant parties and socialist parties; the role of Soviet Russian military, political and economic intervention; the levers of power used by the communists; the exploitation by Moscow and by local communists of national conflicts; and the significance of differences of social structure. Finally it is worth devoting a little space to the case of Czechoslovakia, which has certain specific features of interest.

PEASANT AND SOCIALIST PARTIES

The peasant parties were the first objects of communist attack. They represented, in reality or potentially, the majority of each nation. They must therefore be discredited and split. Some of the things that the communists said against them were true. It was true that in the past the peasant parties had devoted more energy to national than to social issues. It was true that urban middle-class elements were very influential in the Hungarian Small Farmers' Party and the Roumanian National Peasant Party. It was true that those peasant parties which had had power during the inter-war period had used it to the advantage of the wealthier minority of the peasants rather than of the peasants as a whole. But these defects were not the reason for the communist attack on the peasant parties: the communists were concerned not with the rights of the poor peasants but with their own lust for power.

In Roumania there was for a time a genuine reaction against the National Peasant Party. The Ploughmen's Front, a left peasant group that had been founded in 1934 but whose influence had been confined to a few counties of Transylvania, gained mass support in a large part of the country. But when it became clear that the Ploughmen's Front was being used by the communists to split the peasantry, and indeed that through its subservient leader Petru Groza it was controlled by the Communist Party, it lost support, and the old National Peasant Party and its veteran leader Maniu became more popular than ever. A similar group in Hungary, the National Peasant Party, played a less important part, as its leaders were not willing to be used by the communists, and the communists thus had little incentive to publicise or support it.

Communist manœuvres against the peasant parties in Eastern Europe recall Lenin's trick in producing an artificial split in the Socialist Revolutionary Party in 1917.[2] But the East European communists were less successful: the East European peasants were politically more experienced, and more loyal to their leaders, than the Russian peasants had been. The official communist version of the splits that were eventually engineered is that the left wings, the truly peasant elements as opposed to the urban bourgeois elements, those who sincerely believed in the revolutionary alliance of the toiling masses of town and country, followed the leadership of the communists; while the right wings, the bourgeois, the *kulaks* and the traitors to peasant interests opposed the will of the people. This is even less true of the East European peasant parties than it had been of the Russian Socialist Revolutionaries. In Hungary in the spring of 1947 it was precisely the genuine peasants among the parliamentary representatives of the Small Farmers' Party who opposed the communists, and a section of the party's intellectuals who supported them. In Bulgaria in 1945 it was from the compromised right wing of the old Agrarian move-

[1] See above, p. 36.

ment that the communists recruited their stooges, while the peasant masses remained loyal to Petkov. In Poland a hetero-geneous clique of disgruntled persons collaborated with the com-munists, while the peasants, as long as they had any opportunity to express their feelings, showed their devotion to Mikołajczyk. In Roumania only insignificant groups could be detached from Maniu's party, and even in the Ploughmen's Front the true peasant leaders were purged in favour of intellectuals bribed or terrorised into obedience to Moscow. The turning-point in the development of the Bulgarian and Hungarian peasant parties was marked by direct Soviet military intervention: in February 1945 the Soviet general demanded the removal of Dr. G. M. Dimitrov from office in the Bulgarian Agrarian Union, and in February 1947 the Soviet military police arrested the General Secretary of the Hungarian Small Farmers' Party, Béla Kovács. The difference between the pro-communist minorities and anti-communist majorities in the East European peasant parties was not social but political. The theory of a class struggle in the villages between poor peasants allied with the workers and the communists, and rich peasants allied with the bourgeoisie was, as in Russia in 1918 and 1929, nothing but a myth. The only real difference was between those who would accept Moscow's orders and those who would not.

In the relationship between communists and socialists too, there is a communist myth and a quite different reality. The myth is that the proletarian masses, aware of the harm done in the past by workers' disunity, imposed unity against the wishes of the small clique of right-wing traitors to socialism and lackeys of the inter-national bourgeoisie in general and of its British Labour agents in particular. All that is true in this is that the workers were eager for unity: the horrors of Nazism were too fresh in their minds for them to feel otherwise. But the workers remembered that the old disunity had been at least as much due to communist as to socialist errors. Unity to them did not mean capitulation. But that was all it meant to the communists, who were impatient to lay their hands on the relatively efficient machinery of the socialist parties and socialist-dominated trade unions. For Moscow the only aim was to create a reliable instrument of its policy.

This first became obvious in Poland. Already in 1944 the socialist party, which had played an honourable part in the Home Army and the civil resistance to the Germans, was heavily purged of persons regarded by Moscow as 'anti-Soviet', and key positions were given to people whom Moscow hoped that it could trust.

But even the purged party strongly resisted communist—which meant direct Soviet Russian—pressure. The demand for 'fusion' was evaded. Only in March 1948 did the malleable Cyrankiewicz suddenly announce, without previously consulting the party's central committee, that fusion would take place. Even after this, further mass purges were necessary, including for example the removal of the whole committee of the party for Łódź, Poland's largest industrial city, before the ceremony was performed, at a 'congress of unification' held in Warsaw in December 1948.

If the Polish 'fusion' was the result of four years of terror and blackmail, in East Germany 'fusion' was suddenly decided in Moscow, and was imposed, by a combination of threats, blackmail and lies, in a few weeks, in April 1946. The new party was named Socialist Unity Party (S.E.D.). The most eminent Social Democrat who joined S.E.D. was Otto Grotewohl, joint chairman with Dr. Kurt Schumacher (resident in the British zone) of the S.P.D. for the whole of Germany. The formation of S.E.D. split German socialism, for the S.P.D. not only in the western zones but also in the western sectors of Berlin retained its separate existence. Many socialists of the Soviet zone had been persuaded that in the new party socialist influence would predominate, and that by forming S.E.D. they were striking a blow against communist influence. The contrary however proved to be the case. Supported by the might of the occupying army, the communists were able to concentrate in their hands all key positions in the party. The process, accompanied by purges throughout the zone, took several years to complete. By 1952 though Grotewohl himself remained nominally prominent, socialist leaders had been removed from the upper and medium levels of the party, and former membership of S.P.D. was a black mark against a party member. S.E.D. was in practice a well-Stalinised communist party.

In Hungary the right wing of the pre-war socialist party was purged in 1945, and the leadership was divided between a 'left' which obeyed communist orders and a centre which, while socially very radical, wished to preserve the independence of both the party and the country. In Februrary 1948 the leaders of the centre, Antal Bán and Anna Kéthly, were expelled from the party, and in June 1948 the ceremony of 'fusion' took place. Only two years later the 'left' socialists suffered the same fate as had overtaken the centre: some were merely removed from their posts in the party, others were also arrested.[1]

[1] These included the former leader of the socialist party, and for a time President

In Czechoslovakia the Social Democrat Party, which before 1938 had been stronger than the Communist Party, was far surpassed by it: at the parliamentary election it won only 13 per cent of the votes in the Czech lands, to 40 per cent for the communists. This much reduced party was divided between those who wanted an independent party and those who bowed before the communists. The subservient wing, led by Zdeněk Fierlinger, was at first dominant, but at the Brno congress of the party in November 1947 he was overthrown by the party's right and centre. In the 'revolution' of February 1948 Fierlinger was reinstated by communist force, and in the summer he duly led the rump party into 'fusion'.

The Roumanian socialist party had always been very small and weak: it won some importance in 1945 only because it was less disliked by the Roumanian workers than was the Communist Party. But communist pressure, reinforced by Soviet military power, quickly brought it to heel. At a congress held in March 1946 the party split, the opponents of the communists forming a separate party which had but a short life. In November 1947 'fusion' took place. The Bulgarian socialists were also not numerous, but they were tougher than their Roumanian comrades. In the summer of 1945 the subservient wing, with communist physical support, seized the party's newspaper and co-operatives, but the majority, bravely led by the elderly Kosta Lulchev, opposed the government until forcibly suppressed at the end of 1948.

SOVIET INTERVENTION

Soviet intervention in East European affairs has been of three types—direct political action based on the threat of military force, indirect political action, and economic action. Hitherto however it has stopped short of the formal incorporation in the Soviet Union which was the fate of the Baltic states in 1940.

East Germany has been more subject and for longer to the first type of intervention than the other countries. The whole political life of the Soviet zone has been determined by Soviet policy. The Soviet authorities decided when to set up *Länder* governments, when to create zonal authorities, and when to set up a separate East German state. These decisions were, it is true, affected by the policy of the Western Powers in their zones of occupation, but from the beginning the initiative has been rather with the Soviet

of the Republic, Arpád Szakasits, and the chief exponents within the socialist ranks of unity with the communists, György Marosán and Zoltán Horváth. Hungary is the best example to date of the fate that overtakes the 'fellow-travellers' of a socialist party when communists have complete power.

than with the Western governments, and of the Soviet intention from the first to Stalinise the eastern zone there can be no doubt. In Poland direct intervention has been very important, from the creation of the Lublin committee in 1944 to the nomination of the Soviet Marshal Rokossovski as Commander-in-Chief of the Polish Army in 1949. In Roumania Soviet intervention was decisive in February 1945 when Vyshinski flew from Moscow to Bucarest to order King Michael to appoint Groza Premier and so hand over power to the communist-controlled 'National Democratic Front'.

In Bulgaria and Hungary Soviet action was usually more discreet, though the removal of Dimitrov and Kovács, already mentioned, were acts of direct menace. In Czechoslovakia Soviet action was still more discreet. The presence of Soviet troops in 1945 enabled the communists to seize important positions in the local administration and police, but the withdrawal of all Soviet units in December 1945 removed the main source of intimidation. It seems probable however that the presence of the Soviet Vice-Minister of Foreign Affairs, Zorin, in Prague in February 1948 was not unconnected with the technique of Gottwald's 'revolution'.

Soviet economic pressure was an extremely important weapon. In Roumania and Hungary reparations were not only designed to compensate the Russian state for part of its war losses, but were also used to crush national opposition to Soviet and communist political aims. A special device were the so-called 'joint companies' set up in Roumania and Hungary, in which Moscow nominally had an equal share with the Roumanian or Hungarian government, but which in fact were controlled by Moscow. Joint companies possessed a monopoly of air, river and maritime transport in both countries, besides owning substantial shares of such important resources as Rumanian oil and timber and Hungarian bauxite.[1] In East Germany the Soviet government acquired enormous industrial interests, confiscated from the German state, the Nazi Party and other illegal organisations, and from Germany's wartime allies. These were organised as 'Soviet corporations' (S.A.G.). It is estimated that in 1947 they accounted for 25 per cent of the total industrial output of the Soviet zone, and that in the period from January 1946 to June 1948 they deprived the German economy of goods to the value of two milliard *Reichsmark* valued in 1936 prices.[2] Even in allied Czechoslovakia the Soviet

---

[1] These are briefly described in Margaret Dewar, *Soviet Trade with Eastern Europe*, 1951, pp. 62–6, 79–82.
[2] P. Nettl, *The Eastern Zone and Soviet Policy in Germany*, 1951, pp. 220–4.

government acquired a valuable economic interest, the Jachymov uranium mines. The Soviet government was also able to put pressure on the East European governments by its trade policy, imposing unfavourable prices on governments which it was working to disrupt or to subject. An important example is the agreement with Poland of September 1945 by which Polish coal was to be sold to Russia at a price one-tenth of that offered by Denmark.[1] Perhaps the most striking of all cases of Soviet economic pressure for political purposes is the order given to the Czechoslovak government to refuse the invitation to the preliminary conference in Paris on the Marshall Plan in July 1947, though the government had already accepted the invitation, with the consent of Gottwald himself.

LEVERS OF POWER

Already in the first phase of Stalinisation the communists seized certain key positions. The most important of these was the Ministry of Interior, which controlled the police. This post was held by a communist already in 1945 in all these countries except Poland and Hungary, and there too control of the security police was in communist hands.[2] The Ministry of Justice, controlling the formal judicial machinery, was considered less important, but was held by communists in certain cases. Control of broadcasting was seized at an early date. Great efforts were made to control and to create youth and women's organisations. In industry, communists were placed in key positions in the management of nationalised factories and in trade unions.

Land reform was made an instrument of communist power. In Hungary, where redistribution of the landlords' estates was long overdue, and was desired by all the democratic parties, the Ministry of Agriculture, and so the supervision of the land reform, was put in communist hands. In Czechoslovakia and Poland land reform consisted of the expropriation of German peasants in the western borderlands. The confiscated lands provided an invaluable fund of patronage to the communists: Czech or Polish peasants who received such land were expected to support the communists, and to a large extent did. Already long before the third stage of

[1] S. Mikołajczyk, *The Pattern of Soviet Domination*, 1948, pp. 158-9.
[2] In Poland the Ministry of State Security was separate, and was held by a communist. In Hungary the Under-Secretary in charge of political police was a communist. After the autumn election the Ministry of Interior itself was taken by a communist. For details, see F. Nagy, *Behind the iron curtain*, New York, 1948.

Stalinisation had been completed in either country, the western borderlands were communist-ruled states within the state.

Finally, the communists attempted to remodel local government on Soviet lines. The local authorities were to be 'people's committees' representing the broad masses but controlled by the communists. In this aim the communists were not successful. The committees did not resemble the bodies of the same name in Yugoslavia, or the soviets in Russia in 1917. The attempt to capture the masses through new local organisations, which had been so successful in the rise to power of Lenin, Mao Tse-tung and Tito, failed in Eastern Europe. The East European communists got control of local government only after, with Soviet support, they had seized power at the centre. The remodelling of local authorities on Soviet lines was the result, not the cause, of their triumph.

NATIONAL PROBLEMS

Communist treatment of national problems was entirely opportunist. Their ultimate aim was to apply Stalin's nationality policy, to reduce all nationalities to the same level of subjugation to Moscow, to create a 'culture national in form and socialist in content'. But where the exacerbation of national conflicts offered Moscow temporary advantages, this was preferred to a policy of national reconciliation. The most obvious example is the German question. The natural hatred of Poles and Czechs for their German oppressors was deliberately magnified by the communists in order to widen the gulf between the Germans and their eastern neighbours, to make Poles and Czechs feel that their only defence against German revenge was Russia, and so to place them at the mercy of Soviet foreign policy. This conviction on the part of the Czechs goes far to explain the unwillingness of Czech democratic politicians to do anything that might antagonise Moscow, and this in turn limited the vigour of their opposition to the communists.

The communists also made good use of the friction between Czechs and Slovaks. In 1945 the Slovak communists posed as champions of Slovak autonomy against Prague: in 1947 the Czech communists outdid the Czech nationalists in denunciation of Slovak nationalism, rightly believing that the execution of the quisling ex-president Tiso, desired by Czech nationalists and fiercely opposed by the majority of the Slovak people, would dig an unbridgeable gulf between Czech and Slovak democrats, and so help themselves to power.

Moscow was also eager to prevent a reconciliation between

Czechoslovakia and Hungary, the two countries in which in 1946–7 the democrats were strongest and communist and Soviet influence was weakest. The Slovak communists were therefore instructed to outdo the Slovak nationalists in hostility to Hungary, and the Hungarian communists to reply from Budapest in similar tone. The insincerity of this nationalism was revealed when the third phase of Stalinisation was completed throughout Eastern Europe. In 1949 Czechoslovak-Hungarian reconciliation was permitted as both countries were firmly held by communists.

Since the foundation of the 'German Democratic Republic' (D.D.R.) in October 1949, Moscow has instructed its Polish, Czech and East German disciples to proclaim their friendly feelings for each other. The watchword has become 'proletarian internationalism', by which is meant uniform adoption by all of nationalism on behalf of Soviet Russia. In short, in the period of seizure of power national antagonisms were intensified for tactical advantage, but in the period of consolidation of power they are being choked down in order to facilitate domination of all nations alike by Moscow.

THE CASE OF CZECHOSLOVAKIA

Though Soviet intervention, and timely infiltration of communists into key positions, were the decisive factors in the Stalinisation of Eastern Europe, internal social factors played their part. It is not without significance that the process was quickest in the countries whose social, political and cultural background was most like that of pre-1917 Russia, and slowest in the country of which this was least true.

In Roumania in 1944 great landowners were less powerful than in Russia in 1917, but in all other respects the two social structures were very similar. The supremacy of a bureaucracy that was often corrupt and brutal, always incompetent and arrogant, was a factor shared by both Roumania and Bulgaria with the old Russia: another was the intangible but persuasive influence of the Orthodox Church. Russian cultural influence was far greater in Bulgaria than in Roumania, whose cultural connections were with the West, especially with France. But the social position of the intelligentsia, and the cultural and political frustration thereby engendered, were in both countries extremely similar to those that had existed in the last decades of Imperial Russia. To sum up, socially Roumania was nearer to old Russia than Bulgaria, culturally Bulgaria was nearer than Roumania, but in their political systems both were equally near.

Hungary was in general more 'western'. It is true that its social structure—and especially the strong position of the landowners—recalled that of Russia. It is also true that a considerable part of the Hungarian intelligentsia suffered from the same type of frustration as the old Russian. But the political system, the nature of the bureaucracy, and the whole cultural tradition, linked Hungary not with Russia but with the West—with Austria and even with the lands beyond. The influences of both Catholicism and Calvinism of course reinforced this tendency. Much the same is true of Poland. A century and a half of subjection to Russia had of course established some Russian cultural influence, and the Polish bureaucracy owed more to the old Russian model than Poles liked to admit. But these influences were more than counteracted by national antagonism to Russia. The Stalinisation of Poland was, as we have seen, even more due to Russian military force, and even less to internal factors, than the Stalinisation of the other countries.

Czechoslovakia alone among the East European states was a predominantly industrial country. In the Czech lands, if not in Slovakia, the social structure resembled that of a western country. The urban middle class was numerous and influential, the skilled formed a high proportion among the workers, and the peasants were as prosperous and as skilled as those of western lands. The level of education approximated to that of the West, and the intelligentsia found employment for its talents and an honourable place in society. The practice of parliamentary democracy was firmly rooted. The electoral success of the communists in 1946 was due to the same causes as in France—belief that the communists stood for the material interests of the workers, and enthusiasm for Russia. It was not due to bitter revolutionary feeling. Between 1945 and 1947 the old methods of government largely reasserted themselves against communist lawlessless. Yet when the crisis came in Februrary 1948 the resistance of the democrats collapsed.

Some reasons for this have already been given—previous infiltration by the communists into the police and local administration, communist control of the western borderlands, communist exploitation of hatred between Czechs and Germans and of friction between Czechs and Slovaks. To these may be added the tactical mistakes of the democrats. The cabinet ministers representing the Czech People's, Czech Socialist and Slovak Democrat parties resigned in February 1948 in protest against the failure of the communist Minister of Interior, Vaclav Nosek, to carry out the cabinet's directive to him to stop packing the police with communists. But they resigned before they had made sure of the support of either the social democrats—which was necessary in order to have a majority against the communists in parliament—or of President Beneš. They also made no attempt to contact the opponents of the communists in army or police. The communists defended themselves with both constitutional and extra-constitutional means. They induced the social democrats to support them and bullied the President into accepting the resignations of the democratic ministers. They seized the radio and the newspaper offices, paraded armed detachments of workers through the streets of Prague, and set up 'Action Committees' of communists and stooges which took over the powers of the local authorities. Neither the resigning ministers nor the president could address the people. Generals subservient to the communists kept the army immobile. There was no resistance. Gottwald's 'revolution' was made with the help of the police: it resembles Mussolini's march on Rome by sleeping-car or Hitler's acceptance of office from President Hindenburg rather than any genuine revolution. Indeed there is a certain tragic similarity between the roles in these two crises of the ageing Hindenburg and the ailing Beneš—two men whose careers have otherwise nothing in common.

The international background to the Prague 'revolution' is most important. Soviet Assistant-Foreign Minister Zorin was in Prague, and Soviet troops surrounded four-fifths of the Republic's frontiers. The willingness or ability of the United States to help the Czechs resist was highly doubtful. Whether, if Beneš and the non-communist ministers had stuck together and had prepared their action in consultation with the army leaders, the communists would have secured power, and whether, if the communists had been defeated, Soviet forces would have invaded Czechoslovakia, is also doubtful. But neither Beneš nor the Czech politicians were in a mood to take these risks. The catastrophe of Munich had left its mark on them. They had the habit of surrender and they were accustomed to regard the Western Powers as unreliable friends. Britain's war record had not wiped out the 'Munich legend', sedulously fostered by the communists and swallowed in good faith by millions of Czechs who were not communists. Nor had the extremely modest achievements of wartime Czech resistance increased the Czechs' confidence in themselves. Perhaps most important of all was the fact that the Czechs did not wish to oppose Russian wishes. The Czechs still regarded Germany as the enemy, Russia as a friend. It took some years of Gottwald's regime to show them that indirect Russian rule could be more unpleasant than direct Nazi rule. The uncritical admiration of most Czechs for all things Russian disarmed the Czech people in the moment of crisis. This is seen more clearly when events in Czechoslovakia are compared with events in Finland.[1] The refusal of the Finns to accept even cultural influence from Russia protected them. Only three months after the Prague 'revolution' the Finnish parliament forced the communist Leino to resign from the Ministry of the Interior. Shortly after this free parliamentary elections were held, at which the communists' poll fell by one-quarter, and in the new government the communists were not represented. Finland was not less exposed to Russian armed intervention than was Czechoslovakia. But the Finns risked the danger which they clearly saw, and emerged unscathed.

As long as the communists had observed the constitutional rules and had remained loyal to the genuine coalition of the People's Front, the democrats had preserved their independence and Czechoslovakia had been a relatively free country. But when the communists forced a crisis, the various factors enumerated above operated to their advantage. These factors were however so peculiar to the Czechoslovak situation that they make it an unique event. Czechoslovakia is the only western industrial state that communists have captured, but its experience does not provide any general conclusions on the ability of communists to capture industrial states.

'POPULAR DEMOCRACY'

In the words of former Comintern General Secretary Dimitrov, 'the Soviet regime and the Popular Democratic regime are two forms of one and the same system of government . . . Both are based on the dictatorship of the proletariat.'[2] The Hungarian communist leader Rákosi described Popular Democracy as 'dictatorship of the proletariat without the soviet form'. This distinction is pedantic. As we have seen, the Comintern from its foundation attributed magic qualities to the institution of soviets, which in fact already by 1919 had lost what importance it had once had.[3] Whether the organs of government in the Stalinised East European countries are called soviets or people's committees or people's councils is of no practical importance. They have been since 1948 tools of the communist parties. The East European regimes are dictatorships of the proletariat in the same sense in

[1] See below, pp. 301–3.
[2] Speech at the 5th Congress of the Bulgarian Communist Party, December 1948.
[3] See above, pp. 69, 79–80.

which the Soviet-Russian regime is a dictatorship of the proletariat: all are dictatorships of the communist party, that is dictatorships of Stalin. In fact the East European regimes are im-
perfect copies of the Soviet Russian regime, and the imperfections
are being removed with all possible speed.

The hierarchical organisation of the communist parties is of
course essentially the same as that of the Soviet Communist Party.
The communists control the organs of central and local government as in the Soviet Union. The constitutions of the East European states are closely modelled on the Soviet Constitution of 1936.
Parliaments are elected by direct, equal, secret, universal suffrage,
but there is only one list of candidates, and the parliaments only
meet for a few days every year. Between sessions, legislative
business is carried on by the Presidiums, whose members are still
more rigorously selected by the communists than are the members
of the parliaments. Local authorities are elected in a similar way,
and are similarly controlled by the party. As in Soviet Russia, they
are strictly subordinate to the central authorities. The judicial
hierarchy is equally controlled by the party, its members being
elected by the corresponding levels of the political hierarchy, that
is, by bodies nominated by the party. As in the Soviet Union, great
powers are held by the separate hierarchy of procurators controlled
from above by the senior procurator, himself a member of the
party and appointed by the parliament. Communist control over
the police is complete. In the armed forces control is exercised
partly through the hierarchy of the 'political administration',
with its political commissars and *politruks*, and partly through the
secret police departments of the armed forces, themselves staffed
by members of the party. Political control in this narrow sense is
supplemented by control over the so-called 'mass organisations'
—especially youth and women's movements. Special attention is
paid to the hierarchy of education, from primary school to university, and to sports—or 'physiculture'.

The communists have done their best since 1948 to remodel the
economic hierarchy on Soviet Russian principles. Here progress
was quicker in the industrial than in the agricultural field. Both
the managerial and the trade union pyramids were firmly held by
the party. Managerial policy was based on the practice of the later
Stalinist era rather than of the early period of Bolshevism. There
was much less persecution of pre-revolutionary experts than in
Russia. Efficient managers who were willing to submit to the
communists retained their jobs, and were even admitted into the

party, as well as enjoying the social privileges established in Russia since the late 1930's. The agricultural hierarchy was also closely copied from the Soviet Russian model. Collective farm managements and M.T.S. were subject to the control of the party. In Poland and Bulgaria *politotdely* in M.T.S.[1] were introduced at the end of 1950. The purpose of collectivisation in Eastern Europe was the same as in Russia—to increase food supplies for the increasing non-agricultural population and to organise the recruiting of labour from the villages to the new industries, mines and public works. With the exception of Bulgaria, however, the pace was slower in Eastern Europe than in Russia, and—with the same exception—there were few cases of destruction of livestock or clashes between peasants and police. Of the trend there could be no doubt. At least by the late 1950's it was intended that East European agriculture should be collectivised. The trend of industrial planning was also the same as in Soviet Russia. First priority was given to capital goods industries, and especially to metallurgy and engineering: if conditions were good, and resources were available, there would also be great progress in consumers' goods industries, but if not these would be sacrificed.[2]

The position of the social classes in Eastern Europe has been approaching that in Soviet Russia. The workers were subjected to the same pressure as in the Soviet Union. Trade unions represented the interests of the State against the workers, not of the workers against the boss. Differential piece rates, Stahanovism and 'socialist competition' were encouraged. Welfare services were admirable on paper: in practice when economic conditions dictated economies the welfare services were the first to be cut. Severe penalties were imposed for lateness at work or minor breaches of discipline, and more was heard from official spokesmen of the doctor's duty to prevent malingering in the factory than of the worker's right to medical attention.

The position of those intellectuals who were not technicians or managers, was precarious. Their special knowledge was in demand, and even received high material rewards, but their pre-revolutionary educational background caused them to be treated with suspicion. Meanwhile the communists busily prepared a new intelli-

---

[1] See above, p. 158.
[2] Early in 1951 the Polish, Czechoslovak and Hungarian plans were 'revised'. Much higher targets were set in all fields, including consumption goods. But the priority of capital goods over consumers' goods was further stressed. The motive for the 'revision' was undoubtedly Moscow's desire to strengthen the war potential of the three economies in the light of the more dangerous international situation that followed the Korean war.

gentsia, recruited from children of workers, peasants and party bureaucrats, closely watched for ideological orthodoxy and trained in the new schools whose organisation and curriculum were dictated by the party. Such elements of a liberal education as had existed under the pre-revolutionary regimes of Eastern Europe were swept away: they were replaced by a combination of technical instruction with Marxist indoctrination. Press, radio and book publication were of course controlled by communist censorship, and the latest teachings of Zhdanov, Lysenko and Stalin on literature, art, philosophy, genetics and linguistics were introduced. Communist control of education inevitably brought conflict with the Christian churches. Religion was excluded from all but the narrowest field of worship and dogma, and even in this field its future remained uncertain. To outward appearance at least, Eastern Europe was being rapidly organised under a totalitarian hierarchy, whose dominant groups—it is still premature to use the words 'ruling classes'—were, as in Soviet Russia, a combination of party bureaucrats and technical managers.

TITOISM AND PURGES

In the first years the communist parties were far from homogeneous. Their ranks included many opportunists, whose support was useful to the leaders when their aim was to overawe their opponents by a display of numbers, but who could not be considered reliable once power had been won. They also included a number of fascists, of whom some were genuine revolutionaries converted from brown to red, others were careerists, and others again just toughs in search of an employer who wanted heads broken. More dangerous in Moscow's eyes were the idealist communists, who had fought and suffered in the underground and resistance movements, and had taken seriously the wartime talk about the future independence and greatness of their countries. These men might be expected in future to show themselves reluctant servants of the teacher of genius of all progressive humanity.

The conflict between Moscow and the 'resistance' communists was revealed to the world by the Cominform's denunciation of Tito in June 1948. The Cominform statement accused Tito of various doctrinal sins, in particular of favouring the peasants at the expense of the workers, of subordinating the Communist Party to the People's Front, and of maintaining a despotic regime within the party instead of the true principles of democratic centralism. There was some truth in some of these charges, but most of them were less applicable to the Yugoslav Communist Party than to the parties of neighbouring lands.[1] Some time after the breach, evidence was published which showed that there had been serious disagreements between the Yugoslav and Soviet governments about the organisation and equipment of the Yugoslav army, and about the status of Macedonia and Yugoslav-Bulgarian relations.[2]

But underlying all these disputes was the fundamental cause of enmity. Moscow knew that the military and civil bureaucracies of Yugoslavia had been created by Tito and his comrades during the Yugoslav national and civil war, not by Soviet military and political experts. Tito had built his own state machine without being supervised by Stalin's emissaries. He had even conversed with British officers without Soviet citizens or Soviet agents being present: who could tell what anti-Soviet conspiracies he had plotted with the cunning scoundrels of the diabolical British intelligence service? This uncertainty and suspicion caused Moscow to place the most sinister interpretation on the most trivial incidents. When Soviet citizens in Yugoslavia were watched by the Yugoslav secret police, or when Yugoslav officers objected to the fact that Soviet officers of equal rank received far higher pay, from the Yugoslav budget, for jobs which they themselves could do more efficiently, this could only mean that Yugoslavia was preparing, together with the western imperialists, some action hostile to the Soviet Union. Moscow therefore decided to break with Tito. As Tsar Alexander III in the 1880's had been convinced that friction between Bulgaria and Russia could only be the result of Austrian and British intrigues, that the Bulgarian people was loyal to Russia, and that when he had withdrawn Russian officers from the Bulgarian army it would collapse, so Stalin and Molotov believed that friction between them and Tito could only be due to intrigues

[1] The Cominform statement, and several of the letters exchanged between Belgrade and Moscow, are contained in the pamphlet published by the Royal Institute of International Affairs in 1949 under the title *The Soviet-Yugoslav Dispute*. One of the sins imputed to Tito was that he did not stress the leading role of the Communist Party, that he kept it in the background, hiding behind the façade of the 'mass organisation', the People's Front. This accusation was true. The reason for this curious behaviour by the Yugoslav communists, who remained secret and conspiratorial after they had assumed full power, has never been explained. It is however certainly not true that the Yugoslav Communist Party merged itself in the Front, and so allowed the Front to rule. The truth is that the Communist Party held all real power. The Front was its creature and its tool.

[2] This subject is discussed by the Yugoslav communist leader Mosha Piade in some of the articles and speeches contained in *Izabrani govori i članci, 1948–9*, Belgrade, 1950, pp. 223–39. Further light on the conflict can be found in the interesting official biography of Marshal Tito, *Tito speaks*, by Vladimir Dedijer, 1953. It is especially instructive on Stalin's intrigues to set the Balkan states against each other, and on the Soviet policy of economic exploitation of Yugoslavia.

of the British with Tito, that the Yugoslav masses were devoted
to the Soviet Union, and that when he had shown his displeasure
by withdrawing the Soviet military and political experts from
Yugoslavia, the 'healthy forces' •in the Yugoslav Communist
Party and the Yugoslav people would assert themselves and overthrow Tito. But Alexander III had been wrong, and Stalin was
wrong. Both in 1885 and in 1948 Russian arrogance had antagonised a patriotic Balkan nation, and Russian bullying strengthened
its resolve to resist. Tito had loyally followed Moscow's lead:
not he but Stalin picked the quarrel. For a year Tito remained
aloof from the Western Powers: only the economic blockade
imposed by Russia and the East European 'popular democracies'
forced him to seek economic support in the West. But Yugoslavia survived the Soviet and Cominformist pressure. The cause
of the survival of Tito's regime was the same as the basic cause
of the breach: Tito had created his own army and civil administration, he had made the careers of his officers and his bureaucrats,
and with a handful of exceptions they remained loyal to him.

The absence of this basic condition in the other countries explains
why there was no 'Titoism' there. Only Albania was in a position
to follow Tito's example. But here national conflicts were decisive.
The Albanians resented Yugoslav arrogance and domination in
much the same way as the Yugoslavs resented Russian. Albania
also had long-standing territorial aspirations at Yugoslavia's
expense. Since 1944 the Albanian communists had been silent about
this, but Enver Hoxha now took the opportunity to acquire merit
simultaneously among his own subjects and in Moscow: he supported the Cominform. The other 'popular democracies' never had
the chance to follow Tito. In the improbable event that Bierut,
Gottwald, Dimitrov, Rákosi or Anna Pauker had wished to break
with Moscow, they could not have done so, for they had no military
or civil machine of their own. Their armies and bureaucracies had
been built under the supervision of Soviet experts. If forced to
choose between them and Stalin, these officers and bureaucrats
would have chosen Stalin.

Even so Stalin took no chances. Communists regarded as
'nationalist deviationists' were arrested, and some were made to
play the leading role in show trials for treason that recalled the
Moscow trials of 1936–8. To what extent they were 'guilty' of
this 'crime' it is hard to judge. It is probable that the Albanian
Koçi Xoxe, executed as an agent of Tito, was in fact the leader of
the pro-Yugoslav faction within his party. There is evidence that

the Pole Gomułka expressed sympathy for Tito and was impatient of Russian tutelage.[1] Whether the Hungarian Rajk, the Bulgarian Kostov, or the Roumanian Pătrăşcanu were disloyal to Moscow remains a mystery. What is certain is that these men were active in the resistance or underground movements in their countries, while the leaders of their parties—Râkosi, Dimitrov, and Pauker—returned home with or after the Soviet Russian Red Army. Moscow had decided that wartime resistance leaders were less reliable than persons who had spent long years under close supervision in Moscow. Whether in fact these individuals had planned, still more whether they had committed, treason, was a minor detail: in Bolshevik conceptions of law, to belong to a category capable of treason is as important as to commit treason,[2] and preventive action is more valuable than punitive.

Since the autumn of 1951 further purges have taken place in East European communist parties whose significance was less obvious. The first important victim was Rudolf Slansky, General Secretary of the Czechoslovak party. The second was Vasile Luca, one of the leading Roumanian communists. Both men were violently denounced in the official press. In May 1952 Anna Pauker herself was removed from her offices in the party and strongly criticised, though she was not arrested and was not described as a traitor. Both Slansky and Pauker were notorious for their subservience to Moscow. Both were also Jews. The public 'trial' of Slansky in November 1952 was the closest reproduction of the Moscow trials of 1936–8 yet staged outside the Soviet Union. The anti-semitic element in the case was strongly emphasised.[3]

THE EVOLUTION OF YUGOSLAVIA

Meanwhile certain changes had taken place in the Yugoslav regime. Yugoslav communist writers began to denounce the Soviet

[1] The Gomułka case is well discussed by A. Ulam, *Titoism and the Cominform*, Harvard, 1952, pp. 146–88.   [2] See above, p. 172.

[3] Together with Slansky was tried his enemy, the Slovak communist Clementis, former Foreign Minister, a man of the Gomułka-Kostov 'nationalist' type rather than of the 'internationalist' or 'Muscovite' type represented by Slansky. On the Slansky affair three points may be made. First, if Moscow required scapegoats for the economic troubles of Czechoslovakia, it was more likely to pick on persons universally detested: the fact that these were the most loyal of all its stooges was unlikely to affect its decision. Secondly, Jews are always good scapegoats in Central and Eastern Europe. Thirdly, it is quite possible that the disgrace of Slansky was connected with personal struggles for power within the Soviet party: in the absence of hard evidence, however, this can be regarded only as an hypothesis. All three points apply equally to Pauker and Luca in Roumania, and would apply to the Jewish and unpopular leaders of both the Polish and the Hungarian parties. It would be no surprise if while this is in the press sensational events should occur in those two parties. The effect of Stalin's death cannot yet be estimated.

internal regime. Their analysis was essentially the same as that of Trotski: the faults of the Stalinist state were due to bureaucratic degeneration of the revolution. Stalin had turned his back on Lenin's doctrine of the withering away of the state. The nationalisation of industry by the Bolsheviks in 1918 had introduced state capitalism. From this point onwards one of two courses was possible—to strengthen the forces of bureaucratic state-capitalism, or to strengthen the role of the direct producers. The first course led to reactionary bureaucratic dictatorship, the second to socialism and the withering away of the state. Soviet Russia had followed the first course, but Yugoslavia was following the second. In any economically backward country the state was bound to play a larger part in the period of transition to socialism than in an economically advanced country. In any such country therefore the danger of bureaucratic degeneration would be great. Yugoslavia's leaders were subject to the same temptations as the leaders of Soviet Russia had faced, but they were aware of them, and claimed that they would not succumb.[1]

Yugoslav official spokesmen frequently stress the differences between their regime and the Soviet. Since 1950 the machinery of economic planning in Yugoslavia has been decentralised. In the factories power is wielded by works' councils, elected by the workers themselves. In 1952 local government was reorganised, on the basis of representation for producers' association. A new Constitution was prepared, which applied the same principles to national government.[2] The federal organisation of the country into six republics[3] is, the Yugoslav communists claim, a reality, whereas the 'federalism' of the U.S.S.R. is a fiction. The Yugoslav leaders are well aware of the exploitation of the non-Russian nationalities by Moscow: they deny that there is any similar exploitation of the nationalities of Yugoslavia by Belgrade. They are also aware that the rural hierarchy created in Russia by the collectivisation of agriculture is designed to exploit the peasants in the

[1] Milovan Djilas, 'Savremene Teme' (Contemporary Themes), published in E. Kardelj and M. Djilas, Nova Jugoslavija u savremenom svetu, Belgrade, 1951.

[2] The Constitution (which came into force in 1953) has two main features. One is to give representation to producers in a new Second Chamber—the Council of Producers, which replaces the old Council of Nations. In this Second Chamber factory workers receive disproportionately high representation, peasants disproportionately low. The second main feature is that the executive and legislative functions are separated more clearly from each other. Policy is made by the leaders, and administration is carried out by departments whose heads have the title of State Secretary.

[3] Serbia (with the 'autonomous region' Voivodina and the 'autonomous province' Kosovo-Metohija, containing respectively Hungarian and Albanian elements); Croatia (including Dalmatia); Slovenia; Bosnia-Hercegovina; Macedonia; Montenegro.

interest of the state. In the words of Milovan Djilas, one of the
ideologues of 'Titoism', Soviet agricultural policy is 'a struggle
with the collective working peasantry for absolute rent'. This,
the Yugoslav communists claim, is not the case in Yugoslavia,
where 'labour co-operatives' are voluntary associations of agricultural producers. Finally, they claim that their Security Police,
U.D.B.,[1] is quite unlike the Soviet M.V.D. Aleksander Ranković,
the Minister of Interior, claimed in a speech in June 1952 that
U.D.B. had 'avoided the slippery path of bureaucracy'. Though
justly merciless towards the enemies of the state, U.D.B. had
never, like the M.V.D., set itself up as a power above the heads
of the people. It was the people's servant and guardian, not its
master. The cause of the difference lay in the contrast between
'productive relations' in Yugoslav and Soviet society. The Soviet
Union was dominated by its bureaucracy, while in Yugoslavia the
role of the producers was steadily increasing.

A non-Marxist observer is bound to express a little scepticism
at this picture. The decentralisation of economic planning and the
powers of works' councils are likely to have small effect as long as
both planning and councils are controlled by the Communist Party,
and it is organised on familiar principles of 'democratic centralism'.
The same applies to the equal status of the federal republics. It is
indeed unlikely that the present regime has perpetuated the pre-
1941 Greater Serb hegemony over Croats, Macedonians and
others. But the removal of the old form of nationalist discrimination does not mean that national antagonisms have disappeared,
that the republican governments have any real self-government, or
that the various forms of discontent aroused by the Tito regime
no longer take nationalist form. All friends of Yugoslavia of course
hope that antagonism between Serbs and Croats, Serbs and
Macedonians, is vanishing. But past experience of Eastern Europe
makes it almost certain that in a country of mixed nationalities any
discontent, whatever its cause, and whether it be just or unjust,
will be canalised in a nationalist direction. Ranković's claims on
behalf of U.D.B. must also be taken with a pinch of salt. Ranković
himself in June 1951 had admitted that the police had abused its
powers, and that in 1949 nearly half of all persons detained had
been unlawfully arrested. Democratic critics of the regime,
arrested during the period of subservience to Moscow, were still
in gaol in 1952. Finally the claim that Yugoslav 'labour co-operatives' are voluntary associations of agricultural producers cannot

[1] Administration of State Security.

be taken seriously. When in the summer of 1951 peasants who had voluntarily joined 'labour co-operatives' for three years in 1948, claimed the right to secede again, a stream of governmental invective made it clear that they would not be allowed to do so. In the summer of 1952 important economic concessions were made to the peasants, and in certain mountainous and infertile areas 'labour co-operatives' were even dissolved. But in the main grain-producing areas they were maintained, by forces stronger than the enthusiasm of the peasants.

It is not necessary to doubt the sincerity of the Yugoslav communist leaders in order to feel sceptical about their policies. Almost all the things that they say about bureaucracy have been said before, not only by Trotskists but also by Stalinists. The Soviet press is as full of denunciations of bureaucratic degeneration as is the Yugoslav. Like the Yugoslavs, the Soviet spokesmen insist that the communist party should confine itself to general leadership and not dictate the details of administration.[1] Soviet justifications of the M.V.D. are couched in almost the same phrases as Ranković's speeches. Both Soviet and Yugoslav writers attribute the defects of their systems to the wickedness of individual bureaucrats, and point the way to the future by loose use of quasi-economic phrases which they treat as magic formulae.

But the defects are not due to individual wickedness, and there is no remedy in Marxist incantations. The defects are due to two main causes. One is the attempt to enforce, at an impossible pace, a programme of economic construction for which neither the human nor the material resources are available. In order to achieve a part of the targets set, and in order to conceal the fact that only a part has been achieved, a vast machinery of coercion and lies is needed. The second cause is more fundamental. It is that the people are unable to exercise a choice of rulers. That absolute power tends to corrupt absolutely, is still more true in a backward society, in which rulers and ruled live in different centuries, than in an advanced society. Sudden introduction of complete liberty of choice in Yugoslavia is hardly a possible task, and if by some miracle it could be achieved, it would probably let loose reactionary and disruptive forces which would not only hinder economic progress but threaten the existence of the state. Yet to maintain political monopoly in the hands of a group of despots, however noble in intention, who know that they are subject to no popular choice, is to perpetuate all the faults which Tito, Djilas and their friends sincerely

[1] See above, p. 81.

deplore. A way must be found between these two extremes.

It is not impossible that the Yugoslav leaders are seeking such a way, and may have the courage to take it if they find it. It would be unjust to suggest that there is no difference between the Soviet and Yugoslav regimes, simply because the pictures painted of their own system, and the abuse showered at their enemy's by the spokesmen of each country, are so similar. Reality must be distinguished from propaganda. The political structure, and the role of the communist party, in Yugoslavia and in Russia closely resemble each other. The economies are substantially different. Yugoslav industrial policy from 1947 to 1949 was based on the experience of the Stalinist Five Year Plans. Agricultural policy was designed to similar ends, but was pursued with greater caution, than the Russian collectivisation. Since the Cominform blockade started in June 1949, and western economic aid became essential to Yugoslavia's survival, a more realistic character has come into Yugoslav planning.

The obstacle to further realism was for a long time the suspicion that the purpose of economic advice offered from the West was to retard Yugoslavia's industrialisation in order to preserve the country as a 'colony of western capital'. As this suspicion was gradually reduced, the Yugoslav planners began to learn that it is possible to give economic incentives to workers and peasants without abandoning the aim of industrialisation. In the political field, too, changes will become possible when the Yugoslav leaders have rid themselves of the quite unjustified suspicion that the Western Powers wish to 'destroy socialism' in Yugoslavia and to restore by force or fraud the dictatorship of the inter-war years. Already it must be admitted that there is greater freedom of speech. The removal of the obligation to adulate all things Russian and to spit at western culture lifted a great weight from Yugoslav schools and universities, and revived the fruitful intellectual life of this gifted and intelligent people. Yugoslavia is going through a period of transition, which will not necessarily end in the establishment of a 'western democracy', but may produce new political and social forms. Existing trends permit of hope. The result, whatever it be, will be instructive not only for Yugoslavs.

CHAPTER FOURTEEN

The Chinese Revolution

THE surrender of Japan found the Kuomintang forces confined to southern China, the communists in the north-west and in their 'anti-Japanese war bases' north of the Yangtse, the Japanese in the eastern cities, and the Russians in Manchuria. The question was, which faction was to get the Japanese equipment and to occupy the Japanese-held areas. The communist military commander Chu Teh issued an order to communist forces on 12th August to disarm Japanese forces throughout north China and Manchuria. Chiang Kai-shek ordered the communists to remain in their territory: the central government, he said, was making all necessary arrangements to disarm the enemy and liberate the country The desire of both parties to seize strategic positions and military supplies, which might prove decisive in the forthcoming struggle for power, was to some extent restrained by the dependence of each party on the goodwill of the Great Powers, which at this time still proclaimed their unity of purpose as victorious allies.

Already in November 1944 the American Ambassador to China, General Hurley, had held discussions both with the Chinese government and with the communists, with the aim of reconciling the two, both for the last stages of the war against Japan and for the future.[1] The essence of the dispute was that the communists demanded a change of political regime before they surrendered their powers to the central government, while Chiang insisted that the authority of the central government must be recognised by all, including the communists, before political reforms could be made. The communists stressed the need to end the existing one-party dictatorship by the Kuomintang. They also claimed that any military reorganisation should apply to the Kuomintang forces as well as to the communist armies. Chiang demanded that the armed

---

[1] These negotiations are recorded in the official American publication, *United States' Relations with China*, Washington, 1949, pp. 73–111.

forces and civil administration of the communist-held areas should subordinate themselves to the central ministries and military command of the National Government: when this had been done, he would recognise the communist party as a legal party. Neither side trusted the other. Chiang believed that the communists were seeking facilities to undermine his regime throughout China, that they would surrender nothing and seize what they could. The communists believed that Chiang was trying to trap them into placing themselves at his mercy, that he would relinquish none of his power but destroy theirs. Probably each side was right in its view of the other's aims.

On 14th August 1945 was signed the Soviet-Chinese treaty. Chiang Kai-shek's government was obliged to restore to Russia the special privileges which imperial Russia had had in Manchuria until 1905, of which she had ceded part to Japan after defeat in war, and sold the rest to Japan thirty years later.[1] The days when the Bolsheviks proudly renounced imperialistic advantages seized by the Tsars from weak Asian nations were long past. For its part the Soviet government recognised Chiang's administration as the legal government of China. This obliged the Chinese communists to treat Chiang with greater courtesy. Mao Tse-tung himself accepted Chiang's invitation to discuss with his government, and came to Chungking at the end of August. In the six weeks of negotiation that followed some points were settled. In principle the communists recognised that the Kuomintang was the leading party in China, and promised to co-operate with it during the transition to democratic government.

Meanwhile however communist forces had been regrouped, and were moved both from Shensi and from the former 'war bases' into Manchuria, where they united with communist guerrilla bands, both Chinese and Korean, which had been active under Japanese rule. These various forces were allowed by the Russian authorities to acquire Japanese surrendered equipment. At the same time Soviet industrial experts systematically robbed Manchurian factories. Millions of pounds' worth of valuable machinery, on

[1] Russia acquired the Chinese Eastern Railway rights in 1896; the naval base of Port Arthur and the right to build the South Manchurian Railway in 1898. She ceded Port Arthur and the S.M.R to Japan in 1905; and sold the C.E.R to Japan in 1935. In 1945 she recovered half-ownership of the two railways, now known as the Changchun Railway, and the lease of Port Arthur as a naval base. By the treaty signed with Mao Tse-tung's People's Government in 1950, the Soviet government undertook to return Port Arthur at the end of 1952. By the further agreement of September 1952, the railway was returned to China, but Port Arthur remained in Soviet possession until a peace treaty should be signed between Japan, the Chinese People's Republic and the Soviet Union—i.e. until a remote future.

which the Chinese government had counted for the reconstruction of its battered economy, were removed by the Russians as 'war booty'. On 1st November Kuomintang representatives signed an agreement with the Soviet military command, by which Soviet troops were to be withdrawn to the Soviet zone in Korea, to the Port Arthur base or to the territory of the Soviet Union, and government troops were to be allowed to land at ports in the gulf of Liaotung.[1] When the government troops arrived, they discovered that the Soviet troops had indeed been withdrawn, but that Chinese communist troops, strongly entrenched, were ready to resist them by force. The government forces were landed further south, and after fighting a severe battle at Shanhaikwan pass, forced their way through the communist defences and penetrated into Manchuria at the end of November.

Events took a turn towards conciliation when on 15th December President Truman made a statement on American aims in China. These, he said, were to stop the fighting and to call a conference at which the main political groups should work out a plan for the unification of China. A week later General George Marshall, whom the President had appointed as a special ambassador of goodwill, arrived in Chungking. Within the next two months three important agreements were made. The first was that there should be an armistice from 13th January 1946. An Executive H.Q. was set up in Peking, headed by one representative each of the Chinese government, the Chinese communists and the United States government. It was to supervise the execution of the armistice. Meanwhile government troops were to move freely into Manchuria. The second agreement was achieved by the Chinese Political Consultative Conference, in which communists were represented and which concluded its business on 31st January. It agreed that a National Assembly would be convoked in May, and that meanwhile a State Council representing Kuomintang, communists and minor parties should have general powers, which were not however precisely defined. The third agreement concerned the proportion of communist to government divisions in the new national army. The promise of these agreements, which for a time aroused optimism among the Chinese people, was not fulfilled. During February fighting again broke out in Manchuria. Marshall's attempts to send teams of investigators responsible to the Peking Executive H.Q. were blocked by the Kuomintang commanders.

[1] At Dairen, the best port, which was under Soviet administration, they were not allowed to land.

For their part the communists did not keep faith. They continued to move troops from north-west China into Manchuria after the armistice. The Soviet authorities as usual 'interpreted' their obligations in the manner most convenient to themselves. They allowed Kuomintang forces to enter the two chief cities of south Manchuria—Mukden and Changchun—at the end of December 1945, but they did not withdraw their own forces until the spring. They arranged their evacuation of Harbin, the centre of northern Manchuria, in April 1946 in such a way as to enable the communists to seize it before government troops could arrive. During this time the communists were given ample opportunity to acquire ex-Japanese arms and equipment. The communists chose to regard the fact that the Americans transported government troops in their ships—under existing arrangements between allied governments —as evidence of American intervention in the civil war on the Kuomintang side. For their part, Chiang and the Kuomintang commanders used every opportunity of abusing the authority of the Americans, in order to increase their own prestige among the Chinese people by the belief that the United States stood behind them.

By the early summer hopes of agreement had far receded. On 22nd April the communist spokesman Chou En-lai declared that his party would not take part in the National Assembly that was due to meet in May. The government, he said, had maintained the one-party dictatorship of the Kuomintang, and had not allowed the civil liberties without which no genuine Assembly could perform its task. Meanwhile government troops won victories in Manchuria, and on 5th June even captured Harbin. Communist propaganda was now bitterly attacking the United States. Marshall's impartiality as a mediator was questioned, and there were repeated denunciations of American interventionism and imperialism. In the autumn government troops penetrated north-west China, and on 10th October captured Kalgan. On 15th November the National Assembly, which had been postponed while there still seemed slight hopes of peace, at last met, without any communists and with a vast preponderance of Kuomintang members. It adopted various democratic policies, which had absolutely no relevance to the situation. Power remained in the hands of Chiang and his close friends. In January 1947 Marshall finally gave up his mission. In the face of communist distrust and Kuomintang obstruction he had become powerless.

The Marshall Mission was a well-meaning attempt to reconcile irreconcilables. Many supporters of the Kuomintang, many sympathisers of the communists, and many Chinese who had not made up their minds, had wished him well. But neither the cadres of the communist party nor the bosses of the Kuomintang sincerely sought agreement, or were sincere with Marshall. Each had sought to abuse him for their own purposes. Each had refused the concessions he asked whenever they thought that a momentary advantage was on their side. Chiang never really moved from his basic view that the communists were rebels who must accept his orders before there could be discussions. Marshall's arguments, that the communists were too strong to be quickly and decisively crushed by military force, and that if war continued for long the economic strain would destroy the regime, were ignored by Chiang and his government.[1]

During 1947 the government held its positions in Manchuria and made some gains in the north-west, capturing the communists' former 'capital' Yenan in March. But the countryside between the main cities and lines of communication was escaping its control. The communists held the hinterland of Manchuria. During 1948 they conquered a large part of Northern China. The government's harassed garrisons found it increasingly difficult to maintain communications with each other. At the end of the year collapse came suddenly. Mukden surrendered without more than token resistance. In January 1949 the commanders of Peking and Tientsin handed over their cities after bargaining with the communist general Lin Pao. After this the Kuomintang regime disintegrated all over China. The process took some months only because there were large distances to cover. Few shots were fired. As in 1926, when the Kuomintang had marched triumphantly to the north, so now, when the communists marched triumphantly south, they were greeted in town and village as liberators, and there was much comment on their discipline and courtesy. The mandate of heaven had clearly passed from the Kuomintang: it crumbled beneath the curses and insults of the people.

[1] The Marshall Mission forms the subject of the greater part of *United States' Relations with China* (pp. 127–219). The picture presented in these pages appears to an outside observer convincing. It does not however satisfy the extreme American admirers of Chiang Kai-shek, who blame General Marshall and his advisers for their defeat. It has been suggested that the Mission in fact did more harm to Chiang than to the communists, by holding back the Kuomintang forces at a time (the first six months of 1946) when they had a good chance of crushing the communists. It has also been suggested that this was in part due to the influence in the U.S. State Department of communist sympathisers. It is certain that accusations against the State Department by irresponsible demagogues have reached fantastic dimensions. But it does not follow from this that all the accusations are false. The question must be regarded as open.

The communists won partly through the weaknesses of their enemies and partly through their own strength.

The Kuomintang leaders had attempted too much with too few resources, They had sought to establish their power in Manchuria, the most distant region, before it was firm in central China. Even in the south and south-west, where they had been in control all through the eight years of war with Japan, the Kuomintang had only a mediocre civil administration. They had few competent bureaucrats to spare for the eastern provinces and cities surrendered by the Japanese, let alone for Manchuria. They also lacked economic resources. Revenue from taxation had been insecure even in the south-west, and the government had resorted to the printing-press. There could be no question of efficient tax-collection in the newly liberated areas. Economic aid received from U.N.R.R.A. was largely wasted in corruption and nepotism, and these were largely due to the general economic misery. Economic difficulties were aggravated by the Russian robbery of Manchurian industrial plant, by waste of gold and foreign currency in an import spree of luxury goods for the wealthy few, and by needless interference and obstruction which crippled the little business activity that was still attempted. No less than civil servants and economic resources, the Kuomintang lacked popular support. As poverty and discontent grew together, police repression became more cruel, and hatred more intense. The regime knew how to arrest and maltreat malcontents, but it did not know how to explain its policy to the people. Communist propaganda filled the gap. The whole people longed for peace, and the arguments of the communists combined with the silence or empty phrases of Chiang's men to convince the people that the obstacle to peace was the Kuomintang regime. In the last year of the civil war the general demoralisation affected the army, and ultimately the political bosses themselves. Chiang himself seems to have maintained a strong will to the end, but he was unable to inspire his subordinates. In the last stages apathy and defeatism were almost universal.[1]

The communists were better strategists. They did not stretch their lines of communication. They concentrated their forces in the north, enormously assisted by the wealth of Japanese war material which the Russians gave them or allowed them to take. Their troops in Manchuria included a large number of local men, while

---

[1] A vivid impression of the atmosphere of Kuomintang China in disintegration emerges from the travel book of a brilliant British newspaper correspondent— Patrick O'Donovan, *For Fear of Weeping*, 1950.

the Kuomintang garrisons consisted mostly of southerners. In the Manchurian countryside, which the Kuomintang never wrested from them, the communists carried out sweeping land reforms and won over the peasant masses. The intelligentsia of the north, especially the university students and teachers, were mostly on their side. As the civil war dragged on, the intelligentsia of Kuomintang territory too came over to them.[1] Above all, the communists possessed a single leadership, an efficient party discipline, and considerable trained cadres, capable of taking over the administration of new areas. During nearly two decades of guerrilla experience, in the 'liberated areas' of rural China, Mao Tse-tung had created a military and civil state machine that was a match for his opponent.

The destruction of the Chinese state machine by the Japanese, followed by the collapse of the Japanese themselves, had given the Chinese communists their opportunity. The cadres, trained during the guerrilla years in Leninist ideology and the principles of democratic centralism, provided the human instruments. The Japanese stores handed over by the Russians provided the material weapons. The folly of Chiang provided Mao with victory.

CHINESE COMMUNISTS IN POWER

The policy of the victorious Chinese communists is based on 'the teachings which unite the theories of Marxism-Leninism with the actual practice of the Chinese revolution—the Thought of Mao Tse-tung'.[1] The essence of the Thought is to be found in the pronouncements of Mao in the last decade on the New Democracy.[2] The general principles are not startlingly original. They repeat the slogans of the 1920's, which were derived from a mixture of Lenin's *Two Tactics* of 1905, his *Imperialism* of 1916, the N.E.P. programme of the 1920's, and the theses on colonial revolution of the early Comintern congresses. The General Programme of the Constitution of the Communist Party of China, adopted by its 7th Congress on 11th June 1945, and avowedly based on the Thought of Mao Tse-tung, states: 'The Chinese revolution at the present stage is a bourgeois-democratic revolution of a new type in character—the New Democratic Revolution of the broad masses of the people, led by the proletariat, and directed against imperial-

[1] Programme adopted by the 7th Congress of the Communist Party of China, May 1945, quoted in full in Liu Shao-chi, *On the Party*, Foreign Language Press, Peking, 3rd edition, 1951, p. 143.

[2] The most important pronouncements are collected in Mao Tse-tung, *La nouvelle démocratie*, Paris, Editions Sociales, 1951.

ism and feudalism. . . . At a future stage, when the Chinese national-democratic revolution has won a complete victory, the task of the Communist Party of China will be to take the necessary steps for the realisation of a system of Socialism and Communism in China, in accordance with the requirements of China's social and economic development and the will of the Chinese people.'[1] The New Democracy, or People's Democratic Dictatorship, is government by the People. The People however is not simply identical with the population of China. The People consists of all who are not Reactionaries. The distinction is dressed up in 'social' categories by stating that the People consists of four classes—workers, peasants, petty bourgeoisie and national bourgeoisie, while the Reactionaries consist of landowners and bureaucratic bourgeoisie. Whether an individual bourgeois was to be regarded as 'national' or 'bureaucratic' depended in practice not on his economic or social position, but on his political attitude. If he opposed the communists, he was a bureaucratic capitalist and a Reactionary. If he supported the communists he was a national capitalist, and qualified as a member of the People.

The economy of the New Democracy was to have three sectors —'A state economy—the directing element; an agricultural economy, evolving step by step from an individualist economy to a collective economy; an economy of small industrialists and independent traders and of small and medium private capitalists'.[2] The national bourgeoisie would be 'firmly and unhesitatingly protected'. Everything would of course depend on the practical application to individuals of such conveniently vague terms as 'medium capitalist' or 'bureaucratic bourgeoisie'.

Despite some differences in vocabulary, this was a Chinese version of N.E.P. There is no need to accuse the Chinese communists of copying Russian models. They no doubt had Russian experience in mind, but the similarity of their policy to N.E.P. was mainly due to the similarity of the situations. Chinese communists on the victorious conclusion of their civil war, Lenin on the victorious conclusion of his civil war, and East European communists on receipt from their Soviet patrons of political supremacy, all faced similar tasks. The policy of all three was to take the 'commanding heights of the economy' for the state, and to allow private enterprise in agriculture, trade and small industry. The

---

[1] *The Present Situation and Our Tasks*, speech of 25th December 1947 to the Central Committee of the party, printed in full in Mao Tse-tung, op. cit., pp. 99–122. This quotation is from p. 115.   [2] Mao Tse-tung, op. cit., p. 115.

commanding heights, it is true, were rather different. In Poland or Hungary they included much modern industry, in Russia in 1921 a number of efficient though damaged factories and mines. In China there were very few big industrial enterprises: such as there were, however, together with the means of transportation, were taken over, in fact and in many cases also in name, by the state. They became the first sector, the 'state economy'. The 'moderation' noted with such pleased surprise in 1949 by 'Old China Hands', and regarded by many of them as a 'peculiarly Chinese' feature of communism, was in no way peculiar to China. Had they added to their immense knowledge of China just a little knowledge of Russian or East European experience, they would have spared themselves some illusions and some disappointments. The same 'moderation' had been practised by the Bolsheviks from 1921 to 1928 and by the East European communists from 1945 to 1948 or even later. It was only a temporary phase. The only question was, how long the phase would last.

Agrarian policy passed through several stages. In the first year of civil war the moderate policy of the Yenan period was abandoned. The peasants were no longer contented with a reduction of rents, and the communists no longer needed to conciliate the Kuomintang. A directive of the party of 4th May 1946 authorised the confiscation of landlords' estates. This was applied with special fervour in Manchuria. Here there were larger estates than in other parts of China, and the landlords were associated with the former Japanese regime. Land seizure in Manchuria, like land seizure in Russia in 1917–18, was violent and disorderly. The peasants took the law into their own hands, the communists subsequently approved it, and thereby gained peasant goodwill. As the communists prepared to move south, they once more decided to be more moderate. A 'national agrarian conference' for communist-held territory was held in September 1947, and drew up a 'basic programme of Chinese agrarian law'. The two main principles laid down were that 'the demands of the poor peasants and agricultural labourers must be satisfied', and that 'unity with the medium peasants must be preserved and their interests not harmed'. These phrases recall the slogans endlessly repeated during the Russian civil war and during the party controversies of the mid-twenties. It seems probable that they reflected a similar reality and similar contradictions. In February 1948 a more complicated series of instructions was formulated, distinguishing between different parts of the country and making some concessions to landlords and rich peasants.

After the conquest of the whole country a Reform Law was passed in June 1950. It contained a great number of special cases and exceptions, and was to be put into practice over a period of years. As in Russia, it was found necessary to tax the peasants heavily in order to ensure food supplies to the armed forces and to the towns. The war in Korea, and consequent maintenance of a large army, caused the pressure to continue. This side of agrarian policy was of course less popular than was the redistribution of land. In 1952 came the first signs of collectivisation. Several hundred state farms had been created in Manchuria. A few individual collective farms, run by volunteers, were extolled in the Chinese press. The campaign to convince the peasants of the advantages of collective farming grew more intense, but in 1952 it was only in an early stage. An intermediate form of organisation, the 'mutual aid team', was rapidly developed. It was clear that the pace achieved had required methods of persuasion that made it 'voluntary' only in the special communist sense of the word. In March 1953 the official Chinese news agency claimed that 80 per cent of the peasants of North-East China had joined mutual aid teams, and that in the other provinces the percentage varied between 20 and 65.[1]

The future pace of collectivisation in China will depend on the needs of the towns for food and of industry and public works for labour, and these will depend on the speed of industrialisation set by the Peking government and, possibly, by Moscow. This in its turn will depend on the view taken in Peking and Moscow of the international dangers. Even more than in the Balkans or Russia, in China the absence of equipment and skilled labour will force the planners of industrialisation to rely on the use of great hosts of unskilled labour. This will require increasing pressure on the peasantry. Russian experience has shown that the collective farm and the machine tractor station are the best coercive apparatus yet devised for extracting food and recruits from peasants. It seems improbable that China can escape the consequences.

The organisation of the working class has followed the same lines in China as in Russia. Vast trade unions have been created, and they are well controlled by the party. Their tasks are to get as much effort as possible out of every worker, and to weld the unskilled peasant sons into an industrial labour force. Stahanovism and socialist competition are being introduced, especially in

[1] New China News Agency, 19th March 1953.

Manchuria. The same tyranny and exploitation of the worker must result as in Russia, not because the union leaders are wicked or even callous, but because the economic tasks that they are set can only result in exploitation.

The fine promises made to the 'national bourgeoisie' were not kept for long. Foreign business-men were the first victims. They were compelled to employ a large labour force at comparatively high wages, even when the business could not produce for lack of raw materials or sell for lack of a market. This was a cheap method for the government to appease the workers. As long as the business had any capital the government need not provide for the workers: when the business was finally ruined, the workers' difficulties could be attributed to sabotage by the reactionary capitalists. This was no 'peculiarly Chinese' device: it had been adopted by the Roumanian and Hungarian communists to industrialists in 1945-8. With the Korean war, pressure became severer. On the one hand the xenophobia and spy-mania deliberately stirred up by the authorities caused business-men, Chinese as well as foreign, small as well as big, to be regarded as potentially disloyal. On the other hand the government's financial needs grew more acute, and to rob business-men was an easy way out. The result was two mass campaigns in the first months of 1952—the 'Three Anti' and the 'Five Anti'. The first was directed against 'corruption, waste and bureaucracy' in government offices, the second against 'bribery, tax evasion, theft of state wealth, use of less workmen and inferior material, and stealing of economic intelligence' in private business. There were mass 'accusation meetings' and public confessions. Business-men were forced to confess to crimes, then assessed at enormous sums in fines. The campaign was very profitable to the authorities.

The political structure of the Chinese People's Republic was to outward appearance complicated. The supreme executive organ was a large body called the Central People's Government Council. Subordinated to it were the Revolutionary Military Council, which commanded the armed forces; the Administrative Council, which controlled most of the civil and economic ministries; the Supreme Court; and the Supreme People's Inspection Bureau, whose functions were similar to those of the Soviet *Rabkrin*, or Ministry of State Control.[1] Mao Tse-tung was Chairman of both the C.P.G.C. and the Revolutionary Military Council, while the post of Chairman of the Administrative Council, which has been com-

[1] See above, pp. 83–4, 232.

pared with that of a Prime Minister, was held by the veteran communist Chou En-lai.[1]

The system is in fact less cumbrous than it seems because all political power is held by the communist party, and it is organised on the usual basis of democratic centralism. The Constitution of the Communist Party of China closely resembles, though it is not identical with, that of the Bolshevik Party. The supreme body is nominally the Congress, which is to meet once in every three years.[2] The Congress elects the Central Committee, which holds plenary meetings twice a year. The Central Political Bureau is the 'central leading body of the party, and directs all the work of the party during the intervals between the plenary sessions of the Central Committee'. The Central Secretariat 'shall attend to the daily work of the Central Committee according to the decisions of the Central Political Bureau'. There is thus no doubt that the Secretariat is subject to the *Politburo*. The chief officer in the party is not, as in Russia, the General Secretary, but the Chairman of the Central Committee, who is concurrently Chairman of both *Politburo* and Secretariat. The holder of this position is of course Mao Tse-tung, who also holds the highest position in both the civil government and the military hierarchy. Among the Deputy Chairmen of the principal government organs are several members of the *Politburo*.[3] Thus, as in the Soviet Union and the Popular Democracies, the hierarchies of state and party are interlocked at the top. This fusion of party and state ensures unity of purpose in the apparently complicated machinery of government.

The People's Government was allegedly based not on the monopoly of the communist party but on an alliance of parties and of non-party personalities. Communist spokesmen emphasised the part played by 'progressive intellectuals' who were not communists. The genuine welcome given by educated Chinese, and especially by students, to the new regime, was one of the features of the revolution which most favourably impressed sympathetic foreign observers.[4] But like the concessions made to the 'national

[1] Chou En-lai was one of the earliest members of the Chinese Communist Party, which he joined after returning from studies in France. He was closely connected with Li Li-san in 1928–30, but successfully transferred his allegiance to Mao (see Schwarz, op. cit., pp. 157, 165).

[2] Constitution of the Communist Party of China, printed in full in Liu Shao-chi, op. cit. The passages dealing with the higher authorities in the party are on pp. 163–6.

[3] For example, Chu Teh and Liu Shao-chi are vice-chairmen of the Central People's Government Council; Tung Pi-wu is a vice-chairman of the Administrative Council; and Chu Teh, Liu Shao-chi and Chou En-lai are vice-chairmen of the People's Revolutionary Military Council.

[4] For example, G. van der Sprenkel, M. Lindsay and R. Guillain, *New China: Three Views*, 1950, pp. 53–70.

bourgeoisie', this was but a passing phase. The atmosphere of freedom, inhaled with such enthusiasm by nostrils freed from the stink of the Kuomintang corpse, was quickly replaced by a totalitarian hot-house.

The lenient treatment of former Kuomintang supporters ceased with the outbreak of the Korean war. Witch-hunts for reactionaries and running-dogs of imperialism assumed vast proportions. The authorities organised mass meetings, at which alleged reactionaries were exhibited before a mob audience, which was encouraged to bring accusations against them. Incited by communist cheerleaders, the 'popular masses' clamoured for death or confiscation of all property or a sentence of forced labour, and the 'judges' duly 'bowed to the people's will'. When public executions took place, gangs would go round the city forcing people to come and watch, to applaud the executioners and scream insults at the victims. The deliberate purpose of the regime was to implicate as many persons as possible in the executions, to make them feel that the blood of the dead was on their hands. During 1950 and 1951 tens of thousands were executed, and millions took part as spectators of 'accusation meetings' or executions. This particular form of organised mob terror had no parallels in the history of Soviet Russia or the People's Democracies: it was a 'peculiarly Chinese' feature.

It was not enough to suppress real or suspected enemies: all thought had to be controlled by the party. The intellectuals whose sympathy had been so valuable to the party during the civil war, whose acceptance of communist propaganda had done so much to undermine the will to resist of the Kuomintang, now had to be 're-educated' in the Thought of Mao Tse-tung. Soviet procedures of criticism and self-criticism were adapted to Chinese conditions: the main difference seems to have been that the meetings were more numerous, lasted longer and were even more wearisome.[1] In the schools and universities, religion and much of traditional Chinese culture were rejected. What was preserved was drastically purged. Chinese history was distorted on familiar lines. Still more than in Eastern Europe, in China the various stages of the Bolshevik and Stalinist revolutions were imposed simultaneously. The iconoclasm of 1917 was combined with the aggressive nationalism of 1949. Russian Bolshevism had needed a whole generation to grow into the full flower of totalitarianism. Thirty

[1] Some case-histories are given in E. Hunter, *Brain-washing in Red China*, New York, 1951.

years separated the November revolution from the pronouncements of Zhdanov on literature, art and philosophy. China became totalitarian at once. As in Soviet Russia in the Zhdanov period, it was not enough to submit to the regime: positive enthusiasm was required. Under Chiang Kai-shek there had been the old-fashioned tyranny of warlords and police, but the private life of the individual Chinese was his own. Under Mao Tse-tung family relationships, personal emotions and personal tastes were equally subject to the vigilant eyes of the party.

Eminent sinologists have pointed out that parallels can be found in Chinese history to many features of the communist regime.[1] The founders of the Han and Ming dynasties, who reunited China after periods of confusion, were themselves peasants, and their armies, like that of Mao Tse-tung, were peasant armies.[2] Past dynasties in China were great when they had the support of two sections of the population, the peasants and the scholars: these the communists have. The Chinese have never had the habit of democracy as it is understood in the West. They are accustomed to be ruled by a learned oligarchy, and this is what they have today. Marxist-Leninist learning and the Thought of Mao Tse-tung have replaced Confucian learning. Even 'thought-control' has its place in Chinese history. China, these experts argue, is a vast country, with enormous capacity for absorption. The Chinese have conquered their conquerors before, they will do it again.

The student of communism can hardly argue with the expert sinologist on the latter's ground. Whether the Chinese are 'capable of appreciating freedom' I would certainly never presume to decide. This argument has been and is used about other peoples besides the Chinese, and it always seems to me a dubious one. That the Chinese are not interested in western parliamentarism one may readily concede. That they are willing to give political power to their rulers is probable: that they are ready to surrender their personal lives, and accept the savage and systematic destruction of the values associated for millennia with the Chinese family, even one whose knowledge of Chinese history is scanty and third-hand, may venture to doubt. The comparison between the communist party leaders and the traditional Chinese scholar administrators is

[1] The most sophisticated and learned presentation of this case is C. P. Fitzgerald, *Revolution in China*, 1952. It is a brilliant work, of great value, not only to the orientalist, but to the student of communism. I presume however to believe that its basic political argument is wrong.

[2] Liu Pang, who founded the Han dynasty in 206 B.C., and Chu Yüan-chang, who united China and liberated it from the Mongols in A.D. 1368, were both peasants' sons. See Fitzgerald, *China: a short cultural history*, pp. 149–52, 453–4.

not entirely convincing. The honeymoon between the party and the intelligentsia broke down in 1950. The party cadres are as distinct from the intelligentsia as they are from the peasants or from the workers. They are a caste outside and above social classes. The distinctive characteristic of the communist is an ideology which is neither of Chinese origin nor confined in its application to China.

Should the communist regime survive for several generations in China, then it is probable that it would become 'more Chinese', and that ultimately China would conquer her conquerors. But meanwhile the communist leaders possess an efficient coercive machine, well designed to mobilise the Chinese people for the purposes of world communism. The actions of Mao Tse-tung since he assumed power suggest that it would be prudent to assume that for the predictable future his regime will show itself 'more communist than Chinese'.

PEKING AND MOSCOW

If the regime of Mao Tse-tung remains more communist than Chinese, it does not necessarily follow that it will be subservient to Moscow.

The factor which caused the breach between Moscow and Tito, and which enabled Tito to survive the breach, is present also in China. The Chinese communists won their own victory. During the long years of guerrilla and civil war Mao created his own military and civil state machine. The party officials, army officers and civil bureaucrats who owe their careers to Mao, would place their loyalty to Mao before their loyalty to Moscow, should they be compelled to choose. But whether they will be compelled, depends on the decisions of Moscow and of Mao. The existence of a state machine built without the interference of Moscow is not inevitably a cause of conflict. The conflict occurred in the case of Yugoslavia because Moscow chose to provoke it. Though Moscow has never openly admitted that it made a mistake, it is probable that it knows it did. The evidence suggests that the Soviet leaders are extremely anxious to avoid any breach with the Chinese. Nor does Mao appear to desire a breach. Yet objective causes of conflict certainly exist.

The most obvious concern the relations of the Soviet and Chinese states. Russian imperialism is an old enemy of China, and has threatened it in Mongolia, Sinkiang and Manchuria. China has accepted the independence of the Mongolian People's Republic, which in all but name is a part of the Soviet Union. In Sinkiang, where for many years Soviet influence was predominant, Chinese authority appears to have been established.[1] Far more important than these two large but sparsely populated regions is Manchuria. Its population is overwhelmingly Chinese and it has great industrial and agricultural wealth. It forms a bulge separating eastern Siberia from the Far Eastern territories of the Soviet Union. Through it run railways, of which one is far the shortest link between Moscow and Vladivostok, and the other is Russia's outlet to the China seas. Not only the future of Port Arthur and Dairen, but the management of the railways, are serious sources of friction for the future. Russia is in fact the only 'imperialist Power' which by 'unequal treaty' still maintains economic and strategic advantages on Chinese soil.[2]

Against the conflicting interests must be set the common interests. Whether or not the Soviet leaders engineered the Korean war, it has certainly benefited them by embroiling China in armed conflict with the West. The whole modern history of China shows not America but Russia to be China's enemy, but today it is American troops that are fighting Chinese near the frontiers of China, and American naval power that prevents China from reconquering Formosa. In the south sympathy for a communist movement and traditional Chinese imperialism combine to commend support to the Vietminh forces at war with France. As long as America and her allies defend Korea and Indochina from communist invasion, China will regard the West as its enemy and Russia as its friend. But the West cannot take the risk of abandoning Korea or Indochina to communism, for this would mean that Japan, Malaya and Indonesia were in danger, and both Australia's contact

[1] Sinkiang, whose people are mainly of Turkish extraction, akin to the people of Russian Turkestan, passed from Soviet to Kuomintang control in 1941. From 1944 to 1948 a compromise between Moscow and the Kuomintang made possible an autonomous regime under which the local people came nearer to governing themselves than they had for many generations. With the victory of the communists in China, the Soviet government no longer had an interest in supporting Turkish autonomists. It handed over the province to the tender mercies of the Chinese, sacrificing those whom it had earlier supported, when Chinese centralist rule had meant Kuomintang rule. This story has been told at some length by one of the participants, Mehmet Emin Buğra, in a book entitled, *Doğu Türkistan*, published in Instanbul, 1952, which is reviewed at length in *Türkeli*, 1952, No. 5–6. Since the victory of Mao, China has offered Sinkiang the Bolshevik type of 'autonomy'. The mineral resources of Sinkiang, which include oil, are likely to be important for Mao's industrialisation plans. It is not improbable that Sinkiang will be an apple of discord between Moscow and Peking.

[2] See above, p. 272, footnote. The management of the Manchurian railways was formally restored by the Soviet authorities to the Chinese at the end of 1952. It would however be rash to assume that this has ended all friction.

with the West and America's position in the Pacific threatened.

This situation can be changed only by the reappearance of Japan as a major Power. This would take part of the burden from America and her European allies, and would place a burden on Russia. At present Russia, freed by the preponderance of China in eastern Asia from any major commitment in that area, has her hands free for any action or any pressure she may choose to exert in Europe or the Middle East. The reappearance of Japan would tie down a part of Russia's forces and energies in the East. It would also give China a freedom of choice which she does not at present possess. Japan would not only discourage Chinese aggression but would also be a potential trade partner to free her from excessive dependence on Russia. The threefold conflict of interest between Russia, China and Japan in the Manchuria-Korea area should give a certain freedom of manœuvre to the diplomacy both of the Western Powers and of China. But until Japan has been restored as a major Power, international factors are likely to maintain the dependence of China on Russia.

The second factor of potential conflict between Moscow and Peking concerns the relationship between the two communist parties. Hitherto we have stressed the similarities between the Soviet and the Chinese parties. The internal structure, the method of enlisting mass support, the conduct of revolution and civil war, and the role of the party in the state machine after victory are strikingly similar in both countries. Yet there are differences of *nuance* which may prove significant.

The social composition of the Chinese party has not been very different from that of the Russian. In both, the intelligentsia has provided a large proportion of the leaders, and the recruits have come from both peasants and workers. In both, the cadres of the party have been a professional caste outside social class. But though both parties have been similarly composed, the language used about their social composition has been different. The Russian leaders have always insisted that their party is the party of the proletariat, and have indeed made great efforts to fill its ranks with industrial workers. The Chinese leaders have not only failed to recruit many industrial workers, but have even stated that this is not very important. In his report to the 7th Congress of the party, in May 1945, Liu Shao-chi stated that although the party had only a small percentage of industrial workers among its members, this state of affairs 'cannot alter the fact that our party is a political party of the proletariat'. He enumerated six factors which proved the proletarian character of the party: all were political or ideological, none were social. He summed up:

> The social origin of the party membership cannot determine every-thing. The determining factors are our party's political struggles and political life, its ideological education and its ideological and political leadership.[1]

These words describe a state of affairs that exists in other com-munist parties besides the Chinese, but are not openly stated by leaders of those parties.

Mao Tse-tung has also persisted in his unorthodox views about the peasants, first expressed in his 1927 report from Hunan province.[2] In 1940 he wrote: 'The force constituted by the peasants is the principal force of the Chinese revolution.'[3] A similar remark by Tito in 1946 was treated in the Cominform statement as a major heresy.[4]

Another difference lies in the use of the purge in the Chinese and Soviet parties. Mao was ruthless in the elimination of rivals in the early period of his guerrilla action.[5] In the late 1930's however the Chinese party avoided the convulsions of the *Yezhovshchina*. Mao successfully outmanœuvred such potential rivals as Li Li-san and Wang Ming, but he did not physically destroy them: both men occupied important positions in the new regime in 1950.[6] In 1941–2 the party embarked on a purge which became known as *cheng feng*, or 'Rectification of three styles'. The *locus classicus* of this campaign is a lecture given in July 1941 by Liu Shao-chi to the Party School for Central China and published under the title *On Inner-party Struggle*.[7] The main emphasis in this work is on the need to distinguish between 'principled' and 'unprincipled' struggles within the party, to concentrate argument on matters of real importance and not on personal struggles, to avoid confusion of political and personal issues. Though independent information on the life of the party in these years is lacking, the impression is that Mao was eager to avoid the frantic heresy-hunting which had devastated the Soviet party. There is certainly no evidence that a

[1] Liu Shao-chi, op. cit., p. 18.
[2] Fairbank, Schwarz and Brandt, op. cit., p. 86. See above, p. 150.
[3] Mao Tse-tung, op. cit., p. 78 (from Mao's *New Democracy* article of 15th January 1940).
[4] See above, pp. 150, 263.
[5] Schwarz, op. cit., pp. 177–8.
[6] Li Li-san was a member of the *Politburo* in 1947. In 1949 he was first vice-chair-man of the All-China Labour Federation. Wang Ming (Chen Shao-yu) is a member of the Central Committee and a judge of the Supreme Court.
[7] Liu Shao-chi, *On Inner Party Struggle*, Foreign Language Press, Peking, 1951.

major purge took place within the Chinese party. This difference in practice between the two parties is not a trivial detail.

A third difference is the fact that much greater adulation is extended to Mao than to Stalin. The ideology of the party is stated to be the Thought of Mao Tse-tung, which adapts the teachings of Marx and Lenin to Chinese conditions. Stalin is praised as the great leader of a friendly great country, but not as the 'teacher of genius of all progressive humanity'. In fact, Marx and Lenin are the prophets, and Stalin and Mao are their two great pupils, of equal status. The cult of Mao in China is similar to the cult of Stalin in Russia. History is falsified in the same way. Mao is treated as the leader of the revolution from the beginning, though in fact he was only a secondary figure until the end of the 1920's: similarly Stalin's secondary though distinguished role in the Russian civil war is inflated by Soviet historians. Large claims are made for Mao:

> Our comrade Mao Tse-tung is not only the greatest revolutionary and statesman in Chinese history, but also its greatest theoretician and scientist. . . . In the theoretical field, he was boldly creative, discarding certain specific Marxist principles and conclusions that were obsolete or incompatible with the concrete conditions in China, and replacing them with new principles and new conclusions that are compatible with China's new historical conditions.[1]

Until these words were said, only Stalin had been considered to have the authority to 'discard Marxist principles'.

This challenge to the Pope of communism was followed by a challenge to the monopoly of political wisdom claimed by the Bolshevik party. In November 1949 the same Liu Shao-chi, speaking as Head of the Chinese trade unions to the Trade Union Conference of Asian and Australasian countries in Peking, after paying tribute to the example given by the Bolshevik party to the communist parties of industrial European countries,[2] stated:

[1] Liu Shao-chi, *On the Party*, pp. 33–4.
[2] Whether this is a piece of flattery intended as a consolation prize, or whether the Chinese communists really believe that Russia was a typical industrial country, pointing the way for the proletariat of Europe, is not clear. In fact, as opposed to Marxist theology, Russia was an example not for countries of advanced industrial society but for countries of backward society (see above, pp. 2–9, and below, pp. 332–42). The differences between the social, cultural and political conditions of China in 1949, and of Russia in 1917, are of course very great. But from the point of view of the conditions for seizure of power, the differences between them are far less significant than the similarities. The Russian and Chinese revolutions are two species of the same genus. The prestige as prophets of Stalin and of Mao requires the former to stress the similarities, the latter the differences. Conflicts on the prestige of prophets can however have far-reaching consequences.

The path taken by the Chinese people in defeating imperialism and in founding the People's Republic of China is the path that must be taken by the peoples of the various colonial and semi-colonial countries in their fight for national independence and people's democracy.

It can hardly be imagined that this claim was acceptable to the Soviet leaders. Though outwardly polite, and determined to avoid a breach with China, it is probable that they will resist the claim in practice.[1]

One of the most experienced and penetrating observers of world communism has recently expressed the view that rivalries of this sort are today a more potent source of international conflict than any other of the older types of dispute concerning territory, strategical or economic resources. 'The great power-political struggles of the totalitarian epoch are fought out over control of the Party.'[2] Though he in his turn probably underestimates the importance of traditional forms of imperialism, he is certainly right to emphasise this new factor. He is also right to point out that 'the more basic a political conflict, the longer it takes to appear on the surface—precisely because the implications are so terrifying'. Though relations between Moscow and Peking may today be excellent, and though both may be most profoundly convinced that they will remain the best of friends, yet these fundamental factors of state interest, ideology and party organisation may yet produce the irreparable rupture.[3] There is nothing that the non-communist world can do to influence the protagonists, though it can influence the environment in which they move—for example, by its handling of Japan, India and Indonesia. The first duty of western statesmen, in the face of the complex of problems created by the Chinese Revolution, is to be neither optimists nor pessimists, neither sentimental nor vindictive, but to preserve a cool temper and an open mind.

[1] Hitherto no official Soviet spokesman has denounced the Liu doctrine. It is ignored in an essay on Asian national liberation struggles by the Orientalist E. M. Zhukov, who explains Asian revolutionary successes in terms of the lessons of the October Revolution and the history of the Bolshevik party. (*Crisis of the Colonial system*— reports presented in 1949 to the Pacific Institute of the Academy of Sciences, U.S.S.R. Published in Bombay, 1951). A report by the same Zhukov to a meeting of the Soviet Academy of Sciences, in the autumn of 1951, emphasised that the Chinese example could not be too literally applied to other Asian countries. *Izvestiya Akademii Nauk S.S.S.R.*, (*Seziya istozii i filosufii*), Vol. 9, Part I (1952), pp. 80–7.

[2] Franz Borkenau, *The Twentieth Century*, August 1952, article entitled 'Mao Tse-tung'.

[3] The death of Stalin, and the succession of lesser men, only reinforces these arguments.

CHAPTER FIFTEEN

Communism outside the Zone

THE progress and prospects of communism since the war outside the communist zone (Russia, Eastern Europe and China) can most conveniently be considered by five regions —Europe, Asia, the Middle East, Africa and Latin America.

Three small European countries—Finland, Greece and Austria —though subjected to heavy communist pressure and geographically exposed to attack from Russia or her satellites, have successfully resisted. In northern and north-western Europe communist influence has been negligible. Two great western countries, France and Italy, have large communist parties, sure of a numerous poll at elections to central and local government bodies, yet unable to seize power either by constitutional methods or by force.

In Asia, the south-eastern states, internally weak and geographically exposed, have some of the characteristics historically associated with the south-eastern corner of Europe—the Balkan Peninsula. They remain a promising field for communist action. The two great non-communist independent states of Asia, India and Japan, have not yet faced a serious communist bid for power, yet their economic and social problems provide grounds for alarm to their friends and for hope to communist or other subversive elements. The Middle Eastern countries are socially unsound and politically unstable, but with the exception of Persia they have not yet produced a strong communist movement. In tropical Africa revolutionary politics have made their first appearance, but communist influence is still negligible. In Latin America the old social and racial conflicts remain unsolved, while industrial development has increased the importance of the working class. Communism is still a small force, but it has gained ground.

FRANCE

At the first parliamentary election in liberated France, held in October 1945, the communists won 26 per cent of the poll, the socialists and their dependents 25 per cent and the new party of democratic Catholicism, _the *Mouvement Républicain Populaire* (M.R.P.), 24 per cent. Communists and socialists together would have had a bare majority in the Assembly, and could thus have formed a government alone. This the communists proposed to the socialists. Within the socialist party there was strong feeling in favour of common action with the communists. Both during the occupation and after the liberation there had even been talk of a fusion of the two parties. In December 1944 a permanent *Comité d'entente* had been set up to consider how to increase co-operation with the avowed ultimate aim of complete political unity of the working class. During 1945 it became clear that the differences were too great for fusion to be a practical project. But the proposal for a coalition of the 'two Marxist parties' in October was attractive. Only the personal authority of the veteran Léon Blum persuaded the socialist leaders to decline it, and to insist instead on a coalition of the three main parties—communists, socialists and M.R.P. This decision of the socialists was a turning-point in French history. It was due partly to unwillingness to provoke a direct conflict with General de Gaulle, whose prestige was immense throughout France: it may indeed be doubted whether a communist-socialist Government could have withstood the General with success. It is also probable that the advice of the British Labour Party, which had come to power two months earlier, also influenced the socialists. But probably the main reason was unwillingness to accept an embrace whose probable consequences to socialists were already deducible from the experience of Eastern Europe.

The controversy on the new Constitution of France filled a whole year. At first the socialists were nearer to the M.R.P. than to the communists, but in January 1946 they veered to the side of the communists. The resignation of General de Gaulle a few days later strengthened their desire to co-operate. The first draft, which obtained a majority in the Assembly on 19th April 1946, was the work of the communists and socialists. It was however rejected by the popular referendum of 5th May, by 53 per cent to 47 per cent. In the second Constituent Assembly, elected on 2nd June, the communists again had 26 per cent of the poll, but the socialist vote fell to 21 per cent while that of M.R.P. rose to 28 per cent. The second Assembly produced a document which was a compromise between the claims of the communists and of the M.R.P. These two parties, who together with the socialists had shared power for the last year in an uneasy coalition, were brought together by common fear of De Gaulle, who wished the President of the Republic to have greater powers than any of the three governmental parties were prepared to grant. The second draft Constitution, though supported by the leaders of all three parties, was accepted at the popular referendum of 13th October 1946 only by a small majority (53 per cent of the poll).

At the election to the National Assembly, the first under the new Constitution, held on 10th November, the communists increased their vote to 28 per cent of the poll, while that of the M.R.P. fell to 26 per cent and that of the socialists to 18 per cent. In this Assembly communists and socialists together would not have had a majority, even if the socialists had been willing to form a ministry alone with the communists. A three-party coalition remained the only possibility. The communists, as the largest single party, demanded the Premiership. This was however refused by the majority of the Assembly, though supported by a number of socialist deputies. During their participation in the government— from October 1945 to May 1947, with the exception of two weeks in January 1947—the communists held a Vice-Premiership (Maurice Thorez, the party's leader), and for various periods the Ministries of Industrial Production, Armaments, National Economy and Labour. They had little success in infiltrating the machinery of state. They had few supporters in the higher civil service. Communist ministers gave a new importance to the old institution of the *cabinet du ministre*:[1] its numbers were greatly increased, and it became in fact a sort of soviet of political commissars within departments whose heads were communists, composed of persons selected by the party to advise the Minister and supervise the work of his department. When the communists left the government, however, these unofficial advisers went with them: they left left no permanent mark on the French political system.

From the beginning the communists had found it difficult to take part in governments which they did not control. The traditional communist view of parliaments was that they were a useful forum for propaganda: communist deputies must regard themselves not as legislators but as emissaries of the proletariat within the citadel of the bourgeoisie, their duty to unmask the hollow sham

---

[1] The *chef du cabinet* has some similarity to a private parliamentary secretary in the British system, but his influence already in the Third Republic was more considerable. The communist ministers brought a whole team of party stalwarts, to watch the minister on behalf of the party, preserve his ideological purity, and when possible to take over the functions of his leading civil servants.

of bourgeois democracy. It was not easy to discard this mentality. Denunciation and demagogy were easier and more enjoyable than responsibility. In 1947 the communists' attitude became increasingly equivocal: their leaders remained in the cabinet, but party members both inside and outside the Assembly spoke against the government's policy. The main points of disagreement were the situation in Indochina, the revolt in Madagascar, and wage problems. At the end of April 1947 the communist deputies voted against the government's wage policy, and the *Politburo* of the party made an official statement of support for the workers of the nationalised Renault motor works who were on strike. The communist ministers refused to resign from the government, so the Premier, the socialist Ramadier, dismissed them.

During the summer the communists were in opposition, but in the autumn, after the introduction of the Marshall Plan and the creation of the Cominform, their attacks became more bitter. Control of the C.G.T. was used to organise widespread strikes in the winters of 1947–8 and 1948–9. In some cases strikers used personal violence and committed sabotage, but the government did not lose control of the situation.

The French Communist Party was and remains an impressive force. It can bring to the polls, at a parliamentary election, about 5,000,000 voters, nearly a quarter of the electorate and more than a quarter of those who vote. At the election of June 1951, its vote fell only by one-tenth, though the new electoral law considerably reduced the number of its seats in the new Assembly. The bulk of the working class remained in the C.G.T., which it still controlled. Yet events have shown that it is incapable of seizing power. It has no hope of winning a majority by constitutional means, either through its own strength or through a coalition. It has even less hope of victory by force: the armed forces, police and state machine are in its enemies' hands, and the trade unions are no substitute for these. But though it cannot get power, the party can be a valuable rearguard of Moscow. It can make itself a serious nuisance, both in the industrial and the political field.

The strike weapon can be used, and has been used, to damage economic recovery, and thereby weaken France's defences. But the strike weapon, when misused, brings diminishing returns. The French workers are prepared to strike on behalf of their material interests, when there is a good chance that their demands will be accepted. Strikes for political reasons are less attractive to them. In 1951 and 1952 the response of the workers to political strikes was disappointing, though most workers still remained within the C.G.T. The constant demands of Moscow must have embarrassed the French communist leaders, who could not be unaware that the enthusiasm and sacrifice that the workers might offer for supreme efforts in time of crisis cannot be given to repeated petty efforts that can promise neither victory nor advantage.

The communists' political hold over the French workers is most useful to them through its effect on the socialists. The socialists can only hope to become once more a great and powerful party if they can recover working-class votes from the communists. But this they can never do if the communists outbid them in left-wing slogans and social demagogy. To maintain its present following, let alone increase it, the socialist party must compete with communist demagogy: it must show itself intransigent in all matters affecting workers' interests and that old fetish of the French left, secular education. It must always be denouncing both the industrialists and the Church. This makes it a difficult partner in any coalition, but without socialist support, or at least neutrality, governments are desperately weak.

The French workers are not revolutionary. They vote communist for the same reason that British workers vote Labour—because they have come to think of the party as *their* party, the party that stands for their interests. And without doubt they need someone to defend their interests, for though France has made a remarkable economic recovery since 1945, the workers have suffered and still suffer real hardship. The tragedy is that the desire to defend their legitimate interests has since 1945 caused French workers to vote for a party whose internal organisation gives absolute control to its leaders, and whose leaders are mainly concerned with the interests not of the French workers but of Soviet imperialism.

The limits within which parliamentary government operates under the Fourth Republic are much narrower than under the Third. By voting communist, about a quarter of the French nation places itself outside national politics altogether. The obvious result of this is to shift the political centre of gravity to the right. But for a time a section of the right also placed itself outside national politics. The refusal of General de Gaulle's *Rassemblement du peuple français* to enter a coalition with other parties pressed the limits back leftwards. France could only be governed if socialists, Catholic democrats and moderate conservatives would co-operate. But the socialists could co-operate with centre and moderate right only if they would abandon their hope of winning working-class votes back from the communists by competing with communist social demagogy. In these conditions it seemed that no government was possible at all. The situation was temporarily saved by a split in the R.P.F. Thirty of the General's followers defied his orders, voted for the conservative Antoine Pinay in March 1952, and seceded from R.P.F. in July. Thus was created a conservative-centre majority which could rule without the socialists. The majority was however far from harmonious, and its leaders seemed little qualified to deal with basic social problems. French politics are marked by a general climate of pessimism. It is this pessimism which undermines the strength of the French state, whose great economic and military resources, together with the skill and courage of its citizens, make it potentially a Great, even if not a Giant Power. Frenchmen are weak only because they think that they are. This is in the last resort a greater source of strength to the communists than their grip on the C.G.T. or their five million votes.

ITALY

The first government of liberated Italy reflected the strength of the left in the industrial north. The Actionist Parri was Premier, the communist leader Togliatti was Minister of Justice, while another communist, Scoccimarro, was Minister of Finance. In December 1945 however Parri was succeeded by the Christian Democrat Alcide de Gasperi. This government too was a coalition, based on the same parties. The communists retained their ministries. But the balance of power had shifted to the right. The exalted 'left' mood of the liberation days, when large numbers even of normally conservative-minded Italians had been fired by the vision of a 'new Risorgimento', was rapidly passing away.

In June 1946 a referendum to choose between Monarchy and Republic, and a general election to a Constituent Assembly, were held on the same day. The Republic prevailed, by 12·7 million to 10·7 million votes. In the election the Christian Democrats won 35 per cent of the poll, Socialists 21 per cent and Communists 19 per cent.

At the socialist congress, held in Florence earlier in the year, the different trends of Italian socialism appeared once more united: it seemed that the lessons of the disastrous years 1919–22 had been learned.[1] But the unity did not last. The Italian socialists, like their

[1] See above, pp. 70–1.

French comrades, had to decide their attitude to the communists. The slogan 'working-class unity' was extremely powerful. Though fusion with the communists in one party was not an immediate possibility, a majority of the Italian socialists favoured at least close co-operation. The result was a 'Pact of unity of action' made, with the approval of the majority, by the socialist leader Nenni. The Pact caused a split in the party. In January 1947 one of its leaders, Saragat, formed a separate party, which included somewhat less than half the socialist members of the Constituent Assembly. The result of the split was that the socialists became a second-rate political force, and the Communist Party acquired indisputable leadership of the Italian working class.

During the first months of 1947 friction between left and right in the cabinet increased. The preparation of a Constitution inevitably brought important disagreements. The most difficult issues concerned the relations between Church and State. The Christian Democrats insisted that the Lateran Treaties, made by Mussolini with the Vatican, be incorporated in the Constitution. On this the communists, opportunists as ever, were willing to support them, while the non-communist left voted against. On the issues of civil marriage and state subsidies to private schools, the whole left wing opposed the Christian Democrats, and won its case.[1] Economic disputes proved more serious than constitutional. Premier de Gasperi's proposed measures against inflation were opposed by the left. The Premier wished to strengthen his position by including in the cabinet politicians of the right or 'non-party experts' from the business class. The communists and socialists, as was to be expected, fiercely opposed this. On 14th May de Gasperi resigned. After a long 'governmental crisis', he formed a new government on 31st May, with no socialists or communists and consisting almost entirely of Christian Democrats.

The formation of an Italian government without communists coincided in time with the similar event in France and with the opposite event in Hungary.[2] It preceded by four months the formation of the Cominform and the adoption of an openly anti-

[1] V. Falzone, F. Palermo and F. Cosentino, *La Costituzione della repubblica italiana*, Rome, 1948, pp. 65–77, contains a summary of the debates in the Constituent Assembly on marriage and the family.

[2] The only element of truth in the accusation of a 'plot', which the Hungarian communists and their Soviet patrons brought against the Hungarian Small Farmers' Party, and which they made the excuse for arresting Béla Kovács and dismissing Premier Ferenc Nagy (see above, p. 251), was that some of the Small Farmers' leaders had *talked* of the possibility of ending the coalition government (with socialists and communists) and using their legal 57 per cent majority in Parliament to form a one-party ministry.

western line by all communist parties. It was only after the latter event that the Italian communists assumed a more militant posture. In November 1947 they organised demonstrations and strikes, as part of the general communist offensive in Western Europe against the Marshall Plan. Its chief episodes were armed clashes with police in the southern towns of Bari and Bitonto, the seizure of public buildings by communist-led ex-Partisans in Milan on 28th November, and a two-day general strike in Rome on 11th–12th December. Damage to the economy was small, and the government remained calm and preserved order. The communists' control of the trade union movement (C.G.I.L.) gave them a powerful weapon, but it was not adequate to break the state machine.

During the winter of 1947–8, and in preparation for the first parliamentary election under the new Constitution—which was due in April 1948—the communists busily built extra-parliamentary 'mass organisations'.

The first were the Works' Councils (*Consigli di gestione*). The communists claimed that these should not merely defend the interests of the workers in each factory, but should be responsible for all management, including the purchase of raw materials and sale of the manufactured product. At a congress of *consigli* representatives, held in Milan in November 1947, the former leader of the communist resistance, Longo, argued that they must take over control from the factory owners, who were 'incapable of running their own enterprises'. These tactics recall Lenin's use of factory committees in Russian industry in the summer of 1917. They also recall the ideas of Gramsci and his Turin group of communists during the sit-in strike wave of August 1920.

The second mass organisation was designed for the peasants. In December the communists organised in Bologna a 'Constituent Assembly of the Land', with peasant delegates from various parts of Italy. The peasants were urged to 'make their '48',[1] to seize the land from the landlords. The communist agricultural expert Sereni urged that 'committees of the land' be formed in every village in the country.[2] This too recalled Russian experience. The committees

---

[1] The communists did their best, by sentimental revolutionary rhetoric, to turn to their advantage the centenary of the Italian revolutions.

[2] Sereni's interesting book on the land question in Italy, *La questione agraria nella rinascita nazionale italiana*, Rome, 1946, suffers from an all too obvious attempt to fit the Italian agrarian scene into a Procrustean bed made of Lenin's analysis in 1898 of the Russian economy—*The development of capitalism in Russia*. But that there are striking similarities between the economy and society of Imperial Russia and that of the Italian South it would be foolish to deny.

were to be soviets of peasants' deputies, to put revolutionary pressure on the government. The communists made considerable progress among the peasants. The agricultural labourers of Emilia and the Po valley, old strongholds of Italian socialism, were now the most reliable forces of the communists. More surprisingly, the share-cropping peasants of Tuscany, not a region of great poverty or of long-standing class antagonism, supported the communists. In the South, where peasant poverty was comparable with that of the worst districts of Spain or the Balkans, and great estates belonged to landlords, many of whom were absentees, the influence of the Church and the despotic power of the administration checked, but did not entirely prevent, progress by the communists. The inability of the Christian Democrats, divided between their left and right wings, to enact a radical land reform, also favoured the communists.

Other communist-controlled 'mass organisations', such as the League of Democratic Communes, the Renaissance of the South, and the Association of Partisans (A.N.P.I.), played a lesser part.

At the April 1948 election the Christian Democrats, supported by the influence of the Church throughout this very Catholic country, won 48 per cent of the poll, the People's Democratic Front (communists and Nenni socialists) 32 per cent. It was now clear that the Italian communists would not obtain power either by constitutional or by violent means. The 'mass organisations' had failed to deliver the votes, and would certainly not make a victorious revolution. When in July 1948 an attempt was made on the life of Togliatti, the communists through C.G.I.L. declared a general strike, and minor acts of insurrection took place in Tuscany, Genoa and Turin. The machinery of government was never in danger, and after two days the communists called off the strike. Further strikes in the winter of 1948–9 and since have had even less effect.

Like their French comrades, however, the Italian communists are an important nuisance. They have retained the support of a large majority of the Italian working class. The example of Tito had small effect in Italy. The defection of two leading Emilia communists, Cucchi and Magnani, in 1950 on 'nationalist' grounds, did not produce a split in the party. Nor has either branch of Italian socialism proved a serious rival. The Nenni group for a time reasserted a measure of independence from the communists. During 1952 however the communists successfully infiltrated their agents into it. On all major policy issues the Nenni socialists have supported the communists. The right socialists have also been weakened by internal dissensions. The C.G.I.L., like the C.G.T. in France, remains in communist hands, but like its French counterpart it knows that there is a limit to the demands it can make on its members for purely political strikes.

The rise of parties of the right, and the revival of fascism, which have been features of the last years, have hitherto done more good than harm to the communists. The fascists hate the communists, but they also hate the Western Powers and the Atlantic Pact, the principal objects of communist hatred. The Italian scene has some resemblance with the German scene of 1932. In Italy the centre, both socialist and non-socialist, is weaker than in France, and democratic outlook and habits are much less secure. It is not impossible that unbridled demagogy on extreme left and extreme right may destroy Italian democracy. But whether this would benefit the communists is by no means certain. Here again the example of Germany in 1932 should be borne in mind.

GREECE, FINLAND AND AUSTRIA

For the first year after the Varkiza agreement Greece was ruled by moderate and liberal, though unrepresentative, governments, under which freedom of speech, assembly, press and organisation nominally existed for all, including communists. In practice these freedoms were not observed outside Athens and a few provincial cities. In the small towns and villages police and civil administration were in the hands of the right, and those suspected of left sympathies, whether communist or not, were liable to various types of persecution. This tendency was still more marked after the election of 31st March 1946, which gave a large majority to the right-wing People's Party.

In the autumn the communists once more resorted to open rebellion, and soon set up a 'liberated territory' in Macedonia. This revival of civil war preceded by a year the creation of the Cominform and the world-wide abandonment by communist parties of the Popular Front policy. This suggests that the decision was a response to conditions in Greece rather than to a world-wide communist directive. No doubt the subsequent development of the antagonism between Soviet Russia and the West would in due course have recreated the armed conflict in Greece whatever Greek governments did or did not do: the fact that the conflict broke out in the autumn of 1946 was probably due to the repressive policy of the People's Party government.[1]

The Greek civil war lasted three years. In the areas that they held, the communists undoubtedly enjoyed the support of a part of the population, and compelled by terror the aid of the rest. Supplies sent from the Soviet satellite states through Yugoslavia, Albania and Bulgaria enabled the rebels to hold out, but American aid to the Greek government was more effective. The breach between Tito and the Cominform brought dissensions among the Greek communist leaders, and the closing of the Yugoslav-Greek frontier in July 1949 was a heavy blow. By the end of 1949 the Greek national army had won the war. Marshal Papagos' government, formed in December 1952, is more stable than its predecessors. But widespread poverty still offers communism good opportunities.

In Finland the first post-war government was a coalition, in which the communists played an important part. At the election of 1945 the Popular Democratic League, a group controlled by the communists, won 48 seats out of 200, while the socialists won 50 and the Agrarians 49. The Popular Democratic leader Pekkala became Premier, and the Ministry of the Interior was given to Leino, a communist and the son-in-law of the 'Premier' of Terijoki of 1939, Otto Willi Kuusinen. Events in Finland did not however follow the East European model. Leino failed to pack the State (political) Police with communists. In May 1948 Leino was forced by a vote of censure in parliament to resign the Ministry. In the second parliamentary election later in the same year, the Popular Democrats won only 38 seats, while the Socialists won 54 and the Agrarians 56. The new government was formed by the Social Democrats alone. It was succeeded in the spring of 1950 by a coalition dominated by the Agrarians, to be replaced early in 1951 by a coalition between the two major parties, Agrarians and Social Democrats. Since 1948 there have been no communists in a Finnish government.

In the trade unions the Finnish communists seized some key positions immediately after the war, but the social democrats successfully resisted them, and by 1948 had a slight majority in the central trade union council, which was further increased by the

[1] Dr. Borkenau, op. cit., considers it axiomatic that the revolt was ordered from Moscow, and regards this as evidence of the ascendancy of the extremist element within the Soviet *Politburo*, whose leader he believes was Zhdanov. He may well be right, but hard evidence is needed.

trade union elections of 1951. In short, political organisation and civil liberties in Finland have been throughout these years similar to those prevailing in Scandinavia. The Finnish communists are an important party, with genuine support from a large minority of the working class, which sees in them the heirs to the revolutionary tradition of 1918. But they have absolutely no prospect of winning a majority at a parliamentary election, or of persuading other parties to form with them a coalition which they would dominate, or of seizing power by force without foreign aid. Communist influence in the trade unions is a serious nuisance. Co-ordinated action by communist unions and by the Soviet government through its trade treaty with Finland can damage the Finnish economy,[1] but cannot reduce the country to economic collapse.

That the Finns were able not only to escape sovietisation but even to push the communists out of positions that they had acquired, was due to two sets of reasons, external and internal.

The external reasons are related to the fact that Soviet Russia has not felt it necessary to dominate Finland. Having secured Finland's dependence on them by disarmament and by a treaty of mutual aid signed in 1948, the Soviet leaders have had no cause to fear that Finland could become a base for action against Soviet territory. Unlike the countries to the south of the Baltic, Finland does not lie on the main land routes to the west. The Soviet government appears if not to value Swedish goodwill, at least to wish to preserve Swedish neutrality: a Soviet military occupation of Finland would almost certainly drive Sweden to join the Atlantic Pact. Finally the Soviet military leaders know how unpleasant a job it is, how costly in manpower, to hold down Finns, a nation capable of pitiless guerrilla in their forests.

The internal reasons concern the social structure and the political and cultural traditions of Finland. Social classes are well balanced in Finland, and the habit of parliamentary government is deeply rooted. The Finns possess the tough individualism of a border Protestant nation. Some of these advantages the Czechs also had, but the cultural background of the two nations is very different. In particular the Finns have long been impervious—to the point of wilful ignorance—to any sort of Russian cultural influence,

---

[1] The need to provide the goods specified by the reparations agreement caused Finland greatly to develop her metal and engineering industries. These provided large employment, and contributed to a more balanced national economy. Their costs of production were however too high to allow competition in world markets, and the Finnish home market could not absorb their whole output. They were thus at the mercy of the Soviet Union, which by the 1950 trade treaty with Finland undertook to take a large part of their output after the completion of reparations.

while the Czechs were long enamoured of the idealised image which they had created for themselves of Russian culture. Both Czechs and Finns resisted communism from 1945 to 1948. But the Czechs, who had little or no previous experience of Russia, believed her to be their friend and protector, and lowered all cultural and physical barriers to Russian influence: in the last resort their surrender to Gottwald in February 1948 was due to their desire not to oppose their false friend. The Finns, who had had much previous experience of Russia, had good reason to regard her as their enemy, and treated with suspicion any action or initiative associated with Russia. This, and their extraordinary *courage civil* and spirit of national unity, have hitherto saved them. They are of course still completely at Russia's mercy. But they will not surrender.

In Austria a provisional government was set up in April 1945 with the encouragement of the Soviet authorities. The veteran socialist Karl Renner, who had been Chancellor in 1918, was given the same post in 1945, but the Ministry of Interior was given to a communist. Renner however soon showed that he was nobody's puppet,[1] and the Austrian Socialist Party, emerging from eleven years of persecution, showed that it still commanded the loyalty of the Viennese workers. At the first parliamentary election, held in March 1946, the communists won only four seats out of 165. They were still represented in the government for a year more, but only by the Minister of Fuel. In the autumn of 1947 they left the government, in accordance with the new tactic introduced by the formation of the Cominform. Their departure made little difference: after it, as before, Austria was ruled by two parties, Socialists and People's Party.[2] The presence of western troops in the greater part of Austria has undoubtedly strengthened its government, and it has been fortunate that the Soviet authorities have not sovietised their zone as they have Eastern Germany. But these external factors do not wholly explain the resistance of Austria to communism. Of equal importance have been the remarkable unity, loyalty and courage of the Austrian Socialist Party and the Austrian working class.

In north-west Europe communists have been uniformly weak.

[1] Renner, who had a long and distinguished career in the service of the Austrian working glass, and was also a pioneer in the study of the nationality problem, was also the author of the delightful phrase that the position of Austria under Quadripartite occupation was like that of a man in a small rowing-boat with four elephants on board. This great socialist statesman died in 1951.

[2] The People's Party is the successor to the old Christian Social Party of Dollfuss, but has cast off the fascist heritage of Dollfuss. In the October 1949 election the communists won five seats, in 1953 four.

The slight gains made in the first post-war elections in the Low Countries, Britain and Scandinavia had been lost by 1950.[1] They possess some nuisance value. Examples are the influence of communists in the British coal-mining trade unions, and the strong communist influence in the Swedish iron and ore mining district of Kiruna.[2] But these are problems of security rather than of national politics.

In Western Germany the communists have been extremely weak. The West German communists still bear the name K.P.D., and are nominally distinct from the S.E.D. of Eastern Germany, though in practice subordinate to it. Even in the most industrial of the *Länder* of the West, North Rhine-Westphalia, the K.P.D. has never had as much as 10 per cent of the votes in any elections. The communists can make themselves a minor economic nuisance by their own efforts, and they can hope to derive advantage, for themselves and for the Soviet Union, from the revival of German nationalism in the West. It is however most improbable that they will be able to control or canalise this nationalism.

SOUTH-EAST ASIA

In Asia outside Russia and China, the best communist successes have been won in the South-East, and even where there have been disappointments for Moscow, the outlook has remained not unpromising.[3]

Differences in the development of the communist movements of the different countries are in part a result of differences in the policies of the returning imperial governments towards the nationalist movements. In Burma, after a first period in which an attempt was made to restore in essentials the pre-war system of colonial administration, the British government decided to accept the demands of the nationalists, and recognised Burmese independence. In Malaya the British government proposed to create

[1] Communists have fared as follows in post-war elections:
  Britain: 1945, 2 seats out of 615; 1950, 1; 1951, none.
  Belgium: 1946, 23 seats out of 202; 1949, 12; 1950, 7.
  Holland: 1946, 10 seats out of 100; 1948, 8; 1952, 6.
  Denmark: 1945, 18 seats out of 148; 1947, 9; 1950, 7.
  Iceland: 1946, 10 seats out of 52; 1949, 7.
  Norway: 1945, 11 seats out of 150; 1949, none.
  Sweden: 1948, 8 seats out of 230; 1952, 5.
[2] The revelations at the Stockholm spy trial of June 1952, that Swedish communists had been collecting information about the most important fortress in Sweden—Boden, which dominates the northern frontier region, through which a Russian land invasion from Finland would come, and which is not far from Kiruna—showed that the danger was not negligible.
[3] A useful general survey of the South-East Asian scene may be found in V. Thompson and R. Adloff, *The Left Wing in South-East Asia*, New York, 1950.

a more or less centralised Malayan Union, in which Malays, Chinese and Indians should have equal rights of citizenship, and the powers of the traditional rulers, the Malay sultans, should be greatly reduced. Opposition from the Malay population caused the British to abandon this policy in favour of a federal organisation that would ensure the supremacy of the Malays. This cost the British much support from the Chinese, and meant that the independence of Malaya would be postponed into the far future. In Indonesia the Dutch authorities tried to re-establish the pre-war regime, modified by reforms that fell short of the minimum demands of the nationalist Republicans, who controlled a large part of Java, but claimed authority over the whole of the Netherlands East Indies. The Dutch supported against the Republicans rival administrations based on the outer islands, and at times took strong military action against the Republicans. The Dutch were however subject to strong pressure in the United Nations, not only from the Soviet bloc but also from several western governments,[1] to cede to Republican demands. In the end Indonesia was recognised in December 1949, by the Dutch and other governments, as an independent Republic including all former Dutch territory except West New Guinea.[2] Events in Indochina in some respects resembled those in Indonesia. The French negotiated with the Vietnamese nationalists of Vietminh. As in the case of Indonesia, the dispute concerned not only the extent of self-government to be granted, but the area which it was to cover. Both sides agreed that the western regions, Cambodia and Laos, should have a distinct status, but Vietminh demanded that the three Vietnamese territories of Tonkin, Annam and Cochin-China be united under a single self-governing authority. The French wished Cochin-China, the wealthiest region containing the largest city of Saigon, to remain separate. Negotiations broke down at the end of 1946, since when the French have been engaged in war against Vietminh. France was not subject to pressure from the United Nations or from her western allies comparable to that which was exercised on the Dutch. This enabled her representatives in Indochina to take a firmer attitude, but the firmer attitude stiffened Vietnamese

---

[1] Especially the United States and Australia.

[2] The Indonesian claim to New Guinea is in fact based on little but geographical proximity. It may be argued that imperialism is disreputable, and that the Dutch have no 'right' to be in New Guinea. But in that case, it is not clear why the Javanese should have a territory whose population have nothing in common with them, and are culturally so backward that they would inevitably be a colonial dependency. But in the view of many Asian nationalists, imperialism ceases to be imperialism if the colour of the skin of those who pursue it is not white.

resistance, and enabled the communist leaders of Vietminh to place themselves at the head of a strong patriotic movement.

Comparison of these four countries seems to justify the view that rigid opposition by a Western Power to national demands can only benefit the communists. The example of Indochina seems conclusive. It does not however follow that satisfaction of nationalist demands will remove the danger of communism. Burma, which received its independence quickly, has suffered more from communist rebellion than Indonesia, whose nationalists had to struggle for independence for more than four years. The case of Malaya is inconclusive. Independence was not granted, but this was at least in part because there was no movement or authority to which it could have been granted.

The timing of communist insurrection in South-East Asia suggests some central co-ordination. Hostilities between French and Vietminh, it is true, began nearly a year before the foundation of the Cominform, and while the communists still held ministries in the French government. The insurrections in Burma, Malaya and Indonesia, however, all began in the summer of 1948, about half a year after the foundation of the Cominform and a few months after a 'South-East Asian Youth Conference', held in Calcutta, and attended by communists from Asia, the Soviet Union and some European countries.

With the advent of the Labour government in Britain, negotiations were opened with the Burmese nationalist leader Aung San. These negotiations caused a split first within the ranks of the Burmese communists, and then between them and the A.F.P.F.L. One communist group, the 'Red Flag', was from the first implacably hostile to the British. The Burma Communist Party ('White Flag'), did not oppose negotiation with the British on principle, but rejected the conditions accepted by Aung San. It was expelled from the A.F.P.F.L. in October 1946. In January 1947 Aung San signed in London an agreement with the British government which gave Burma the substance of independence and allowed her to choose whether to remain within the Commonwealth or to separate completely. On his return to Burma Aung San held an election, won a large majority against communist opposition, and proclaimed Burma an independent republic. The assassination of Aung San and several leading members of the A.F.P.F.L. government in July 1947[1] did not bring the collapse of the regime. A new

---

[1] The victims included the A.F.P.F.L.'s peasant leader, Thakin Mya, and four other ministers.

constitution was adopted in September, and the Burmese Republic came into legal existence, with the consent of the British Parliament, on 1st January 1948. The new government was however very weak. The A.F.P.F.L.'s armed force, the People's Volunteer Organisation (P.V.O.), was well penetrated by communists. When the communists raised rebellion in the summer of 1948, the majority of the P.V.O. followed them. The government also had difficulties with the non-Burmese nationalities, of which the most important were the Karens. The government stressed its devotion to Marxism and admiration for the Soviet Union, and made efforts to appease the communists even at the cost of public security. It was rewarded by implacable hatred from the Burmese communists and cool hostility from Moscow and Peking. The government controlled the main cities, and during 1950 and 1951 extended its authority over most of the country, but was unable to break the communist guerrillas, who for their part were unable to establish a firm 'liberated territory'. In 1951 conditions were sufficiently settled to permit an election to parliament. The A.F.P.F.L. won 135 seats out of 233. The chief legal opposition was the Burma Workers' and Peasants' Party, which in turn was controlled by the communists. Placed between the two colossi of the Asiatic mainland, Burma inclined in foreign policy to India. The Burmese government was stronger than its opponents, but it was far from secure.

In Malaya the first two years after the return of the British were marked by a threefold struggle, within legal channels, between communists, British and the non-communist nationalists.[1] The main field of struggle was the trade unions, which both in Singapore and on the mainland were controlled by the communists.[2] Communist attempts to create 'mass organisations' were more successful among the Chinese than the Malays, but two such bodies were set up, one for each community.[3] Peaceful political struggle ended with armed rebellion by the communists in May 1948. The rebellion continued for the next four years despite the efforts of

[1] The Chinese community was divided in sympathy between Kuomintang and Communists. The Malay nationalists were mainly concerned to prevent the Chinese from acquiring equal political status with the Malays.
[2] During the Labour government in Britain, the British authorities in Malaya made efforts to create non-communist trade unions. They had some success, but up till the outbreak of the rebellion the communist-led unions still had more than half the organised labour both in Singapore and on the mainland.
[3] Among the Malays, the Malay Nationalist Party and the United Malay Front (P.U.T.E.R.A.), both of which seem to have had some contacts with Indonesian communists. Among the Chinese, the Malaya Democratic Union and the Pan-Malayan Council of Joint Action. See Thompson and Adloff, op. cit., pp. 142–7.

considerable forces of British troops. The communist guerrillas were unable to establish fixed 'liberated territories', but they were able to operate in the jungle, and to raid settled areas. They received considerable support, some forced and some willing, from the Chinese community. The racial divisions of Malaya were to some extent a factor favourable to the British, since it was unlikely that the Malays would support Chinese communists. On the other hand the persistence of racial conflict prevents a democratic treatment of political and social problems, which alone could remove the causes of revolt. Thus though the situation in Malaya did not warrant extreme pessimism, optimism was equally impossible.

Indonesia is much the most important country of South-East Asia. Its population of more than 70 millions exceeds that of the whole peninsula, Siam included. Its strategic position is also vital, for it commands Australia's communications with India and with Japan. If friendly to the Western Powers, Indonesia can help to protect Southern Asia against aggression from China. If Indonesia were to join the Moscow-Peking Axis, not only would Malaya be lost, but Australia would be in grave danger. That these are real issues has been shown by Indonesian politics since 1945. Indonesia, it will be remembered, had the earliest Marxist movement in Eastern Asia, and communism was a force in Java before it had gained appreciable support in China. The Javanese communist leaders of the 1920's reappeared in Indonesia after 1945. Yet communism has been remarkably unsuccessful in Indonesia. The reasons for this must be found partly in poor communist leadership, but mainly in the strength of nationalism, reflected in the non-communist parties.

The Javanese nationalist leader Soekarno proclaimed the independence of Indonesia on 17th August, without the consent of the Japanese authorities, but without resistance on their part. From the end of September onwards, first British and then also Dutch troops occupied key positions in Indonesian territory, but in a large part of the interior of Java Soekarno's Republican government held effective authority.[1] During October 1945 several political parties began to take shape in Republican areas.[2] First was the Nationalist Party (P.N.I.), whose leaders were recruited from

[1] The first British troops landed at Batavia (Jakarta) on 29th September. Dutch forces arrived in the following months. The main ports of Java and Sumatra were occupied, and Dutch forces took over Borneo, Celebes, the Moluccas and the smaller islands. The stronghold of the Republicans was central Java, in which the three main towns were Jogjakarta, Surakarta and Madiun.
[2] For the development of the parties, see Kahin, op. cit., pp. 155–61.

the Javanese intelligentsia and from Javanese members of the pre-war civil service. Second was the *Masjoemi*, whose political pro-gramme was specifically related to Islamic principles. It was the largest party, and had the strongest influence among the peasantry. It included both traditional conservatives and modernists with socialist inclinations. The third was the Socialist Party, which had, like its European counterparts, a pro-communist and an indepen-dent wing. Fourth was the Communist Party.

The policy of the Indonesian communists from 1945 to 1948 can be divided into three stages.

The year 1946 was marked by great confusion. The official Communist Party (P.K.I.) was led by insignificant persons, and had little influence. More important was the Trotskist group led by Tan Malaka, who played a leading part in the organisation of a Fighting Front, which exploited anti-Dutch nationalism to pursue an extreme revolutionary policy. The refusal of Socialists and *Masjoemi* to follow this policy brought the disintegration of the Front. An attempted *coup d'état* by Tan Malaka's group in July 1946 was also frustrated.[1] During 1946 Republican territory was ruled by a coalition of *Masjoemi*, P.N.I. and Socialists, with the socialist Sjahrir as Premier. In the summer two experienced com-munist leaders, Sardjono and Alimin,[2] returned from exile, and P.K.I. began to assume the shape of a true Stalinist party.

During 1947 the centre of gravity moved to the left. The agree-ment of Lingaddjati, signed between Dutch and Republicans in November 1946, was strongly criticised by *Masjoemi* and P.N.I., and defended by socialists and P.K.I. The communists had a rep-resentative in the government. In November 1946 they won a big success when the two main trade union organisations were united in one body (S.O.B.S.I.), which from the beginning was dominated by communists. In June 1947 there was a further move to the left when Sjahrir was replaced by the pro-communist socialist Sjari-foeddin. His government fell as a result of opposition to the *Renville* agreement with the Dutch of January 1948.[3]

This marks the second stage. The new administration, composed

---

[1] The activities of Tan Malaka and his group are described in some detail in Kahin, op. cit., pp. 170–8, and 183–92.

[2] Alimin had been one of the leaders of the communist movement of the 1920's. Since the rising of 1926–7 he had been in exile (see above, pp. 135 *n.*, 136). Before returning to Indonesia on 12th August 1946, he had spent some time in Yenan.

[3] Under the *Renville* agreement (so called from the name of the U.S. warship on which it was signed), the Republic's foreign relations were to be handled together with those of the Netherlands. The Republic could not make separate agreements with third Powers.

principally of *Masjoemi* and P.N.I., who had most fiercely attacked the *Renville* agreement, now sought agreement with the Dutch on better terms, hoping to enlist the support of other western governments. The left socialists and communists reverted to a policy of extreme 'anti-imperialism' and anti-westernism, which corresponded with the line adopted by communist parties throughout the world since the formation of the Cominform. The Indonesian communists' aim was at first to draw Indonesia into the Soviet camp rather than to start an Indonesian revolution. An Indonesian communist named Soeripno signed an agreement in Prague in January 1948, for the exchange of consular representatives between Indonesia and the U.S.S.R. The Indonesian government however refused to accept this agreement, which was incompatible with existing engagements to the Dutch and would have involved a breach with the West. At the end of February 1948 Sjarifoeddin formed, together with the P.K.I. and various other left groups, a People's Democratic Front. Sjahrir and the moderate socialists refused to join the Front, and the Socialist Party thereby split, on the same lines as in Italy.[1] During the early summer the P.D.F. made great efforts to persuade the government parties to support a Soviet orientation.

The third stage came in September 1948. The veteran communist Moesso, organiser of the 'Illegal P.K.I.' of 1935,[2] arrived from Prague in August. He declared his aim to be a 'Gottwald policy' of peaceful seizure of power. Early in September he began a provincial tour of anti-government propaganda. Probably without his approval, pro-communist troops opened hostilities against government forces in the Madiun area. Once the fighting had begun, the communist leaders, like the K.P.D. leaders in January 1919, had to see it through. The rising was fairly quickly suppressed by loyal troops, and most of the communist leaders were killed.[3] The confusion which followed was used by the Dutch to occupy most of the territory of the Republic. But United Nations pressure for the second time caused the Dutch to yield.[4]

---

[1] See above, p. 297.   [2] See above, p. 194.

[3] The dead included Alimin, Moesso, Soeripno and Sardjono, as well as Sjarifoeddin, who not only had led his left socialist followers into the P.D.F., but had stated on 29th August 1948 that he himself had been a communist ever since 1935, when he had joined Moesso's 'Illegal P.K.I.'. Whether this claim is true, is a matter of some doubt. The Madiun rebellion is described in great detail, and the actions and policy of the communist leaders are carefully analysed, in Kahin, op. cit., pp. 256–303.

[4] In July 1947, following the formation of the predominantly left-wing Sjarifoeddin government, the Dutch had made their 'first police action', invading Republican territory. This action led to intervention by the U.N. Security Council in August 1947. A U.N. Good Offices Committee visited Indonesia in October, and its efforts contributed to the conclusion of the *Renville* agreement. The Dutch 'second police action'

After a further year of negotiations, Indonesian independence was recognised in December 1949.

In the independent Republic the communists have played little part in political life, though they have maintained their influence in S.O.B.S.I., which remained affiliated to the communist-controlled W.F.T.U.[1] The future of West New Guinea continued to provide a source of friction with Holland, and so indirectly with the West as a whole. Overpopulation remained a source of economic instability. Nevertheless communist blandishments have been ineffective in Indonesia. The country's problems are too numerous and too complicated to allow facile optimism. Its prospects in 1953 however seemed better than its neighbours', and in Soekarno and his lieutenants it seemed to possess leaders of a quality superior to most politicians of newly independent Asian lands.

In Indochina, when Japan surrendered the Vietminh seized power. On 20th August Ho Chi-minh was master of Hanoi.[2] On 25th Bao Dai abdicated, and recognised Ho Chi-minh's 'Republican government', which claimed authority over all three Vietnamese provinces. By agreement between the Allied Great Powers, the north of Indochina was to be provisionally occupied by Chinese troops, the south by British. In the south, with British support, the French re-established their authority.[3] In the north, an uneasy relationship existed between the Vietminh, the Chinese, and the Vietnamese troops that enjoyed the sympathy of the Kuomintang. Ho Chi-minh, who feared Chinese imperialism, disliked Kuomintang politics, sincerely loved France, and hoped for support from the French communists and socialists, authorised his military commander to sign, in Hanoi on 6th March 1946, an agreement with the representative of the French general Leclerc. This permitted

---

was undertaken in December 1948. Dutch forces occupied Jogjakarta, and took prisoner Soekarno, his Prime Minister Hatta, the socialist leader Sjahrir and other leaders.

[1] See below, p. 328.

[2] The atom bomb was dropped on Hiroshima on 6th August. Ho Chi-minh gave his forces the name 'Vietnam Liberation Army' on the 7th, and ordered a general insurrection on the 10th. The Japanese forces did not attack them, nor were they attacked. On the 17th Vietminh organised a demonstration of 20,000 persons in Hanoi, while the Japanese looked on. See Devillers, op. cit., pp. 135–40.

[3] Vietminh was in control of Saigon by 25th August. On 2nd September there were anti-French riots and looting. On the 6th the first British forces landed. On the 21st the British decreed martial law. The local French profited from this restoration of order to make numerous arrests of Vietnamese. This action was followed on the 25th by a massacre of French civilians by Vietnamese. The position of French and British troops in Saigon was for a time precarious. During October considerable French forces were landed, led by General Leclerc. After a good deal of fighting with Vietminh guerrillas, the French had made themselves masters of Cochinchina and southern Annam by the end of January 1946. The British handed over all authority to the French on 28th January, and left Indochina on 5th March. Devillers, op. cit., pp. 154–69.

French troops to return to the north, provided that the relationship between Vietnam and France within the French Union should be decided in future political negotiations.[1]

This promising beginning was followed by disappointments. The French settlers and officials were determined not to relinquish their hold over Cochinchina. They were supported by a section of the Vietnamese population, and found a powerful advocate in the High Commissioner in Saigon, Admiral Thierry d'Argenlieu. Ho Chi-minh himself was under fire, both from the extremists within his own party and from the nationalists outside it, who lost no opportunity to denounce as 'treason' any concession to the French. The negotiations continued during the second half of 1946. A personal visit by Ho Chi-minh to France in the summer, and a conference between French and Vietnamese representatives at Fontainbleau from July to September, failed to bring a settlement. Ho Chi-minh however signed on 14th September a *modus vivendi* covering various minor points. In the autumn tension increased. The outbreak of hostilities at Haiphong in November brought matters to a crisis. A last attempt was made to settle the incident peacefully, but the extremists on both sides had their way. On 19th December 1946 Vietminh forces attacked the French in Hanoi by surprise. The French held the city, but Ho Chi-minh and his men retired to the mountains and led a war which has not ceased since then.[2]

The war reinforced the hold of Vietminh over the loyalty of the Vietnamese. A large 'liberated territory' was firmly held in the north, and guerrilla forces also operated in parts of Annam and Cochinchina. When the Chinese communists had advanced to the southern boundary of China, Vietminh had direct contact with a friendly Great Power, and received military and civil supplies from China in much the same way as the Greek communist rebels had received supplies from Albania and Yugoslavia in 1946–8. The

[1] The text of the agreement is in Devillers, op. cit., pp. 225–6. The French recognised the Republic of Vietnam as 'a free state with its government, army and finances, forming part of the Indochinese Federation and the French Union'. The unification of the three Vietnamese provinces was to be decided by a plebiscite of the whole population.

[2] For these negotiations, and for the manœuvres of Admiral d'Argenlieu, the French *colons* and the Vietnamese autonomists in Cochinchina, see Devillers, op. cit., pp. 256–310. The crisis of November–December in Haiphong and Hanoi is described in detail in the same work, pp. 331–57. The author ascribes the responsibility partly to the extremists in Ho Chi-minh's camp, and partly to certain French officers who wished to precipitate a conflict. One of the most fantastic details he reveals is that a conciliatory message from Ho Chi-minh to M. Léon Blum—who assumed the French Premiership at this time—written on 15th December, was held up by the telegraphic censorship in Saigon, and did not reach Paris until 26th December, a week after the final breach in Hanoi (op. cit., pp. 351–2.)

organisation of the 'liberated territory' was not unlike the organisation of Tito's areas in Yugoslavia during the Axis occupation. The Vietminh was as thoroughly controlled by the communists as was the Yugoslav People's Front.[1] In March 1951 the self-dissolved communist party reappeared under the name of Vietnam Workers' Party. Its title recalls the 'unified socialist' parties of East Germany, Poland and Hungary. Based on Stalinist principles of democratic centralism, it was a communist party in all but name, and was all-powerful in Vietminh territory.

The French authorities had rejected an agreement with Vietminh in 1946, when by risking the grant of a large measure of self-government they might have won the confidence of many Vietnamese, and separated the moderate patriots from the communists. Their refusal drove the patriots into the arms of Ho Chiminh and Ho Chi-minh into the arms of his own extremists.[2] In May 1949 the French government tried to retrieve its mistake by conceding something like dominion status to Bao Dai,[3] the former Emperor of Annam. From the first day a mighty orchestra of propaganda, in which not only communist but many sorts of liberal and anti-imperialist instruments were heard, denounced Bao Dai as a puppet and traitor, and French policy as both perfidious and stupid. Undeterred the French and Bao Dai persevered, and in three years they achieved some success. Yet not only the military but also the political situation remained extremely precarious. The French were pressed by their western allies to make real concessions to Bao Dai in order to increase his prestige. But for many Frenchmen the aim was not simply that of their allies, to keep Soviet imperialism out of Indochina: it was to preserve French rule. They were not fighting Ho Chi-minh in order to surrender to Bao Dai. Other Frenchmen were willing to give Vietnam all but formal independence, but rightly insisted that power could not be given to Bao Dai while the war was being fought: control of

---

[1] The Communist Party of Indochina was officially dissolved at a meeting of its Central Committee held in Hanoi on 11th November 1945. Thereafter it was merged in Vietminh, in much the same way as the Yugoslav Communist Party was merged in the People's Front—without however incurring the censure of the Cominform. In May 1946 Vietminh combined with Dong Minh Hoi and V.N.Q.D.D. (See above, p. 227 n.) in a wider organisation, the Vietnam National People's Front (Lien Viet). The real effect of this new move was not to give the nationalists more influence in the government, but to extend the influence of the communists, through Vietminh and Lien Viet, over a still larger section of the Vietnamese population.

[2] The difference between Ho Chi-minh and his extremists should not be exaggerated. Its essence was that he hoped for good results from his contacts with the French communists, while they regarded all Frenchmen as enemies. Both he and they were equally hostile to non-communist Frenchmen.

[3] See above, p. 227.

military operations and of public order must be kept in French hands. Only victories of French arms would convince non-communist Vietnamese that Vietminh would lose, and that it was therefore safe for them to take the risk of supporting Bao Dai. Meanwhile there was some evidence that in Vietminh 'liberated territory' communist rule was becoming oppressive and unpopular. Against this was other evidence that, as in Yugoslavia and China in their wars of liberation, a great wealth of enthusiasm, energy and natural ability, never before brought into the political life of the country, was being exploited by the communists; that in the minds of thousands of young Vietnamese their own careers, the independence of Vietnam, and the communist party were indissolubly connected. And over all hung the sword of Damocles, military intervention from China.

JAPAN AND INDIA

In Japan the democratic legislation imposed by General MacArthur broke up the large landed estates and the *zaibatsu* trusts, permitted the workers to organise trade unions, and allowed the communists to operate as a legal party.

In the trade union field two main organisations appeared, the Japanese Federation of Labour dominated by the socialists and the National Congress of Industrial Unions in which communist influence was strong. Three times in the next three years the intervention of MacArthur's Headquarters checked communist progress. During the second half of 1946 economic conditions were extremely bad, the workers suffered great hardships, and the communists did their best to exploit discontent. The communist-led campaign was designed to culminate in a general strike, planned for 30th January 1947: at the last moment MacArthur forbade it. During 1947 and 1948 the communists made gains among the government workers' unions: in July 1948 a directive from MacArthur's Headquarters expressly forbade strikes in the government service. During 1948 anti-communist groups ('Democratisation Leagues'), encouraged both by the Japanese government and by Allied Headquarters, began to undermine the communist position in the N.C.I.U. unions. A third external blow was dealt in the summer of 1949, when the demand by the American financial adviser Dodge for drastic economies in government service was used by the Japanese government to dismiss public employees known to be active members of communist-controlled trade unions. By the end of 1949 membership of N.C.I.U. unions was slightly more than half of what it had been in 1947.

In the political field the communists, following the world-wide Popular Front tactic, sought an alliance with the socialists. Their aim was, as in Eastern Europe, to make the socialists their prisoners, by the usual methods of infiltration and of bringing into the alliance, as equal partners, miscellaneous small groups in fact controlled by themselves. The Japanese socialists, like the French, Italian, or Indonesian, included both supporters and opponents of co-operation with the communists, but among their leaders the latter were more numerous. During 1946 the radical mood of the workers made it difficult to reject all communist approaches, but events in Eastern Europe strengthened the determination of the socialist leaders to preserve their independence. The mass discontent of the winter of 1946–7 caused General MacArthur to direct the government to hold a new general election, and in this the socialists emerged as the strongest party. The socialist leaders however refused to consider alliance with the communists in a revolutionary opposition. Instead they formed a coalition government with centre groups, excluding both the communists and the right-wing Liberals. In the autumn of 1948 the coalition was reshuffled. Though based on the same groups, its premier was a democrat instead of a socialist. During 1948 the socialists lost popularity. Some of their former supporters went over to the communists, but most swung to the right. In the election of 1949 the socialist parliamentary group fell from 143 seats to 49, the communist increased from 4 to 35, and the right from 133 to 264. Though the communists' share of the left vote had grown, the left vote as a whole had been reduced to little more than half.[1]

To sum up, the communists never had between 1945 and 1949 the least prospect of obtaining even a share in the government of the country, but they made great gains in the trade unions, which only external intervention checked. In the countryside for all their efforts to woo the peasants, the communists made little impression. Among university students, and in general among the younger generation of the intelligentsia, they were much more successful. It was estimated that at the end of 1949 about 40 per cent of all Japanese students were under the influence of the National Federation of Self-governing Student Associations, which was controlled by communists. Thus, though far from power, the Japanese communists had made great progress. As in the 1920's, their support

[1] In October 1951 the Japanese socialists split into two parties. The main difference was on international policy: the left socialists were neutralists, the right were pro-western. In the 1953 parliamentary election the right socialists won 66 seats, the left 72 seats, the communists one.

came partly from workers and partly from intelligentsia. But among both these social groups they were far stronger than they had ever been before.

The problem that most exercised the theorists of the Japanese party in these years was the relative importance to be given to the struggle against the Japanese ruling class or the American 'imperialist occupant'. If purely Japanese considerations might make the first seem the more dangerous enemy, the interests of the Soviet state required that all energies be directed against the second. A turning-point came in January 1950, six months before the Korean War. The Cominform[1] criticised one of the party's leaders, Nozaka, for overestimating the possibility of a peaceful struggle, and for insufficient hostility to the 'imperialists'. In March Nozaka publicly admitted his mistakes. In May a new Thesis of the *Politburo* was circulated to members of the party. In principle it recognised the struggle against domestic reaction and against international monopoly capitalism as equally important, in fact as inseparable from each other. In practice, its chief emphasis was laid on the struggle against the second, which of course meant the struggle against the United States. The party then embarked on a new tactic of anti-American violence, which caused General MacArthur in June to ask the Japanese government to take various measures against individual leading communists.[2]

The outbreak of war in Korea drove the Japanese communists into semi-legality. The party was not formally banned: the Allied authorities and Japanese government took the view that those who committed espionage, sabotage or other crimes should be punished for their offences, not for being communists. The main leaders of the party retired into hiding. The priority of anti-American activity over all other tasks received doctrinal expression during the celebration in July 1952 of the party's thirtieth birthday. A statement of its General Secretary, Tokuda, published in the Cominform journal, clearly adopted the thesis that Japan was no longer an imperialist Power but had become a colony. Though humiliating to Japanese national pride, this slogan had the advantage that it enabled communists to support any form of anti-western nationalism that might appear in Japan. The calculation was the same as in Germany.[3]

[1] See below, p. 328.
[2] The essence of the measures was to exclude the members of the Central Committee and the leading editors of the communist press from any active part in political life. Soon after this 'purge' the leaders went into hiding.
[3] See above, p. 304.

The prospects of Japanese communists are not good. It is true that pressure of population[1] holds prospects of economic misery from which extremists may hope to benefit. But the state machine in Japan is comparatively stable. As the Japanese government takes over power from the Americans, it is likely to be less rather than more tolerant to communists. Among the masses neither communism nor Russia is popular:[2] even among the organised workers the party is certainly much less strong than it was in 1947. Nor does Japanese nationalism seem likely to help the communist cause. Japanese vital interests lie in the Korea-Manchuria area, not in the south seas: they bring Japan into political conflict not with America and Australia but with the Soviet Union and to a lesser extent with China. It is true that Japan needs trade with China. But the development of China-Japan trade need not damage western, or help Soviet, interest: rather it should be of advantage to the West, both in providing an outlet for Japanese industry and in increasing China's freedom of manœuvre in relation to Russia. The economic and military strength of the United States, if supported by tactful diplomacy, should be able to derive advantage from the three-cornered conflict of interests between China, Japan and Russia, and to make of Japan a friend and a fortress of peace.

In India the communists placed themselves in a curious position by their support of the British war effort after June 1941. They thereby received greater freedom of speech and movement than ever before, and gained ground in the trade unions, some of whose non-communist leaders had been arrested for anti-war activity. But in the long term the policy harmed them, for it separated them from the mass movement in India, and convinced many Indian radicals, who had hitherto felt sympathy for them, that they were a mere fifth column of another Power.[3]

When India became independent in 1948, the roles of Congress and communists were reversed. The communists described the new situation as a British imperialist trick, and Nehru and Patel as British agents. The second congress of the Indian Communist Party, held in Calcutta in February 1948, adopted a policy of violence. With new leaders in command, the party organised insurrectionary strikes in Bombay and other cities, and revolts in Madras and West Bengal provinces. Its most ambitious attempts

[1] See below, p. 318 n.
[2] Russia annexed southern Sahalin and the Kurile islands from Japan.
[3] See M. R. Masani, 'The Communist Party in India', in *Pacific Affairs*, March, 1951.

were in the Telengana district of Hyderabad province. The incorporation of this native state in India after the ending of British rule had been accompanied by internal disorders, in which social and religious discontents were mixed. The communists made full use of both. They hoped to establish in Telengana an Indian Yenan, but the regular army of independent India proved too strong for them. In 1950 the policy of violence was abandoned. In 1952 the party's policy was designed to create a Popular Front. Despite the use of 'broad' slogans about a 'bloc of four classes' —modelled on Chinese experience, and including the 'national bourgeoisie'—it attracted few dupes. But under their own label, at the general election of 1952 the communists did comparatively well, especially in Hyderabad territory, where their brief rule seemed to have won them more friends than foes. Though completely dwarfed in parliament by Congress, they won enough seats to form the largest single opposition group.[1]

The outlook of communism in India is uncertain. As in Japan, so in India, rapid growth of population threatens growing poverty.[2] The Indian communists can exploit not only the misery of the masses but also the frustration of the intelligentsia, and the ease with which educated Indians, however cultured and brilliant, succumb to slogans about 'western imperialism' while closing their eyes to the crimes perpetrated by totalitarian Soviet imperialism. The illusions of some Indian statesmen on the nature of communist China make them vulnerable to the more sophisticated type of communist propaganda. It may be that the Indian communists can be most effective in the next years as a law-abiding parliamentary pressure-group on foreign policy. Against the communists are the facts that the state machine bequeathed by the British to India works better than that of any other independent state in Asia except Turkey and Japan; that there is goodwill towards the West in India as well as suspicion; and that communist China threatens Indian security both in Tibet and on the borders of Burma. Much will depend on the ability of the Western Powers to be gener-

---

[1] The communists won 4½ per cent of the votes to the central legislature, less than half as much as the socialists (10½ per cent). But the communists, whose votes were more concentrated, had nearly twice as many seats (23, to the socialists' 12, in a House of 489, in which Congress held 362). In the provincial assemblies the communists had some successes, winning 62 seats out of 375 in Madras, 28 out of 238 in Bengal, and 42 out of 175 in Hyderabad. See article by W. H. Morris Jones, 'The Indian Elections' in *Political Quarterly*, July-September 1952.

[2] The population of India in 1947 was about 332 million. The yearly increase is estimated at nearly 5 million. The density of agricultural population is especially severe in certain provinces. The population of Japan has increased extremely rapidly since the war. It was 83 million in 1950, and the yearly increase is about 1·5 million.

ous in economic aid, and to show patient understanding of the special Indian political outlook.

Whereas in South-East Asia—with the exception of Malaya—it is conceivable that communists might obtain power by the disintegration of the state machines, in Japan and India it is most unlikely that they could win except as a result of foreign invasion. But even if they are far from power, the communist parties of two such important countries deserve serious attention. Their future will largely depend on the relations between the communist parties of the Soviet Union and China.

There has been some evidence that Japanese and Indian communist affairs have already caused friction between Moscow and Peking. In Japan, it is significant that when the Cominform saw fit to attack the Japanese party for insufficient activity against the Americans, it should have singled out Nozaka, who of all prominent Japanese communists has had the closest connections with China, and has most stressed the need for Japan to follow the teachings and example of Mao Tse-tung.[1] The Korean war, by providing an obvious common interest between Soviet, Chinese and Japanese communists, probably put an end to friction for the time being. In the case of India, it seems possible that the frequent changes in the leadership of the party since 1947 have been connected with a struggle between groups looking respectively to Moscow and Peking.[2] The 'extreme left' leadership of 1948–9 referred to Mao as an 'opportunist'. Its successors in 1950–1 were alternatively flattering to China and to the Soviet Union. The fourth General Secretary, Ghosh, who was elected in November 1951, laid the greater stress on the Chinese orientation, and was criticised as an 'opportunist' in the Cominform journal by Anna Pauker.

THE MOSLEM WORLD

In the Moslem world, communists have made progress since 1945 only in Persia. But throughout the Middle East unhealthy social conditions, political instability and intellectual confusion have been factors favourable to revolutionary action of some sort.

The overthrow of Reza Shah by Anglo-Soviet invasion in 1941 ended a regime which, for all its abuses, had given Persia twenty

[1] Nozaka however spent many years in Moscow, and so could equally well be regarded as a 'Muscovite'.
[2] See Borkenau, *Mao Tse-tung*, loc. cit.

years of comparative stability. In the consequent confusion, the flagrant injustices of Persian society attracted greater public attention. The freer political discussion and organisation permitted by the occupying Powers gave the extreme left its chance. The *Tudeh* ('Masses') party, founded in 1942, was a communist party in all but name. It won strong support among the radical intelligentsia and among the factory workers and artisans of the few industrial centres. By 1946 it had shown its strength by strikes in Isfahan, Abadan and Tehran.[1] In December 1945, under the protection of the Soviet occupying forces, a revolt broke out in Tabriz, the capital of the north-western province of Azerbaidjan, whose people are mostly not Persians but Turks, akin to those living across the Soviet border. An autonomous government was proclaimed under the leadership of a newly-created 'Democratic Party', whose leading figure was Jaafar Pishevari, the former organiser of the 1921 Ghilan 'republic' and Comintern expert on the Middle East.[2] The Soviet authorities also encouraged Kurdish separatism, a convenient instrument to be used against Iraq and Turkey as well as Persia.[3] The Tabriz regime was able to exploit genuine national and social discontent, though its methods of police terror antagonised many of its subjects. But pressure from the Western Powers and skilful manœuvres by the Persian Premier Qavam es-Sultaneh induced the Soviet government to withdraw its forces from Persia, whereupon the Azerbaidjan and Kurdish regimes collapsed.[4]

This setback to the Soviet and communist cause was not however exploited either by the Persians or by the Western Powers. There was no land reform,[5] and little social progress. *Tudeh* was better organised than any other party, and successfully appealed to idealism, discontent and ambition. Though formally banned after

[1] A. Bashkirov, *Rabochee i profsoyuznoe dvizhenie v Irane*, Moscow, 1948.
[2] See above, p. 129.
[3] The number of Kurds is estimated (1950) at 600,000 in Iran, 1,750,000 in Turkey, 800,000 in Iraq, and 250,000 in Syria. In 1946 a Kurdish 'republic' was established, with Soviet protection, by Qazi Muhammad, which collapsed at the same time as the Azerbaidjan regime. Qazi Muhammad was captured by the Persian troops and executed in February 1947. Another Kurdish leader, Mulla Mustafa of Barzani, escaped in 1947 to Soviet territory. *The Middle East*, R.I.I.A., 1950, pp. 59, 240, 385, 435.
[4] Qavam took three members of Tudeh into his government in August 1946, but they resigned in October when Qavam broke off his negotiations with the Azerbaidjan 'Democrats'. Qavam persuaded the Soviet government to evacuate Persian territory on the understanding that a concession would be granted to it to exploit oil resources in northern Persia. After the Soviet troops had left, however, the Persian parliament voted against the grant of the concession.
[5] A decree by Qavam es-Saltaneh's government, of August 1946, that the tenant's share of the crop should be increased to the extent of 15 per cent of the landlord's share, was not carried out. See R. N. Gupta, *Iran: an Economic Study*, New Delhi, 1947.

an attempt on the Shah's life in December 1949, it was able to survive underground. For their part, the Western Powers failed to win the friendship either of the politicians or of the people of Persia. The advent to power of Dr. Mossadeq and the confiscation of the Anglo-Iranian Oil Company's property in 1951 created an atmosphere of militant xenophobia, and introduced a process of political disintegration which was likely to benefit both Soviet imperialism and *Tudeh*.

Social development in the Arab lands was accelerated by the war. Industry made rapid progress, and the urban population, including factory workers, greatly increased. The intelligentsia became more numerous and more vocal. The military prestige of the Soviet Union caused educated Arabs to take an interest in Soviet institutions and communist doctrine. Public opinion became more aware of social issues. The Arab lands most influenced by modern ideas and institutions were Egypt and Algeria. Less profoundly, yet considerably, affected were Iraq, Lebanon and Tunisia. Traditional social forms and loyalties remained powerful in Morocco, Syria, Jordan and above all the Arabian peninsula.

In Iraq a communist party appeared after the war, and played some part in a strike in the Kirkuk oilfields in 1947. The party was suppressed, and five of its leaders were executed in 1949.[1] In Algeria the communists have a certain working-class following, but there is greater mass support for the nationalist groups.[2] which have at times co-operated tactically with the communists but view them with deep suspicion. In Tunisia the trade unions broke away from the communist-dominated French C.G.T., and formed their own central organisation, *Union Générale des travailleurs tunisiens*, which is affiliated to the anti-communist trade union international I.C.F.T.U.[3] In Egypt, though social, cultural and political conditions seemed extremely favourable for the development of communism, at the end of 1952 there still appeared to be

[1] Khadduri, *Independent Iraq*, 1951, pp. 273–5.

[2] The *Union démocratique du manifeste algérien*, led by Ferhat Abbas, does not reject completely the idea of partnership with France within the French Union, but insists on much greater self-government for the Algerians. The *Mouvement du triomphe des libertés démocratiques*, led by Messali Hadj, is more radical. It recognises little, if any, cultural affinity between Algeria and France, and stresses the links of Algeria with the whole Arab world. Messali Hadj began his political career as a communist, but broke with the party. The fullest account of North African politics is C. A. Julien, *L'Afrique du nord en marche*, Paris, 1952. On Algeria, there is some unsystematic information, and some useful documents, in P. E. Sarrasin *La crise algérienne*, Paris, 1949. There is also some information on French North Africa in R. Letourneau, *L'Islam contemporain*, Paris, 1950. A French communist analysis of Tunisia is P. Sebag, *La Tunisie*, Paris, Editions sociales, 1951.

[3] See below, p. 328.

no effective communist organisation. The growth of communist sympathies among university students was an omen for the future rather than a political force in the present. In Syria, Lebanon and Arabia communism was negligible. In Israel it had small support. In pre-war Eastern Europe persecuted Jews might well have hopes of communism, but with their own homeland to create, their energies were more constructively employed. Persecution of any form of Sionism in the Soviet Union or 'popular democracies' still further reduced the appeal of communism in Israel.[1]

The explosive force in the Arab countries is not communism but nationalism. It is compounded of national pride, religious fervour, desire for modernisation and social revolt. It is directed against Britain and France, which still hold territories or military positions in Arab lands, and against the United States which is regarded partly as the protector of Britain and France and partly as a monstrous symbol of imperialism and capitalism. Arab nationalism has its own revolutionary organisations, wholly or partly conspiratorial. The most important of these, the Moslem Brotherhood, has points of resemblance to such right-wing revolutionary organisations as the Roumanian Iron Guard and the Japanese 'young officers'.[2] The real political conflicts about which Arabs feel strongly are those which set them against the Western Powers—the problems of Israel, Suez, the Sudan, Tunis and Morocco. Even in Algeria, where many Arabs sincerely recognise French culture as a positive influence, the massacres of 1945 created bitter hatred.[3] In the widespread mistrust or loathing of the West that pervades most political groups and social classes in the Arab world, the fear of Russia and of communism is forgotten. Forgotten too is the terrible fate of some thirty million Moslems oppressed by totalitarian Stalinism.

The important exception in the Moslem world is Turkey, whose people not only support a foreign policy aligned with the West, but are practically invulnerable to communist influence. Having enjoyed real independence for thirty years, the Turks are less easily intoxicated by nationalist slogans than the Arabs. As a secular

---

[1] The left socialist party, *Mapam*, has been fiercely attacked by Soviet and East European spokesmen, though it has urged a neutralist policy weighted in favour of the Soviet bloc. The moderate socialist party, *Mapai*, the government party in Israel, is of course detested by all communists. The Slansky trial and the 'poisoner-doctor' affair in Moscow, marked a more pronouncedly anti-semitic phase in Soviet policy. In February, 1953, the Soviet government broke off diplomatic relations with Israel.

[2] See above, pp. 135 and 190.

[3] Riots took place in Constantine province in May 1945, in which several hundred Frenchmen were killed. In the subsequent repression by French troops, it is estimated that thousands of Algerian Moslems perished.

state, Turkey is little influenced by the idea of Islamic solidarity with the Arab lands. The recent re-emergence of Moslem influence in Turkey has had no apparent influence on Turkey's relations with the West.[1] Geographical and historical factors make Turks suspicious of all things Russian. Finally the Turks, unlike the Arabs, are close kin of the peoples of Azerbaidjan and Turkestan, and know well both that Stalinist imperialism is a deadly threat and that they can escape it only with the help of the West.

The largest of all Moslem states, Pakistan, has been fully absorbed in its own immediate problems—its racial complexity, the different interests of its western and eastern halves, its claims to Kashmir, and its quarrels with Afghanistan. But it will certainly exert a growing influence in the Moslem world. Much will depend on whether the rulers of Pakistan choose boldly to face the danger which from the north threatens them and the whole Moslem world, or to earn cheap popularity from the mob by diatribes against an unreal bogey of 'western imperialism'.

That communism is weak throughout the Moslem world is no cause for complacency in the West. Arab and Persian nationalists are doing Moscow's job for it without needing an ounce of gold or a word of advice from Moscow. They are engaging the attention and the resources of the West at a time when these are in short supply, and they are undermining the state machine and social framework of their own countries. If the Arab and Persian Kerenskis do their duty, the road to power for the communists will be solidly laid and smoothly paved. There may today be no communists to walk the road, but when the moment is ripe they will be found. The Moslem peoples will escape disaster only if they will open their eyes to the Stalinist threat and to the fate of the Moslems under Stalinist rule. It is no less true that the western nations can help the Moslem peoples to save themselves only if they will treat them as equal partners. Western diplomacy requires in the Moslem world a combination of strength, generosity and persuasiveness seldom achieved in human history.[2]

AFRICA

In Africa south of the Sahara communism is practically unknown. Yet here too the social and cultural forces from which it can

[1] See article by Professor Bernard Lewis, 'The Islamic Revival in Turkey', in *International Affairs*, January 1952. A more general survey is an article by Richard D. Robinson, 'The Lesson of Turkey', in *Middle East Journal*, Autumn 1951 issue.

[2] These issues are brilliantly and originally discussed by A. Hourani, 'The decline of the West in the Middle East', in *International Affairs*, January and April, 1953.

emerge are coming into being. In West Africa, both British and French, urban centres already exist, though industry is still very small. In these cities an African intelligentsia has emerged as a political factor. In Central and East Africa society is still primitive. The urban and skilled element is European, Indian or Arab. In Kenya the presence of European farmers, economically a valuable element, but socially an alien privileged group, complicates the political situation. South Africa is in a category by itself. Here the Europeans form nearly a quarter of the population but are bitterly divided between English- and Afrikaans-speaking; the economy has been transformed during the last twenty years from one based solely on agriculture and mining to one in which factory industry plays an important part; and economic development has created an African intelligentsia and an African industrial proletariat. The last trend has also made some slight progress in recent years in the mining regions of Belgian Congo and Northern Rhodesia.

The most important political party of French West Africa, the *Rassemblement démocratique africain* (R.D.A.), founded after the war, was at first closely connected with the French Communist Party. Later the majority of the party, led by its founder Houphouet, broke with the communists. The African workers of the Ivory Coast—the colony where R.D.A. is strongest—are divided in their attitude to the communist-controlled C.G.T.[1] In the Gold Coast, the nationalist leader Nkrumah was at one time influenced by communism, but since his party obtained substantial political power under the new constitution he has been more concerned with practical politics and less with demagogic slogans. Nigerian politics remain at the slogan stage. The nationalist leader Dr. Azikiwe ('Zik') has flirted with communism, and there may have been some communist influence behind the riots in the Enugu coalmines in 1950. But nationalism, not communism, is the dominant issue.

In South Africa all the conditions required for communist success are present, except one: organised communist leadership. This

[1] The R.D.A. was founded in October 1946 at Bamako in French Sudan by the deputy Houphouet. Its main strength has lain in the Ivory Coast. In 1946 it was closely linked with the French Communist Party. In 1950 Houphouet broke with the communists. The original intention, that R.D.A. should be an all-West African movement, was not achieved. The party's early success was in part due to support received from a part of the French administration. Its later failures were caused partly by the withdrawal of this support; partly by local patriotism; and partly by the hostility to communism of the Catholic Church, which had many of its believers among the followers of R.D.A. In Senegal the French Socialists had a considerable following. Large areas of French Africa were unaffected by any political activity.

great country offers fine prospects for every type of professional merchant of hate. Official South African politics is a contest not so much of English against Afrikaner, as of industrial capitalism, with a weak dose of old-fashioned liberalism, against rural paternalism with a strong dose of fascism. The Afrikaner Nationalists oppress the Africans from a religious conviction of racial superiority: the United Party business-men exploit the African worker from economic convenience. The former wish to deny the African all education and all political rights, the latter to grant him just as much as they think will increase his efficiency as a cheap labourer. The position of the African working class in the Union today recalls that of the Russian working class before 1905. The African intelligentsia suffers from the frustrations of the Russian intelligentsia of 1880, aggravated by the intolerable humiliations of the colour-bar. National and social hatreds of European against European, European against African, and of all against Indian, give every chance to the hatemongers of communism, fascism and black racialism. Across the ocean is the rapidly growing great power of India, with 300 million citizens, talented and enduring, capable of the highest technical and military achievement. Communism is only one—and not the most likely—of the disasters that could overtake South Africa in the next decades.

African nationalism is an explosive force that will cause ever more trouble. It has made its appearance not only in the west and south, but also in Sudan, Uganda, Madagascar and Kenya.[1] It is reflected in the threefold struggle between the claims of African intelligentsias; the counter-claims of European settlers in Algeria, Tunisia, Kenya or Rhodesia; and the liberal consciences of the British Colonial Office or French National Assembly. The opposite poles of policy are the experiment in African self-government in the Gold Coast and the *apartheid* doctrine of Dr. Malan.[2] The problems of the Sudan, Nigeria and Central African Federation

[1] In Madagascar an armed revolt took place in March 1947. It was led by three deputies of the French parliament, who in 1946 had founded a party called the *Mouvement démocratique de rénovation malgache*. After the revolt the French government dissolved the M.D.R.M. The deputies were condemned to death, but reprieved. In Kenya, African opposition to the white settlers has not taken the form of a precise political party. During 1952 a secret society called Mau-Mau committed a number of violent crimes, and became a serious danger to public security.

[2] The most objectionable feature of *apartheid* is that the share of South African territory and economy which it proposes to allot to the African four-fifths of the population is immensely smaller and poorer that than reserved to the European one-fifth. There may or may not be something to be said for segregation of Europeans and Africans. Ruthless exploitation by a minority of a majority which every year grows more numerous and poorer is morally indefensible, economically inexpedient and politically dangerous.

are all examples of the conflict between European interests and African aspirations. As in the case of the Moslem world, so also in Africa, local explosive forces embarrass and threaten Moscow's international rivals without any need for Moscow to intervene.[1] At a later stage, when the explosive forces have done their work, Moscow may well hope that communism will have its day.

LATIN AMERICA

In Latin America the victory of the Allies, and the increased prestige of the Soviet Union, brought a swing to the left.

In the June 1945 election in Peru, A.P.R.A. had the largest number of parliamentary seats of any single political party, and for a time exercised a strong influence on the President, Luis Bustamente. In October 1945 in Venezuela a group of outlook similar to A.P.R.A., *Acción Democrática*, came to power. In both countries there was more freedom of speech than for decades, and far-reaching social and educational reforms were planned. In Brazil greater political freedom was granted in 1945, and the Communist Party was able to work in the open. At the parliamentary election which accompanied the presidential election of December 1945, the communists received nearly 600,000 votes, or 10 per cent of the poll. In Chile the communists began to recover lost ground after the Soviet Union was involved in the war. The victory of Gonzalez Videla at the presidential election of September 1946 was in part due to communist support. In his first administration he gave the ministries of Communications and Agriculture to communists.

The swing to the left did not last long. The social forces opposed to reform—landowners, business, church and army—were too strong. The communists were obliged, in accordance with Soviet policy, to attack the United States, and American policy therefore soon discarded the sympathy for the left which it had had at the end of the war. The forces of the right were free to counter-attack without fear of incurring displeasure in Washington. Already in the early summer of 1946 mass demonstrations and strikes by communists in Brazil alarmed the authorities and provoked counter-measures by the police. In May 1947 the Brazilian Communist Party was declared illegal. Its leader Prestes, who had emerged from ten years' imprisonment in 1945, went into hiding.

---

[1] The anti-communist Law passed by Dr. Malan's government in 1950 seems designed, not to combat communism, which hardly exists as an organised force in the Union, but to attack all working-class organisations and to give the Nationalist Party further opportunities of electoral gerrymandering to keep itself permanently in power.

In Chile the communists resigned from the government in the spring of 1947. During the summer they organised several big strikes, and in September several of their leaders were arrested. A year later President Gonzalez persuaded the Congress to ban the Chilean Communist Party, but communist influence remained strong in the trade unions. In Peru tension grew during 1947 between President Bustamente and A.P.R.A. The latter's demands both for land reform and for greater educational and political rights for the Indians aroused fierce opposition from the ruling class. In March 1948 Bustamente openly broke with A.P.R.A . and in September he banned it and arrested as many of its leaders as he could lay his hands on. In November 1948 the *Acción Democrática* regime in Venezuela was overthrown.

Probably the most important development in post-war Latin America has been the Perón regime in Argentine, the most effective power among the states of the continent. The essence of *Perónismo* is a combination of economic nationalism, anti-United States demagogy, and social reform. It is a revolutionary movement of a fascist type. It is, like Moslem or African nationalism, an independent force, in no way controlled, hardly even influenced, by communism or by Moscow, yet doing more serious harm within its region to the enemies of Moscow than any existing communist movement. It is possible that communists will infiltrate, or have already infiltrated, the state machine and trade unions of Argentine. But the Argentine is formidable not because of communist infiltration but because of the explosive forces of anti-United States nationalism and of social revolt, which are united in the person of Perón. The Argentine leader has his own imperialism, directed towards Bolivia, Chile and the small republics of the Plata. In the long term no doubt the greater human and material resources of Brazil will give her the leading position. But for the immediate future Argentine is likely to remain the centre of anti-United States policy in the western hemisphere.

Glaring social injustice, political tyranny and racial oppression remain, as before 1941, sources of revolution all over South America. Whether exploited by local dictators, by Argentine imperialism or by communism, they will cause trouble in the free world and pleasure in Moscow and Peking.

INTERNATIONAL COMMUNIST ORGANISATIONS

With international communist organisation this work is little concerned, but a few words are here needed to round off this brief post-war survey. The Comintern was dissolved, without the formality of a Congress, in 1943. In 1947 appeared the Cominform, an association of the communist parties of the Soviet Union, France, Italy and six of the East European 'popular democracies'.[1] A year later Yugoslavia was expelled from it. It does not appear that the Cominform is in itself an important political factor. Its chief function is to publish a fortnightly journal, curiously entitled *For a lasting peace, for a people's democracy*, which appears formally to lay down the 'line' for communist parties all over the world. The functions of a Far Eastern Cominform may be performed by the Asian-Australian branch of the communist-controlled trade union international, the W.F.T.U., which held an important conference in Peking in November 1949.[2]

Moscow certainly placed great hopes in the W.F.T.U., which was founded at the end of the war, and at first represented powerful non-communist trade unions. The communists however had a majority in it from the beginning, and persisted in using their majority to support not the economic interests of the working class but the political aims of Soviet foreign policy. The inevitable result was that the non-communists broke away, and W.F.T.U. ceased to be a world trade union organisation and became a mere instrument, recognised as such by all, of communist international policy. It is still of some use to Moscow in parts of Asia and Africa, and in Latin America, where it controls the *Confederación de trabajadores de America latina* (C.T.A.L.), originally founded in 1938.

In December 1949 was created, at a congress in London, a rival world organisation, the International Confederation of Free Trade Unions (I.C.F.T.U.). It set up its own regional organisations for Asia and Latin America during 1950 and 1951.[3]

The other international organisations set up under communist auspices at the end of the war, the 'world federations' of 'democratic youth' and 'democratic women', and the International Union of Students, are of little importance. More spectacular success has been won in recent years by the communist-sponsored 'peace campaign'. But it too has lost ground since its aims, to propagate hatred of Moscow's rivals, and to maintain bellicose hysteria among nationsruled by Stalin and his puppets, became obvious.

---

[1] Czechoslovakia, Poland, Hungary, Roumania, Yugoslavia, Bulgaria.
[2] It was at this conference that Liu Shao-chi's statement, discussed above (p. 290) was made.
[3] The *Asian Federation of Labour* was created by a congress held in Ceylon in January 1950; the *Organisacion regional interamericana de trabajadores* by a congress in Habana in January 1951.

International communist organisations receive no more than this brief mention, as they have little bearing on the social conditions and political systems that favour or hinder communist action, or on the methods used by communists to seize power, which are the subject of this book. Not mysterious international agencies or sinister Cominform emissaries, but the conditions within each country and the balance of international power, are the factors that decide the victory or defeat of communist as of other revolutionaries.

CHAPTER SIXTEEN

Communism, Social Classes and Power

I N the half-century that has passed since the split in the Russian Social Democratic Party which gave birth to Bolshevism, the pupils of Lenin have had victories and defeats, most of which have been briefly described and analysed in earlier chapters. It remains to draw some general conclusions concerning the political, social and other factors which favour or hinder communist movements.

Communist victories can be divided into three categories— those won principally by their own efforts, those obtained by armed intervention from outside, and those in which there is an element of both. Of the first type there are four examples only—Russia 1917–20, Yugoslavia 1941–4, Albania 1943–4, and China 1946–9. In the last three cases external help—from the Russian Red Army to the Yugoslavs and Chinese, and from the Yugoslavs to the Albanians—played a part, possibly a greater part than is yet clearly established. But the main effort was made by the Yugoslav, Albanian and Chinese communists themselves. Of the second type of victory there are many examples. The Soviet forces invaded and occupied Azerbaidjan, Armenia and Georgia in 1920–1, Mongolia in 1922, the Baltic states of Latvia, Estonia and Lithuania in 1940. Soviet intervention in the internal affairs of Poland in 1944–5 and of Roumania in March 1945 belong to the same category. In Eastern Germany and North Korea, occupied enemy territories, the Soviet authorities installed by threat of force communist-led puppet regimes. In the third or marginal category are Bulgaria, Hungary and Czechoslovakia. Here Soviet intervention was indirect, and in the Bulgarian and Czechoslovak cases supported by a strong local communist movement. But the Soviet intervention was in fact decisive. The distinction between the second and third categories is thus rather blurred.

Communist failures may be divided into two categories. The first are cases where the communists took power, but were overthrown, the second cases where the attempt to seize power was unsuccessful.

Of the first category, far the most important was Hungary in 1919, the second most important Greece in 1944. Both these movements had strong local support, and a comparatively efficient machinery of coercion against their internal enemies. They were overthrown by external force—Roumanian in Hungary, British in Greece. If this force had not been used, they might have established themselves for a considerable time. The other examples in this category are unimportant—Bavaria and Latvia in 1919, the puppet governments of Białystok in 1920 and Terijoki in 1939, and Persian Azerbaidjan in 1946. The Bavarian soviet was a mere flash in the pan; the Latvian soviet regime had strong support in Riga but faced both overwhelming external force and hostility from most of its own peasantry, which it was never in a position to coerce. The Persian Azerbaidjan regime was installed by force and overthrown when the external force was withdrawn, yet undoubtedly enjoyed for a time a measure of local support. Białystok and Terijoki were brief inglorious episodes.

The second category includes some important cases. The first was Berlin in January 1919. Here the reason for failure was that the majority of the Berlin workers did not support the revolutionaries. Had they been supported by the workers, and obtained power, other factors—which have been discussed elsewhere[1]— would have come into operation to overthrow them: as things were, they did not even reach that stage. This is still more true of Germany in 1921, 1923 and 1932: on the first two occasions a pitiful attempt was made, on the third not even that. The Bulgarian rising of 1923 was a hopeless venture, undertaken after the indispensable peasant ally had been rendered helpless. The Chinese disaster of 1927 was probably due chiefly to the superiority of the enemy forces, but was also at least in part due to the failure of the communist leaders to exploit the revolutionary factors that were undoubtedly present: this failure was the failure of the Comintern and of Stalin rather than of the Chinese leader Chen Tu-hsiu who got the blame for it. The Spanish Popular Front must be included in this category. The communists had an insignificant part in the making of the Front, but the course of the war gave them opportunities to infiltrate the state machine of Republican Spain, and they used the opportunities well. Military defeat prevented them from enjoying the fruits of their labour, and this was

[1] See above, pp. 53–8.

in large part the result of foreign intervention. The last important examples in this category are France and Italy in 1944–7. The presence of armies, whose leaders were not likely to favour communist revolutions, yet had to be publicly treated as friends and allies, deprived the communists of the hope of seizing power at the time when the internal balance of forces was most favourable to them. Later they were frustrated by their inability either to win a majority for themselves alone at the polls, or to persuade other strong parties to become their dupes. No less decisive was the fact, demonstrated by the strikes of 1947, that command of the organised workers is not, in an advanced industrial society, a weapon strong enough to capture or to smash the state machine.

The communist bid for power in Indochina cannot yet be fitted into any of these categories, as the struggle is not over. It may end either as a failure of the type of Greece in 1944 or as a victory of the type of Yugoslavia or China.

THE STATE MACHINE

The political factors that have been decisive for the victory or defeat of communists have been the resistance or collapse of the state machine and the international balance of power.

The phrase 'collapse of the state machine' is unsatisfactory, but no other has yet been devised that describes this very important phenomenon. Its essential feature is the destruction of the nerve centre of the body politic. The heads of the administration, and their political chiefs, are either removed from their posts or rendered powerless by a paralysis of will which makes them unable to command obedience, or even to give orders. The loyalty of their subordinates, and of society outside the hierarchy, ceases to exist. The lower ranks of the bureaucracy may continue to perform their routine tasks in a normal manner, but the state machine as a single machine has collapsed. This condition existed in Russia for most of the period between the February and October revolutions, in Hungary in the winter of 1918–19, in Yugoslavia during most of the Axis occupation, and in most of China from the surrender of the Japanese armies until the triumph of the communists. It did not exist in Germany in November 1918, or in France in 1947.

This condition has been brought about, during the three decades with which we are here concerned, only by the direct or indirect effects of war. One should not draw from this the dogmatic conclusion that nothing but war can produce this condition. It is possible to imagine, at least in a country of backward society, the slow disintegration of a state machine through a combination of corruption, social division, incompetence and demagogy. Persia during 1951 and 1952 pointed the way. It is possible that while these pages are in the press, Dr. Mossadeq will have demonstrated that one does not need defeat in war to play the role which a cruel fate imposed on the unfortunate Kerenski.

But in a country of advanced industrial society it seems unlikely that this condition can be produced by other causes than defeat in war. The relations between state and people are not the same in an advanced industrial society as in a backward and mainly agrarian society. In a backward society the state machine is something imposed from above. It is separate from society. The people has, or feels it has, no part in it. It presses down vertically on the shoulders of the people. The classic example of this was the bureaucracy of Imperial Russia. In an advanced society the state machine is linked horizontally, at all levels, with the different strata of society. At any given moment, a majority of the people may detest the government in power. But the state is theirs. The state is inextricably connected with the people, the people with the state. The greater power of European governments to prevent revolutions in the twentieth century, as compared with the nineteenth, has often been explained in terms of the perfection of modern weapons. Street crowds, it is pointed out, cannot fight against tanks. This is of course true, but it is less than the whole truth. Perfection of weapons is only one aspect of a wider phenomenon, the centralisation of power in all fields of life. The last fifty years have been the age of the masses—of mass armies, mass trade unions, mass-circulation newspapers, mass politics. The relationship between the politician and the mass is complex, and there are many variations between the opposite poles of totalitarian *Führer* and freely elected leader. But governments of industrial societies have a weapon more powerful than the tank—the art of manipulating the masses.

It is believed by some that economic slumps can smash an industrial state. Communists in Western Europe have long placed hopes in slumps. But the great slump of the early 1930's helped not the communists but fascists. In industrial societies the main support of communists comes from the working class. But in a slump, with mass unemployment, the workers are weak, the bosses strong. Power is for the boss to dispose of, not for the trade unions. If normal methods of government break down in a slump, the heads of the bureaucracy, armed forces and business world are not likely to hand over power to communists: they are much more likely to give it to fascists. Germany in 1933 is the classic case.

Examples can be found, in industrial states of the last three decades, of the early stages of political disintegration, of the beginnings of a collapse of public order not caused by defeat in war. One is Italy in 1921–2. Armed bands of fascists terrorised the Po valley, and met with half-hearted resistance from socialists. But the Italian state machine was not really on the point of collapse. The armed forces were in reserve, and the civil administration functioned in most of the country. In the end they handed over to the fascists. They would not have accepted communists. The second example is France in 1934–6. The fascist leagues became a menace to public order: the reaction of public opinion to this menace produced the Popular Front. But the majority of those Frenchmen who voted for the Popular Front wanted to restore democratic government, together with some social reforms: they did not want a revolution from the left. The political and social forces of France restored the equilibrium disturbed by the fascist leagues. But the state machine was never in danger of collapse. The most striking example of political disintegration without war in this period was Germany in 1932. Street battles between Nazis and communists were a regular feature of the life of German cities. This situation was largely the result of the slump, and the men who fought the battles were largely unemployed. But here again the state machine did not collapse. The civil bureaucracy, *Reichswehr* and business bosses had the situation under control, and when parliamentary government had broken down they handed over, in good order, to Hitler, who they hoped was their saviour but proved their devourer.

Defeat in war however has produced many instances of the collapse of the state machine. The accumulated effects of the disastrous war paralysed the will of Nicholas II and his clique, and after his overthrow made the task of the Provisional Governments difficult and of the disruptive Bolsheviks simple. War smashed the bureaucratic apparatus of the Yugoslav state, substituting for it a multiplicity of Axis military and quisling authorities who knew little of the tasks of governing Yugoslavia, and this gave the communists their chance. War smashed the Chinese Kuomintang bureaucracy in the territories occupied by the Japanese, and the communist guerrillas found the Japanese and the quislings less skilful enemies than the old bureaucracy had been. The communists were able to exploit Chinese patriotism in the occupied areas. In the unoccupied areas the accumulated effects of war produced in the Kuomintang administration a paralysis of will similar to that which had affected Nicholas II. This became still more marked after the defeat of the Japanese.

These three situations were well exploited by the communists, who in these three countries had able leaders and efficient cadres. In Eastern Europe in 1944–5 the military collapse of Germany involved the collapse of the state machine in various forms.[1] The dominant factor thereafter was not the local communist movements, which in all cases except Bulgaria and Czechoslovakia were weak, and even there faced very strong and resolute popular opposition, but the conquering Russian army, which by direct or indirect intervention placed the communists in power.

In France and Italy the state machine disintegrated during the last stages of German occupation until it reached collapse. But the Anglo-American armies proved a factor of order. They did not, like the Russian armies in the East, intervene to place their favourites in power. Their presence ensured that no bid for power by the violence of a minority could succeed. They helped the French and Italians to rebuild their state machine by democratic means.[2] In the Asiatic territories reoccupied by western armies there was no single pattern. In Malaya and the Philippines the old state machine was restored: in the Philippines this was followed by the grant of independence, in Malaya it was not. In both countries the state machine was later shaken by communist armed revolt, but it was not broken. In Burma independence was granted before the

---

[1] The Roumanian and Bulgarian state machines emerged from the war comparatively unscathed; they were then undermined by the communists with Soviet advice and help. The Hungarian state machine was destroyed; in its place the Soviet authorities helped the Hungarian political leaders to rebuild another. Though the communists occupied key positions in it from the beginning, it cannot be said that they completely controlled it: only after they had crushed their political rivals in the spring of 1947 did they take it over. In the Czech lands the Germans had made use after 1939 of the old state machine, but by 1945 it had been very drastically purged. In Slovakia a new state machine had been created by the Tiso regime. Both the Czech quisling and the Slovak state machines collapsed in 1945. Here too the Soviet authorities helped rebuild a state machine which was mainly non-communist: only after the 'February revolution' of 1948 did the communists take it over. In Poland the Germans smashed the state machine of 1939. The Polish resistance movement created a 'shadow' state machine, ready to take over from the Germans: this was smashed by the Red Army. In its place the Soviet authorities created a state machine that was from the first controlled by communists. To sum up. In Poland the communists proceeded at once to install their own regime after their Russian protectors had destroyed the real Polish state. In Roumania and Bulgaria the transition was from the old regime (semi-fascist) to the communist state machine. In Hungary and Czechoslovakia there was an intermediate stage, in which the communists first built up a state machine and then knocked it down again.

[2] Communists will no doubt say that the Americans, and their French and Italian agents, created dictatorships of the bourgeoisie, subservient to Wall Street. The facts do not support this view.

FROM LENIN TO MALENKOV

state machine had been fully rebuilt. The new Burmese state was thus extremely weak, and its ability to withstand communist revolt remained uncertain. In Indonesia the Javanese nationalists built, partly on the foundations of the old, a state machine of their own which later withstood the shock of communist rebellion. In Indochina the old state machine was restored in the south and centre, but in a large part of the north never. Here the collapse of Japanese authority was used by the Vietnamese communists to as good effect as the collapse in Russia, Yugoslavia or China.

The second political factor, the international balance of power, requires little explanation. Communists have succeeded when Soviet military force was available to support them, and have failed when anti-communist or non-communist military force was present in overwhelming strength. But there is a third type of situation, of which the only self-made communist victories are examples. This situation can perhaps best be described as one of effective remoteness from external armed intervention. Either the armies of Ludendorff or the armies of Foch could have smashed the Russian Red Army if they had been used against it. But the German army was beaten by the Allies, and after victory the French, British and American peoples demanded peace and 'normality'. Any French, British or American politician knew that if he tried to keep the armies mobilised to fight the Bolsheviks he would lose the forthcoming elections. The 'Allied intervention' of which communist propaganda has screamed for thirty years was an insignificant effort which barely affected the outcome of the struggle. Effective remoteness also operated in favour of the Yugoslav and Albanian communists in 1941-4. The Germans had commitments on many fronts. There was a limit to the forces which they could spare against Balkan guerrillas, and only certain parts of the occupied Balkan territories—the main lines of communications and certain important economic resources—had to be defended. There was thus a limit to the effort they were prepared to make to exterminate the communist guerrillas in their mountain and forest fastnesses. This effort was formidable, but it was not enough. The same was true of China. The Japanese needed troops not only to fight the main Pacific war, but also to guard the Manchurian frontier against the Soviet Union and even to fight Chiang Kai-shek's regular troops. What was left to fight the communist guerrillas was not sufficient. This fact does not of course detract from the fine qualities of courage and leadership displayed by Yugoslav, Albanian or Chinese guerrillas.

This factor of effective remoteness did not operate in favour of the Hungarian revolution in 1919. The Roumanian army was strong enough to defeat the Hungarian Red Army, despite the latter's undoubted heroism. Whereas French and British public opinion did not believe it mattered to them what kind of regime Russia might have, the Roumanian leaders knew well that the regime in Hungary was of vital concern to them.[1]

'BACKWARD' SOCIETIES

An analysis of the social factors that favour or hinder communist movements must consider separately the two main types of society—the 'backward', predominantly agrarian, with little modern education, and the 'advanced', predominantly urban, in which the great majority of the people receive a modern education. It must be repeated that there are many variations. Such countries as Italy, Spain, Japan or the Argentine contain within their frontiers regions of each of these types. Nevertheless for our present purpose this oversimplified division into two types will suffice.

Communist movements in backward societies have recruited their leadership mainly from the intelligentsia and their mass support from peasants and from nations suffering from one form or another of subjection or national humiliation. These three social or national groups may of course overlap—a peasant's son belonging to a subject nation may become a member of the intelligentsia—but as groups they are distinct.

The role of intellectuals in the leadership of communist movements has been stressed repeatedly in earlier chapters.[2] The Russian, Yugoslav and Chinese movements are the classical examples. Others include Greece, Indochina, Persia, Bulgaria and India. The combination of idealist and personal frustration has also been discussed above.

Peasants have provided the mass support for communist-led movements in backward countries, and in certain circumstances have provided a large part of the cadres of the communist party.

[1] Nevertheless they made a big mistake. Having overthrown the communist regime which they rightly regarded as a threat to themselves, they allowed the counter-revolutionary extreme right to overthrow the moderate socialists, thereby placing in power the most implacable nationalist enemies of Roumania.

[2] There is a subdivision of this social category to which I hope that sociologists will devote great attention in future, the semi-intelligentsia, of the half-educated with intellectual pretensions. From it have emerged to plague us in the last generation, the cobbler's son of Gori, the customs official's son of Braunau, and the blacksmith's son of Forlì.

China and Yugoslavia are the best examples of this. It is no coincidence that both Mao Tse-tung and Tito have publicly stressed the role of the peasants in the revolution to the point of implicit disparagement of the role of the industrial proletariat. This lapse from orthodox Marxist doctrine made Mao unpopular with the Comintern for many years, and was one of the main doctrinal sins imputed to Tito by the Cominform.[1] Mao and Tito were right in the circumstances in which they were fighting, that is, at a time of disintegration or collapse of the state machine. In backward societies whose state machine is still strong, it is more difficult to win peasant support, and such support is less useful. But in such a society the peasants are so much more numerous than the workers, and so large a proportion of workers still retain the mental habits of peasants, that no revolutionary movement can hope for success unless it enlists a considerable number of peasant supporters.

This does not mean that in countries of backward society peasants are better revolutionary material than workers. It seems rather that working-class support is essential to revolutionary movements in such countries, at some stage in their development, but that it is insufficient for victory unless reinforced by substantial peasant support. The pattern of these movements has often repeated itself. The first stage is the emergence of a revolutionary leadership, without any mass support at all. The second stage comes when this leadership, drawn from the intelligentsia, makes its first contact with the masses. The masses which it reaches are the most accessible and most easily organisable masses—the urban workers. This stage came in Russia in the years 1902–5, in Bulgaria on the eve of the First World War, in China in 1921–5.

But this is an early stage of the revolutionary movement, and it is also an early stage in the development of the working class. The workers of Russia in 1905, of Bulgaria in 1913 and of China in 1922 were unskilled workers recently arrived from the villages. Most still had close personal contact with the peasants, and their mentality was in most cases that of peasants rather than of a new industrial proletariat. They suffered not only materially but also spiritually. They had left the rural society, with its customs and loyalties, in which for all its poverty and injustice they had their place. They had not yet found a place in urban society, whose customs they had not learned to understand, and whose loyalties they had not accepted. This bewilderment, this uncertain position

[1] See above, pp. 150 and 253.

between two worlds, is a characteristic of working classes in an early stage of industrialisation. It can be seen in India or Egypt or South Africa today. It was found in England at the time of the Chartists. Material hardship and spiritual bewilderment combine to make the workers revolutionary material at this stage in social development.

But the combination of revolutionary leaders and urban masses is not strong enough to seize power in a country of backward society as long as the state machine is strong. Much greater mass support is needed, and only the peasants can provide it. But peasants are often ill disposed to revolutionary movements. In Eastern Europe and Asia in the twentieth century the peasants have suffered from poverty and injustices, which would make them listen to revolutionary propaganda. Against this, however, must be set the influence of religion, patriotism and traditional loyalties. As long as the state machine functions normally, these forces operate against revolutionary movements. If however the state machine is shaken, or destroyed by a blow from without, the revolutionaries have better opportunities. The weakness of the state machine removes the main obstacle that has prevented access by revolutionaries to the villages. If the collapse of the state machine is followed by foreign conquest, then the revolutionaries can exploit patriotism, and even in some cases religious loyalties, to win the peasants to their cause. This was what happened in China from 1927 onwards, and in Yugoslavia from 1941 to 1945. In China the state machine had been weak ever since 1911. In the remote provinces in which Mao Tse-tung built his armies after the disasters of 1927, he had no serious rivals, and his own armed strength was sufficient to ensure him control over considerable areas. The peasant support which Mao organised, compensated the Chinese communists for their complete loss of the first mass support that they had won, that of the Shanghai workers, who after 1927 turned away from them. From 1937 onwards, the war with Japan enabled the communists to exploit patriotism on a massive scale. The Yugoslav communists were able to do the same. So were the Greek and Albanian parties. In south-east Asia patriotic slogans are the most powerful weapons of the communists. But they have produced the best results in those areas where the collapse of the old colonial regimes under Japanese invasion enabled the communists to establish direct contact with the peasants. Without this collapse of the state machine, the communists would not have had access to the peasants.

The existence of an intelligentsia both ideally and personally frustrated, of a peasantry suffering from overpopulation and land hunger, of an exploited and bewildered unskilled working class, and of national humiliation or colonial subjection, give communists their opportunity. But they do not necessarily ensure communist victory. In such conditions revolutionary movements of some sort are almost certain to appear, but they need not be communist, or even 'left'. They may take the form of fascism, anti-semitism or some kind of religious traditionalism. What form they will take, will depend on the intellectual climate in which the intelligentsia, which will provide the revolutionary leadership, has grown up. In present times, it will depend largely on the national attitude to Russia or China or their enemies. Between the world wars, sympathy for Russia contributed largely to incline radical young Serbs and Bulgarians towards communism, while dislike of Russia, and jealousy of the Jews in their midst, inclined radical young Roumanians of very similar social background and emotional attitudes towards Nazism. In Japan in the 1930's militarism and imperialism were the most attractive ideologies: today communism is stronger. In Egypt a combination of technical modernism and Moslem traditionalism still seems to appeal more strongly than communism to the intelligentsia.

'ADVANCED' SOCIETIES

In countries of advanced societies, the social group in which the communists make most converts is certainly the working class. But West European or North American workers in 1952 are very different from the proletariat of the Chartist age. The workers who most resemble those described by Marx are those of backward societies, for example Egypt or South Africa. One reason for the paradox that communists have been most successful not in the countries of the industrial West where Marx expected revolutions, but in the agrarian East to which Marx paid little attention, is that it is precisely in the countries of the East that the condition of the working class most resembles that of which Marx wrote. Since Marx wrote the Communist Manifesto, the West European workers and capitalists have both gone a long way. The workers have grown prosperous and have ceased to be a revolutionary force. The capitalists have found that they can make better profits by paying high wages and introducing machinery than by exploiting the cheap labour of the unskilled.

Marxist-Leninist dogma will not allow communists to face these facts. There must be some other explanation. Communists account for their frequent failures to capture western industrial workers by the theory of the 'labour aristocracy'. The best-paid workers, the communists assert, have sold themselves to the bourgeoisie and become their agents: only the broad popular masses of really poor and exploited workers provide the foundation for the 'party of the proletariat', the communist party. This theory simply is not true. Communist parties include as high a percentage of well-paid workers as do socialist or other working-class parties. Communist parties of course also include many of the poorest workers: so also do socialist parties, liberal parties or fascist parties. The theory of the labour aristocracy is as artificial as the theory of the class struggle within the peasantry. The truth is that as countries become more thoroughly industrialised, the workers become more prosperous and less revolutionary. There are still poor workers in countries of advanced society. There are however no exploited proletariats such as the British proletariat of 1840 or the Persian proletariat of 1952.

Where, despite a generally high level of prosperity, the majority of workers have supported communism, this has been for political and cultural reasons, not for economic. Economic interests will induce them only to support some party which speaks in the name of the workers: which party they choose is decided by other factors. In France the communists have profited from the old mental habit of *pas d'ennemis à gauche*. In both France and Italy the communists profited from the resistance movement, which gave them both a reputation for heroism and an opportunity to infiltrate the trade unions. In both countries they profited from the bad discipline, personal quarrels and doctrinal disunity of the socialists. Once installed in the trade unions, the communists controlled the machinery which enabled them to present themselves to the workers as the party that best defended workers' interests. In Austria the socialists remained firmly united, and the behaviour of the Russian armies in Vienna and Lower Austria told heavily against the communists. In Germany the socialists controlled most of the trade unions, and after 1922 were not split: right up till 1933 they commanded the loyalty of most German workers. Since 1945 hatred of the Russians in Western Germany has deprived the communists of influence. In Britain and Scandinavia the labour movements have a long and successful record, the habit of parliamentary institutions is deeply rooted, and the Protestant tradition for at least two centuries has operated against either religious or anti-religious fanaticism. The political and cultural climate of these countries is highly unfavourable for communists.

But even in those countries where the majority of workers support communist parties, it is wrong to imagine that the workers are a revolutionary force. Most French or Italian workers vote for the communists because they expect them to defend their material interests, not because they want a revolution. In a catastrophic slump workers will support a revolutionary party, but the events of 1932–3 in Germany show that this need not be a 'party of the left'.

The role of the intelligentsia in communist movements is much smaller in advanced than in backward societies. This is partly because in advanced societies intellectuals have fewer grounds for frustration, and more attractive outlets for their energies, and partly because the workers enjoy a much higher level of education, and do not need to the same extent the tutelage of intellectuals. But intellectuals are to be found in western communist movements. Some cases can be chiefly explained by personal ambition or a personal sense of grievance. But there are also more general political attitudes among the western intelligentsias which give communists an opening. In France the long tradition of the opposition of educated men and women to the powers that be, operates in favour of the communists, though not only of them.[1] In Britain too there is a small but influential intelligentsia that clings through thick and thin to the slogan *pas d'ennemis à gauche*. Its essential feature is a guilt complex. As long as Britain has a colony, as long as there is social injustice or race hatred in any part of the British Commonwealth, or in any country with which the Commonwealth is associated, they have, they believe, no moral right to resist aggression by communists. They feel less strongly about the colonial exploitation of Uzbeks, Letts or Hungarians, or the economic exploitation of Russian workers. The mentality is the same as that which prevailed among a rather different section of the British intelligentsia in the 1930's, which argued that as Versaille had been an unjust treaty, we had no right to oppose Hitler. This group was well cultivated by Nazi propaganda in the 1930's, and the corresponding group today are well cultivated by Soviet and communist propaganda.

[1] The *fronde* of the French intelligentsia against the state has of course also taken the form of sentimental conservatism. *Action française* is the classic example.

CLASSLESS COMMUNIST CADRES

From these groups are formed the communist parties' cadres. In backward countries the cadres come from peasants, workers, subject nationalities and the intelligentsia, but principally from the intelligentsia. In advanced countries they come from the working class and the intelligentsia, but principally from the workers.

But the communist cadres, though formed from several social classes, belong to none. Whatever their social origin, communist leaders form a caste of professional revolutionaries, and stand outside class. In democratic countries, communists do not always attain in practice to the exalted ideal of a Leninist professional revolutionary. In democratic conditions a worker who is a leading communist may go on living like other workers, or a middle-class intellectual who is a leading communist may go on living like other middle-class intellectuals. This is because in free countries the conditions of the struggle are not arduous, and many communists consciously or unconsciously accept as normal the climate of 'bourgeois democracy' for which in public they show so much scorn. But wherever communists are persecuted by the forces of the state—whether it be a state of advanced or backward society—communist cadres become members of a separate, dedicated caste.

It is an easy but dangerous error to identify Italian communists with the Italian workers' movement, Chinese communists with the Chinese peasants' movement, or Indian communists with the Indian radical intelligentsia. But communist cadres must not be confused with the social classes from which they derive support.

How far the communists themselves are aware of this it is hard to judge. Communist social analysis is almost worthless. The cant phrases about proletariat, proletarian aristocracy and Lumpenproletariat; rich, middle and poor peasants; petty, national and bureaucratic bourgeoisies; compradores and feudal elements; big, bad and patriotic landlords, are repeated *ad nauseam*. Sometimes the communists seem genuinely to be trying with these cant phrases to explain social facts: at other times they are simply using 'social' phrases as terms of abuse. But whatever their intentions, they do not help the student of social problems.

Communist dogma lays down that the leading revolutionary class is the proletariat. In fact in the thirty years since the foundation of the Comintern there have only been three cases of communist parties which have been 'the party of the proletariat' in the sense that they have had the freely expressed support of a large majority of the industrial working class of their country. These are the French party since 1945, the Italian party since 1948 and the Czechoslovak party between 1946 and 1948. Even these examples, as we have seen, are subject to qualifications.[1] Other communist parties are, or have been, parties of part of the proletariat. Others again have been parties without the proletariat. The Chinese party after 1927 is the best example of the latter. Even in 1945 the Chinese communists found it necessary to claim that their party was a 'party of the proletariat', but as we have seen they interpreted the phrase in a peculiar manner.[2]

The truth is that ever since Lenin, the claim of the communists that their party is the party of the proletariat has rested on the assumption that the party alone understands and pursues the interests of the proletariat. The interests of the proletariat are simply defined as whatever at a given moment the communist party is trying to do. Most communist statements about the proletariat are true when we translate the word 'proletariat' as 'communist professional revolutionary caste'. They are true but tautological.

STALINIST SOCIETY

In the Soviet Union, Eastern Europe and China the communist caste holds power. It is a caste of professional communists, but hardly of professional revolutionaries: a revolution is the last thing that it wishes. Members of this ruling caste enjoy privileges and power which, if compared with the lot of their fellow-citizens or subjects, are greater than those of any ruling group anywhere in the world. The occupational risks are however also very high. Since 1945 there has been nothing in the Soviet Union to compare with the *Yezhovshchina*, but there have been purges. In the satellite countries the turnover has been more rapid. The examples of the Kostov-Rajk type of 'patriotic' communist and of the Slansky-Pauker type of 'servile' communist are equally instructive.

Under communist regimes a section of the working class has improved its material position. The improvement is clearly greater, the more backward the country. The workers of Czechoslovakia have not improved their lot. It was the support of the workers that enabled Gottwald to make his police-'revolution', but since then

[1] See above, pp. 258, 294–5, 299–300.
[2] See above, pp. 287–8.

the exploitation of the Czechoslovak economy by Soviet imperialism has imposed growing hardships. The discontent, and even passive resistance, of the Czech workers was clearly shown in the low output in the Ostrava coal and metallurgical industry during 1952. Economic exploitation by the Soviet imperialists has also adversely affected the standard of living of the workers of the other European satellite states, and probably of Manchuria. In short, some workers have gained, others have lost. It is probable that what has been gained could have been gained without paying the price that the communists and Moscow are exacting. Throughout the Soviet and Chinese empires the unending emphasis on war industry, capital goods and vast public works maintains pressure on the workers' standard of living, limits their leisure and threatens their social amenities. At the worst, it involves a combination of the economic exploitation of early capitalism with the political terror of modern totalitarianism. The absence of any free elections, in central or local government or in factories, deprives the workers of any safeguard against exploitation.

The treatment of peasants by victorious communists seems to follow the same pattern everywhere. First comes the redistribution of land, for which the peasants are grateful, accompanied by heavy taxation and requisitions, for which they are not. Whether the balance shows a gain, depends on local circumstances and the action of individual communist local organisers. This stage occurred in Russia in the civil war, in parts of Eastern Europe after 1945, and is being completed in China in 1953. After an interval (in Russia eight comparatively happy years of N.E.P., in Eastern Europe and China periods varying from four to seven) collectivisation sets in. It seems that the catastrophic errors of Russia in 1929–33 are being avoided in Eastern Europe and China, but it is not sure that they will be avoided to the end. Whatever the method, the result of collectivisation is to create a new centralised coercive machine, ruling the lives of the peasants more directly and more pervasively than any tyranny of the past, to deprive them of the fruit of their labours, and to impose a new form of serfdom. It should however be clearly understood that this is the consequence of Stalin's *recipe*: it is not the inevitable consequence of any form of co-operative farming. On the contrary, there is much to be said for co-operative farming, on both economic and social grounds, provided that it is combined with political conditions which enable farmers to choose the men and women who are to give them orders. Danish experience shows this.

The position of the intelligentsia—in the usual sense of the free professions, not in the special sense of the Soviet 'toiling intelligentsia'[1]—is tragic under communist rule. Having joined or supported the communist movement for ideal motives, to fight tyranny and social injustice, they are deprived of what freedom they had under the pre-revolutionary dictatorship. Those who possess unusual technical or scientific qualifications, or enjoy international fame as writers or artists, may survive if they will perform the prescribed number of kowtows to Stalin or Mao. The others are destroyed, some immediately, most after a long agony of humiliation and self-betrayal.

The prospect for nations struggling for independence is hardly more encouraging. The Chechens and Crimean Tatars were destroyed as nations. The deportations of Balts are on such a scale as to threaten their national existence. The land of the Central Asiatic peoples is colonised by Russians, their economic resources exploited to the advantage of Moscow, their Islamic religion persecuted, their history falsified. The peoples of Eastern Europe are transformed into colonies.

In the Soviet Union, as we have seen, there is a tendency for the privileged group to make its privileges hereditary. There are also grave tensions within the privileged group. Both managers and party officials belong to a new generation. The caste of classless revolutionaries who seized power in 1917 is gone.

In Eastern Europe, Lenin's and Stalin's revolutions are superimposed on each other. Power is held by the revolutionary caste, but these are men who have been trained in a Stalinist school. The non-party managerial element, which plays an important part and enjoys privileges, is of the pre-revolutionary generation: there has not yet been time to form post-Stalinist managerial cadres. The social tensions are not less acute than in the Soviet Union, but they are of another kind. They are kept in check by Soviet military domination.

In China too there are elements of both Lenin's and Stalin's revolutions and policies. Power is held by the revolutionary caste, but these are men who have acquired their experience in their own country and their own wars. In China too the problem of the pre-revolutionary generation of experts is important. But the future social development of China cannot be predicted by one who does not know China. The Chinese revolution was of the communist type. Post-revolutionary Chinese policies have been Stalinist

[1] See above, pp. 238-9.

policies. But in future the social and cultural traditions of China will no doubt also help to shape events.

THE MENACE OF STALINIST IMPERIALISM

Stalinist totalitarianism threatens the existence of free men and women, as individuals and as nations. It deludes millions who, suffering victims or indignant spectators of some racial, social or political oppression, seek a sudden and miraculous redemption. But of all communist myths none is more absurd than that of the historical inevitability and invincibility of communism. The victories of communism have been won as a result of certain political and social conditions. These conditions can be prevented or removed.

Resistance to Stalinism has three aspects—external defence, internal defence, and the treatment of social conditions.

The external threat can be met only by the possession of over-whelming military force. Defeat in war, which experience shows is the communists' best opportunity, can be best avoided by avoiding war itself, and the best way to ensure this is to convince the Russian and Chinese communist leaders that if they go to war it is they who will be defeated. They will be convinced of this only if they see that their prospective victims are both well armed and united. The widespread belief that social reform removes the need for armaments is a fallacy: prosperity invites aggression. It is of course true that there are limits to the strain that armaments can place on an industrial economy, and that excessive hardships produce disaffection. It may also be true that the Soviet leaders will not deliberately launch a major war. But to stake the future of the free nations on the assumed probability that Moscow desires peace would be a foolish gamble. To increase social justice and economic prosperity in one's country is in itself an essential task of policy, but it is no substitute for defence. To balance the claims of defence and prosperity is the task of practical statesmen. But when in doubt defence should come first. It is more important, for both individuals and nations, to be alive than to be prosperous.

The strength that will deter Soviet or Chinese aggression is not only a matter of armaments: diplomacy is also an essential weapon. It is also a weapon which *all* the free countries must use. The widespread belief that there are only two Powers in the world, and that all other states are helpless and can only submit to the will of one giant or the other, is a fallacy. These two without doubt overshadow the others. But the others have an increasingly important part to play. Their friendship or hostility can turn the balance decisively against either giant. The place for diplomacy is not so much in the relations between the giants as in the relations of the lesser but considerable Powers with each other. An important task of the United States is to win over these lesser Powers. Certainly the main single force that can withstand Soviet imperialism is the might of America. Certainly every democratic statesman who wishes his country to remain free from Soviet imperialism must regard the United States as his friend. 'Third force' manœuvring and 'neutralism' invite disaster. But no less certainly the United States would lose the world struggle—'cold' or 'hot'— if it did not have the support of those lesser Powers whose resources or strategic position are most important.

This is no place to discuss the main tasks of western diplomacy —the problems of Germany, Japan, India, Indonesia and the Middle East. Some mention has been made of them in earlier pages. But all concerned with resistance to communism should give them careful thought.

The free world must have armed strength and skilful diplomacy in order to survive. But survival is not enough. The aim of western policy must be to liberate the peoples oppressed by totalitarian Stalinist imperialism. This does not mean that the West must launch a crusading war. It cannot be too often stressed that preventive wars are incompatible with democratic principle and democratic practice. To talk as if a preventive war were a possibility is both foolish and dangerous. It is foolish because it may encourage false hopes among conquered nations. It is dangerous because it may encourage aggressive adventures by the communist world. No western statesman would subject his nation to the uncertain horrors of atomic war. It is well that the Soviet leaders should know this, provided that they also know that the West would defend itself if attacked.

To reject preventive war does not however mean to accept the Stalinisation of half humanity as a permanent fact. The communists, and their conscious and unconscious instruments, make great efforts to persuade public opinion in the free world that they must choose between preventive war and recognition of the present conquests of Stalinism. This choice is false, and must be resolutely rejected. The means by which Stalinism can be forced back, and the oppressed peoples, including the Russian people itself—the greatest martyr of the last thirty years—can be liberated, are not clear today. This does not mean that they will not become clear, or that they do not exist. Both bellicosity and defeatism are fatal errors. The only policy that will save the free world is to be patient and strong, to search for every opportunity and to keep an open mind.

THE INTERNAL MENACE—REALITY AND ILLUSION

The internal threat of communism is in part a police problem. Nothing has been said in these pages of communist espionage and sabotage, not because these are not important subjects but because we are here concerned with the political and social aspects of communism, not with its conspiratorial technique. Police problems can only be handled by the police, and one can only hope that they will do their job well.

The question is however sometimes asked, whether a free society can permit the existence of a communist party.

Certain arguments used against the banning of communist parties are unconvincing. One is that, if banned, the party 'will go underground'. The answer to this is that the party has gone underground already. Ever since the Twenty-One Conditions of the Second Comintern Congress of 1920,[1] all communist parties operating in democratic states have been bound to maintain a clandestine organisation, parallel with the legal party which functions normally under the law. The banning of a party would deprive it of its overt activities, and make its underground work not less but more difficult.

There is also no need to take seriously the protests of the communists themselves. None will whine so piteously as the communists, when they see themselves threatened with the loss of those civil liberties of which, should they ever be placed in power by the 'liberating' Soviet army, they would enthusiastically deprive 95 per cent of their compatriots. Whatever other considerations have to be taken into account in forming an opinion on this issue, the wishes of the communists themselves do not.

There are circumstances in which communist parties may have to be banned—during war against a communist state, or perhaps in certain special emergencies involving immediate threat of war. It is also arguable that communist activity cannot be tolerated in countries whose people, through lack of education, are mentally defenceless against communist propaganda. The question can only be decided on the facts of individual cases. And even in emergencies or special conditions, there are arguments, based on expediency,

[1] See above, pp. 73–4.

which weigh heavily against suppression. The example of France in 1939–40 shows that anti-communist action can become, or can be considered to be, anti-working-class action. Suppression will weaken the communists, but if it turns the working class against the rest of society, more will have been lost than gained. The argument that uneducated people cannot be exposed to communist propaganda is also liable to abuse. The anti-communist law passed by the South African Nationalists is the classic example. This law was designed not so much to stop communism, of which there was very little, as to smash the trade unions and persecute persons of any opinions inconvenient to the government.

Except in special emergencies—and even then only with strong safeguards—the suppression of communist parties in democratic countries is objectionable on grounds not of expediency but of principle. The persecution of any minority is objectionable to democrats. Not for their sakes, but for the sake of our own principles, we must be exceedingly reluctant to put communists outside the law. To deny communists employment in positions that affect the security of the state, is a perfectly justifiable, and indeed imperative, measure of national defence. To suppress communist parties is a dangerous infraction of the civil liberties not only of the communists—who spit on all liberties—but of the whole body of citizens. Thus, while not excluding it in absolutely all circumstances, one should view it with the strongest suspicion.

It is important to understand that mass witch-hunting, even if conducted by eminent persons and accompanied by floods of self-righteous rhetoric, is a poor method of dealing with the communist danger, and exposes democratic society to other dangers no less insidious. Between the world wars the politicians of Eastern Europe inveighed interminably against Marxism, communism and judeo-bolshevism. Their eloquence was usually inspired less by moral condemnation of Soviet practices than by fear of the social discontent of their own impoverished and bullied subjects. It was usually based on a very thorough ignorance of communism in practice or in theory. Anti-communism served as a respectable mask for the satisfaction of personal grievances, and for petty acts of injustice and revenge. It delivered the politicians into the hands of Nazi propagandists, and Hitler led their countries to ruin.

Some of these politicians escaped from the advancing Red Army, and crossed the Atlantic. There they lose no opportunity of pointing out that, like the late Adolf Hitler, they have spent a large part of their adult lives in the verbal or physical annihilation of communists. It would be unfortunate if their claims were taken too seriously by their new hosts. *Non tali auxilio, nec defensoribus illis. . . .*

During the 1930's thousands of democrats in Western Europe fell into the trap of the Popular Front. Fascism was a real menace, and the communists, who loudly proclaimed their hatred of fascists, and put it into practice on the battle-field of Madrid, seemed brave and loyal allies. In 1939 the communists swallowed all their words, and applauded while Stalin shook Ribbentrop's hand. But the resistance redeemed their reputation. Both the Popular Front and the resistance were used by the communists to infiltrate themselves into strong positions, to make thousands of young converts, and to dupe hundreds of thousands of good democrats. The last years have shown how dangerous to freedom can be the communist positions won by deceit of the innocent and the enthusiastic.

With this sad example before them, the free nations should be able to avoid falling into a similar trap held out by the fascists. There is no doubt that communism is a deadly menace to freedom, and there is no doubt that fascists hate communists, and are both brave and efficient. But fascists must not be allowed to take the leadership of the struggle against communism, as the communists once took the leadership of the struggle against fascism. This does not of course mean that everyone who has once been a fascist should be for ever banned from the society of democrats. In most European countries there are decent citizens who were once led astray by fascist slogans. Nor does it mean that the alliance of any state should be rejected because its government is fascist.[1] It does mean that in a democratic country democrats should treat with the gravest suspicion any organisation which pursues fascist aims, and that persons who have been leaders of fascist groups in the past, and have given no solid proof of repentance, should be excluded from the political company of free men and women. Many of the fascist criminals of Central Europe, and their literary sycophants, are still at large, in Spain or South America. Among them are Roumanian Iron Guardists, who butchered Jews, tortured British oil engineers, and robbed and murdered their own countrymen. Among them is Ante Pavelić, whose record as a mass murderer can bear comparison with that of the late Adolf Hitler himself. Pavelić could display his talents only in a small country, but he displayed

---

[1] The problem of relations with Spain should be considered on a basis of international realities, not of emotional *ressentiment*, whether of Popular Front nostalgia or of conservative nostalgia.

them to good effect. He escaped unscathed and is no doubt plotting further villainies. Not by Beelzebub shall we cast out devils.

The fascist danger is at present as remote as was the communist danger in the 1930's. But democrats must watch for any sign of its revival. They cannot afford to be duped again.

There are two divisions in the world today. One is between the communists and the rest. The other is between those who regard slavery, torture and massacre as permissible methods of political struggle and those who do not. The first division is the more publicised, the second the more fundamental.

The social causes of communism are frustration of the intelligentsia and poverty of the masses. Something can be done at least to diminish these.

It is frequently said that mass poverty breeds communism. This is only half true. Populations living in the most abject misery are not usually the most revolutionary: the Indian *rayot* and the Egyptian *fellaheen* have been passive factors in history. But if revolutionary agitators are at hand, there is no doubt that they can exploit poverty for their ends. Action designed to reduce poverty helps also to reduce communism. Yet it should be understood that there are limits to the political value of 'economic aid to undeveloped countries'.

Firstly, a large part of any such funds will be dissipated in various forms of corruption, nepotism and luxury. However the funds may be controlled, they will be administered at some stage by underpaid officials with numerous family connections. Until these have had their slice of the cake, few crumbs will reach the masses. Secondly, the western benefactors will be hated. The most odiously selfish motives will be attributed to them by the fertile imagination of the recipients, and communist propaganda will further inflate every calumny and every scandal. The more the western experts labour to ensure fair methods, the more will they be accused of imperialistic exploitation. Here the communist agitator and the extreme social reactionary will work hand in hand. American experience in Kuomintang China and in Greece can provide copious examples. Thirdly, even in the most ideal conditions, western economic aid can only very slightly diminish eastern poverty. The notion that it is possible, by vast expenditure of dollars, to hand over ready-made to Nigerians, Burmese and Paraguayans a prefabricated twentieth-century welfare state plus complete 'solutions' of all social problems, plus an American standard of living, is a harmful fantasy. It is harmful because it is creating, every day and in every land, expectations that can never be fulfilled, and whose non-fulfilment will produce further oceans of xenophobia and quasi-Marxist rhetoric. Fourthly, even if there is some slight reduction of poverty in some areas, it will not last long, for the improved standard of living will soon be outpaced by the increase of population. Suggestions that births be limited are interpreted as sinister schemes to perpetuate the domination of the imperialist exploiting white race. Communist propaganda makes full use of the natural desire of man and woman to have many children. Communists deny that there is any problem of overpopulation in the world. Their doctrines on this subject are a mixture of eighteenth-century rationalist optimism with an unceasing hunt for scapegoats. Poverty is due solely to the wickedness of capitalists, landowners and western imperialists: annihilate these, and all will be well. This idiotic dogma is doubtless sincerely believed by the faithful. It also has tactical advantages. Togliatti's desire for more Italian babies has the same motive as had Mussolini's. Rapid growth of population yields further millions of soldiers and forced labourers, cannon-fodder and factory-fodder in the Stalinist third of the world, civil-war-fodder outside the zone.

The level of skill, education and prosperity enjoyed by North America, the Pacific Dominions and—until recent times—the greater part of Europe, were achieved by centuries of toil, carried out in relatively favourable conditions of climate and of public security.[1] They cannot be handed ready-made to the rest of humanity. Of all obnoxious commodities that the West has exported to the East, none is more harmful than the belief that every man and woman is entitled, of right, to be presented with the standard of living of a Chicago business man.

Economic aid to backward countries can achieve big results provided that it is treated as an economic proposition. Investments that make the best use of available manpower, skill and raw materials can serve a useful purpose. Resources poured out either as a gigantic dole or as part of some romantic scheme based on the Stalinist *mystique* of heavy-industry-at-once-at-any-cost, will be wasted.

The frustration of the intelligentsia is a more immediate cause

[1] The security was of course largely due to the fact that the western nations were free from the invasions which spent their force on the backs of Poles, Hungarians, Moldavians or South Slavs. The immunity was due not to superior virtue but to good fortune. Nevertheless, the difference in social and cultural evolution remains a fact.

of communist and other anti-western revolutionary movements than is the poverty of the masses. Can anything be done to remedy this scourge of the twentieth century?

The obvious answer is that the system of education should be improved. It has often been pointed out that the education systems of countries of backward society produce too many lawyers and journalists, too few doctors and agricultural experts. This is equally true of the Balkan universities in the 1930's and of those of Egypt, India or West Africa today. The need for a more practical system of education, more linked with the life of the people, was pointed out, for example, by Lord Curzon as Viceroy of India at the beginning of the century. But the problem is easier to state than to solve. A western legal education possesses for Asian or African minds an almost magic prestige. Proposals for educational reform are interpreted as a sinister trick by the imperialists to deprive Asians and Africans of the elixir of political power. Moreover there is in Asian and African societies a more effective economic demand for lawyers and journalists than for doctors or engineers. It is always profitable to minister to cupidity and hate: skills designed to remove disease or ignorance command a lower market price. Finally, it does not follow that the best technical training available in western medical or engineering schools is always best suited to the Asian or African environment. For example, though it is undeniable that modern agricultural science can benefit Asian and African agriculture, yet its practical application to Burmese or Uganda peasant holdings will not be the same as to large, extensive and highly mechanised farms in the United States or Britain.

But despite these difficulties, it cannot and must not be impossible to devise educational systems that will produce the right kind of experts in the right place, that will enable Asian and African and Latin American intellectuals to serve their peoples' welfare, that will remove the frustration that devours them, and will make them less inclined to seek salvation in messianic short-cuts. This field of educational reform is one in which the experts of European countries, of European colonies, and of independent Asian and Latin American states can help each other. If the United Nations had not become above all a forum for demagogy and hatred, it would have provided facilities for the fulfilment of this common task. There is incidentally no field in which economic aid to undeveloped countries can be more fruitful than this.

No less important than practical economic and educational measures are tact and courtesy. Personal slights, often exaggerated by excessive Asian or African sensibility, have done and still do unmeasured political harm. London landladies who refuse lodgings to African students are worth a company of troops to Stalin: Dr. Malan and his *apartheid* are worth several army corps.

In countries of advanced society the intelligentsia is not a separate social category. Intellectuals are to be found in many different occupations and in all political groups. The revolutionary intelligentsia as a distinct political factor does not exist. But certain false values diffused by the intelligentsia contribute to the undermining of the western world. One is the belief that every man and woman has a right to be looked after by society, and that those who talk about obligations are 'reactionaries'. Modern welfare services are regarded, not as the fruit of the toil and struggle of past generations, to be guarded and defended and reconquered by our own, but as an unconditional gift. Bread and cinema tickets are the birthright of western man. It is forgotten that the difference between a higher and a lower standard of living is less important than the difference between the life and death of men and women and nations. Another false value is the obsession of 'debunking' which became so widespread in the West in the 1920's. At first a healthy reaction against Victorian cant, against the complacency of the generation that led Europe to the slaughter of 1914, it grew into a perverse distortion of reality. It became allied to the guilt complexes about the Versailles peace, or about imperialism, which have morally disarmed two generations of intellectuals in Britain and France. The numerous scandals, imperfections and injustices of western society were equated with the horrors of Hitlerian or Stalinist totalitarianism. Western neo-Marxists forgot the Marxist doctrine of the transformation of differences of quantity into differences of quality. A British magistrate sends a poor labourer to gaol for poaching a rich man's pheasants. Stalin starves to death a million Ukrainian peasants and a million Kazah nomads. Both, the debunker will argue, are examples of class prejudice. There is injustice in both Britain and Russia.

Western intellectuals must stop being ashamed of their own civilisation, and become aware of the difference in quality between it and totalitarianism. Defeatism is no less deadly than cant. Certainly western society is full of evils against which honest men and women must fight. But the western achievement is also something to defend with pride. No difference of class or creed within western society is comparable in reality with the gulf that divides western from Stalinist society. Classes and creeds must fight each other within western society: without such a struggle freedom loses its meaning. But in the last resort the classes and political groups within western society—excepting only the classless cadres of the Stalinist fifth column—belong to each other, and the western nations belong to each other. This is the reality. Yet the fantasies that are in the minds of men and women can prevail over reality. If western men and women insist that they hate each other more than they hate Stalinism, they have it in their power to hand themselves over, bound hand and foot, to the Stalinists.

The western nations can make reality prevail over fantasy. This is a human duty, not a party slogan. Conservatives can no more afford to arrogate to themselves a monopoly of patriotism than socialists to consider 'the nation' an invention of 'the reactionaries'.

There will be no sudden, miraculous and sensational victory over the powers of darkness. Even the dollar cannot prefabricate a Complete Utopia to outwit the Kremlin. Even the most high-minded ideologists cannot manufacture 'a new faith' to convert those wooed by communist propaganda. But much less than this can ward off the Stalinist onslaught. The western nations have sufficient military, diplomatic and economic resources to force Stalinism back and to accelerate its collapse, without war. They will achieve this if they will remember three things: that their own freedom must be defended; that the Russian and other enslaved nations are not their enemies but their friends; and that only they themselves can remedy the evils that infect their own society.

Every blow against injustice in a British or French village or workshop is a blow against Stalinism. But the blow should be struck, not because it will weaken Stalinism but because it will lessen the volume of injustice in the world. Those who see in social and political reforms no more than tricks to defeat communism, will achieve few reforms, will do their countries small good, and will perhaps not even defeat communism. Poverty and tyranny, social oppression and race hatred are evil things. These every man of good will should fight, in his own country or outside it, as long as mind and limbs have strength.

Bibliography

THE following list contains the names of works that I have found useful, or can recommend as useful to readers who wish to pursue the subject further. As those readers who have read my footnotes will already have noted, and as will become still more clear to those who peruse the list, there are comparatively few studies of individual communist parties, but many studies of internal or international politics or economics which contain useful material relevant to the study of communism. The list has been divided into four main sections—European Background; European communism; the Soviet Union; and Asia, Africa and Latin America. The sections have been subdivided by periods. But several works contain material on more than one of these main regions, and more than one period. In the case of works published in Great Britain, only the date of publication is given, in all other cases the place and date.

A. EUROPEAN BACKGROUND

The following is a convenient short list of secondary works giving the immediate historical background, before 1914, of the main European countries. Halévy's masterpiece is still unsurpassed. Eliot's description of the Balkans at the turn of the century can still instruct and delight the reader. Of the more recent works, those of Thomson, Taylor and Brennan can be specially recommended. The last of these also covers the years between the world wars.

Bonomi, I. *La politica italiana da Porta Pia a Vittorio Veneto*. Rome, 1944.
Brennan, G. *The Spanish labyrinth*. 1943.
Clapham, Sir J. *The economic development of France and Germany*. 1945.
Eliot, Sir C. *Turkey in Europe*. 1900.
Ensor, R. C. K. *England 1870–1914*. 1936.
Halévy, E. *Histoire du peuple anglais*, Epilogue, 2 Vols. Paris, 1926.
Plamenatz, J. *The revolutionary movement in France*. 1952.
Robinson, G. T. *Rural Russia under the old regime*. New York, 1949.
Salomone, A. *Italian democracy in the making*. Pennsylvania, 1945.
Seignobos, C. *L'évolution de la troisième république*. Paris, 1921.
Seton-Watson, H. *The decline of Imperial Russia*. 1952.
Taylor, A. J. P. *The Habsburg monarchy*. 1948.
Thomson, D. *Democracy in France*. 1946.
Ziekursch, J. *Politische Geschichte des neuen deutschen Kaiserreiches*, 3 Vols. Frankfurt, 1925.

The following works deal with the labour and socialist movements in individual European countries. Those marked with an asterisk deal also with the period between the world wars.

358 FROM LENIN TO MALENKOV

Arhiv Komunističke Partije Jugoslavije, Vols. 3 and 4. Belgrade, 1950.
Bauer, O. *Die Nationalitätenfrage und die Sozialdemokratie*. Vienna, 1907.
Blagoev, D. *Prinos k'm istoriyata na sotsializma v B'lgariya*. Sofia, 1906.
Dan, F. *Proiz'hozhdenie bolshevizma*. New York, 1946.
Dolléans, E. *Histoire du mouvement ouvrier*. Paris, 1946.
Feldman, J. *Geschichte der politischen Ideen in Polen*. Munich, 1917.
*Hansson, and Landqvist, O. *Arbetarrörelsen i Sverige*. Stockholm, 1947.
Lapčevic, D. *Istorija socializma u Srbiji*. Belgrade, 1926.
Lenin, V. I. *Sochinenia*, 3rd edition. Moscow, 1930–3. Vols. I–XVI.
Louis, P. *Histoire du socialisme en France*. Paris, 1946.
Luxemburg, R. *Kwestja polska a ruch socjalistyczny*. Cracow, 1905.
Martov, Y. and Dan, F. *Geschichte der russischen Sozialdemokratie*. Berlin, 1926.
Mehring, F. *Geschichte der deutschen Sozialdemokratie*. Stuttgart, 1913.
Mitrany, *Marx against the peasant*, 1951.
*Paasivirta, J. *Arbetarrörelsen i Finland*. Stockholm, 1949.
Perl, F. *Dzieje ruchu socjalistycznego w Polsce*. Warsaw, 1910.
*Renaudeau, F. *Le parti travailliste de Grande-Betragne*. Paris, 1947.
*Petrescu, C. Titel. *Socialismul în România*. Bucarest, 1945.
Rezler, G. *A magyar nagyipari munkásság kialakulása*. Budapest, 1945.
Venturi, F. *Il popolismo russo*, 2 Vols. Rome, 1952.

B. COMMUNISM IN EUROPE

(1) *Comintern publications*

III Internatsional 6–7 marta 1919 g. Moscow, 1919.
2. *S'yezd Kommunisticheskovo Internatsionala*. Moscow, 1920.
Le 5e Congrès de l'Internationale communiste. Paris, 1924.
Protokollen des 6ten Weltkongresses der K.I. Hamburg, 1929.
The 7th World Congress. 1935.
Kommunisticheskii Internatsional. v dokumentah (ed. B. Kun). Moscow, 1931.
The Second and Third Internationals and the Vienna Union, conference of the executives in Berlin, 1922.
Communist International. Moscow.
Kommunismus. Vienna (1920–2).
International Press Correspondence ('Inprecorr').
Dimitrov, G. *The People's Front*. 1937 (speeches and articles).

(2) *Works about the Comintern*

Balabanova, A. *My life as a rebel*. 1938.
Borkenau, F. *The Communist International*. 1938.
Borkenau, F. *Der europäische Kommunismus*. Munich, 1952.
Lazitch, B. *Lénine et la troisième Internationale*. Paris, 1950.

(3) *Germany*

Bullock, A. *Hitler: a study in tyranny*. 1952.
Carr, E. H. *German-Soviet relations between the world wars*. 1951.
Fischer, R. *Stalin and German communism*. New York, 1948.
Flechtheim, O. *Die KPD*. Offenbach-am-Main, 1948.

Görlitz, W. *Der deutsche Generalstab*. Frankfurt-am-Main, 1950.
Krivitsky, W. *I was Stalin's agent*. 1939.
Levi, P. *Unser Weg wider den Putschismus*. Berlin, 1921.
Luxemburg, R. ('Junius'). *Die Krise der Sozialdemokratie*. Berlin, 1915.
Luxemburg, R. *Die russische Revolution*. Berlin, 1922.
Noske, G. *Von Kiel bis Kapp*. Berlin, 1920.
Rosenberg, A. *The birth of the German Republic*. 1931.
Rosenberg, A. *The history of the German Republic*. 1936.

Krivitsky's book is also interesting on the Soviet purges (see section C of this bibliography). Levi's pamphlet deals with the March fiasco of 1921. Luxemburg's pamphlet on the Russian revolution was published by Levi three years after her murder.

(4) The Hungarian Revolution

Böhm, W. *Im Kreuzfeuer zweier Revolutionen*. Munich, 1924.
Garami, E. *Forrongó Magyarország*. Vienna, 1922.
Jászi, O. *Revolution and counter-revolution in Hungary*. 1924.
Révész, M. *Vázlatok a magyar munkásmozgalom történetéröl*. Budapest, 1946.

(5) France

Danos, J. and Gibelin, M. *Juin 36: masses et militants*. Paris, 1952.
Goguel, F. *Les partis politiques sous la troisième république*. Paris, 1945.
Montreuil, J. *Histoire du mouvement ouvrier en France*. Paris, 1945.
Walter, G. *Histoire du parti communiste français*. Paris, 1949.
Werth, A. *France in ferment*. 1938.
Zévaès, A. *Histoire du socialisme et du communisme en France*. Paris, 1947.

(6) Other Countries 1918–1939

Arhiv komunističke partije Jugoslavije, Vol. 1. Belgrade, 1950.
Bauer, O. *Die österreichische Revolution*. Vienna, 1923.
Bojan-Blaziewicz, W. *Przewrót majowy w Polsce*. New York, 1926.
Borkenau, F. *Spanish cockpit*. 1938.
Buell, R. L. *Poland, key to Europe*. 1939.
Cole, G. D. H. *A History of the Labour Party from 1914*. 1948.
Macartney, C. A. *The social revolution in Austria*. 1926.
Nenni, P. *La storia di quattro anni*. Rome, 1946.
Orwell, G. *Homage to Catalonia*. 1938.
Roberts, H. L. *Roumania: the politics of an agrarian state*. Yale, 1951.
Rossi, A. *The rise of Italian Fascism*. 1937.
Seton-Watson, H. *Eastern Europe between the wars*. 1945.
Trotski, L. D. *Where is Britain going?* 1926.

Among these works Borkenau's report on the early phases of the Spanish civil war, Orwell's picture of the rivalry between anarcho-syndicalists and communists in Catalonia, and the surveys of Roumania by Roberts and of Poland by Buell deserve special commendation. Rossi's account of the rise of Fascism is a classic. Nenni's account of socialist policy during the same years is also of great interest.

(7) *The Second World War*

Amery, J. *Sons of the eagle*. 1949.
Beneš, Dr. E. *Paměti, od Mnichova k nove válce a k novemu vitězství*. Prague, 1948.
Bénouville, G. de. *Le sacrifice du matin*. Paris, 1945.
Bilmanis, A. *Latvian-Russian relations*. Washington, 1944.
Bór-Komarowski, J. *Secret Army*. 1950.
Cadorna, R. *La riscossa*. Milano, 1948.
Clissold, S. *Whirlwind*. 1949.
Lazić, B. *Titov pokret i režim*. 1946 (no place stated).
Longo, L. *Un popolo alla macchia*. Rome, 1947.
Michel, H. *Histoire de la résistance*. Paris, 1950.
Oras, A. *Baltic eclipse*. 1948.
Rossi, A. *La physiologie du parti communiste français*. Paris, 1949.
Rossi, A. *Les communistes français pendant lad rôle de guerre*. Paris, 1951.
Rossi, A. *Les cahiers du communisme*. Paris, 1952.
Soustelle, J. *Envers et contre tout. D'Alger à Paris*. Paris, 1950.
Stavrianos, L. *Greece*. Chicago, 1952.
Tito, J. *Borba za oslobodjenje Jugoslavije*. Belgrade 1946.
Tito, J. *Report to 5th Congress of C.P.Y*. Belgrade, 1948.
Verax, C. *Lituania entre fuego cruzado*. Buenos Aires, 1944.
Woodhouse, C. M. *Apple of discord*. 1948.

Rossi's studies of the French communist party are of special value. The accounts of Amery, Clissold and Woodhouse are the three best authorities on the Albanian, Yugoslav and Greek resistance movements. General Bór-Komarowski's testimony on the Warsaw rising, which he himself led, is an important contribution to history.

(8) *Eastern Europe since 1945*

Armstrong, H. F. *Tito and Goliath*. 1951.
Betts, R. R. (ed.). *Central and South-East Europe, 1945–8*. 1950.
Dedijer, V. *Tito speaks*. 1953.
Fejtö, F. *Histoire des démocraties populaires*. Paris, 1952.
Friedman, O. *The break-up of Czechoslovak democracy*. 1950.
Georgescu-Cosmovici, A. *Au commencement était la fin*. Paris, 1951.
Gluckstein, Y. *Stalin's satellites in Eastern Europe*. 1951.
Kardelj, E. and Djilas, M. *Nova Jugoslavija u savremenom svetu*. Belgrade, 1951.
Mikołajczyk, S. *The pattern of Soviet domination*. 1948.
Nagy, F. *Behind the iron curtain*. New York, 1948.
Nettl, P. *The Eastern Zone and Soviet policy in Germany*. 1951.
Pijade, M. *Izabrani govori i članci*. Belgrade, 1950.
Ripka, H. *Le coup de Prague*. Paris, 1949.
Seton-Watson, H. *The East European Revolution*. 1950.
Ulam, A. *Titoism and the Cominform*. Harvard, 1952.

(9) *Western Europe since 1945*

Aron, R. *Le grand schisme*. Paris, 1950.
Aron, R. *Les guerres en chaine*. Paris, 1951.

Einaudi, M. (ed.) *Communism in Western Europe*. Cornell, 1951.
Falzone, V. and others. *La Costituzione della repubblica italiana*. Rome, 1948.
Fauvet, J. *Les forces politiques en France*. Paris, 1951.
Lefranc, G. *Les expériences syndicales en France de 1939 à 1950*. Paris, 1950.
Scandinavia (RIIA study group). 1951.
Schütz, W. W. *Deutschland am Rande zweier Welten*. Stuttgart, 1952.
Sereni, E. *La questione agraria nella rinascita nazionale italiana*. Rome, 1945.
Taylor, E. O. *The Fourth Republic of France*. 1951.
Wright, G. *The reshaping of French democracy*. 1950.

C. SOVIET UNION

(1) The Revolution

The literature of this subject is of course vast. The following are works of some importance. Suhanov, a left-wing Menshevik, is a detailed diary. Kritsman is an invaluable survey of the economy of Bolshevik-held territory during the period of 'War communism'.

Carr, E. H. *The Bolshevik Revolution*, 2 Vols. 1951–2.
Chamberlin, W. H. *The Russian Revolution*, 2 Vols. 1935.
Kritsman, L. *Geroicheskii period velikoy russkoy revolyutsii*. Moscow, 1924.
Lenin, V. I. *Sochinenia*. 3rd edition, Moscow, 1930–3, Vols. XVII–XXIX.
Milyukov, P. N. *Istoriya vtoroy russkoy revolyutsii*. Sofia, 1921.
Milyukov, P. N. *Rossiya na perelome*, 2 Vols. Paris, 1927.
Suhanov, N. *Zapiski o revolyutsii*. Berlin, 1923.
Trotski, L. D. *The history of the Russian revolution*, 3 Vols. 1933.

(2) Party congresses and resolutions

The following are the congresses of whose minutes I have made use· I have not been able to find copies of the minutes of the 12th or 13th Congress. Of the following, the 10th and 14th are the most important. The collection of the resolutions of the party is an essential reference work.

VKP(b) Rezolyutsiah. Moscow, editions of 1936, 1 Vol., and 1941, 2 Vols.
10 *S'yezd RKP (b)*. Moscow, 1921.
14 *S'yezd VKP (b)*. Moscow, 1926.
15 *Konferentsiya VKP (b)*. Moscow, 1927.
15 *S'yezd VKP (b)*. Moscow, 1928.
16 *S'yezd VKP (b)*. Moscow, 1930.
17 *S'yezd VKP (b)*. Moscow, 1934.
18 *S'yezd VKP (b)*. Moscow, 1939.

(3) The rise of Stalin to power

The works of Stalin and Trotski listed below are important sources. Souvarine and Eastman contain some material not easily available elsewhere. Bazhanov was Stalin's secretary in 1924. Serge's book is interesting for its impressions of the mental climate of opposition circles in Moscow and Leningrad in 1925–7.

362   FROM LENIN TO MALENKOV

Bazhanov, B. *Avec Staline dans le Kremlin.* Paris, 1930.
Deutscher, I. *Stalin, a political biography.* 1949.
Eastman, M. *Since Lenin died.* 1925.
Serge, V. *Mémoires d'un révolutionnaire.* Paris, 1950.
Souvarine, B. *Staline.* Paris, 1935.
Stalin, J. V. *Sochinenia.* Moscow, 1946–1951, Vols. I–XIII.
Stalin, J. V. *Voprosy Leninizma,* 11th edition. Moscow, 1939.
Stalin, J. V. and Kamenev, L. B. *Leninizm ili Trotskizm.* Moscow, 1925.
Trotski, L. D. *Uroki oktyabrya.* Berlin, n.d. (? 1925.)
Trotski, L. D. *My Life.*
Trotski, L. D. *The Stalin school of falsification,* Selected Works, ed. M. Schachtman. New York, 1936, Vol. 2.
Trotski, L. D. *Stalin.* 1947.

(4) *The period of the Five Year Plans*

The literature of this period too is vast. The Congresses and the works of Stalin contain valuable material. The following list includes some surveys of the Soviet economy (which are not confined to the period of the Plans, but are especially useful on them), and some accounts by eye-witnesses. Scott and Littlepage, American engineers, worked in Soviet industry. Ciliga is a Yugoslav who was imprisoned and then exiled in Siberia, having gone to the Soviet Union as a communist. Tchernavin, a Russian professor, was in a forced labour camp during part of the First Five Year Plan period and escaped with his family to Finland.

Baykov, V. *The development of the Soviet economic system.* 1946.
Bienstock, G., Yugov, A. and Schwarz, S. *Management in Soviet industry and agriculture.* 1944.
Ciliga, A. *Au pays du grand mensonge.* Paris, 1950.
Ciliga, A. *Sibérie, terre d'exil et d'industrialisation.* Paris, 1950.
Deutscher, I. *Soviet trade unions.* 1950.
Dobb, M. *Soviet economic development since 1917.* 1948.
Gordon, M. *Russian workers before and since Lenin.* 1944.
Hubbard, L. *The economics of Soviet agriculture.* 1939.
Jasny, N. *The socialised agriculture of the U.S.S.R.* Stanford, 1949.
Littlepage, J. D. *In search of Soviet gold.* 1939.
Mertsalov, V. S. *Tragedia rossiiskovo krestyanstva.* Frankfurt, 1951.
Prokopowitsch, S. N. *Russlands Volkswirtschaft unter den Sowjets.* Zürich, 1944.
Scott, J. *Behind the Urals.* 1942.
Tchernavin, V. *I speak for the silent.* Boston, 1935.
Trotski, L. D. *Die wirkliche Lage in Russland,* Dresden, n.d. (? 1930).

(5) *The purges*

The following Soviet publications give the official case:
History of the CPSU (b), short course, Moscow. 1943.
Sudebny otchot po dyelu anti-sovyetskovo trotskistskovo tsentra. Moscow, 1937 (Radek-Pyatakov trial).
Sudebny otchot po dyelu anti-sovyetskovo i pravo-trotskistskovo bloka. Moscow, 1938 (Buharin-Rykov-Yagoda trial).

The evidence of the Zinoviev and Radek trials was analysed by an independent Commission headed by the American philosopher John Dewey, which issued its report.

Not Guilty, 1938

Of the considerable literature by persons who have escaped from the Soviet Union, dealing with the *Yezhovshchina*, or with the Stalinist regime during the period of the *Yezhovshchina*, the following are perhaps the most useful.

Beck, F. and Godin, W. *Russian purge.* 1951.
Lipper, E. *Onze ans dans les bagnes soviétiques.* Paris, 1950.
Ouralov, A. *Staline au pouvoir.* Paris, 1951.
Trotski, L. D. *The Revolution betrayed.* 1938.
Weissberg, A. *Conspiracy of silence.* 1952.

The following three works of fiction, all three by former communists, are psychologically revealing, though they cannot be regarded as historical evidence in the strictest sense.

Koestler, A. *Darkness at noon.* 1940.
Plisnier, C. *Faux passeports.* Paris, 1938.
Serge, V. *L'affaire Toulaev.* Paris, 1950.

(6) *The Second World War*

The following three works, two by Germans and one by an anti-Stalinist Russian, throw valuable light on German policy in occupied Soviet territory and on the Vlasov movement. The third is the most useful of the three.

Kazantsev, A. *Tretya sila.* Frankfurt, 1952.
Kleist, P. *Zwischen Stalin und Hitler.* Bonn, 1950.
Thorwald, J. *Wen sie verderben wollen.* Stuttgart, 1952.

(7) *The non-Russian nationalities*

The following periodicals contain some useful material.

Revolyutsia i Natsionalnosti. Moscow.
Revolyutsionny Vostok. Moscow (also for communism in Asia).
Svobodny Kavkaz. Munich (anti-Soviet Caucasian exiles).
Türkeli. Munich (anti-Soviet Turkestani exiles).

The following non-Soviet and anti-Soviet works are of value in this much neglected field. The best single work is Kolarz. The Ukrainian encyclopaedia contains a good historical summary, more concrete and less rhetorical than most Ukrainian publications. The historical studies by Reshetar, Kazemzadeh and von Mende, relating to the Revolution or pre-revolutionary period, are solid and useful. Avtorhanov's short book on the Chechen people, ending with its national annihilation by the Stalinist police, is an important document of our time.

Avtorhanov, A. *Narodoubiistvo v SSSR.* Munich, 1952.
Chokay-oglu, M. *Turkestan pod vlastyu sovyetov.* Paris, 1935.

Entsiklopediya Ukrainoznavstva. Munich, 1951.
Kautsky, K. *Georgia, a social-democratic peasant republic*. 1922.
Kazemzadeh, F. *The struggle for Transcaucasia*. New York, 1951.
Kolarz, W. *Russia and her colonies*. 1952.
Kowalewski, M. *Polityka narodowościowa na Ukrainie sowieckiej*. Warsaw, 1938.
Mazepa, L. *Ukraina v ohni i buri revolyutsii*. Augsburg, 1950.
von Mende, G. *Der nationale Kampf der Russlandtürken*. Berlin, 1936.
Reshetar, J. *The Ukrainian Revolution 1917–1920*. Princeton, 1952.
Resul-zade, M. E. *Das Problem Aserbaidschan*. Berlin, 1938.

(8) *The Stalinist regime*

The following works concern aspects of the political, social and cultural regime of Stalinism. The Constitution, the Criminal Code and the textbook of 'state law' are essential documents. Achminow's book is an interesting study of the social forces behind the regime, influenced by Burnham's theory of the 'managerial revolution' but an original, though controversial, contribution. Redlich, a theoretician of the exiled NTS group, is especially concerned with totalitarian propaganda. Avtorhanov's small book on historical studies in the Soviet Union and Mehnert's study of the political significance of Stalinist falsification of history, are of considerable interest. Yelagin writes from personal experience of the Stalinisation of the theatre and of music in the Soviet Union. Gollwitzer, a German Protestant pastor who was for four years a prisoner in the Soviet Union, has some penetrating observations on the regime. Rounault, a Frenchman deported in error from Roumania to the Donets Basin, is interesting on the mentality of Soviet industrial workers.

Achminow, H. *Die Macht im Hintergrund*. Ulm, 1951.
Avtorhanov, A. *Polozhenie istoricheskih nauk v SSSR*. Munich, 1952.
Berman, R. *Justice in Russia*. Harvard, 1951.
Fedotoff White. *The growth of the Red Army*. Princeton, 1944.
Gollwitzer, H. *Und führen, wohin du nicht willst*. Munich, 1952.
Mehnert, K. *Stalin versus Marx*. 1952.
Moore, Barrington. *Soviet politics: the dilemma of power*. Harvard, 1950.
Osnovy gosudarstvennovo prava. Moscow, 1947.
Redlich, R. *Ocherki bolshevizmovedenia*. Frankfurt, 1952.
Rounault, J. *Mon ami Vassya*. Paris, 1949.
Timasheff, V. *Religion in Soviet Russia*. 1943.
Towster, J. *Political power in the USSR*. New York, 1948.
Ugolovny kodeks SSSR. Moscow, 1938.
Yelagin, E. *Ukroshchenie iskusstv*. New York, 1952.

(9) *Soviet foreign policy*

On the first decade Fischer is still the only comprehensive work. It should be read critically, for it gives the benefit of many doubts to the young Soviet government. On the later period Beloff is a reliable guide, hampered of course by the absence of access to any confidential diplomatic documents from the Soviet side. The German documents published in Washington are invaluable for the years 1939–41.

Beloff, M. *The foreign policy of Soviet Russia*, 2 Vols. 1946–8.
Degras, J. (ed.). *Documents on Soviet foreign policy.* 2 Vols. 1950–2.
Fischer, L. *The Soviets in world affairs*, 2 Vols. 1930.
Nazi-Soviet Relations. Washington, 1948.

D. ASIA, AFRICA AND LATIN AMERICA

(1) *BACKGROUND*

(a) *General*

Peterson, A. D. *The Far East: a social geography.* 1949.
Wint, Guy. *The British in Asia.*
Zinkin, M. *Asia and the West.* 1951.

(b) *The Moslem world*

Antonius, G. *The Arab awakening.* 1938.
Brockelmann, C. *Geschichte der islamischen Völker.* Munich, 1939.
Gibb, H. A. R. and Bowen, H. *Islamic society and the West.* 1950.
Gupta, R. N. *Iran: an economic study.* New Delhi, 1947.
Issawi, C. *Egypt: An economic and social analysis.* 1947.
Kirk, G. E. *A short history of the Middle East.* 1948.
Luke, Sir H. *The making of modern Turkey.* 1936.
Warriner, Doreen. *Land and poverty in the Middle East.* 1948.

(c) *Southern Asia*

Boeke, J. N. *The structure of the Netherlands East Indian economy.* New York, 1942.
Bousquet, G. *La politique musulmane et coloniale des Pays-Bas.* Paris, 1939.
Desai, A. R. *The social background of Indian nationalism.* Bombay, 1948.
Furnivall, J. S. *Educational progress in South-East Asia.* New York, 1943.
Furnivall, J. S. *Colonial policy and practice.* 1948.
Harvey, G. E. *British rule in Burma.* 1946.
Moreland, W. H. and Chatterjee, Sir A. *A short history of India.* 1944.
Rawlinson, H. G. *India: a short cultural history.* 1943.
Robequain, C. *L'évolution économique de l'Indochine française.* Paris, 1939.
Schuster, Sir G., and Wint, G. *India and democracy.* 1941.

(d) *East Asia*

Allen, G. C. *A short economic history of Japan.* 1946.
Chen Han-seng. *Landlord and peasant in China.* New York, 1936.
Fitzgerald, C. P. *China: a short cultural history.* 1942.
Grousset, R. *Histoire de la Chine.* Paris, 1942.
Holcombe, A. N. *The Chinese revolution.* Harvard, 1930.
Reischauer, F. *Japan: government and politics.* New York, 1939.
Sansom, Sir G. *The Western world and Japan.* 1950.
Tawney, R. *Land and labour in China.* 1937.

(e) *Africa*

Macmillan, W. M. *Complex South Africa.* 1930.
Macmillan, W. M. *Africa emergent.* 1949.

Marquard, L. *Peoples and policies of South Africa*. 1952.
Walker, Eric. *History of South Africa*. 1941.

(*f*) *Latin America*

Humphreys, R. A. *The evolution of modern Latin America*. 1946.

The works listed above concern the background to communism in the sense that they deal mainly either with history before 1920, or with economic or cultural problems that lie at the root of revolutionary politics, but are distinct from them. They are not mainly concerned with politics after 1920. Partial exceptions to this are the works of Kirk, Bousquet, Desai, Schuster and Wint, Holcombe, Reischauer and Marquard. But these too are essentially background works for the student of Asian or African revolution.

(2) RECENT POLITICS AND COMMUNISM

(*a*) *The Moslem World*

Agabekov, G. *Die Tscheka bei der Arbeit*. Stuttgart, 1932.
Bashkirov, A. *Rabochee i profsoyuznoe dvizhenie v Irane*. Moscow, 1948.
Hollingworth, Clare. *The Arabs and the West*. 1952.
Julien, C. A. *L'Afrique du nord en marche*. Paris, 1952.
Khadduri, M. *Independent Iraq*. 1951.
Lenczowski, G. *Russia and the West in Iran*. New York, 1949.
Letourneau, R. *L'Islam contemporain*. Paris, 1950.
Sarrasin, P.-E. *La crise algérienne*. Paris, 1951.
Sebag, P. *La Tunisie*. Paris, 1951.

All these make some reference to communism. Persian communism is described critically by Lenczowski and with orthodox approval by Bashkirov. Agabekov, a deserter from the GPU, has something to say of Soviet activities in Persia and Afghanistan. Julien is an admirable survey of French North African politics. Sebag treats Tunisia from a communist standpoint. Sarrasin contains some important documentary material. Khadduri is a thorough study of Iraqi politics up to 1948. Hollingworth and Letourneau are broader surveys.

(*b*) *Southern Asia*

Devillers, P. *Histoire de Vietnam de 1940 à 1952*. Paris, 1952.
Hayden, J. R. *The Philippines*. New York, 1942.
Kahin, G. McT. *Nationalism and revolution in Indonesia*. New York, 1952.
Mus, P. *Le Vietnam chez lui*. Paris, 1946.
Mus, P. *Vietnam, la sociologie d'une guerre*. Paris, 1952.
NEI Information Service. *Communism in the Indonesian Republic*. 1948.
Thompson, V. and Adloff, P. *The left wing in South-East Asia*.
Van Mook, H. *The stakes of democracy in South-East Asia*. 1950.

The most comprehensive factual surveys are the books by Devillers and Kahin. Thompson and Adloff also cover Burma and Malaya. Dr. van Mook writes with the authority of his experience as Governor-

General of the Netherlands East Indies. The works of M. Mus are thoughtful and interesting.

(c) Japan

Byass, H. *Government by assassination*. 1944.
Colbert, Evelyn S. *The left wing in Japanese politics*. New York, 1952.
Eydus. *Yaponiya ot 1-oy do 2-oy mirovoy voiny*. Moscow, 1946.
Swearingen, R. and Langer, P. *Red flag in Japan*. Harvard, 1952.
Wakefield, H. *New paths for Japan*. 1948.

Byass is an interesting study of the young officers' terrorist groups of the 1930's. Swearingen and Langer give a competent picture of the Japanese communist movement, with the main emphasis on the post-1945 period but with considerable information also on the inter-war years. Mrs. Colbert covers some of the same ground, with much detail but less analysis. Eydus is a 1946 Stalinist version of inter-war Japanese politics, with special emphasis on the communist party.

(d) China

Agrarian Reform Law of the People's Republic of China. Peking, 1951.
Fairbank, H., Brandt, R. and Schwarz, B. *A documentary history of Chinese communism*. 1952.
Fitzgerald, C. P. *Revolution in China*. 1952.
Culture and education in new China. Peking, 1951.
Hu Chiao-mu. *Thirty years of the Communist Party of China*. Peking, 1951.
Hunter, E. *Brain-washing in Red China*. New York, 1951.
Isaacs, H. *The tragedy of the Chinese Revolution*. 1938.
Jones, F. C. *Manchuria since 1931*. 1949.
Land Reform in China, 'Background books'. 1952.
Liu Shao-chi. *On the Party*. Peking, 1951.
Liu Shao-chi. *On inner-party struggle*. Peking, 1951.
Mao Tse-tung, *La nouvelle démocratie*. Paris, 1951.
Roy, M. N. *Revolution and counter-revolution in China*. Calcutta, 1948.
Schwartz, B. L. *Chinese communism and the rise of Mao*. Harvard, 1950.
Snow, E. *Red star over China*. 1937.
Stalin, J. V. *Ob oppozitsii*. Moscow, 1928.
Trotski, L. D. *Summary and perspectives of the Chinese Revolution* (*1928*), (Selected works, ed. M. Schachtman. New York, 1936).
United States Relations with China. Washington (DC), 1949.
Van der Sprenkel, G., Lindsay, M. and Guillain, R. *New China: three views*. 1950.

The works of Fairbank, Liu, Mao, Trotski and Stalin are essential documentary sources. Schwartz's book is a piece of first-class research and analysis, absolutely indispensable to students of communism. Isaacs and Roy are also of great interest. Fitzgerald shows great knowledge of China but little understanding of communism.

(e) Africa

Crocker, W. R. *Self-government for the colonies*. 1949.
Davidson, Basil. *Report on southern Africa*. 1952.
Deschamps, H. *L'éveil politique africain*. Paris, 1952.

Leakey, L. S. *Mau Mau and the Kikuyu*.
Sachs, S. L. *The choice before South Africa*. 1952.

Crocker's book deals mainly with British West Africa, Deschamps mainly with French tropical Africa. Both are concerned both with social problems—in particular the rise of an African intelligentsia—and with recent politics. The short work by Leakey on the Mau-Mau is based on many years' experience of the Kikuyu. Sachs is a South African trade unionist: the most valuable part of his provocative work is that which deals with the labour movement. Davidson is a newspaper correspondent of the extreme left: his account contains much factual material. Communism is barely mentioned in any of these works, as it hardly exists in Africa. For the understanding of the social factors that produce communism, however, they are of real value.

(f) Latin America

Butland, G. J. *Chile*. 1951.
Haya de la Torre, R. *El Antimperialismo y el APRA* Santiago, 1936.
Hunsche, K. H. *Der brasilianische Integralismus*. Stuttgart, 1938.
Loewenstein, K. *Brazil under Vargas*. New York, 1942.
Stevenson, J. R. *The Chilean Popular Front*. Philadelphia, 1942.
Tannenbaum, F. *Mexico: the struggle for peace and bread*. New York, 1944.

Communism does not bulk large in these books, though there is some mention of it. They throw light, however, on the Latin American social and political scene. Haya de la Torre's exposition of the doctrines of APRA, and the account by the German Nazi Hunsche of the Brazilian fascist ideological movement are from this point of view interesting.

(3) PERIODICALS

The following periodicals have been of use to me at times, and often publish articles bearing on the communist movement. Particularly useful is *Pacific Affairs*, far the best source on post-war Asian politics for those who, like myself, cannot use material in Asian languages.

African Affairs. London.
L'Afrique et l'Asie. Paris.
Aussenpolitik. Stuttgart.
Bolshevik. Moscow.
For a lasting peace, for a people's democracy. Bucarest.
Foreign Affairs. New York.
Fortnightly. London.
International Affairs. London.
Middle East Journal. Washington (DC).
Der Monat. Berlin.
Pacific Affairs. New York.
Politique Etrangère. Paris.
Twentieth Century. London.

Indispensable sources of information are *The Times*, the *Manchester Guardian*, *The Economist*, the *New York Times*, the *New York Herald Tribune*, *Le Monde*, *Die Neue Zürcher Zeitung*, of all of which I have made frequent use on many subjects.

Index of Persons

Abdul-Hamid, Sultan, 125
Adler, Friedrich, 63
Aguirre, President of Chile, 199, 208
Alekseev, General, 40
Alessandri, President of Chile, 199
Alexander, King of Yugoslavia, 108
Alexander III, Tsar, 264–5
Alfonso XIII, King of Spain, 183
Alimin, 135n., 309, 310n.
Amanulla, Emir of Afghanistan, 130
Andreyev, A. A., 170
Antonov-Ovseenko, 186n., 187
Aung San, 226, 306
Azikiwe, Dr., 324

Baden, Prince Max of, 53, 55
Badoglio, Marshal, 223–4
Bagirov, M. D., 171
Bakunin, Michael, 16
Bán, Antal, 252
Bao Dai, Emperor, 227, 311, 313–14
Barthou, Louis, 177
Bauer, Otto, 19, 63
Bekr Sidki, 193
Beneš, President, 203, 259
Beria, L. P., 171, 231
Berzin, General, 185, 187
Besteiro, Julian, 188
Bierut, Bolesław, 265
Bissolati, Leonida, 18n.
Blagoev, Dimiter, 14
Blucher, Marshal, 140, 145
Blum, Leon, 181–2, 193, 203, 292, 312n.
Blumkin, Yakov, 167n.
Bonomi, Ivanoe, 223–4
Boris, King of Bulgaria, 108, 188
Borodin, Michael, 140, 145
Brandler, Heinrich, 103–4
Buharin, N. I., 82n., 133n., 146, 165, 167–9, 170, 175

Caballero, Largo, 186
Cabet, Etienne, 1
Cadorna, Raffaele, General, 224
Cardenas, General, 197
Carol II, King of Roumania, 190, 199
Casado, Colonel, 188
Chamberlain, Neville, 200
Chang Hsueh-liang, 191–3
Chang Tso-lin, 145, 191n.
Chautemps, Camille, 182

Chen Tu-hsiu, 137, 138–9, 145–6, 149, 331
Chiang Kai-shek, 141–9, 152, 191–3, 206–7, 271–2, 274–7, 284, 336
Chou En-lai, 192, 274, 282
Chubar, V. B., 168n.
Chu-Teh, 150, 152, 271, 282n.
Chu Yuan-chang, 284n.
Clémenceau, Georges, 61, 98, 168
Clementis, Vladimir, 266n.
Cucchi, Aldo, 299
Cuno, Wilhelm, 101–2
Curzon, Viscount, 354
Cyrankiewicz, Jozef, 252

Daladier, Edouard, 182, 200
Darlan, Admiral, 219
Daszyński, Ignacy, 65, 218n.
Denikin, General, 40, 45–7
Diaz, Porfirio, 196
Dimitrov, George, 178n., 260, 265–6
Dimitrov, Dr. G. M., 251, 254
Djemaladdin Al-Afghani, 124n., 125
Djilas, Milovan, 268–9
Dobrogeanu-Gherea, 14
Dodge, 314
Dollfuss, Dr., 171, 183, 303n.
Dzierzhinski, Feliks, 72, 218

Eberlein, Hugo, 69, 171n.
Ebert, Friedrich, 57
Eihe, R. I., 168n.
Eisner, Kurt, 58

Feng Yu-hsiang, 144–5
Ferdinand, King of Bulgaria, 67
Fierlinger, Zdeněk, 253
Fischer, Ruth, 105–6
Foch, Marshal, 39, 47
Fourier, Charles, 1
Franco, General, 185, 187–8
Fröhlich, Paul, 53, 56
Frossard, L.-O., 105
Frunze, M. V., 97, 172
Fukumoto, Kazuo, 133n.

Gamarnik, Y. B., 170
Gandhi, Mahatma, 126
De Gasperi, Alcide, 296–7
De Gaulle, General, 203, 218, 221–2, 292–3, 295–6

369

Index of Subjects